WHITE FREEDOM

WHITE FREEDOM

The Racial History of an Idea

Tyler Stovall

PRINCETON UNIVERSITY PRESS

PRINCETON & OXFORD

Requests for permission to reproduce material from this work
should be sent to permissions@press.princeton.edu

Published by Princeton University Press
41 William Street, Princeton, New Jersey 08540
6 Oxford Street, Woodstock, Oxfordshire OX20 1TR

press.princeton.edu

ISBN 978-0-691-17946-9
ISBN (e-book) 978-0-691-20536-6

British Library Cataloging-in-Publication Data is available

Editorial: Eric Crahan & Thalia Leaf
Production Editorial: Ali Parrington
Text Designer: Karl Spurzem
Jacket Design: Derek Thornton, Notch Design
Production: Danielle Amatucci
Publicity: Maria Whelan & Kate Farquhar-Thomson
Copyeditor: Anne Cherry

Jacket art: Shutterstock

This book has been composed in Arno Pro with Janson Text display

Printed on acid-free paper. ∞

Printed in the United States of America

10 9 8 7 6 5 4 3 2 1

For Justin

CONTENTS

If we are lucky, there comes a time in the life of every historian of the modern world when the histories we study and our own life experiences begin to intersect. I remember at one point in the late 1990s introducing my course on twentieth-century Europe by saying I'd been teaching the course since before the fall of the Berlin Wall, prompting many students to regard me as an ancient relic. This is true of my experience writing this book, in more ways than one. Its final chapter mostly deals with events that happened during my lifetime. I was born a few months after the *Brown v. Board of Education* Supreme Court decision that marked the start of the civil rights movement, and involvement in that movement shaped much of my childhood and youth. Like everyone I knew, I grew up the child of a World War II veteran, in my case one who boasted of having seen opera in La Scala and who kept a German Luger in the house. As a graduate student in French history I chose to study the Paris suburbs, and over time saw that area emerge as the new symbol of multicultural France in the twentieth century. I lived through the collapse of the Soviet Bloc in Europe and the rise of the New Right here in America. Much of my life has thus been shaped by changing ideas of freedom and race and the intersections between them.

These personal reflections help explain why I came to write this book, why I felt I had to. I did so not just because I regarded the subject as critically important for our past, present, and future, but equally because the idea simply would not leave me alone, waking me up in the middle of the night more than once to ponder the subject. In the end, so much of what I and many other historians and scholars have studied seemed to come down to different visions of these two key concepts, so

I decided it was worth trying to write a history of them, and of the relationship between them.

White Freedom deals with a subject at once personal, national, and global, belonging both to the past and the present. It explores the ways in which two seemingly opposite philosophies, liberty and racism, are in significant ways not opposites at all, and its explorations cover two centuries, from the Enlightenment to the present. Global in scope, at the same time it devotes particular attention to two countries where this opposition has loomed largest in modern history, France and the United States. In doing so, it attempts to offer new perspectives on some very old problems and concerns, to help us understand not just the interactions of freedom and race over time but the making of the modern world in general. I certainly admit this is an ambitious undertaking: whether or not it has succeeded is up to the reader to judge.

* * *

If history and my life as an historian have taught me one thing, it is that no one can do this alone. Many people and institutions played a role in bringing *White Freedom* to the light of day, and I am privileged to express my gratitude and indebtedness to all of you. First and foremost I should thank my editors at Princeton University Press, who helped me take a vague idea, or hope, and transform it into a book. Brigitta van Rheinberg first listened to my idea and shepherded me through developing a proposal and starting to write the book. Since she moved on to other responsibilities I've been very fortunate to work with Eric Crahan, who has consistently encouraged me along while at the same time challenging me to write my ideas as effectively as possible. I'd also like to thank Thalia Leaf, who has been a godsend in dealing with some of the more technical aspects of publishing a book as well as contributing her own solid critical ideas. All in all, working with the people at Princeton University Press has been a dream, and I am honored to be one of their authors.

Friends and colleagues in France made a major contribution to making this book a reality. I have been extremely fortunate to have found a group of colleagues at the Université de Paris VIII, probably the leading academic institution in France when it comes to the study of race. I gave my first presentation based on this material as part of their groundbreaking *Seminaire sur l'histoire sociale des populations noires en France*, and ever since then have remained in close contact with them. In particular I would like to thank Emmanuelle Sibeud, Sylvain Pattieu, Audrey Celestine, Michel Giraud, and Sarah Fila-Bakabadio for making Paris my academic home away from home, for giving me a sense of intellectual comradeship so important to me while writing this book.

Colleagues and friends at my own institution, the University of California at Santa Cruz, have also earned my thanks and my gratitude for helping make *White Freedom* possible. The Center for Cultural Studies graciously let me present some of my findings at their weekly seminar; I would like to thank Anjali Arondekar, Maya Peterson, Mayanthi Fernando, Gail Hershatter, Alan Christy, Hunter Bivens, Wlad Godzich, Jodi Greene, and the other attendees for their suggestions and encouragement. I was particularly honored that the directors of The Humanities Institute, Nathaniel Deutsch and Irena Polic, chose to adopt the idea of freedom and race as the organizing theme for the institute's academic program one year; I learned a lot from the various seminars and talks held at Santa Cruz on the subject. I wrote this book while serving as dean of the Humanities at Santa Cruz, and I am especially grateful to the divisional staff for all their efforts on behalf of my work on this book. In particular I'd like to thank Judy Plummer, Katie Novak, Julie Kruger, Jay Olson, and Amy Bruinooge for all their help. I also want to thank the Humanities Division and the Academic Senate of UC Santa Cruz for their support of my research.

During this period I also served as president of the American Historical Association, which gave me my first opportunity to publish my findings from this project in the pages of the *American Historical Review*. I am very grateful to the staff of that journal for the work in publishing my article. I'm grateful to Oxford University Press for allowing me to use material from that article in my book. More generally, I would like to thank James Grossman, the AHA executive director, for constantly encouraging my work and never letting me or anyone else forget why history matters.

Finally, and most important, I want to thank my friends and family. I have been privileged to work with graduate students at both Santa Cruz and Berkeley, and my former students remain some of my closest intellectual peers. Michael Vann invited me to give my first talk on this project at CSU-Sacramento, embarrassing me with his effusive introduction, and Naomi Andrews recruited me to give a keynote address at the Western Society for French History. Both Robin Mitchell and Felix Germain have remained close colleagues and friends, their own scholarship inspiring my own work. In Paris, Jim Cohen, Richard Allen, and Elizabeth Altschull have always laid out the welcome mat for me, facilitating not only my research but my understanding of France in general. I thank you all.

Above all, I am grateful to my wife, Denise Herd, and our son, Justin Stovall. Throughout the years Denise has done all she could to support my research, including keeping the home fires burning during trips to conferences and for research. Her own very important scholarship on race, Black culture, and public health remains an inspiration to me. When I started this book Justin was just entering middle school, and now he is a sophomore in college; the boy has become a man. I owe him more than I can ever say, or perhaps even understand, but let me just thank him for constantly reminding this historian devoted to the study of the past that it's the future that really counts.

My thanks to you all! I hope you enjoy this book and find it worthy of your investments in me over the years. It could not have happened without you.

WHITE FREEDOM

INTRODUCTION

Freedom and Its Dark Sides

We hold these truths to be self-evident: that all men are created equal;
that they are endowed by their Creator with certain unalienable rights;
that among these are life, liberty, and the pursuit of happiness.

—AMERICAN DECLARATION OF INDEPENDENCE, 1776

Men are born and remain free and equal in rights.

—DECLARATION OF THE RIGHTS OF MAN AND THE
CITIZEN, PARIS, 1789

Free, white, and twenty-one.

—TRADITIONAL AMERICAN SAYING

At the dawn of the twenty-first century the American Congress appointed a task force to investigate the veracity of a persistent rumor that the US Capitol Building, among other official structures in Washington, DC, had been built by the labor of Black slaves. Rumors to this effect had existed for some time, but recent revelations of receipts for payments for slaves found in the Treasury Department had lent them new credence. Accordingly, Congress created the Slave Labor Task Force, in order to investigate the rumors and decide what, if anything, the federal government should do in response to them. In 2005 the task force released its report, entitled "History of Slave Laborers in the Construction of the United States Capitol," concluding that the rumors were true:

> Soon after it was finished in the 1820s, the Capitol began to be called the "Temple of Liberty" because it was dedicated to the cherished ideas of freedom, equality, and self determination. How, then, can a building steeped in those noble principles have been constructed with the help of slave labor? The first step in the Capitol's evolution was taken in the last decade of the eighteenth century and was, in fact, assisted by the toil of bondsmen—mainly slaves rented from local owners to help build the Capitol and the city of Washington. . . .
>
> The irony of slaves helping to build America's "Temple of Liberty" is potent. It is instructive, however, to recall that other landmarks of American freedom were also built with a similar labor force or in other ways intertwined with the institution of slavery. Faneuil Hall, for instance—Boston's celebrated "Cradle of Liberty"—was given to the city by a slave owner whose fortune was founded on the slave trade. America's oldest lending library, the Redwood Library in Newport, Rhode Island, was founded in 1747 with the help of New England's largest slaveholder, Abraham Redwood. Two well-known Massachusetts leaders, Cotton Mather and John Winthrop, were also slave owners. Independence Hall was built at a time when slavery was widespread in Pennsylvania. Indeed, the colony's Quaker founder, William Penn, was also a slave owner.[1]

The report's conclusions led Congress to take several actions to rectify the historical record and acknowledge the role played by African slaves in building the Capitol. Unlike most congressional activities at the time, they represented a bipartisan effort, reaffirming the accord of both Democrats and Republicans. In 2007 Congress agreed to rename the Great Hall of the Capitol Visitor's Center "Emancipation Hall," in honor of the slaves who helped build it. As Congressman Jesse Jackson Jr. argued, "Emancipation is the great, enduring theme of our nation's still unfolding story. Without emancipation, our house divided

FIGURE 1. "Emancipation Hall." Scott J. Ferrell/Congressional Quarterly/Getty Images.

would not have stood. We would not be a beacon of freedom and democracy around the world. We would never have had, in the words of
Abraham Lincoln, 'a new birth of freedom.'"[2] Both the House and the
Senate overwhelmingly approved the measure in November 2007, and
President George W. Bush signed it into law the following January. Two
years later, on June 16, 2010, congressional leaders from both parties
unveiled two plaques in Emancipation Hall that honored the work of
enslaved African Americans in building the Capitol.[3]

The story of Emancipation Hall in many ways tells an inspiring and
moving story of a nation's willingness to come to terms, across party
lines, with its slave heritage. But it also raises some interesting and ultimately rather unsettling questions. Why would one name a building
constructed by slaves Emancipation Hall as a way of honoring their
legacy and history? They certainly weren't emancipated when they
worked there. Freedom undoubtedly represented the aspiration of
those whose forced labor built the Capitol, and so much of America,
but it was definitely not their reality and did not express the nature of
their lives. Probably very few of them lived to see the end of slavery.

How could naming the structure they built Emancipation illustrate the nature of lives lived without freedom? If one really wanted to acknowledge them, why not call the building Slave Hall? Why would it be impossible to imagine an official government building in a country that claimed freedom as its greatest value with that name? Did the name Emancipation Hall, far from honoring the slaves who helped build it, instead represent yet another denial of their own history? If so, why did all of official Washington, including African American legislators descended from slaves, rush to embrace it?

Questions like these inspired and lay at the heart of this book, *White Freedom*. This study considers two seminal values in the modern world, freedom and race, and the relationship between them.

The relationship between freedom and race has been one of the key themes of modern society and politics in the Western world. Scholars and social commentators have long noted that the era of the Enlightenment, which emphasized the importance of freedom and in many ways codified our modern understandings of the idea, also witnessed the height of the transatlantic slave trade.[4] The enduring presence of racism in the history of America, a nation built simultaneously upon ideas of liberty and upon African slavery, Indian genocide, and systematic racial discrimination, has provided one of the most dramatic (but certainly not the only) example of this complex relationship.[5] To take one specific example, historians of the American Revolution have struggled for generations to conceptualize a war for liberty that preserved and reinforced slavery, and the debate has by no means come to an end.[6]

Commentators have often portrayed the relationship between freedom and race in paradoxical terms, as the quotation from the 2005 Congressional report cited above makes clear. If liberty represents the acme of Western civilization, racism—embodied above all by horrible histories like the slave trade and the Holocaust—is its nadir. The two classic statements of freedom that open this introduction illustrate this contradiction: the first was written by a man, Thomas Jefferson, who owned slaves;[7] the second was written by representatives of a nation that owned one of the greatest slave colonies, Saint-Domingue, the world had ever seen.[8] Some argue that one represents the essence of modern societies while the other is more peripheral;[9] others (for example, Black nationalist Malcolm X) contend the reverse, that racism is the true inescapable reality of Western culture and society.[10] In general, however, perspectives on freedom and race tend to posit them as opposites, and the relationship between them as paradoxical and ironic, one due more to human inconsistencies and frailties than to any underlying logics.

White Freedom takes issue with this consensus, suggesting instead that the relationship between liberty and racism is not necessarily contradictory but rather has its own internal consistency. In short, I reject the idea of a paradoxical relationship between the two; to my mind there is no contradiction. The central theme of this study is that to an important extent, although certainly not always, ideas of freedom in the modern world have been racialized. In particular, many have considered whiteness and white racial identity intrinsic to modern liberty. Models of autonomy and self-empowerment have often come with a racial dimension, as reflected in the popular saying, "free, white, and twenty-one." To be free is to be white, and to be white is to be free. In this reading, therefore, freedom and race are not just enemies but also allies, *frères ennemis* whose histories cannot be understood separately. Put baldly, at its most extreme freedom can be and historically has been a racist ideology.

The example with which I began this book, Emancipation Hall, illustrates this point nicely. As I will discuss later in this introduction, scholars of various persuasions have long argued that slavery and the treatment of nonwhites in general fundamentally contradicted Western ideas of freedom, and as a case in point would point to the use of slave labor to build the US Capitol building. The dedication of part of the building as Emancipation Hall in memory of the slaves who built it shows, however, that one cannot simply extend the narrative of freedom to those who were not free without making a mockery of their own history. This approach in effect seeks to preserve traditions of liberty grounded in whiteness, rather than to unpack the role played by race in creating and maintaining those traditions. It tries to integrate African American ideas of freedom into a building constructed in violation of them as a way of embracing a multicultural vision of liberty, but can do so only by ignoring the dominant narrative that saw freedom as embodied in whiteness.

White Freedom thus challenges the idea that freedom and race are necessarily opposites, arguing instead that both historically and in the present day they have worked together to construct white identity. The pages that follow will show the many different ways in which freedom has functioned as an essential part of white identity, and by contrast the ways lack of freedom and the lack of white racial identity have gone together. Rather than see this relationship as paradoxical, it argues that in many cases it has been absolutely essential to what it means to be white (and therefore to be nonwhite). The book will therefore consider not just different examples of white freedom but more generally its evolution as concept and practice over the two hundred-plus years from the Enlightenment to the present day.

One can easily anticipate objections that many might make to such a thesis. Two in particular stand out in my mind. First, how can one condemn as racist, or even racialized, a broad human goal that has stood for the best in mankind, that has motivated millions and millions of people throughout history to fight and die for the rights of all? Let me state from the outset that this study does not aim to condemn the desire for freedom, to sully it by labeling it racist. Rather, I wish to consider the ways in which the ideal of freedom, like many other aspects of modern human politics and society, has had a racial dimension. Notably, the notion that whites in particular should be (and have been) free, and that freedom foregrounded the interests and goals of white populations, is one this study will explore.

The second objection also bears a lot of weight. Given that so many movements *against* racism have embraced an identity as freedom struggles (decolonization and the civil rights movement are perhaps the most prominent examples of these), how can one refer to freedom as a racist ideology? How can one characterize as white an ideal that inspired so many people of color to sacrifice everything for it? My answer to that is that freedom has never just been white; there are many political variants of human liberty. In particular many great popular struggles have been waged in the modern era to bring freedom to all men and women. But in many ways that is my point: peoples of color have had to fight for inclusion into the idea of freedom, in fact not just struggling to be part of white freedom but to overthrow it as a concept and as a social and political reality. Those struggles have had their victories but also their defeats, and have never succeeded in completely destroying the relationship between freedom and race in the modern world.

To a certain extent both these objections rest upon a foundational belief that freedom is a positive human value, whereas racism is its evil antithesis. I certainly believe in human liberty and reject racial discrimination, as do probably most people in the contemporary world. But also, as an historian I understand that such convictions are not only not universal, but have also changed over time. As I will discuss more extensively in chapter 1, people have not always viewed freedom as a positive value, and there are important ways in which that is still true. One need only substitute *anarchy* for freedom, for instance, to understand that the idea of liberty can have serious negative connotations. Similarly, the idea of the *libertine* represents a person whose freedom is immoral, destructive, and ultimately self-destructive. The contrast between ideas of a political activist understood as a *freedom fighter* versus a *terrorist* shows how warriors for liberty can be seen in both positive and negative terms.[11] A central theme of the history of freedom, one which this book will consider, is how as a social and political value it was in effect domesticated, embedded in governmental systems that limited the autonomy of the individual for the effective functionality of the collectivity.

If freedom has not always been good, equally race and racial discrimination have not always been seen as bad. Obviously, this was true in fundamentally racist societies like Nazi Germany and the antebellum American South, but the idea of racial differentiation as a positive value—one that emphasized the biological differences between peoples—also existed in cultures that did not embrace overt racism. A belief in racial difference did not have to necessitate racial oppression, for example, but could be seen instead as a way of maximizing the inherent and distinct qualities of each race. Ideas of race were intimately intertwined with the rise of nationalism in nineteenth-century Europe, for example, to the extent that the modern nation was seen as a political formation that could affirm and advance the racial interests of a people. Romantic literature also embraced a frequently positive vision of race, as one can see in novels like Sir Walter Scott's *Ivanhoe* or James Fenimore Cooper's *The Last of the Mohicans*.[12] Finally, the rise of racial pride movements such as Black nationalism often served to mobilize and empower members of ethnic minority groups.[13] The response to racial discrimination has been as much racial pride as antiracism, and the two have at times gone together.

Very few people willingly embrace what they perceive to be evil. The construction of white freedom rested on the idea that both liberty and white racial identity were not only positive values but also in many ways inseparable. This history will explore the rise of this phenomenon across the modern period, considering how a belief in freedom developed in the context of increasing racial differentiation. This study will explore, for example, how the first represented a reaction to the second, and also how the two phenomena interacted and even mutually reinforced each other.

The chronological scope of this study is the modern era, from roughly the eighteenth century to the end of the twentieth, in particular the two hundred years from 1789 to 1989. Although freedom and racial difference have existed for a long time, they came together in the modern era, and together they have played a major role in shaping the world we know today.

In terms of geography, it lies somewhere between comparative and world history. As a generation of transnational historians has argued, the story of mankind is not limited by the boundaries of the nation-state, and so we must consider the ways in which those boundaries are transgressed or even ignored as much as created and maintained.[14] In fact, one type of freedom, freedom to migrate elsewhere in search of a better life, directly speaks to the global nature of liberty. At times, therefore, this study will look at the relationship between freedom and race in different parts of the world, considering how particular issues played out in a variety of geographical settings.

At the same time, however, this is not a world history per se. It does not systematically pursue the history of freedom and race on a global scale. Rather, I generally focus on two areas: Europe, and within Europe

France in particular; and the United States. An American born and bred, I trained professionally as an historian of France and have during the course of my career written books and articles that consider the intersections of both national histories. For me, a comparative approach to history is a fruitful way to consider transnationalism, one that considers not the absence of nation-states but their interactions.

There are other justifications for focusing a transnational history of freedom and race on France and the United States. There now exists a significant historical literature comparing the world's two great republics, one that has made important contributions to comparative and world history.[15] In particular, France and America are both countries for whom the ideal of freedom is absolutely central to their national identities. For the French, liberty is intimately associated with their national history. The Germanic tribes who settled post-Roman France called themselves Franks, which meant free in their language, and gave the name to their nation. Modern France is of course grounded in the experience of the French Revolution, whose classic slogan, *Liberté, égalité, fraternité,* gives freedom pride of place.[16]

Equally, most Americans would argue that the United States stands for freedom more than anything else, and perhaps more than any other nation. As historian Eric Foner states in the preface to his seminal study *Give Me Liberty! An American History*: "No idea is more fundamental to Americans' sense of themselves as individuals and as a nation than freedom. The central term in our political language, freedom . . . is deeply embedded in the record of our history and the language of everyday life."[17] Moreover, in both countries the idea of freedom has generally had a universal character: all peoples should be free, not just their own, a belief that at times has guided imperial expansion, foreign policy, and participation in the great wars of the modern era.[18] At the same time, as this study will explore, the histories of both France and the United States have been shaped by racial difference, highlighting the perceived contradictions between freedom and racism in the modern world as a whole. In both cases these two concepts and practices often represent the best and the worst of their national histories.

The modern histories of France and the United States, and the comparisons between them, thus form the meat of this book. However, they are not its exclusive focus. One could hardly write a study of freedom and race in the modern era without considering the history of imperialism, for example, and that means attention to other imperial formations, especially Britain and the British Empire.[19] Similarly, twentieth-century fascism also speaks to this complex history in a variety of ways, so one must take into consideration the history of fascist Italy and especially Nazi Germany.[20] Moreover, in the twentieth century conflicts between capitalism and communism helped shape debates about both freedom and race, especially (but not only) in the era of decolonization and the cold war, so that one must also explore that history. Ultimately, of course, there are few aspects of modern world history that do not touch upon the themes of race and/or freedom to some degree, so as this project grew I found myself frequently venturing into unfamiliar territory. It is a measure of the importance of this topic that I nonetheless managed for the most part to keep it at the center of my narrative.

Finally, I should note that my thinking about the relationship between freedom and race has been strongly influenced by ideas of whiteness, and the scholarly literature on whiteness studies.[21] Whiteness scholars have shown how racial identity belongs just as much to socially dominant strata as to the oppressed, and it makes sense to consider the history of an ideology that generally symbolizes empowerment in this light. Consequently, this book's analysis of freedom links it not so much with racial categories of all sorts, but more specifically with racial superiority, i.e., whiteness. One could easily imagine a negative image of freedom as savagery, and that idea of freedom being associated with blackness; I will in fact consider aspects of this possibility in chapter 1. But for the most part this study will consider the ways that positive ideas about freedom interacted with, both drawing upon and promoting, ideas of white racial identity as an elite social and political status.

White Freedom, then, explores the modern history of two seminal concepts, freedom and race, and the relationship between them. In particular it considers how our ideas about freedom have been shaped by racial thinking, arguing that for much of the modern era liberty and white privilege have frequently been strange bedfellows at worst, soul mates at best. It certainly does not argue that white freedom is the only kind of freedom, that all modern visions of liberty are racist. It does suggest, however, that belief in freedom, specifically in one's entitlement to freedom, was a key component of white supremacy. In societies governed by racial hierarchy, the whiter one was, the more free one was. Conversely, those who could not claim white identity were in many cases those who lacked freedom. The contrasts between white citizens, nonwhite colonial subjects, and Black slaves provide the most obvious examples of this, but they are not the only ones. As this study will show, the nature of white privilege and freedom certainly changed over time, but the link between the two remained tight enough to accentuate its continued existence as an historical phenomenon.

Ultimately to chronicle the history of white freedom is also to chronicle the history of struggles against it, struggles for a more conclusive idea of liberty that would free all women and men. This study focuses more on the former than the latter, primarily because I feel this story is less familiar, but both are of crucial importance. To explore the history and power of white freedom is hopefully to give a better sense of what those who fought against it were up against, a better understanding and appreciation of their heroic efforts. If whiteness and freedom are frequently allied in modern history, so are struggles against both racism and the lack of freedom, and not necessarily just for peoples of color. In exploring how freedom was limited and shaped by racial difference, one must also consider the history of those who insisted on freedom for all. This too, in the end, is part of the history of white freedom.

Defining White Freedom

So far I have discussed white freedom as the relationship between two seminal concepts, but the time has come for a more organic, concise statement of definition. What is white freedom? How can one define a concept born of such different and contrasting ideas?

For the purposes of this study, I therefore define white freedom as the belief (and practice) that freedom is central to white racial identity, and that only white people can or should be free. Such a definition can lend itself to several different interpretations. At one level, white freedom seems merely another version of white supremacy, the belief that whites are superior to other peoples on racial grounds. From this perspective, freedom seems the ultimate symbol of white racial superiority and privilege. Whites are free because they are smarter, more powerful, or more morally deserving than other peoples. Such an argument can easily slip into a kind of circular logic: whites are freer than other races because they are better, and they are better than others because they are more free. White supremacy did not in modern history necessarily imply racial hostility; one can portray whites as better than others without attacking those others (as we shall see, much writing about race during the Enlightenment did exactly that). In practice, however, the idea that one must subjugate other races in order to preserve the freedom of whites has played a central role in the development of white freedom, just as the example of such subjugation has served to affirm the association of freedom with whiteness.

Ultimately, however, the meaning of white freedom transcended racism and white supremacy, emphasizing instead how ideas of liberty in general were grounded in whiteness. The classic exploration of this is Edmund Morgan's *American Slavery, American Freedom*. In this seminal study Morgan considers how African slavery contributed to the development of the idea of freedom in colonial Virginia, a key aspect of what he terms "the central paradox of American history."[22] He shows not only how slavery lay at the root of the prosperity that made visions of freedom and independence in colonial America possible, but also how the creation of a massive slave population (forty percent of the residents of colonial Virginia by the eighteenth century) enabled the unity of elite and working-class whites around ideas of freedom. According to Morgan, whites in colonial Virginia prized freedom so much precisely because they could see every day what it meant to live without it.[23] As he argued in his conclusion:

Racism thus absorbed in Virginia the fear and contempt that men in England, whether Whig or Tory, monarchist or republican, felt for the inarticulate lower classes. Racism made it possible for white Virginians to develop a devotion to the equality that English republicans had declared to be the soul of liberty. There were too few free poor on hand to matter. And by lumping Indians, mulattoes, and Negroes in a single pariah class, Virginians had paved the way for a similar lumping of small and large planters in a single master class.[24]

Although grounded in the racist belief that slaveholding America was a land of free people because African slaves were not people, this idea of white freedom emphasized the identity of whites rather than the oppression of Blacks. In fact, for it to function as a hegemonic creed of what it meant to be American, the position of African Americans and other peoples of color had to be reduced to inconvenient exceptions in a grand narrative of freedom, or preferably ignored altogether. In this sense, therefore, white freedom transcended, or at least sought to transcend, white supremacy and racism by casting freedom as a universal value. As scholars of whiteness have shown, portraying white identity as universal served to mask the very real relations of power that made it possible. I argue that in fact the juxtaposition of white freedom and Black slavery was not a paradox, precisely because it arose out of the immutable facts of race. As this book will show, celebrations of liberty in the modern world often had a racial dimension, and the refusal to recognize this dimension played a key role in the development of white freedom.

White freedom thus lay at the heart of the constitution of whiteness as a social and ultimately political identity. As an ideology it argued that to be white meant having control of one's own destiny, of being free from domination by others. The myth of the freeborn Englishman or the ideal of the yeoman American farmer rested above all on not being a slave, and in the modern era that increasingly meant not being a Black slave. And it also meant a sense of natural rights that by the nineteenth century more and more people viewed as universal. Analyzing the history of white freedom thus means uncovering the racial dimensions of a concept usually defined as belonging to all members of the human race. It means remembering that to be human itself has often been defined in racial terms.

Freedom and Race in Historiography and Theory

As Eric Foner has pointed out in his sweeping history of freedom in America, the idea of liberty is so popular that virtually every significant political movement in American history has embraced it as an identification and a goal.[25] Freedom seems universally valued and sought after, not just in the United States but throughout much of the modern world, yet it is at times difficult to define. What, after all, does it mean to be free, and how have the meanings changed according to time and place?[26]

In one sense, of course, women and men have been writing about freedom as long as they have been free to write. Many eras of human history, notably ancient Greece and Rome, the Renaissance and Reformation, and the Enlightenment, have produced major texts about liberty.[27] In this book, however, both for reasons of economy and because of my particular topic, I will discuss modern historical and theoretical writers about freedom. This modern historiography really begins with John Stuart Mill's *On Liberty* (1859), followed by the essays of Lord Acton in the late nineteenth century, and then is carried on by a number of writers in the mid-twentieth century, notably Isaiah Berlin.[28] The fall of the Berlin Wall in 1989 and the collapse of Soviet communism spurred a new interest in the history of liberty.[29]

A number of scholars have written general histories of human freedom, seeking to reveal the basic outlines of this idea across historical time. A few basic themes and traits characterize much of this historiography. Much of it has a teleological orientation, charting the evolution of humanity from oppression to freedom. Often this goes along with the story of the rise of the West, starting with the ancient Greeks and Romans and culminating with contemporary liberal democracy. In the preface to the first volume of his massive study *Freedom*, sociologist Orlando Patterson observes, "No one would deny that today freedom stands unchallenged as the supreme value of the Western world. . . . There is now hardly a country whose leaders, however dubiously, do not claim that they are pursuing the ideal. The very hypocrisy and absurdity of many of these claims attest to the enormous power of this ideal. People may sin against freedom, but no one dares deny its virtue."[30]

Closely aligned with this emphasis on freedom as a key factor in the making of the modern world is a strong emphasis on the politics of freedom, and of liberalism in particular. For many writers on the topic, freedom and classic liberal philosophy are virtually indistinguishable, and the basic principles of liberalism largely define modern ideas of freedom. This is especially true of the many books about freedom written during or after the collapse of Soviet communism and the resurgence of neo-liberal politics at the end of the twentieth century.[31] In *Freedom: A History* (1990), Donald W. Treadgold sees freedom as characterized by a few essential traits: political pluralism; social pluralism and diversity; property rights; the rule of law; individualism.[32] Similarly, in a book publishing the results of a conference comparing liberty in France and the US, editors Joseph Klaits and Michael H. Haltzel make the evolution of liberalism in both countries key to the history of freedom.[33] Some writers see not just liberalism but also democracy, especially in the form of liberal democracy, as integral to the history of freedom.[34]

Another important approach to the history of freedom is the story of freedom struggles. Historians of minority and oppressed groups have also frequently crafted those histories as narratives of overcoming discrimination and achieving freedom. A classic example of this is one of the first major studies of African American history, John Hope Franklin's *From Slavery to Freedom*, which cast the long fight against racism and for racial equality as a freedom struggle.[35] Both the civil rights movement and anticolonial struggles for national independence during the decades after World War II adopted the idea of freedom as a key way of defining their movements, and this vision has characterized much of the historiography of these movements as well.[36] Other movements against discrimination and for equality in the postwar era adopted the banner of liberty: both feminist and gay struggles frequently used the term *liberation* to characterize their goals.[37]

Some scholars have written about freedom as essentially the opposite of slavery and have seen the history of the two as deeply intertwined. No one has embraced this perspective more thoroughly than Orlando Patterson, whose earlier works on slavery led him to explore its relationship to the idea of liberty from the ancient Greeks to the modern era in his massive history of freedom. Another major study, David Brion Davis's *The Problem of Slavery in Western Culture* (1966), explored at length the paradox of slavery and freedom in human history, noting that John Locke and other advocates of liberty at times supported the institution of human bondage.[38] Other historians have noted the extent to which the call for freedom often assumed the form of a rejection of servitude, even among slaveholders themselves.[39]

The historical discussion of the relationship between slavery and liberty brings us close to my own reading of the rise of white freedom. Before exploring this in more depth I now wish to turn to the other relevant historiography, that of race and racial thinking, in the modern world. Like liberty, race has been explored and analyzed from many different perspectives, resulting in a rich and complex body of scholarly literature. As I will argue below, the two intellectual traditions at times parallel and intersect with one another, exhibiting important differences as well as a good deal in common.

Like that of freedom, the historiography of race has taken different forms over the years, and also like freedom, race as a concept has proved notoriously difficult to define. Discussions of physical, biological, and cultural distinctions between peoples go back to the ancient world, notably Aristotle's differentiation between the superior northern races (Greeks) and the barbaric "Eastern" races.[40] But, much more so than is the case with the historiography of liberty, most historians of racial thinking see it as the product of the modern era. In his pathbreaking synthetic study *Race: The History of an Idea in the West*, Ivan Hannaford argues that the word *race* did not enter into general use in northern Europe until the sixteenth century, and was not fully conceptualized until the eighteenth.[41] In general, contemporary historians of race have been at pains to reject the idea that racial thinking is a universal part of the human experience, instead linking it to the specific history of modernity.[42]

Intellectual history has often taken the lead in the historiography of race, again similar to the history of freedom. Hannaford's seminal study starts with the ancient world and proceeds through the Middle Ages considering texts by Aristotle, Socrates, Cicero, Saint Augustine, Maimonides, and Shakespeare before arriving at the birth of modern racism in the seventeenth century. Other authors have adopted a similar trajectory, looking at the roots of racial thinking in early recorded history but arguing that racism itself begins with the European discovery and conquest of the Americas. The Enlightenment has been a major focus of intellectual historians of race; some have argued that the great thinkers of the eighteenth century rejected both slavery and racism, while others see the era as a seminal one in promoting the idea of classifying humankind along racial lines.[43] Scholars of anti-Semitism and the Holocaust have also made major contributions to the historiography of race. George Mosse's *Toward the Final Solution* and Leon Poliakov's *The Aryan Myth*, for example, ground modern anti-Semitism in the evolution of racial thinking since the Enlightenment, arguing that it differed fundamentally from the religiously based hatred of Jews in the past.[44]

Such studies on the intellectual history of race have produced what is by now a standard historical chronology, which sees racial thinking as originating in early modern Europe, being developed by the Enlightenment in the eighteenth century and the rise of scientific racism in the nineteenth century, combining with the rise of the nation-state and nationalist culture to produce virulent forms of racism, and culminating with the Holocaust, the example par excellence of racial genocide and the racial state. Like the historiography of freedom, therefore, it tends to adopt a teleological narrative of racial thinking.

Similarly, just as many studies of liberty have concentrated on freedom struggles, so too has a considerable body of scholarship on race focused on the condition of nonwhites and those racially Othered. Virtually all of the history of African Americans, and to a large extent that of peoples of African descent in general, takes questions of race as a central issue.[45] The scholarly disciplines collectively known as ethnic studies take as their subject racialized communities and population groups.[46] The tremendous expansion of this scholarship since the 1960s has made studies of race far more central to the intellectual life of American universities than before, and increasingly has established a presence far beyond the boundaries of the United States. These fields of study are usually interdisciplinary, combining perspectives from various fields in the social sciences and humanities, and interdisciplinarity in general has often stimulated new approaches to the academic study of race.[47]

A central paradox of the historiography of race is the fact that while racial thinking, especially scientific racism, was overwhelmingly repudiated after the Holocaust, the scholarly study of race has become more prominent than ever. From the heated battles over affirmative action in the United States[48] to questions of universalism versus difference in France[49] and controversies over race relations in Britain,[50] politicians, public intellectuals, and activists have wrestled with how to deal with a phenomenon that almost all agree has no objective or scientific reality.[51] As we shall see below, the histories of both race and freedom are replete with paradoxes, a topic I will take up in chapter 1.

* * *

I have organized *White Freedom* in three sections, of two chapters each. Part 1 deals with both broad theories and specific practices of white freedom, organized thematically rather than chronologically. Chapter 1 considers alternate ideas of freedom, notably those related to piracy and childhood, and how they were increasingly suppressed and relegated to the margins of modern bourgeois society in Europe and America. Both children and pirates represented a kind of racialized "savage" freedom, attractive and easily romanticized yet nonetheless at odds with white freedom in the modern era. Chapter 2 takes as its subject a specific case study, the Statue of Liberty. Probably the most famous symbolic image of freedom in the world, the Statue of Liberty also represents ideas of freedom in both France and the United States. This chapter explores the racial history of the great statue, from its forgotten and suppressed links to antislavery to its changing relationship to immigration. Together, the two chapters give an overview of the main outlines of the book.

Parts 2 and 3 proceed chronologically. Part 2 looks at the relationship between freedom and race in the late eighteenth and nineteenth centuries, from the Enlightenment to the outbreak of the Great War. Chapter 3 considers the Age of Democratic Revolution and how it brought together liberty and whiteness. It examines the Enlightenment, the American Revolution, the French Revolution, and the Saint-Domingue Revolution, to show the many ways in which struggles around both white freedom and Black slavery intersected. This chapter concludes by arguing that the crusade for freedom at the beginning of the modern era ended up by emphasizing the links between liberty and race. Chapter 4 deals with the rise of modern industrial and bourgeois society and the rise of liberal democracy in Europe and America. In Europe it explores the link between the rise of mass democracy at home and the growth of massive empires in Africa and Asia, producing polities organized around white citizenship and nonwhite subjecthood. In America the chapter considers the rise of mass democracy, the Civil War, and Reconstruction, showing how the struggle against Black slavery ended up reaffirming white freedom. It also investigates the history of immigration and whiteness at the turn of the century.

Part 3 of *White Freedom* focuses on the twentieth century. Chapter 5 discusses the history of the two world wars and the interwar years. It explores the ways in which World War I brought the planet together into one global social and political unit, and how that unit was segmented along racial lines. The chapter considers the history of fascism and how it interacted with racialized ideas of freedom, and then analyzes the great antifascist crusade for freedom and the racial dimensions of that crusade. It ends by looking at how the struggle against fascist racism undermined the idea of white freedom. This leads into Chapter 6, which considers the fall and rise of white freedom in the latter half of the twentieth century. Beginning with decolonization and the civil rights movement in America, it notes the triumph of struggles against white freedom up to 1965, then the return of that ideological practice in the 1970s and 1980s. It concludes with the fall of European communism in 1989, a date justly celebrated as a banner year for freedom but one that had its own racial implications.

Such is the story of *White Freedom*. It intends not to condemn the idea of liberty but rather to explore a rarely considered dimension of that ideology, its relationship to ideas of race and racial difference in the modern world. I hope this book will inspire other studies on the complex nature of liberty in our history and ultimately help us to understand how we can make all the world's peoples more free. If it can do that, or even if it simply inspires and provokes debates about race and freedom in our time, I feel it will have served its purpose.

PART 1

CHAPTER 1

Savage Freedom

PIRACY, CHILDHOOD, AND ALTERNATE RACIAL VISIONS OF LIBERTY

Some of the most intriguing characters in J. M. Barrie's 1904 play *Peter Pan* are the "lost boys," refugees from Victorian childhood living in the magical world of Neverland. Consisting of male infants[1] who had fallen out of their baby carriages and found their way to this alternate realm, the lost boys live a carefree life of eternal childhood alongside other beings sheltered from historical time: Captain Hook and his pirates; the Native Americans (or "redskins") and their Tiger Lily.[2] They ally themselves with the ultimate lost boy, their leader Peter Pan, whose entire existence revolves around a refusal to grow up. The lost boys have much in common with these two groups, camping out in the woods, dressing up as animals, and in many ways living like primitives. As Barrie notes in chapter 5, "On this evening the chief forces of the island were disposed as follows. The lost boys were out looking for Peter, the pirates were out looking for the lost boys, the redskins were out looking for the pirates, and the beasts were out looking for the redskins. They were going round and round the island, but they did not meet because all were going at the same rate."[3] The lost boys do not go to school or have to obey adults in general. Like Native Americans, pirates, and animals, they represent an image of savage freedom.

After a climactic battle in which Peter Pan and the lost boys kill the pirates, the boys return with the young heroine Wendy to the real world of middle-class England. They slay the pirates and leave behind their Native American allies and animal familiars to embrace all the pleasures of bourgeois childhood, and in doing so kill the primitive beings inside themselves. By the time the play ends, sometime in the future, the primitive boys have grown up to become white Englishmen with beards and jobs, at home in Edwardian middle-class society. Pirates must die and children, especially male children, must grow up as a part of the triumph of Western civilization. In *Peter Pan,* and in the world that produced it, savage freedom inexorably gives way to white freedom.[4]

Few concepts loom larger in the history of modernity and Western civilization more generally than freedom, on the one hand, and race on the other, and yet few seem more intrinsically different and opposed to each other. The idea of liberty is almost universally praised and seen as a key part of human progress, endlessly celebrated and reaffirmed. Few words in English or many other languages have a more positive connotation. Ideas of race and racial difference, in contrast, are generally condemned and considered something to be refuted or overcome. If the one represents the highest strivings and achievements of modernity, the other symbolizes its underside, how far Western civilization has to go in realizing its full potential. One stands for the potential of the individual to realize all of his or her potential and desires, the other the limits imposed by biology, community, and destiny. One represents light, the other darkness.

In this chapter I consider points of intersection between these two so radically different and opposed ideas in order to explore the idea that the coexistence of racism and freedom in the modern world is less a contradiction than the articulation of the variegated nature of both concepts and their manifold interactions over time. The fact that freedom could symbolize resistance to oppression and at the same time create its own types of racialized injustice speaks to the power and complexity of the idea, and the impossibility of considering it in isolation from other central modern concepts like race. I will explore how the amalgam of liberty and racial thought I call white freedom could arise out of the affinities between the two, how it is a product of their textual and theo-

retical interstices. The theory and historiography of both race and freedom is far from Black-and-white.[5]

In considering this complex relationship, the bulk of this chapter will
focus on two very different groups and histories that illustrate alternate
experiences of liberty, models that deviated from liberalism and ultimately had to be suppressed in order to create a liberal ideological and
political order, and that represented a racial challenge to the idea of
white freedom. I first will consider the history of piracy in the modern
and contemporary eras. Piracy has represented a rejection of the integrity and laws of the liberal nation-state, while at the same time often
symbolizing a romantic idea of freedom. The suppression of the first
aspect of piracy helped create the second, so that piracy presented a dual
aspect that remains potent to this day.

The second is the history of childhood. The romantic idea of children
as free and carefree has gone hand in hand with increasing regulation of
childhood in the modern era, creating a fascinating dichotomy between
ideas of liberty and authoritarian realities. This dichotomy has frequently sparked revolts by children and especially by teenagers, so that
many have regarded adolescence as a particularly turbulent time of life.
Like piracy, the idea of childhood freedom was both a romanticized
fantasy and a racialized reality that had to be suppressed to enable the
triumph of liberal ideas of freedom.

This chapter will thus consider the histories of childhood and piracy
as examples of racial alternatives to white freedom, visions of "savage"
freedom that had to be suppressed. As I will explore in greater detail
below, in the modern era both pirates and children represented a departure from, even a rejection of, increasingly racialized ideas of freedom. In
both cases it was not a great leap from the rebel to the barbarian, from the
political and cultural outsider to the racial Other. In particular, the dominant society portrayed both as savages, groups that one must either
civilize or eliminate. Children would hopefully grow into a mature idea of
freedom, facilitated by the rise of an extensive infrastructure of formal
education. Civilized society must eradicate piracy, either by capturing and
executing the actual pirates or by integrating their economic practices

into the broader structures of liberal capitalism. Both piracy and child-hood represented the kind of savage liberty white freedom must ulti-mately destroy.

As noted above, freedom has not always been a positive value nor has it always followed the strictures of liberal political theory; as Isaiah Ber-lin observed, "Freedom for the wolves has often meant death to the sheep."[6] Liberty was thus not automatically benevolent but had to be made so by suppressing the negative aspects of the idea, and the process of constructing a positive image of freedom had a strong racial dimen-sion. This chapter will briefly consider that process, arguing that liberty became white by divesting itself of qualities seen as primitive or retro-grade. True freedom belonged to the civilized, and civilization was itself increasingly defined in racial terms during the modern era: the barbar-ians of the jungle might revel in a spirit of anarchy, but only those of culture and enlightenment could build a society based upon freedom. Racial difference was built into the very definition of liberty, therefore, in ways that would both foster and result from racialized ideas of free-dom as white.

Liberty and Race

Similarities, Differences, Intersections

I began this chapter by noting how freedom and race are both extremely important ideas in Western civilization, and how at the same time they seem to be so different from each other, one positive, one negative. In particular, the historiography of racialized minorities has embraced the idea of freedom as freedom struggles; an individual or a group becomes free by overcoming racism and the limits of racial identity. The end of racial difference is the triumph of freedom.[7] Upon closer examination, however, the Manichean polarity between liberty as good and race as bad tends to break down. Race became a powerful means of categoriz-ing humanity precisely because so many people, scholars as well as or-dinary women and men, saw it as useful and beneficial. At the same time freedom has had its own negative aspects; as Orlando Patterson has observed, liberty has not been the most important concept in many cultures throughout human history. The concept of white freedom challenges the polarity between liberty and race as good and evil, underscoring the ways in which modern political cultures integrated a racialized view of the world into their ideas of freedom.

The trauma of the Holocaust, the crusade for Black civil rights in the United States, and the tidal wave of decolonization that swept the globe in the twenty years after the end of World War II all combined to craft an image of racial thinking as an unmitigated evil. It is important to emphasize, however, that this was not always the case. From the late seventeenth until the mid-twentieth century racial categorization was viewed as very much a part of progressive science, further illuminating the relationship between humanity and the natural world. The emphasis of Enlightenment intellectuals like Kant on classifying and ranking different human races, the social Darwinism and scientific racism of the nineteenth century, all illustrated the importance of racial thinking. One must also stress the fact that racial science did not necessarily equal racism: Count Arthur de Gobineau, for example, rejected anti-Semitism and he and other racial theorists opposed slavery. For many, the study of racial difference would enable scientists to improve the lives of all racial communities by understanding their biological potentials and limitations.

Another important positive dimension of racial thinking lay in its relationship to the rise of nationalism in the nineteenth century.[8] The mingling of ideas of nation and race represented a sharp departure from the tradition of racial thought in Europe, which had first become prominent as a way of characterizing the aristocracy, a group linked by blood and certainly not by national identity.[9] Yet the rise of Romanticism in the early nineteenth century highlighted the importance of national character shaped by history, turning the idea of the nation into an organic cultural unit rather than simply a political structure.[10] *Völkisch* ideology in Germany is the most salient example of this new view of the nation as race, but it hardly stood alone.[11] Even Ernst Renan, the French scholar whose famous 1882 essay "What Is a Nation?" challenged the German philosopher Johann Gottlieb Fichte and others who championed racial nationalism, saw France as a mixture of racial types rather than characterized by their absence.[12] Moreover, Renan's portrayal of France as united around history and spiritual principle in effect tended to racialize the nation.[13] By the end of the century the increased predominance of the nation-state as a political and cultural construct made racial pride an important part of national patriotism.

Racially subordinate groups have also embraced the ideal of racial pride, usually as a response to and rejection of racial oppression. The processes by which peoples who are lumped together according to stereotypes and discrimination develop a positive sense of group identity are extremely complex; like nations, racial minorities must be constructed over time. Scholars have studied how slaves from a variety of places in Africa gradually became Black Americans in the United States, or how modern Zionism crafted a new nation from diverse Jewish populations.[14] The point is that such processes involved creating a positive sense of racial identity, often modeled on that of the nation: the term *Black nationalism* is no accident. From the idea of the "race man" as someone dedicated to Black community empowerment to the "Black is Beautiful" movement of the 1960s, racial pride has constituted not only a key African American ideology but also a powerful weapon against racism.[15]

Many other peoples have embraced a sense of racialized identity as a rejection of racial oppression: for example, in 1933 famed German composer Arnold Schoenberg renounced his conversion to Lutheranism and reembraced the Judaism of his birth as a defiant response to Nazi anti-Semitism.[16] Many things tie racialized communities together, including at times cultural traditions, residential closeness, and a sense of a common history, but a shared history of racist victimization often plays a key role. To give one example, current debates in France about the identity of French Blacks have wrestled with how to define as a unified community people who come from a variety of different backgrounds and histories. The most popular solution, one championed by historian Pap Ndiaye, has been to argue that all those who suffer racial discrimination as Blacks are in fact Black. In this case, as in many others, the negative fact of racial categorization and bigotry is transformed into a group assertion of identity, one that gives the very idea of race a positive dimension.[17]

Racial thinking has therefore been considered by many people, both historically and in the present day, as an important dimension of social identity. That people often believe this for different, even diametrically opposed, reasons does not diminish the fact. Such ambivalence also exists in modern ideas about freedom. The near-universal praise accorded the concept of liberty in the modern world tends to obscure the fact that political freedom was not always viewed in such a positive light. Struggles for freedom have often been so dramatic and difficult precisely because many—and not just evil despots—have opposed them. Even campaigns for national liberation, often portrayed as the battle of a united people against an oppressive outsider, have usually involved major internal conflicts, often amounting to civil wars; for example, up to twenty percent of white American colonists fought for the British during the US war of independence.[18] For all the allure of freedom, throughout history many people have firmly rejected its clarion call.

Much of this conflict, of course, arises from the fact that people often have different ideas of what constitutes freedom. But the opposition to liberty at times goes deeper than that: the very etymology of terms like *freedom* and *liberty* is revealing in this regard. For example, whereas the *Oxford English Dictionary* defines *freedom* as the ability to act without restraint, its definitions of *licence* and *libertine* are very similar: *licence* it defines as "Freedom to behave as one wishes, especially in a way which results in excessive or unacceptable behaviour"; *libertine* as either a religious freethinker or "a person . . . who freely indulges in sexual pleasures without regard to moral principles."[19] Both *licence* and *libertine* generally denote undesirable qualities and behaviors. Their similarities to the idea of liberty thus suggest that freedom, by itself, uncontrolled by morality or moderation, is in many ways a negative phenomenon. This of course has been a staple argument of liberal ideas about liberty: a free society must be controlled by the rule of law, by principles that will guarantee freedom for all and prevent the strong from oppressing the weak. At the same time, however, liberal ideas of political freedom have emphasized the importance of negative freedom, freedom *from*, as central to the ideal of liberty. The modern world has built political structures, notably parliamentary government and liberal democracy, to make freedom an institutional reality, but the essence of liberty remains much more complicated and paradoxical.

This helps to explain why movements for political liberty have had a controversial history. The history of modern republicanism provides a useful example. Republicanism, the idea that the people of a nation or other political unit are sovereign, has a long history going back to ancient Greece, the Roman republic, and the city-states of the Italian Renaissance—Venice, Florence, etc. In the modern era republicanism has been closely associated with political liberty, above all in the United States, which as an independent nation has always been a republic. Yet it has also often been associated with instability and revolution. Oliver Cromwell's Commonwealth during the English Revolution and the Jacobin Republic during the French Revolution both executed kings and abolished their respective monarchies to affirm the centrality of popular sovereignty, but these actions convinced many that republicanism was a radical and dangerous ideology that, far from promoting freedom, brought its own type of oppression. In both cases revolutionary regimes gave way to restorations of the monarchy. Similarly, in the Americas, although the United States demonstrated that a republic could be moderate, the instability of the Latin American republics that followed the overthrow of Spanish rule in the New World seemed to confirm skeptical views of the ideology.

As a result, liberalism during the nineteenth century tended to reject republicanism in favor of constitutional monarchy, most notably in Great Britain but elsewhere as well. Not until France established the Third Republic in 1870 did a major European nation embrace a conservative vision of republican rule, and even in the twentieth century the collapse of many of the republican governments established after World War I revealed the weakness of this type of regime. As the fate of Germany's Weimar Republic demonstrated so tragically, the republican ideal of freedom was by no means universally accepted or viewed as positive.

The history of anarchism provides an even more dramatic example of negative liberty. As an ideology, anarchism has always emphasized a rejection of authority, especially state authority, and the complete liberty of the individual as the heart of all political structures. Like republicanism, its pedigree goes back to the ancient world, not just Greece and Rome but also Taoist China. In the modern era anarchism came to mean not just the absence of the state but also a communal organization of society based on freedom, equality, and common property. Pierre-Joseph Proudhon in France and Peter Kropotkin in Russia made anarchism a key part of struggles for socialism and revolution. By the late nineteenth century anarchism had become associated with terrorism, as anarchist militants staged a spectacular series of assassinations of heads of state throughout Europe and America in the 1880s and 1890s. A movement that emphasized individual freedom thus turned into one that seemingly justified murder. Anarchism became more known for lawlessness and chaos than for resistance to oppression; as one dictionary defines it, anarchy is "a state of disorder due to the absence or nonrecognition of authority."[20] Here again, freedom is a social problem rather than a solution.[21]

Both liberty and race therefore have positive and negative connotations, both historically and in the present. They are similar in some other important ways as well. Both have a significant universal quality, seeking to explain essential aspects of the human condition as a whole. Both are strongly rooted in intellectual history, especially that of the modern era. Both have also inspired important political movements, at times dominating entire states. Finally, as we have seen in the discussion above, both are extremely varied and open to multiple interpretations, interpretations that often reflect the social and political positions of those that hold them. Freedom and race have been adopted equally by dominant authorities and by subordinate groups opposing them. In both cases, the diversity of these two concepts has been an important source of their power.

There are of course important differences between the two ideas as well, especially when one considers their evolution in the modern era. Although, as I have tried to show, the idea of freedom as universally good versus race as primarily racism and therefore evil has not always existed, is in fact fairly recent, nonetheless this polarity shapes much of current thought about the two ideas and the relationship between them.

It is precisely this polarity that white freedom undermines, showing how much these two great ideas have in common.

The rest of this chapter will consider two examples of alternate visions of freedom, piracy and childhood. In ways that are both strikingly different and curiously parallel, these two conditions offer insights into how the modern world has conceived of liberty and how, in particular, it has developed a circumscribed vision of that ideal. Both represent the kind of primitive freedom that had to be excluded in order to develop this circumscribed vision. As a result, both childhood and piracy help illustrate how part of the limits of modern liberty could be racial, leading to the creation of white freedom.

Liberty's Stepchildren

Freedom on the High Seas

What does it mean to be free, and when do we feel the most free? The two questions will often elicit very different responses. Do we feel more free standing in a voting booth or driving a fancy new car down a picturesque, uncrowded highway on a brilliantly sunny day? To give another example, a staple of political freedom in the United States is the right to a trial by jury, but probably most Americans feel more free when they get out of jury duty than when they serve on it. Political and personal liberty are perhaps two different things, but since the point of the former is to facilitate the latter, one can hardly treat them in isolation from each other. How do we consider cases where, as in the second example, the two seem dissonant, even opposed? In part this speaks to the classic need to create a society of freedom for all by restricting the ability of individuals to do whatever they want. It also, however, illustrates the existence of many alternate visions of liberty not necessarily represented in the realm of liberal political theory. Such visions can certainly reinforce the ideology of political freedom, but they can also challenge it. In different ways both piracy and childhood represented alternate ideas of freedom, and the rest of this chapter will explore how both fed into a racialized vision of liberty.

One of the most famous visual representations of the ideal of liberty is Eugène Delacroix's 1830 painting *Liberty Leading the People*. An iconic image in the history of modern France and in Romantic art, Delacroix's painting represents freedom as a militant goddess leading a national revolt against monarchy and tyranny. A century earlier, however, a Dutch artist created a strikingly similar image that gives a very different portrait of liberty. The *Historie der Zee-Rovers*, published in Amsterdam in 1725, included as a frontispiece an engraving of the famed English female pirate Anne Bonny.[22] Like the image of Marianne in *Liberty Leading the People*, this image centers around a bare-breasted woman holding a sword and brandishing a flag, in this case the skull and cross-bones. The painting is much rawer than Delacroix's, the woman's face displaying a passion that seems as much sexual as militant. Nonetheless the two paintings have a great deal in common. It is fascinating that the image of a female pirate, one who transgressed norms of gender as well as law during her life, should resemble so closely one of the classic symbols of modern freedom.[23]

Maritime piracy has of course existed ever since mankind had the skills to take to the sea in boats. It bedeviled the ancient world, leading the great Roman writer Cicero to define piracy as a crime against civilization and pirates as the enemies of all nations. Throughout much of human history piracy has afflicted the commerce of the Mediterranean in particular. The heroes of Homer's epics were often nothing but pirates, seizing ships and raiding coastal settlements. The Roman Empire waged a series of military campaigns against Mediterranean pirates, at its height successfully enforcing the *Pax Romana* over much of the high seas.[24]

The height of Mediterranean piracy came during the early modern era. From the sixteenth century until the French conquest of Algeria in 1830, pirates based in North African cities like Tunis, Tripoli, and Algiers regularly raided shipping throughout the Mediterranean, stealing cargoes and enslaving crewmen and passengers. Known as the Barbary pirates, they were nominally subject to the Ottoman Empire, but in practice often functioned independently of the sultan's wishes. Their attacks against the ships of Christendom thus combined religious antagonism, Ottoman foreign policy, and a search for profits. In addition

FIGURE 2. Eugène Delacroix, *Liberty Leading the People* (1830). Musée du Louvre, Paris, www.Eugene-Delacroix.com.

to capturing ships from Europe, Barbary pirates frequently raided coastal settlements, not only in the Mediterranean but as far afield as Britain, Ireland, and Denmark, seizing captives to be used or sold as slave labor.[25]

The Barbary pirates had a tremendous impact on Europe and beyond before their demise; America's first overseas war was its campaign against them in the early nineteenth century.[26] Nonetheless, no era and place have had a greater impact on our ideas of what it means to be a pirate than the early modern Caribbean. During what historians have called the golden age of piracy, from roughly the 1620s to 1725, a variety of pirates, corsairs, privateers, and buccaneers established settlements in places like Tortuga, Hispaniola, and Port Royal, Jamaica, and raided established shipping across the Caribbean and Atlantic. The contemporary image of pirates, complete with peg legs, parrots, and the skull and crossbones flag, comes down to us from that era.[27]

HISTORIE DER ZEE-ROOVERS.

FIGURE 3. Anne Bonny, Pirate, *Historie der Zee-Rovers* (1725). JCB Archive of Early American Images; Call number D725 D314hA. © John Carter Brown Library, Box 1894, Brown University, Providence, RI.

Caribbean piracy arose in the context of European colonization of the New World; many pirates were Europeans adrift in the Americas, shipwrecked sailors, debtors, or escaped servants in search of a new life; others were escaped African slaves or native Americans fleeing the destruction of their communities. Many, notably the great privateers like Sir Francis Drake, worked as agents of the English, French, and Dutch governments, charged with raiding and harassing the great Spanish treasure fleets.[28] Others attacked any and all shipping, searching above all for profits and owing loyalty to no one other than themselves. In the early eighteenth century piracy began to decline as nations developed more regular naval forces, and as the burgeoning profitability of the Atlantic slave trade led the British and Spanish governments to agree on new arrangements to share the wealth. By the time the British Royal Navy caught and killed the notorious pirate Blackbeard off the coast of North Carolina in 1718, the golden age of piracy had essentially come to an end.[29]

The pirates of the Caribbean, as the success of several Disney movies bearing that name makes clear, have been remembered ever since. No other era of piracy in human history has had the same impact on the modern imagination. The golden age of piracy remains attractive for several reasons. Pirates symbolized an exotic, untamed world, one in which fantasy and reality still coexisted. They lived in a lush tropical natural landscape and seascape, representing all the physical allure of the Caribbean. In addition, they embodied a powerful masculine warrior tradition, in which men won battles through individual skill, strength, and courage rather than overwhelming firepower. Finally, the piracy of the seventeenth century is close enough in time to be documented but distant enough to seem hazy and romantic; from our perspective, for example, the celebrated peg leg represents a dramatic costume rather than physical pain and mutilation.[30]

Above all, and central to this study, the pirates of the golden age stand for freedom. As the early-eighteenth-century Welsh pirate captain Bartholomew Roberts, the famed "Black Bart," proclaimed: "In an honest service there is thin commons, low wages, and hard labour. In this, plenty and satiety, pleasure and ease, liberty and power; and who would

FIGURE 4. "Caribbean Pirates, Bartholomew 'Black Bart' Roberts." Lebrecht Music & Arts/
Alamy Stock Photo.

not balance creditor on this side, when all the hazard that is run for it, at worst is only a sour look or two at choking? No, a merry life and a short one shall be my motto."[31]

Several aspects of Caribbean piracy in the early modern era highlight this emphasis on pirates as free men. Many fled to the pirate ships to escape slavery or other types of servitude, and several Black pirates rose to the rank of captain. The decline of Caribbean piracy in the early eighteenth century took place at roughly the same time as the rise of the Caribbean plantation economy and society, so that in this region slavery and freedom existed cheek by jowl.[32] Pirate captains took part in the slave trade, often capturing slave ships and selling their captives, but sometimes they also gave them the opportunity to join the pirate crews. Some pirates also referred to themselves as "maroons," adopting the name given to rebel slaves in the colonial Caribbean. The image, and frequently the reality, of the pirate ship as a refuge from slavery thus underscored the idea of piracy as freedom.[33]

Pirate ships were also often governed by a rough practice of democracy, very much in contrast to both colonial society and emerging national navies. Many pirate captains were elected by their crews, according to the principle of one man, one vote, and could be deposed by popular vote as well. Pirate ships also practiced the separation of powers, vesting significant authority in other officers like the quartermaster. Only during actual battles did the captain exercise absolute authority.[34] On some ships a rough racial democracy prevailed; Blacks were by no means equal in general, and many worked as servants or even slaves aboard pirate ships, but certainly they enjoyed much more power and respect than on land in the Caribbean and the Atlantic world during this era. Historians Marcus Rediker, Peter Linebaugh, and others have argued that pirates often took part in political struggles for liberty during the eighteenth century constituting a kind of *sans-culotte* society at sea.[35]

However, the linkage between piracy and freedom arises equally from the place of pirates in modern popular culture. There is a clear connection between the decline of piracy as an actual threat to seagoing commerce in the early eighteenth century and the rise of fictionalized accounts about it: the first major study of pirates during the golden age, Charles Johnson's *A General History of the Pyrates*, appeared in 1724.[36] It was enormously popular and gave colorful portrayals of leading pirates like Blackbeard and Anne Bonny. The popularization of fictional pirates really took off in the nineteenth century, with the publication of Byron's poem "The Corsair" in 1814 and Sir Walter Scott's novel *The Pirate* in 1822. Perhaps the most influential of all fictional works about piracy, Robert Louis Stevenson's *Treasure Island*, appeared in 1883.

Nineteenth-century writers and their twentieth-century successors bequeathed to modern popular culture an image of pirates as symbols of adventure and romance. To be a pirate in the contemporary imagination means to sail one's own ship across the shimmering blue waters of the Caribbean, to become rich by finding legendary hoards of gold and jewels, and to drink rum and carouse without stopping. Perhaps most important, it means being able to do whatever one wants whenever one wants, not to have to obey any rules, or as one popular children's book put it, never having to change diapers.[37] In American culture in particular, the pirate Jolly Roger waves alongside the Confederate Stars and Bars as the emblem of the rebel,[38] a beloved figure of popular culture that expresses resentment of and resistance to the increasingly routinized and bureaucratic character of modern society.[39] The pirate symbolizes, in short, the spirit of freedom.

This idea of piracy as freedom has not only survived but thrived in the contemporary world. While in many respects the world of wooden ships and the skull and crossbones seems utterly different from that of smartphones and laptops, the rise of Internet piracy in the twenty first century has suggested an important link between the two. In the words of Internet historian Aram Sinnreich, for example:

> In 1390, an army of crusaders set out to wage war on piracy, with disastrous consequences for the soldiers themselves, their nations, and the entire Western world. . . . Over six hundred years later, we are in the midst of another, very different crusade, which nonetheless shares many similarities with Mahdia and may threaten to wreak just as much havoc and destruction over the long term. In this instance, it is Hollywood, rather than Genoa, playing the role of the righteous crusader, with the US government as its military ally, and digital technology innovators and their millions of online users cast in the role of the "pirates." . . . The similarities between today's piracy crusade and its fourteenth-century predecessor are more than superficial, and more extensive than a cursory comparison might suggest.[40]

Online piracy, or the downloading and sharing of Internet content in violation of copyright and other laws, really began in 1999 with the founding of Napster in the United States. A computer software program that facilitated peer-to-peer (P2P) file-sharing, Napster enabled consumers to download music, videos, and other types of files without paying for them. Not surprisingly it achieved instantaneous popularity: by 2001 millions of Internet users were using Napster to download over 2.5 billion files per month.[41] Four years later Internet users in Sweden created The Pirate Bay, which became very popular in Europe. Defenders of file sharing viewed it as a question of free speech and civil liberties versus capitalist profits. A popular image associated with the movement

FIGURE 5. "You call it Piracy, We call it Freedom." https://twitter.com/Sector404_Arg
/status/292354243791306752.

featured a pirate ship with a cassette tape mounted over a crossbones on its mainsail, and the slogan *You call it Piracy, We call it Freedom*.

The global music industry, which saw a sharp decline in profits during the first decade after the founding of Napster, certainly disagreed, and launched a major legal campaign against file-sharing networks, which at different times managed to shut down both Napster and The Pirate Bay.[42] In both the United States and Europe government agencies and courts scrambled to ban file sharing, culminating with the Anti-Counterfeiting Trade Agreement (ACTA) of 2011, signed by eight nations. As fast as industry and political authorities could suppress such services, however, new ones sprang up to take their place, so that P2P file sharing has remained a presence in the Internet to the present day.

The politicization of Internet piracy by industry and government authorities provoked a political reaction by the pirates themselves. Thousands of protestors took to the streets of European cities in 2012 to protest the ACTA, and the European Parliament eventually refused to ratify it. At the beginning of 2006 activists in Sweden founded the Swedish Pirate Party, devoted to freedom of communication and the Internet. A government raid on The Pirate Bay that summer sharply increased its profile and its popularity; by 2009 it managed to win a seat in the Euro-

pean Parliament and its youth group became the largest political organization of young people in Sweden. The same year saw the birth of the
Pirate Party of Germany, which soon became even more successful,
winning 8.5 percent of the vote and 15 seats in the 2011 Bundestag elections.[43] In 2010 pirates created the Pirate Party International, which now
has members and affiliates in over forty European countries as well as
some American states. Drawing on the precedent of the Green Party
movement in Europe, the pirate parties represented a major new force
in global politics.[44] The movement even developed a spiritual side: in
2010 a Swedish philosophy student founded the Church of Kopimism,
which saw file sharing as a sacred act of devotion and won recognition
from the Swedish government two years later.[45]

Pirate politics emphasized freedom above all, freedom of communication and expression, freedom from control by corporations and the
state. As the Swedish Pirate Party argued in its 2006 manifesto:

> The development of technology has made sure Sweden and Europe
> stand before a fork in the road. The new technology offers fantastic
> possibilities to spread culture and knowledge all over the world with
> almost no costs. But it also makes way for the building of a society
> monitored at a level unheard of up until now. . . . The right to privacy
> is a corner stone in an open and democratic society. Each and every
> one has the right to respect for one's own private and family life, one's
> home and one's correspondence. If the constitutional freedom of in-
> formation is to be more than empty words on a paper, we much [*sic*]
> defend the right for protected private communication.[46]

If the pirates of the early modern Caribbean and Mediterranean represented a challenge to and rejection of the nation-state in the era of its
rise to global power, the pirate parties opposed modern nations in a
postmodern and transnational era.

The history and current state of the Internet piracy movement thus
highlights the powerful association of piracy with freedom as well as
with plunder. This image of liberty stands opposed to the standard political narrative of liberal freedom in two important respects. First, this
vision of freedom is one of escapism rather than political engagement,
flight from oppression rather than commitment to building a free society.

It is a classic vision of negative freedom, freedom *from*, as outlined by Isaiah Berlin and so many others, but it doesn't grapple with the problem of making negative freedom work in a large and complex society to ensure the rights of all. Instead, it embraces a dream of individual autonomy and rebellion, rebellion directed in the modern world precisely against liberal society. Its popularity illustrates the central contradiction within negative freedom, namely that relative liberty for all can be attained only by limiting the rights of each; otherwise put, a free society must contain both positive and negative aspects of liberty.

Second, the image of the pirate as free man directly contradicts the centrality of the rule of law to political liberalism and the liberal ideal of freedom. Pirates were at bottom criminals, and the view of them as romantic rebels tends to ignore that fact. But the paradox of this vision of liberty goes much deeper. There is ample room in Western libertarian tradition for breaking laws viewed as unjust or overly oppressive; Victor Hugo's *Les misérables* is a classic case, as is Dr. Martin Luther King Jr.'s "Letter from Birmingham Jail." But squeezing the pirates of the early modern Caribbean into such a tradition, let alone seeing them as romantic rebels from contemporary perspectives, is more difficult than it may first appear. Pirates often behaved with great brutality, at times slaughtering not only their military opponents but innocent men, women, and even children as well.

Perhaps more to the point, piracy was above all a crime against *property*. Most liberal accounts of freedom see the rule of law and the right to private property as essential to modern liberty, and pirates directly opposed both. This is of course precisely the main criticism of Internet piracy by the music and entertainment industries today: that it practices the theft of cultural products.[47] The relationship between piracy and slavery also reveals this. Slaves constituted a significant share of property in the Atlantic world during the seventeenth and eighteenth centuries,[48] and seizures of slave ships and their cargo formed an important and illicit part of the pirate economy. Moreover, the fact that many pirates were themselves runaway slaves itself contravened the rules of property at the time.[49] The very existence of piracy thus challenged the property rights so crucial to liberal ideas of freedom.

The piracy of the early modern Caribbean thus represented both a powerful model of freedom (then as now), and at the same time a sharp departure from the standard narrative of political liberty. A final important aspect of piracy as alternate vision of freedom has to do with its association with childhood during the modern era. Like many other parts of traditional cultures, as piracy ceased to be a real presence and threat it was gradually relegated to the realm of childhood fantasy, leading to the contemporary era's pirate-themed birthday parties, television shows, and amusement park exhibits.[50] The first major example of this was Robert Louis Stevenson's 1883 novel *Treasure Island*. The hero and narrator of the novel is Jim Hawkins, a youth in his early teens who encounters a series of pirates and other motley maritime characters as the son of a tavernkeeper in an English port. He goes to sea aboard a ship that is seized by pirates, led by Long John Silver, and ends up having a number of adventures culminating in the successful recovery of a treasure hoard from a deserted Caribbean island. *Treasure Island* introduced many of the classic tropes of pirate romance, not only the legendary character Long John Silver himself but also "X marks the spot," the peg-legged pirate, and the talking parrot.[51]

Especially compared to the romanticized images of pirates that followed, *Treasure Island* is relatively realistic. A particularly striking aspect of the novel, however, and one that represents a significant departure from previous pirate literature, is the presence of a boy as its central character. In some respects Jim Hawkins is not a typical child, or rather represents a premodern and preromanticized era of childhood: his age is indeterminate and he is in many ways treated like an adult. Nonetheless, *Treasure Island* soon became not only a classic children's adventure story but also forged an important link between childhood and piracy.

This link became far more powerful with the appearance some twenty years later of J. M. Barrie's *Peter Pan*, where piracy departs entirely from the real world to become a part of children's fantasy. In the play, which premiered in 1904, a group of middle-class London children, Wendy Darling and her younger brothers, are whisked off by the mysterious and playful sprite Peter Pan to the magical realm of Neverland, populated by fairies, mermaids, Native Americans, and pirates, notably the sinister Captain Hook. Both the pirates and the Native Americans represent peoples who exist in fantasy because they are no longer a real threat to the advance of modern civilization, but at the same time stand for freedom from the increasingly controlled character of that civilization.[52] Peter Pan and his fellows, the lost boys, are children who magically refuse to grow up, wishing to hold onto the wonder and freedom of childhood. After a climactic battle scene in which Peter Pan slays Captain Hook, however, Wendy decides she does want to grow up after all and returns with her siblings and the lost boys to the conventional domesticity of bourgeois London. But Peter Pan refuses to stay and remains a free spirit outside the world of mature society. The story ends ambiguously, with Wendy accepting her decision to grow up and yet still yearning for the freedom Peter Pan represents.[53]

In *Peter Pan* Captain Hook and his fellow pirates represent evil, but they also symbolize a certain type of freedom, that of a child's imagination. Moreover they, and the story in general, suggest that childhood *is* freedom, the absence of the constraints imposed by society upon individuals (and accepted by those individuals) as they mature into responsible adults. Wendy, her siblings, and the lost boys cannot leave the realm of fantasy to return to England until Captain Hook dies, for example. In Neverland children can fly, do as they wish when they wish, have exciting adventures, and do not worry about what adults want them to do. Not only the lost boys but all of Neverland's inhabitants represent beings who have not grown up; both pirates and Native Americans are adults trapped in a childlike state, having failed to mature along with society in general. When Peter Pan defiantly proclaims, "I won't grow up!" he, like the pirates and other residents of Neverland, insists that true freedom consists in remaining a child.[54]

Immature Freedom

The association of piracy with children is part of the transformation of childhood in the modern era, and in particular the rise of the concept of the Age of Innocence.[55] The classic text on the history of children remains Philippe Ariès's *Centuries of Childhood*. In this enormously influential study Ariès argued that the idea of childhood as a separate stage of life arose only in the modern era, that in the Middle Ages people generally regarded children as little adults, when they paid attention to them at all. His argument inspired a generation of historians to challenge his work and bring a new depth of research to the historiography of childhood. Ariès also argued, however, that the transition to modern ideas and practices of child-rearing tended to make children less free, to give them greater protection and security at the price of limiting their autonomy.

> The school shut up a childhood which had hitherto been free within an increasingly severe disciplinary system, which culminated in the eighteenth and nineteenth centuries in the total claustration of the boarding-school. The solicitude of family, Church, moralists and administrators deprived the child of the freedom he had hitherto enjoyed among adults. . . . But this severity was the expression of a very different feeling from the old indifference: an obsessive love which was to dominate society from the eighteenth century on.[56]

Just as the modern nation-state strove to eliminate the freedom of pirates, so too did it harness and restrict the freedom of children. It did so not just to protect young people but also to protect society in general. As J. M. Barrie realized, pirates and free children inhabited the same world, one that modern society was determined to stamp out.

The idea of children as special beings to be cherished and protected rather than smaller versions of adults began in Europe and America during the seventeenth and eighteenth centuries, and it focused primarily on the offspring of the middle and upper classes. Economic, social, and cultural factors played a role in this new perspective. The increasing importance of capitalism buttressed the need to invest in children's education and skills to prepare them for success as adults, success that could not necessarily rely on inherited wealth. If the aristocracy looked to the past the middle classes looked to the future, and nothing better symbolized that future than the next generation. The religious convulsions of the early modern era likewise played a role by gradually weakening the doctrine of original sin, as one could now view children as innocent and benign rather than born evil. Finally, by the mid eighteenth century infant and child mortality rates began to drop significantly, facilitating the ability of parents to bond emotionally with their children.[57]

By the eighteenth century the issue of child-rearing had become a major concern of European Enlightenment intellectuals. In particular, both John Locke and Jean-Jacques Rousseau wrote extensively about the subject. Locke's enormously influential *Some Thoughts Concerning Education* (1693) viewed the child as an innocent being to be carefully molded by education and moral principles into an upstanding adult and member of society.[58] Rousseau's great novel of education, *Émile* (1762), also embraced the idea of the innate natural goodness of children, opening with the famous sentence, "Everything is good as it leaves the hands of the Author of things; everything degenerates in the hands of man."[59] Locke and Rousseau thus struggled with how to preserve the innocence and benevolence of childhood in an imperfect society.

Both authors wrestled with the question of freedom, and their perspectives illustrate changing ideas of childhood liberty. Locke in particular argued that children are born with a love of freedom, in particular a love of playing freely, and that educators should use this to imbue them with a taste for learning and reason by making them seem like play.[60] The issue of freedom is of course one of the great themes in the writings of Rousseau (see chapter 3 for more on this), and in *Émile* he devotes considerable attention to how to train the young Émile to grow up into a free, self-sufficient man. More than Locke, however, Rousseau emphasized that children had to be trained to be free, they could not simply rely on their own desires. For both authors, therefore, the idea of childhood freedom rested upon adult authority and control.[61]

The Romantic era of the late eighteenth and early nineteenth centuries brought to fruition the ideal of childhood as innocent and idyllic, in the context of the triumph of bourgeois society in Europe and America. In 1788 the English painter Joshua Reynolds completed his classic painting *The Age of Innocence*. The young girl portrayed in the painting is beautiful and adorable, protected, safe and secure; she is also motionless, passive, mute. *The Age of Innocence* offers a portrait not just of a child but of the modern idea of childhood in general, reflected in

FIGURE 6. Joshua Reynolds, *The Age of Innocence* (c. 1778). Tate Britain.

the classic phrase "children should be seen and not heard." The painting's subject seems well taken care of and loved. Whether she is free or not seems less evident.[62]

The modern vision of childhood thus sacrificed freedom and autonomy for security and adult authority. The middle-class child in particular became in effect a bird in a gilded cage, and in some ways has remained so down to the present. Few people today have less autonomy than children, after all; their parents and elders tell them what to eat, what to wear, and how to spend their days. Moreover, whereas in most societies in the past children have worked for a living, often starting at a very young age,[63] the modern era has generally replaced work with school, formal education imposing its own constraints.[64] Most laws guaranteeing freedom, including of course the right to vote, do not apply to those under eighteen. To the extent that children enjoyed freedom, it was negative freedom, freedom from cares or wants. The Age of Innocence created an image of the child as a being without cares or concerns, his or her every need and want met by loving parents. Innocent children should be free from all the problems that challenged adult life.[65] Contemporary debates around the overbearing nature of "helicopter parents" and their restrictions on their indulged and controlled children only highlights the difficulties modern society has in coping with the idea of children as free.[66]

Not surprisingly, this image of childhood freedom has not gone unchallenged. Most notably, the benevolent authoritarianism of modern parenthood sparked a counterreaction among children themselves, a demand for freedom. This became most obvious with the rise of modern adolescence in the West. The existence of a gap between physical and social maturity, between puberty and full-fledged adulthood, has been a major characteristic of childhood long before the twentieth century, and "youth" have often been noted for social and political turbulence. In France, for example, young people created a Bohemian youth culture in Paris during the 1830s, and young artisans played a prominent role in the revolutions of 1848.[67]

Until the early twentieth century, however, most young people worked for a living. The rise of modern adolescence, like that of children as innocents, occurred as an aspect of middle-class society, of the increasing prominence of families that could afford to keep their physically mature children out of the labor market. In particular, it developed in tandem with mass secondary education. During the nineteenth century America and Europe largely succeeded in creating compulsory primary education for its children, but secondary education, as exemplified by Britain's "public" schools, remained the privilege of social elites until well into the twentieth. Once that changed, however, masses of young people, usually postpubescent and sometimes bigger than their teachers, were nonetheless still subject to school discipline and treated like children in general. The modern teenager was born.

The twentieth century in particular witnessed the triumph of modern adolescence, and to a significant extent the concept achieved particular prominence in the United States. In 1904 the American psychologist G. Stanley Hall published *Adolescence*, the first scholarly treatment of the subject, and Americans coined the term *teenager* during World War II. Not for nothing did John Lennon state during the 1960s that "America had teenagers and everywhere else just had people."[68] Yet the rise of adolescent groups and movements went far beyond the boundaries of the United States. The two great world wars, which brought millions of young people together, helped spur the sense of adolescence as a stage of life apart. Mass conscription became one of the biggest examples of youth mobilization, and outside the military many nations organized official youth movements. Nazi Germany's Hitler Youth, for example, enrolled millions of young people under the Third Reich.[69]

Yet the heart of adolescent culture in the twentieth century was social and cultural, as well as increasingly commercial, and frequently involved revolts against established authority. The 1920s brought the excitement of the Jazz Age, leading young people in Europe and America to defy the social and sexual taboos of their parents. As the world plunged into a new world war during the 1930s, groups of young people like the Swing Kids of Nazi Germany, the *Zazous* of Vichy France, and the Black and Latino Zoot Suiters of wartime Los Angeles challenged the cultural and political authority of the established order, sometimes at great risk to themselves.[70] Most dramatically, during the 1960s the postwar baby boom generation exploded in a series of campus and urban protests, including the near overthrow of the French government in May 1968, as well as creating a vibrant youth counterculture.[71] In the United States in particular, the revolt against the draft and the Vietnam War constituted a particularly sharp rejection of adult authority.[72]

Teenagers, physically mature yet still controlled and treated as children, became prototypical rebels and adolescence widely viewed as a turbulent time of life.[73] More generally, the image of free children, whether as members of youth gangs, beggars, or truants, became another negative idea of liberty.[74] Like piracy, childhood presented an idea of freedom at odds with some basic tenets of political liberalism. In modern societies in particular, children lacked the economic autonomy so often seen as a precondition for freedom. In this respect, childhood represented the antithesis of liberty.

At the same time, the political project that created liberal democracy during the nineteenth century in America and Europe closely tied freedom to education and maturity, that is to say, to the end of childhood. The shift from work to school was inspired not only by new visions of childhood and revulsion against the abuses of child labor during the Industrial Revolution but also by the conviction that only educated men could be free and responsible citizens.[75] The Third Republic in France, which made primary secular education free and mandatory during the late nineteenth century, considered the education of young children central to its liberal republican mission.[76] Schools also provided discipline: as one British school inspector noted in the late nineteenth century, "if it were not for her five hundred elementary schools London would be overrun by a horde of young savages."[77] Here, as in many other aspects of modern childhood, responsibility and freedom stood at odds to each other.[78] As *Peter Pan* made clear, growing up meant the end of a child's vision of liberty.

Both piracy and childhood thus represented alternate visions of freedom, visions that had to be suppressed or relegated to the realm of fantasy in order to make way for the hegemony of the modern liberal political order. At the same time, as I noted at the start of this chapter, both childhood and piracy had a significant racial, or racialized, dimension. I have already considered the relationship between piracy and the resistance to slavery, for example. More generally, the pirates of the early modern Caribbean were generally viewed as savages, a perspective grounded both in their brutality and in their odd, picturesque way of life.

The idea of the pirate as savage looms much larger in the case of piracy in the Mediterranean. Unlike the corsairs of the Caribbean or Internet piracy today, few have viewed the Barbary pirates as symbols of freedom. The historian Adrian Tinniswood makes this point sharply in the introduction to his *Pirates of Barbary*, stating:

In the West . . . neither group [Barbary or Somali pirates] has been able to boast the glamour of the buccaneers of America—the Henry Morgans and the Captain Kidds, the swashbuckling Errol Flynns of old romance. *Those* pirates have been held up by historians as heroic rebels without a cause, cheerful anarchists or ardent democrats, proto-marxists or proto-capitalists, promoters of gay rights and racial equality, praiseworthy dissidents rather than villains.

The pirates of Africa, past and present, have not. The white West regards them as the irreconcilable Other—not rebels against authority but plain criminals, not brave Robin Hoods . . . but cowardly thieves.[79]

More so than their Caribbean equivalents, the corsairs of the Barbary Coast were the inveterate enemies of white freedom precisely because racialized views of them did not permit their enemies to associate ideals of freedom with them at all.

Two points illustrate this. First, the very word *Barbary* came from the ancient Greek word for "barbarian," and even though the Islamic cultures they represented in many ways stood superior to those of Christian Europe for many centuries, the name and concept of the North African pirates as racial barbarians stuck. The fight against the Barbary pirates thus became a fight for Christian, or white, civilization. Second, the slave practices of the Barbary pirates represented the last time in modern history that nonwhites enslaved masses of white Europeans. As Gillian Weiss has argued, for the West in general and France in particular, the idea of "white slavery" became increasingly intolerable by the early nineteenth century, leading ultimately to the French conquest of Algeria in 1830 and the end of the Barbary pirate era. The fight against Mediterranean piracy was thus literally a fight for white freedom.[80]

Four years before *Liberty Leading the People*, Eugène Delacroix completed another canvas that uses the image of a woman to speak to issues of freedom, but in a very different way. In 1826 Delacroix painted *Greece on the Ruins of Missalonghi* in tribute to the Greeks' current war of independence against the Ottoman Empire, a war that won tremendous support from European intellectuals down to its triumph in 1830. The painting,

FIGURE 7. Eugène Delacroix, *Greece on the Ruins of Missalonghi* (1826). Musée des Beaux-Arts de Bordeaux, www.Eugene-Delacroix.com.

like *Liberty*, centers around a white woman, but in this case she is defeated and bloodied, not victorious. In the background stands the menacing figure of a Black warrior. It represented a narrative of white slavery that drew upon both the Greek conflict and the Barbary pirates, making the scene even more extreme by suggesting the rape of a white woman by a Black man. Delacroix thus integrated support for Greek independence into opposition to white slavery; in 1830 both the victory of the Greeks and the French occupation of North Africa would mark a definitive triumph for a racialized vision of liberty.[81]

In making this point, however, one must note another: the fact that one could represent the pirates of the seventeenth century Caribbean as white does not so much reflect historical reality as underscore the processes of racialization germane to the rise of white freedom. The actual pirates of the era came from many different races, including former Black slaves; most probably did not look like Errol Flynn or Johnny Depp. One of the most striking characteristics of films like *Pirates of the Caribbean* is that one can watch them without ever realizing that most people in the region are of African ancestry. The modern era of white freedom has room for romantic rebels only if they are white, or made to seem so; in this sense, Tinniswood's remarks above apply just as much to the actual buccaneers of the early modern Caribbean as they do to Barbary pirates. The romantic whitewashing of Caribbean piracy thus played an important role in integrating that tradition into narratives of white freedom.

Moreover, one should emphasize the fact that the decline of Caribbean piracy after 1715 coincided with the triumph of the Caribbean slave economy during the eighteenth century. Suppressing the "Black" freedom of piracy went hand in hand with perhaps the greatest example of Black slavery in history, a social and economic phenomenon that provided a significant share of the wealth that fueled American and European societies during the Enlightenment. This suppression thus helped create, as we shall see in chapter 3, the theoretical and ideological framework of modern liberty. It not only overwhelmingly benefited white planters in the Caribbean but more generally underwrote the prosperity of the Western world as a whole. The end of Caribbean piracy thus formed a key aspect of the historical triumph of white freedom.[82]

If the piracy of the early modern era has links to current cyberpiracy, these links also have a certain racial dimension. Certainly, most Internet pirates see themselves as progressives in the tradition of the Green movement, embracing racial and gender equality, environmentalism, and respect for LGBTQ communities. Yet the issue of the digital divide along racial lines remains real, with whites in general having greater access to the wonders of the Web than nonwhites. At the end of 2016 a report, *Digital Denied*, detailed the existence of the divide in America: "In this report, we demonstrate that communities of color find themselves on the wrong side of the digital divide for home-internet access— both in terms of adoption and deployment—in a manner that income differences alone don't explain. Once we control for other economic and demographic factors that contribute to this divide, the data illustrate persistent broadband adoption and deployment gaps for people of different races and ethnicities."[83]

This gap appears much more significant on a global level. A 2016 article in the online business journal *Strategy + Business*, "Why Are 4 Billion People without the Internet," noted that only seventeen percent of the population of South Asia and eleven percent of the population of sub-Saharan Africa could afford to use the Internet.[84] The membership of the Pirate Party International remains overwhelmingly European. For all its universal idealism, the world of Internet piracy nonetheless has definite links to the practice of white freedom.

The image of children as savages who need to be forced into civilization also has a long history. Especially during the modern era, philosophers and educators often drew parallels between educating children and civilizing colonial natives; one trained both natives and children to be enlightened, refined human beings, in effect by making them grow up. It was perhaps no accident that Jules Ferry, one of the great statesmen of France during the Third Republic, made his mark primarily in two areas: the expansion of childhood education at home and of empire abroad.[85] As Karen Sands O'Connor, a scholar of children's literature, has argued, "Educators and psychoanalysts examined childhood in the same ways that so-called primitive races were being viewed. Edwardian children's authors combined the approaches, creating works that concentrated on contrasts between childhood and savagery on one hand, and adulthood and civilization on the other. The end result was children's literature that consciously privileged white, British children over all others."[86]

At the same time, paternalist imperial ideology often treated the colonized as children, people who also needed to be civilized by force of arms if necessary; not for nothing did Rudyard Kipling famously characterize the native as "half devil and half child."[87] For example, in *On Liberty* John Stuart Mill argued that freedom should be restricted to the "mature races."[88] In her discussion of what she calls "the child-savage trope," Elisabeth Wesseling notes how this parallel often became a reality for colonial administrators: "As an outgrowth of the child-savage trope, colonial regimes in the overseas territories were often patterned after parent-child and teacher-child relationships in the metropolis. Raising children and ruling natives were structured as kindred practices."[89]

Both observers of adolescence and teenagers themselves frequently compared their cultures to those of nonwhites. The nineteenth century Parisian aesthetes who called themselves Bohemians used the term to refer to the Gypsies, exotic and nonwhite outsiders in modern Europe.[90] Cultural commentators on youth culture during the American Roaring Twenties labeled fashionable young men "sheiks," following the runaway success of Rudolph Valentino's 1921 movie *The Sheik*.[91] Native Americans in particular became symbols of youth culture. Paris in the Belle Époque confronted the social problem of street gangs known as *les Apaches*. Both the German *Wandervogel* and the British Boy Scouts drew upon romanticized visions of Indian traditions, and during World War II one German youth gang in Cologne labeled itself the Navajo.[92] Youth movements in twentieth-century Europe and America often privileged influences from African American culture, especially African American music. In a celebrated 1957 essay, "The White Negro," American writer Norman Mailer explored this relationship:

So no wonder that in certain cities of America, in New York of course, and New Orleans, in Chicago and San Francisco and Los Angeles, in

FIGURE 8. "Encore les rôdeurs! Rencontre d'Apaches et d'agents de police sur la place de la Bastille." Supplément illustré du *Petit Journal*, August 14, 1904.

such American cities as Paris and Mexico, D.F., this particular part of a generation was attracted to what the Negro had to offer. In such places as Greenwich Village, a ménage-à-trois was completed—the bohemian and the juvenile delinquent came face-to-face with the Negro, and the hipster was a fact in American life. If marijuana was the wedding ring, the child was the language of Hip for its argot gave expression to abstract states of feeling which all could share, at least all who were Hip. And in this wedding of the white and the Black it was the Negro who brought the cultural dowry.[93]

It seems appropriate that the powerful youth movements of the 1960s occurred in conjunction with freedom struggles by peoples of color in both the United States and the colonized world. In short, a rejection of whiteness constituted a key dimension of the adolescent search for freedom.

In essence, in the modern world pirates and children have at times stood for a vision of liberty that not only challenges and departs from liberal orthodoxy but is also racialized as Other, a kind of "Black," or

savage, freedom. In the case of piracy, the decline of such savage freedom in the Caribbean and of white slavery in the Barbary coast both
coincided with the rise of transatlantic slavery, and Black slavery had as
its inevitable opposite white freedom. In the case of children, the embrace of savagery and nonwhite cultures represented their immaturity
and their need to grow into a white model of liberty.

Such alternate visions of freedom were both threatening and alluring
at the same time, thus doubly dangerous; the continuing attraction of
primitivism in Western culture illustrates the enduring appeal of savage
freedom.[94] The project of translating liberal ideas of freedom into the
institutional framework of liberal democracy involved suppressing such
alternate ideas of liberty, of in effect rendering them Other. The increasingly powerful template of racial difference in the modern era provided
an influential way of doing so. Ultimately, the antidote to savage liberty
was white freedom.

Conclusion

This chapter has endeavored to challenge the contemporary polarity
between liberty and race by considering the historical evolution of both
concepts, to illustrate both differences and also affinities between them.
The result has been different forms of liberty, often far removed from
the ideas of classic liberal political theory. Pirates and children represent
two important examples of this: both are in some senses doomed to
perish, either by elimination or by maturation, with the rise of modern
society, yet both also retain a strong appeal precisely because of their
instability. The tremendous popularity of Internet piracy today suggests
that such alternate visions will never completely disappear. In making
my central argument that modern concepts of freedom have often been
racialized I suggest that white freedom is one of those forms, one result
of the intersection between two of the most foundational ideas in modern history.

The next chapter will approach the history of that intersection by considering perhaps the most famous representation of freedom in the world
today. The Statue of Liberty symbolizes not only the idea of freedom in

general but more specifically the fundamental national character of the United States as the "land of the free." As I will show, this great icon of freedom has an important racial dimension, rarely acknowledged but nonetheless present and in many ways central to its symbolic presence. Analyzing the Statue of Liberty from this perspective will offer new insights into the complex relationship between freedom and race, and the ways in which white freedom arose out of those interactions.

CHAPTER 2

Lady of Freedom,
Lady of Whiteness

THE STATUE OF LIBERTY AS
SYMBOL OF WHITE FREEDOM

The Statue of Liberty is a fake.

According to a persistent rumor among African Americans, the sculpture that rises grandly from Liberty Island in New York Harbor is not the original Statue of Liberty. The true original was modeled after a Black woman and had African features. In addition, the point of the statue was to honor not immigrants but rather the abolition of slavery in America by the Civil War, and in particular the service of Black Union soldiers. The statue carried broken chains to symbolize emancipation. Furthermore, the legend goes, the current white statue was substituted for the original when American politicians objected to portraying Liberty as a Black woman. Some have even argued that the original Black statue still exists, either in France or hidden somewhere in the catacombs of New York.[1]

No evidence exists to verify this legend, but its mere existence illustrates the racialized nature of America's most famous monument. Of all the memorials to freedom throughout the world, none is more important or widely known than the Statue of Liberty. Towering majestically over the entrance to New York Harbor since 1886, the great statue has become, more than any other monument or physical site, the symbol of

FIGURE 9. View of the Statue of Liberty from Liberty Island (2008). Daniel Schwen/CCA-SA-4.0.

both human freedom and American national identity. Originally a gift from France to the United States, it also represents the historical ties between the two great republics and the significance of liberty as a global phenomenon. Endlessly reproduced as a tourist object, commercial symbol, or nationalist icon, the Statue of Liberty is one of the great monuments of the modern world.[2]

National monuments not only have but are power. They represent a combination of myth and history: frequently representing historical events, such as the great war monuments of the twentieth century, they generate their own myths around them that bring together and are embraced by national communities.[3] They thus exemplify what literary scholar Lee Bebout has termed the "mythohistorical," which he considers the intersection of myths and history to build a sense of identity and community.[4] Through this combination national monuments build a sense of national community. The Statue of Liberty has functioned as one of the greatest monuments in America by building what it means to be American around the myth of freedom, thus enabling Americans as a people to build their sense of national identity on the basis of that myth. It symbolizes the idea that American history is above all the forward march of liberty, for the nation and the world in general.[5]

In this chapter I wish to consider a little-explored aspect of the Statue of Liberty's history, its role as a racial icon, and more specifically as a symbol of whiteness. Most obviously the statue's European physical features, but also the lack (indeed, as we shall see, the suppression) of any markers identifying it with rebel or freed slaves, give it a strong sense of racial identity. Moreover, the symbolic role played by the Statue of Liberty in allowing European immigrants to the US to claim white status affirms its racial character, as does its complicated but largely exclusionary or at best irrelevant relationship to African Americans and other peoples of color. Most important for the purposes of this book, the Statue of Liberty embodies both racial difference as well as an unparalleled representation of human liberation. It is thus the perfect symbol of white freedom.

This chapter will explore the racial history of the Statue of Liberty from both an American and a transnational perspective.[6] Recent studies of the statue have increasingly considered its French origins and the context of French politics and culture in the late nineteenth century, and my study will continue that emphasis, considering how questions of race and class shaped the statue's birth.[7] I will then review the shifting racial meanings associated with the Statue of Liberty in the United States, ranging from its origins to the celebration of its centennial in 1986. Finally, I will briefly look at other statues of liberty throughout the world, notably China's *Goddess of Democracy*, which was associated with that nation's democracy movement in the late 1980s. Throughout, I will argue that the Statue of Liberty is the world's most prominent example of the racialization of modern ideas of freedom.

A Domesticated Vision of Republican Freedom in France

Conceived by French scholar and activist Édouard de Laboulaye and wrought by French sculptor Frédéric Auguste Bartholdi, the Statue of Liberty not only represents the admiration of the people of France for America but equally illustrates the changing nature of liberty, including its racial dimensions, in French history. The idea of France as a land of freedom has been central to modern French identity, summarized by the famous slogan of the French Revolution, *Liberté, égalité, fraternité*, which ranked freedom first.[8]

In particular, the ideal of freedom has taken the political form of republicanism, emphasizing popular sovereignty and the rejection of aristocratic rule. Emerging out of the cauldron of the French Revolution, republicanism espoused a new vision of France, and indeed of all humanity, centered around individual liberty and political democracy. By the beginnings of the twentieth century a republican ideology dominated French political culture, and it continues to do so to this day.[9] The creation of republican hegemony took decades, however, involving a series of tumultuous political struggles throughout the nineteenth century. The Statue of Liberty was conceived and constructed during this era of republican apprenticeship in France, eventually symbolizing not just freedom in America but also the triumph of the republican ideal in the land of Liberty's birth.

Republicanism as a political idea goes back to antiquity, notably the Roman Republic, and played a prominent role during the Renaissance with the rise of the republican city-states, Florence, Venice, etc. In the early modern era republican nation-states emerged in the Netherlands and in revolutionary England under Oliver Cromwell.[10] During the Enlightenment, French intellectuals such as Montesquieu and Rousseau developed republican political philosophy in opposition to absolute monarchy, at times aligning it with liberal ideology.[11] But it was the French Revolution that created the first republican political movement in France, one destined to shape the future of the nation in the modern era. It also emphasized a key theme in the history of republicanism, its association with political extremism and violence. Like Cromwell's seventeenth-century Commonwealth, the first French Republic of 1794 grew out of regicide; the people became sovereign by executing the king as well as abolishing the monarchy. Radical measures like the deestablishment of the Catholic Church and the abolition of slavery in France's colonies also gave republicanism a revolutionary air. The overthrow of the republic by a military dictator, Napoleon, further underscored the violence and instability of the movement.[12]

Throughout the nineteenth century, republicanism in France struggled with its revolutionary heritage. French political history in the 1800s seems like a crazy quilt of republics, dictatorships, and empires, constantly interrupted by revolutionary upheavals: rebels overthrew the national government in 1830, 1848, and 1870.[13] At the base of the turmoil, however, was the core tension between republicanism and liberalism, between the emphasis on democracy and the stress on individual freedom. Not for nothing did the liberal prime minister of the July Monarchy, François Guizot, scornfully dismiss those campaigning for universal suffrage by saying that if they wanted to vote they should get rich.

How could the radical vision of democracy championed by the Jacobin republic and the *sans-culottes* of the French Revolution coexist with property rights, the rule of law, and civil liberties?[14]

The contrast between these two visions of republicanism formed part of the broader struggle throughout Europe and beyond to reconcile popular sovereignty and private property, a struggle that would ultimately create the powerful compromise we know as liberal democracy. In order for republicanism to win the allegiance of the affluent bourgeoisie in particular and the majority of the French population in general, it ultimately had to shed its revolutionary trappings and come to terms with the nation's established order. The ideal of "the social republic," a republicanism that emphasized social equality and justice, had to be suppressed, by force of arms if necessary.[15] Not until the creation of the Third Republic in 1870 did French republicanism succeed in making this key ideological shift, and not until the republicans' victory in the Dreyfus Affair at the end of the century did republicanism become the uncontested dominant political ideology and culture in France.

This struggle came to a head during the early years of the Third Republic. In 1851 Napoleon's nephew, Louis Napoleon, had violently suppressed the Second Republic created by the revolution of 1848. A year later he proclaimed himself Emperor Napoleon III, establishing the Second Empire and driving republican forces into an underground opposition movement. Perhaps the most curious of modern French regimes, the Second Empire oscillated between iron-fisted repression and progressive ideas; it made trade unions legal in France, for example, and maintained the tradition of universal manhood suffrage established in 1848. Yet the liberalism of the Second Empire failed to mollify its republican critics, so that when the emperor was ignominiously taken prisoner after a major defeat in the Franco-Prussian war, a new Parisian revolution overthrew his regime and established the third of France's republican governments.[16]

The challenge for the new Third Republic was to make republicanism respectable. Caught between the radical republican Left and the powerful monarchist Right, as well as facing defeat at the hands of the Prussians, its prospects at first seemed bleak. Many republican leaders argued that the new regime could only survive if it renounced its radical heritage; as the new provisional president, Adolphe Thiers, proclaimed, the republic must be conservative or it would not be.[17] The showdown between these two republican visions came in March 1871 when radicals seized control of the Paris city government and staged the armed uprising known as the Paris Commune. The republican government led by Thiers brutally suppressed the Commune, invading the city and conquering it block by block as the rebels fought back behind barricades and set fire to large parts of the capital. Tens of thousands of Parisians died in the fighting, shot by the forces of a republican regime that had itself come to power through revolution.[18] The defeat of the Commune represented the triumph of bourgeois republicanism in France over its revolutionary alter ego. By the end of the 1870s republican forces had achieved political dominance in the country, and the Third Republic would go on to be the longest-lasting regime in modern French history.[19]

The idea of the Statue of Liberty took shape in this France racked by empire, republicanism, and revolution. The life and politics of Édouard de Laboulaye, the man who more than any other conceived of the idea, illustrates the ways in which the political turbulence of mid-nineteenth century France shaped the statue that would come to dominate New York harbor. Laboulaye was born in 1811, at the end of Napoleon's First Empire, and spent his childhood and youth under the Restoration, the July Monarchy, and the Second Republic. An ardent republican whose hero was the Marquis de Lafayette, Laboulaye was in his early forties when Louis Napoleon smashed the French republic, replacing it with the Second Empire.[20]

Bitterly disappointed by this new turn to despotism in France, Laboulaye focused on the United States as a successful example of republican government and popular sovereignty. A professor of law at Paris's prestigious Collège de France, he became one of the nation's first and most prominent specialists in the study of the United States, publishing studies of American life, giving popular lectures and courses about America, and translating many key American works into French, including the autobiography of Benjamin Franklin.[21] Like a fellow

Frenchman whom he greatly admired, Alexis de Tocqueville, Laboulaye saw in the United States a successful example of moderate and stable republicanism that could serve as a model for France and the rest of Europe.

During the 1860s in particular Laboulaye used his admiration of the United States to criticize France's imperial regime. Much divided the two nations during these years: Napoleon III's regime openly favored the cause of the Confederacy during the American Civil War and also took advantage of that conflict to intervene in Mexico, overthrowing the government of Benito Juarez in favor of a Habsburg puppet, the emperor Maximilian.[22] French censorship prevented Laboulaye from voicing his admiration of the American republic too openly, but he nonetheless made it clear that the United States remained a model of freedom for France. As he wrote in 1862, at the height of the American Civil War, "Frenchmen, who have not forgotten Lafayette nor the glorious memories we left behind in the new world—it is your cause which is on trial in the United States. . . . This cause has been defended by energetic men for a year with equal courage and ability; our duty is to range ourselves round them, and to hold aloft with a firm hand that old French banner, on which is inscribed, Liberty."[23]

The 1865 triumph of the North in the Civil War was followed five years later by the collapse of the Second Empire in France and the advent of the Third Republic. The defeat of the Confederacy removed Laboulaye's one major criticism of the United States, slavery. Like many French liberals a strong abolitionist, Laboulaye had struggled to understand how a regime as noble as the American republic could tolerate such an abomination against human rights. During one of his celebrated lectures at the Collège de France, Laboulaye commented, "Why is it that this friendship [between France and America] has cooled? Why is it that the name of American is not so dear to us as it was in those days? It is due to slavery."[24] For Laboulaye, the Civil War and the emancipation of America's slaves reaffirmed his faith in that nation's republican vision. The overthrow of the Second Empire brought the end of a regime that had antagonized the United States, and France was once again a republic. As a result, Laboulaye ardently hoped for an alliance of the two great sister republics, one that would bring liberty and enlighten-ment to all the peoples of the world.[25]

By the beginning of the 1870s Laboulaye had developed the idea of a giant statue symbolizing liberty that France would give to the United States in honor of the centennial of the American Revolution.[26] At the end of the 1860s he met Frédéric-Auguste Bartholdi, an ambitious young French sculptor devoted to monumental public art who would make his vision a reality. Bartholdi had long been interested in larger-than-life sculptures, influenced by classical works like the Colossus of Rhodes and the great statues of Thebes in Egypt. In the late 1860s he had designed a great statue, *Egypt Bringing Light to Asia*, for the Egyp-tian viceroy, Ismail Pasha, which was intended to stand at the entrance to the new Suez Canal. The project never came to fruition, but in many ways it represented a first exploration of the themes that would culmi-nate with the Statue of Liberty. Most important, the image of a female colossus symbolizing liberty and progress inspired Bartholdi's creation of the American statue.[27]

Why would one give the ideal of liberty a female form? There is a long history of female representations of nations and political ideas, one which, as many feminists have trenchantly noted, has often coincided with the political exclusion and suppression of women in real life.[28] The ancient Romans celebrated the goddess Libertas, and during the early modern era in Europe the idea of freedom as a woman challenged the masculine authority of kings. The French Revolution gave birth to the idea of Marianne as the great symbol of the Republic, and throughout the modern era she has represented both republicanism and the nation of France in general.[29] No representation of modern liberty is better known, or more powerful, than Eugène Delacroix's painting *Liberty Leading the People* (Fig. 2). Created in the year that the 1830 Revolution overthrew the Restoration monarchy, Delacroix's great work portrays Liberty as a powerful woman, armed and bare-breasted, leading the in-surgents of Paris in the fight for freedom.[30]

Marianne is the direct ancestor of the Statue of Liberty, but the American monument incorporated some very important changes, sym-bolizing a different vision of freedom. Most notably, the classic image of Marianne united republicanism and revolution, emphasizing the overthrow of oppression. Key to this vision was the presence on so many Mariannes of the Phrygian cap, the ancient Roman symbol of the freed slave. Throughout the modern era in Europe, as "La Marseillaise" itself demonstrates, the struggle against monarchism and capitalism often adopted the metaphor of the slave uprising.[31] Marianne thus represented not just resistance to oppression but more specifically freedom as the end of slavery. As in Delacroix's painting, many Mariannes also bore weapons, emphasizing that the fight for liberty was a violent struggle. Finally, Marianne often bore a torch of some sort, symbolizing both illumination and also the fires of revolution.

The effort to produce a nonrevolutionary Marianne formed a key part of the fight for a conservative vision of republicanism in France. The Paris Commune also saw the proliferation of Marianne images, usually adorned with red Phrygian caps, and produced its own Mariannes.[32] One of the most dramatic (and for its opponents, horrific) images of the Commune was the *pétroleuse*, or female incendiary; persistent rumors suggested that working-class Parisian women would fill empty bottles with gasoline and use these homemade bombs to attack the forces of order and set fires throughout the city.[33] The *pétroleuse* was Delacroix's *Liberty* come to life, a revolutionary woman holding a flame in her hand. She symbolized everything bad about republicanism, and the French troops that suppressed the Commune summarily executed women throughout the city suspected of being *pétroleuses*, even if their only crime was carrying empty milk bottles.[34]

The new Third Republic sought to craft a more peaceful, less revolutionary image of Marianne after 1870; like the Second Empire before it, it sought to ban the Phrygian cap as part of this symbol.[35] More important for the purposes of this study, the turmoil of the 1870 revolution and the Paris Commune reinforced Laboulaye's and Bartholdi's belief in moderate republicanism and the need to represent it in a monumental symbol. Although neither was actually in Paris during the Commune, both had been close by and were able to witness firsthand the devastation it had wrought. For them, the French civil war highlighted the dangers of the revolutionary republic, which must be suppressed

FIGURE 10. Paul Klenck, *Une Pétroleuse* (c. 1871). Musée Carnavalet, Histoire de Paris (Paris Musées)/AKG-IMAGES.

symbolically as well as in actual combat. Their vision of the Statue of
Liberty consequently emphasized freedom's moderate virtue. The
statue is fully clothed, both majestic and modest, unlike the radical har-
ridans of Paris. It also does not bear a Phrygian cap: as we shall see, the
suppression of any links with antislavery also had an important American dimension, but in the French context it represented the rejection of
freedom as insurrection, so violently embodied by the Paris Commune.
In addition, the Statue of Liberty's torch is carefully contained, a light
and not a fire, or as Laboulaye put it, "a torch and not a flame," to illu-
minate, not to destroy.[36] The French vision of the Statue of Liberty thus
represented a domesticated version of the *pétroleuse*, weaponless and
shorn of all revolutionary intent.[37]

The evolution of the image of Marianne, and the contest between
moderate and radical visions of republicanism, formed part of the struggles around social class that so profoundly shaped life and politics in
nineteenth-century France. The moderate republic was to an important
degree a bourgeois republic, whereas the ideal of the social republic often
symbolized by Marianne wearing a red Phrygian cap played an important
role in working-class politics and culture.[38] French officials after 1870
struggled against popular and working-class desires for a Marianne with
a Phrygian cap on the official buildings of the republic.[39]

At the same time, such conflicts based in social class and class ideologies had an important racial dimension. As I will argue more extensively
elsewhere in this study, differences of race and class have often interacted in modern history, so that working-class Europeans have frequently been racialized as Other.[40] During the nineteenth century,
many leftists portrayed workers as slaves and their struggles as a kind of
slave uprising; Karl Marx himself called the Paris Commune a revolt
against "the would-be slaveholders of France!" and compared it to the
American Civil War.[41] Others considered the Communards savages,
viewing them and Parisian workers in general as unfit for civilization
and liberty. For Count Arthur de Gobineau, France's most prominent
racial theorist, the Commune and French workers in general represented racial degeneration and debasement analogous to Blacks and
other peoples of color.[42]

Perhaps most important, the triumph of bourgeois republicanism in France coincided with imperial expansion overseas. It is one of the ironies of French history that the regime which overthrew the Second Empire would foster the nation's greatest period of imperial expansion. The Third Republic created a massive new empire, expanding and consolidating colonies in Africa, Indochina, and the Pacific, all in the name of republicanism. As I will discuss further in chapter 4, it presented the strange contradiction of a republican empire without an emperor. The essence of this contradiction was of course racial difference, so that republican France became an empire of Black and brown natives ruled over by white citizens.[43]

The great statue France bequeathed to the United States in 1886 was therefore far more than a straightforward symbol of liberty. It represented the changing view of republicanism, and freedom in general, in France during the nineteenth century. In particular, it represented the triumph of a new view of freedom, one that increasingly rejected the concept's more radical history in favor of the rule of law and respect for the rights of property. This bourgeois vision of liberty also had a significant racial component, especially noteworthy because the Third Republic would not only emphasize conservative republicanism but also go on to create the greatest overseas empire in French history, so that when Liberty came to America's shores, this racial dimension already prefigured in France would become more important than ever.

Republicanism and Race in the United States

The America that welcomed the Statue of Liberty stood poised on the edge of global prominence, while at the same time haunted by the shadows of the recent Civil War. To an even greater extent than in France, the political life of the United States centered around republicanism: the birth of the American nation constituted a definitive break with monarchy, and the United States had always been a republic. As in France, however, there were different visions of republicanism in America. America also faced a choice between more and less inclusive visions of the republic, radical versus conservative republicanism. In America the key issue dividing republicans (which is to say political thinkers in general) was slavery, and behind it, racial difference.[44]

Unlike France or any other modern nation, the United States began not just as a republic but as a slave republic, and the intimate entanglement of freedom and race lay at the heart of the American experience from the beginning. The 1790 Alien Naturalization Act limited citizenship to whites,[45] a legal tradition reinforced by the Dred Scott decision of 1857, which held that even free Blacks could not be US citizens.[46] The conflict over slavery led directly to the Civil War, the greatest military conflict in American history, which cost the lives of 600,000 Americans, more than any other war before or since. The importance of the war to American history cannot be overstated: in a sense the true American Revolution, the Civil War made the United States one nation and set the stage for the unprecedented economic growth of the late nineteenth century and the world dominance of the twentieth.[47] Most notably for our purposes, in abolishing slavery and making the freed slaves American citizens, the victory of the Union spelled the end of the white republic.[48]

Or did it? The Republican Party had been founded in 1854 as a political movement opposed to slavery, yet as became clear such opposition could take different forms. For many, including the first Republican president, Abraham Lincoln, opposition to slavery meant hostility to the presence of Blacks, slave or free, on American soil. The republic must reject slavery, but the best way to do so was to get rid of the slaves themselves. Lincoln and many other Republicans had come only reluctantly to support the abolition of slavery, and the Emancipation Proclamation provoked furious hostility throughout the North during the war.[49] By 1865 the Republicans were clearly divided as to how to rebuild a bitterly divided nation and more generally about the shape of the American republic in the future. Moderate and conservative Republicans wanted not only to reconcile with the defeated South but also to prevent social or political equality for African Americans. Their support of Lincoln's successor, the Southern Democrat Andrew Johnson, illustrated these changing attitudes.[50] In contrast, the Radical Republicans insisted on a thoroughgoing political overhaul of the South, one that would give the freedmen full status as American citizens based on the principle that all Americans were equal regardless of race.[51]

The conflict between these two perspectives haunted the Reconstruction era and ultimately brought it to its end. During the decade after the end of the Civil War the Radical Republicans controlled the US Congress, using that control to pass sweeping legislation (including the Thirteenth, Fourteenth, and Fifteenth Amendments to the US Constitution) that sought to empower the former slaves as equal citizens of the republic. Most important, they deployed federal troops throughout the former Confederacy to ensure the freedmen's right to vote, so that during Reconstruction Black legislators often controlled the state governments of the South. These efforts were fought tooth and nail not only by white Southerners and the Democratic Party that represented them but also by Andrew Johnson and other moderate Republicans. Resistance to Reconstruction frequently turned violent, especially after a group of ex-Confederate soldiers founded the Ku Klux Klan in 1866, unleashing a wave of white terror against Black and white Republicans throughout the South. In 1873 white vigilantes massacred some 150 Blacks in Colfax, Louisiana.[52] Two years later similar terrorists killed hundreds of Black men in Mississippi as the Democrats retook control of the state by force.[53]

For most white Southerners, and many Northern Republicans as well, the very idea of Reconstruction state governments dominated by Blacks was an unthinkable outrage contrary to all civilized norms. The fact that such administrations created the first public school systems in the South meant little to their opponents, who condemned them as corrupt and savage.[54] Just as some opponents of the Paris Commune denigrated its members as savages, so too opponents of Reconstruction did not hesitate to tie the Radical Republicans to the forces of red revolution. In April 1871, the *Charlottesville Weekly Chronicle* charged that "The French Reds, like their brethren, the Black Radicals of this country, are appealing to a higher law to justify their crimes. They threaten the guillotine in Paris. [The Radicals] would send halters to the leading men of the South. One set is as bad as the other. There is little choice between them."[55]

The same year that saw the triumph of the moderate Republic in France, 1877, also witnessed the end of the radical Republican Reconstruction in the United States. In 1876 the moderate Republican Rutherford B. Hayes won a very closely contested presidential election, partly on his promise to stop meddling in the affairs of the South. He won Southern Democratic support by agreeing to withdraw federal troops from the region, a promise he kept in 1877. With their departure, little prevented white Democrats and the racist terrorists who supported them from ending Reconstruction and the promise of an egalitarian Republic. Blacks continued to exercise their right to vote for a while, but starting in the 1890s Southern state legislatures passed new constitutions using the poll tax and other means to effectively disenfranchise them. By the first decade of the twentieth century, white supremacy had destroyed Reconstruction and the dream of an inclusive republic.[56]

The end of Reconstruction was perhaps the most obvious example of the increasingly racialized nature of American republicanism in the late nineteenth century. The year 1877 also witnessed a massive series of railway worker protests that turned into the first general strike in American history. While many hostile observers racialized the strikers as inferior Europeans,[57] the strike leaders frequently and increasingly emphasized the whiteness of the movement. Strikers in San Francisco turned the movement into a pogrom against the city's Chinese.[58] In 1882, little more than a decade after laborers from China had helped build the nation's first transcontinental railroad, America passed the first of several Chinese Exclusion Acts, making it a crime for workers to immigrate to the United States from China.[59] The decades after the Civil War also witnessed the final stages of the American wars against Native Americans in the Great Plains, culminating with the Wounded Knee massacre of 1890.[60] Moreover, although to a lesser extent than France or Britain, at the end of the century the United States acquired an overseas empire, annexing Puerto Rico, Guam, the Philippines, and Hawaii in 1898. America's colonies were, like those of France, largely inhabited by nonwhites and subject to authoritarian imperial rule.[61] The Civil War and Reconstruction had brought the hope that republicanism in Amer-

FIGURE 11. Poster for Chinese Exclusion. "The magic washer. The Chinese must go." (1886). Color lithograph. Everett Collection Inc./Alamy Stock Photo.

ica could embrace all peoples, but by the dawn of the twentieth century it was clear that America would remain a racialized white republic for the foreseeable future.

Historians David Roediger and Alexander Saxton have described the racialization of American politics after the Civil War as *Herrenvolk* republicanism, the democratic hegemony of the master race. The battle against slavery had triumphed in the destruction of that institution, but that did not necessarily bring freedom to the slaves. As in other post-emancipation societies throughout the Americas, the antebellum elites of the South managed to preserve their racial hegemony by terrorizing and ultimately disenfranchising the "freed" slaves. Racial difference no longer existed as a function of slavery but now assumed center stage in American political and social life. As a result, by the turn of the twentieth century liberty in America was for whites only.[62]

The nation that welcomed the Statue of Liberty in 1886 was thus one that had embraced its own version of conservative republicanism that was, even more than in France, grounded in racial difference. The image of a Marianne shorn of references to insurgent politics found a ready audience in America. Correspondingly, while Laboulaye and Bartholdi personally supported the abolitionist cause, they designed the statue not to irritate what had become increasingly a sore subject in the United States. By the 1880s the Confederate narrative of the Civil War and Reconstruction, viewing them as an unfortunate mistake at best, a crime against civilization at worst, had gained traction throughout the country and remains influential to this day.[63]

During his tour of the United States to explore support for the statue, the new political context became clear to Bartholdi and influenced his design of his magnum opus. He had originally planned to have the statue hold broken chains in her hand as a symbol of slave emancipation, but he replaced them with a book of law. The Statue of Liberty does in fact include broken chains at her feet, but they are effectively hidden both by her robe and by the pedestal on which she stands. Like the Phrygian cap, therefore, the effective absence of the broken chains distanced the statue not only from slave emancipation but from radical Republicanism in general.[64]

Political dynamics in both France and the United States thus served to distance the Statue of Liberty from republican egalitarianism, and in doing so gave it an important racial meaning. The resplendent white lady standing above New York harbor turned her back on the racialized working masses of Europe and the increasingly marginalized Blacks and other peoples of color in America. When Americans celebrated the inauguration of the Statue of Liberty in 1886 they celebrated a racialized vision of liberty; the original statue may not have been Black, but the one they embraced was certainly white. Right from the beginning of its history in America, therefore, the Statue of Liberty was a powerful representation of white freedom.

White Woman on a Pedestal

As is well known, the United States met France's gift of the Statue of Liberty by funding and building a giant pedestal upon which to place it. Funded by a popular subscription launched by American newspaper magnate Joseph Pulitzer, the massive pedestal and base rise 154 feet from the soil of Liberty Island, slightly taller than the statue itself. The Lady of Liberty thus stands high above New York harbor, lifting her torch to a height of over three hundred feet and to this day dominating the maritime approach to America's largest city.[65]

This image of the woman on a pedestal corresponds to increasingly conservative and dominant images of gender and womanhood during the nineteenth century, in America and throughout the world. We have already seen how the design of the Statue of Liberty represented a more conservative vision of Marianne, illustrating the shift in republicanism in both the United States and France. This shift corresponded to a broader transformation of the image and reality of women's lives during the nineteenth century, one that historians have characterized as the rise of domesticity. Briefly stated, with the spread of industrial society and bourgeois culture middle-class women found themselves removed from the world of paid labor and increasingly relegated to the home. The doctrine of separate spheres assigned to women management of the household and oversight of the children, while making them dependent financially and politically on men. While this new idea of femininity certainly did not reflect the lives of working-class women, the bourgeois standard of female behavior and status increasingly characterized what it meant to be a woman in the modern age.[66]

The image of the woman on a pedestal closely corresponded to the new model of domesticity. It was the image of a woman prized and cherished, even venerated, but also controlled and fixed firmly in place. Many feminists saw in this image an attempt to masquerade the oppression of

women in a gentle guise, praising them as symbols instead of recognizing them as human beings.[67] They rejected arguments of men like Senator George Vest of Missouri, who in 1887 declared on the floor of the
Senate, "It is said that suffrage is to be given to enlarge the sphere of
women's influence. Mr. President, it would destroy her influence. It
would take her down from that pedestal where she is today, influencing
as a mother the minds of her offspring, influencing by her gentle and
kindly caress the action of her husband toward the good and pure."[68]

Scholars have commented on the ambivalent appearance and symbolism of the Statue of Liberty. Perhaps most famously, historian Marvin Trachtenberg observed that though it represented a powerful, monumental image of woman, a "great lady," at the same time "for a fee she is
open to all for entry and exploration."[69] This incongruity corresponded
more generally to new bourgeois ideas of femininity, which rendered the
ideal woman sexless and subservient, while at the same time struggled
to repress sexual desire. Freud's madonna-whore complex, a powerful
representation of this ambivalence about women, thus found expression in the great statue dominating New York harbor after 1886.[70]

As many feminist historians have noted, these new ideals of domesticity often intersected with and were mutually reinforced by the new
racial hierarchies and racism. In both Europe and America, the proper
lady was a white woman who not only kept her distance from subaltern
classes and races, but whose presence could also foster the hegemony
of white bourgeois civilization. During the late nineteenth and early
twentieth centuries the creation of new European empires in Africa,
Asia, and the Pacific emphasized a vision of white womanhood
grounded in domesticity and racial privilege. While European women,
like European men, had long traveled to the colonies in search of wealth,
adventure, or religious service,[71] colonial regimes began promoting the
emigration of white women to their empires as wives and mothers. They
would not only prevent the need for interracial liaisons between European men and native women, but also domesticate colonial society by
centering it around white family life. The rise of white domesticity in
the colonies often corresponded to an increased sense of racial barriers
and discrimination; historians have long debated whether or not this

was due to the women themselves or to colonial society's view of them. Creating white domestic life meant, among other things, segregated white neighborhoods and social spaces in colonial cities. Imperial life thus placed the European woman on a pedestal, coming in contact with the natives below only as a benevolent but distant mistress.[72]

In the United States as well the presence of the white woman stood for bourgeois domesticity and freedom. Very similar to the European colonies, white pioneer women in the American West were seen as crucial to transforming the region from a wilderness populated by savages into a settled and domesticated part of the United States. Wives and mothers, farm women and schoolteachers—not saloonkeepers, prostitutes, or cowgirls—were instrumental to the civilizing of the West.[73] In no area did the racialized cult of domesticity prove more important than the American South, both before and after the Civil War. Rendered famous by *Gone with the Wind*, the cult of Southern womanhood has a complex history, involving both the embrace of patriarchal society and the emphasis on white women's empowerment in a variety of spheres ranging from the church to the plantation. The ideal of the Southern plantation mistress in particular underscored how white women created and symbolized civilization in a society dependent upon the labor of enslaved Black women and men.[74]

The image of the lady on the pedestal was crucial for white Southern women; their gentility depended upon an isolation from the realities of slave society. Above all, it meant the complete absence of sexual relations between white women and Black men; in contrast, sex between white men and Black women was an unacknowledged staple of antebellum Southern society. After the Civil War and the emancipation of the slaves, white Southerners sought to maintain racial dominance by the Jim Crow system of rigid legal and social segregation. Although several Southern states had repealed laws against interracial marriage during the Reconstruction era, they soon reenacted them throughout the region as part of the reestablishment of white dominance. Miscegenation, seen as the worst possible transgression of this system and a literal violation of the white woman on the pedestal, was vociferously condemned and ruthlessly attacked.[75]

During the late nineteenth century this emphasis on white biological and sexual purity became a key component of the form of racial terror known as lynching. White segregationists lynched Black men and women as a way of reestablishing white supremacy throughout the South. It soon, however, also became linked to a defense of white womanhood against the threat of Black rapists. As South Carolina Senator Ben Tillman argued, "We of the South have never recognized the right of the negro to govern white men, and we never will. We have never believed him to be the equal of the white man, and we will not submit to his gratifying his lust on our wives and daughters without lynching him."[76] Although, as contemporary antilynching activists like Ida B. Wells pointed out, most lynchings had nothing to do with sexual contact at all, let alone attempted rape, the idea that white men lynched Black men to preserve the honor of white women became a central theme of Southern life under Jim Crow. At a time when the image of liberty was enshrined in New York harbor as a white woman on a pedestal, racial terror became an important means of preserving that ideal in the states of the former Confederacy. The Statue of Liberty thus represented both freedom and racial segregation, and ultimately the violence needed to preserve racial segregation.[77]

As the ultimate representation of the white woman on a pedestal, the Statue of Liberty could thus symbolize the pure female needing protection from the Black rapist, and at the same time stand for retribution against Black men in general. One Texas journalist, for example, warned New Yorkers about the danger posed to the statue by Black men, saying that "some morning they would find the old girl with her head mashed in and bearing the marks of sexual violence."[78] The ambivalent gender symbolism of the statue, representing both female power and female vulnerability, assumed a more sinister meaning in the context of the racialized politics of late-nineteenth-century America.

In one instance a replica of the Statue of Liberty did play a role in an actual lynching. During the early years of the twentieth century a series of racial assaults forced many of the African American residents of Missouri's Ozarks region to flee for their lives. These culminated on April 14, 1906, when an enraged mob of thousands of whites lynched three Black

FIGURE 12. "O Liberty, What Crimes Are Committed in Thy Name!" (1906). Editorial cartoon, "Suggested to a Post-Dispatch Cartoonist by the Springfield Lynching under the Statue of Liberty." *St. Louis Post-Dispatch*, April 17, 1906.

men, Horace Duncan, Fred Coker, and Will Allen, for allegedly having sexually assaulted a white woman, Mina Edwards. The crowd dragged the three men to the Gottfried Tower, one of the city's tallest structures, which was topped by a replica of the Statue of Liberty, and hung them from it. An editorial cartoon in the *St. Louis Post-Dispatch* entitled "O Liberty, What Crimes Are Committed in Thy Name!" commemorated the grisly event.[79]

As the cartoon's title suggests, the use of the Statue of Liberty in a lynching prompted widespread outrage among both Black and white Americans. There was a sense that the very notion of freedom had been defiled. The governor of Missouri not only condemned the crime but also argued that the statue should be removed from the Springfield public square until justice was done.[80] At the same time, the incident did express some more general aspects of the statue, notably the role played by white womanhood in violence against Black men. The image of three Black men lynched by the Statue of Liberty dramatically illustrated the racialized dimension of America's greatest monument.[81]

The image of the white woman on a pedestal emphasized patriarchal control over women in general: at best it was an idea of protection, not freedom. In both Europe and America, the rise of new racial hierarchies during the late nineteenth and early twentieth centuries created a racialized version of patriarchy, in which the white woman had to be protected from natives of color. That such "protection" entailed strong limits on the agency, social, and sexual freedom of white women merely reinforced the importance of white male dominance over both women and men of color. In this context, the Statue of Liberty represented the kind of white female purity that served to justify the racial and gender hierarchies of the time.

Immigration, Race, and the Statue of Liberty

For most Americans, the Statue of Liberty symbolizes above all the history of immigration to the United States, particularly immigration from southern and eastern Europe during the late nineteenth and early twentieth centuries. In the classic narrative of American history, it represented the nation's welcome to the oppressed from throughout the world, and its ability to turn them all into loyal citizens grateful for the freedom they had found on its shores. As an article for the National Park Service has put it, "Between 1886 and 1924, almost 14 million immigrants entered the United States through New York. The Statue of Liberty was a reassuring sign that they had arrived in the land of their dreams. To these anxious newcomers, the Statue's uplifted torch did not suggest 'enlightenment,' as her creators intended, but rather, 'welcome.' Over time, Liberty emerged as the 'Mother of Exiles,' a symbol of hope to generations of immigrants."[82]

A closer analysis of the famed statue's relationship to American immigrants reveals a somewhat different story. As several historians have pointed out, in the late nineteenth century many Americans viewed and portrayed the Statue of Liberty as a symbol of anti-immigrant sentiment. "More often than not—at least in the early years—the Statue of Liberty stood as a symbol of opposition to immigration rather than of welcome to the 'huddled masses yearning to breathe free.'"[83] Those Americans who embraced nativism and saw the immigrant masses as a religious, racial, and political danger to the republic feared they would overwhelm not only the statue but the country as a whole. Not until well into the twentieth century did the idea of the statue as a welcoming beacon to immigrants become dominant in American society.

In exploring the reasons for this transformation, I focus on the racial identity of the Statue of Liberty, its representation of the ideal of white freedom. Historians of whiteness have studied the ways in which European immigrants were gradually accepted as white in America, and their relationship with the Statue of Liberty is part of this history.[84] In sum, the Statue of Liberty became a welcoming symbol of immigration when European immigrants became white. Those immigrants who gazed rapturously at the magnificent statue upon their arrival in New York harbor may have seen a symbol of freedom and prosperity, but they also saw a vision of whiteness, of what they ultimately could become in America. As this study has argued, whiteness and freedom were closely intertwined, and the changing relationship between European immigrants and the Statue of Liberty dramatically illustrates the history of white freedom.

From the 1880s until World War I, the United States witnessed a wave of immigration unprecedented in both size and origins. During this period more than 20 million immigrants journeyed to America; whereas in the early nineteenth century roughly 125,000 arrived per year, by the

1880s and 1890s the number jumped to nearly half a million. In 1907 alone almost 1.3 million came to the United States.[85] Moreover, they came from different places. Before the late nineteenth century most American immigrants were natives of the British Isles, including Ireland; Germany; and Scandinavia. The new immigrants still came mostly from Europe, but starting in the 1880s they mostly left the eastern and Mediterranean parts of the continent. Some 4 million Italians journeyed to America in the late nineteenth and early twentieth centuries; between 1910 and 1920 alone, more than 3.5 million came from the Russian and Austro-Hungarian empires. Many of these latter were Jews, some 2 million of whom came to the United States from the 1880s to the 1920s.[86]

Thanks to her location in New York harbor, the Statue of Liberty had a front-row seat to witness this massive human drama. Most European immigrants traveling to America by steamship first came to New York. In 1892 federal authorities turned Ellis Island, just upriver from the statue's home on Bedloe's Island, into the nation's largest immigrant processing center. The immigrant ships passed by the Statue of Liberty en route to Ellis Island, where they would formally enter the United States. The sight of the great monument to the left was for many their first sight of America, and one of the most dramatic and enduring.

> To the immigrants who battled tough times and rough seas, the Statue of Liberty was a welcoming beacon, a mystical madonna who made the homeless newcomers weep, pray and dance for joy.
>
> Swathed in a morning's mist, the mesmerizing lady of the harbor appeared off to the left of their ships, hailing their entry to the new world. For many, it was the first time they dared to hope.
>
> "The people were screaming and some of them were crying. It was all kind of a joyous feeling of coming to the land of freedom and a land of love," recalled Clara Larsen of New York City who came from Russia in 1911 at age 13.[87]

By no means did all Americans consider the Statue of Liberty a symbol of welcome to the new immigrants, however. As historian Peter Schrag has pointed out, if America is a land of immigrants, it is also one of anti-immigrant hostility and prejudice.[88] The massive new waves of immigration horrified many Americans, who frequently looked down upon the newcomers as ragged, dirty, ignorant, criminal, and in general unfit to be citizens of the United States. Many turned to nativism, a tradition of hostility to foreigners and immigrants that experienced a major rebirth during this era. Led by Senator Henry Cabot Lodge of Massachusetts, the nativists sought to keep foreigners out of the United States, seeing them as a mortal danger to the country. In an era of heightened racial prejudice it is not surprising that anti-immigrant hostility frequently crossed the line into overt racism. The beginnings of the twentieth century saw the rise of an influential eugenics movement dedicated to preserving the purity of "American blood" by contamination from outsiders. In 1916 Madison Grant published *The Passing of the Great Race*, a popular work of racial science that warned that immigrants from "non-Nordic races" threatened to overwhelm and ultimately destroy America. World War I and the Russian Revolution increased fears of immigrants, now also suspected as dangerous Communists and anarchists. In 1924 nativism triumphed with Congress's passage of the Johnson-Reed Act sharply limiting immigration to America.[89]

Nativists, like many others in American history, adopted the Statue of Liberty to represent their own ideas. If the statue did in fact symbolize America, then it could not belong to the despised immigrant masses thronging into New York. Many argued that in fact Liberty stood opposed to the immigrants, struggling to protect the integrity and purity of the American people. A series of cartoons in the late nineteenth century portrayed Liberty as under siege by motley hordes of foreigners, violent anarchists, or other undesirables. In 1895 Thomas Bailey Aldrich published the poem "Unguarded Gates," summing up the nativist fear of the immigrant threat:

Wide open and unguarded stand our gates,
And through them presses a wild motley throng—
Men from the Volga and the Tartar steppes,
Featureless figures of the Hoang-Ho,
Malayan, Scythian, Teuton, Kelt, and Slav,

Flying the Old World's poverty and scorn;
These bringing with them unknown gods and rites,
Those, tiger passions, here to stretch their claws.
In street and alley what strange tongues are loud,
Accents of menace alien to our air,
Voices that once the Tower of Babel knew!
O Liberty, white Goddess! Is it well
To leave the gates unguarded? On thy breast
Fold Sorrow's children, soothe the hurts of fate . . .[90]

In this interpretation, and from the perspective of nativists in general, the Statue of Liberty did not welcome the new immigrants but in contrast sought to protect America against them.

So how did "the white goddess" end up embracing the immigrants from Europe in the twentieth century? In answering this question, it is important to note that southern and eastern European immigrants were never entirely bereft of white status or privilege. Albeit reluctantly, until 1924 they were allowed into the United States in large numbers, unlike the Chinese, for example. The Johnson-Reed Act imposed strict limits on them, but even stricter ones on hopeful immigrants from Asia or Africa. Nonetheless, it took several decades before European immigrants were fully accepted as Americans, worthy of the benevolent gaze of the Statue of Liberty.[91]

The immigrants themselves, and their descendants, played a key role in this symbolic transformation. Starting with that first spectacular view of the statue rising above New York harbor, many took it as a symbol of all that America had to offer, and those that succeeded in their new land remembered this initial vision of Liberty with gratitude. Joseph Pulitzer, who had arrived penniless in New York during the Civil War and became a leading newspaper publisher, took the lead in launching the campaign to raise funds for the statue's pedestal, calling it "the people's statue."[92] Many other immigrants contributed to the campaign; as one wrote, "I would send you more if I could, as I know how to appreciate liberty, because I am a Jew and emigrated from Russia to this city a few years ago."[93] In 1902 William Flattau, a businessman of Russian origin,

FIGURE 13. "Anti-Immigrant Cartoon, Statue of Liberty" (1890). Color lithograph by Victor. Paris, Musée des Arts et Métiers/AKG-IMAGES.

built a fifty-five-foot high scale model of the Statue of Liberty on the roof of his warehouse in Manhattan.[94] The descendants of the immigrants would in their own turn champion the statue; Lee Iacocca, the chairman of the Ford Motor Company and the son of Italian immigrants, led the planning of the one hundredth anniversary celebration of the Statue of Liberty in 1986.

Nothing more famously symbolizes the idea of the statue as "Mother of Exiles" than the famous poem by Emma Lazarus, "The New Colossus." Lazarus herself came from a well-established German Jewish family in New York, and by her early thirties had carved out a substantial reputation as a poet. Starting in the early 1880s she became aware of and horrified by the anti-Semitic pogroms in eastern Europe and the flight of many Russian Jews to America. Their plight inspired in Lazarus a new attention to her own Jewish identity as well as a determination to do what she could to aid her impoverished co-religionists in New York. Asked by friends to contribute to an art exhibition raising funds for the Statue of Liberty's pedestal, she responded by writing the sonnet that would both become her most famous work and firmly link the statue to the history of European immigration.

> "Keep, ancient lands, your storied pomp!" cries she
> With silent lips. "Give me your tired, your poor,
> Your huddled masses yearning to breathe free,
> The wretched refuse of your teeming shore.
> Send these, the homeless, tempest-tost to me,
> I lift my lamp beside the golden door!"

"The New Colossus" received little attention at the time and played no role in the formal inauguration of the Statue of Liberty in 1886. In 1903, however, it was engraved on a bronze plaque and mounted on the base of the statue.[95]

Emma Lazarus's great sonnet, and the fond memories of millions of new Americans who passed through New York harbor, would ultimately turn the Statue of Liberty into the Mother of Exiles, a symbol of the United States as a nation of immigrants. It took decades, however, before this new vision of the statue would become dominant; Lazarus's poem was largely ignored by the American public until the late 1930s. By then major changes in national life had facilitated this transformation. During World War I the Statue of Liberty became more popular than ever, competing with Uncle Sam as the symbol of American national identity. Pictures of the famous statue were featured prominently on Liberty bonds, at times appealing directly to former immigrants. In August 1918 thousands of American soldiers in Iowa posed for a picture as a living Statue of Liberty before being shipped off to the war in France.[96] With the onset of World War II the desperate plight of Jewish refugees from Nazi Germany brought new attention to "The New Colossus" and America's welcome of an earlier group of immigrant Jews. Many observers noted the contrast between that time and the nation's failure to admit most refugee Jews in the 1930s, although the full tragedy of that decision was not clear until the extent of the Holocaust became known. With the US entry into the war, the idea of welcoming the tempest-tossed huddled masses once again became important to American identity.

Most important, however, was the change in the immigrants themselves. John Higham has argued that the transformation of the Statue of Liberty became possible only with the end of mass immigration in 1924.[97] Americans could romanticize European immigration once it had largely receded into the past and was no longer present in the shape of millions of people speaking strange languages, eating strange foods, and crammed into miserable slums. By the 1930s, a nadir of immigration into the United States, not only were there few newcomers in America's cities and mill towns, but those who had come earlier had adjusted to American life politically, socially, and culturally. Many had learned English, and most of their children had grown up speaking the language fluently. Many immigrants had joined labor unions, and what had been seen as un-American subversion became with the advent of the New Deal in the 1930s a major means of integration into national life. World War II brought new opportunities for national service, along with acceptance as equal citizens. By the war's triumphant end in 1945, the former immigrants were now Americans.[98]

To an important extent, as Matthew Frye Jacobsen and other historians of whiteness have observed, that meant being accepted as white.[99]

Later in this study I will explore in greater detail the history of what Peter Schrag has called "The Great Awhitening," the ways in which immigrants from Europe were gradually accepted as and transformed into white Americans, and the implications of that process for the idea of white freedom. The point here is that this new acceptance of immigrants, and of the Statue of Liberty as a symbol of immigration, were a part of this process. In 1941 the *Detroit Free Press* would publish a cartoon, "Americans All!" about the statue. The cartoon, by Arthur Pronier, shows a maternal, smiling Statue of Liberty embracing a variety of happy children identified as coming from different immigrant backgrounds. Strikingly, all the children are of European origin and white. In this interpretation, Lady Liberty would welcome immigrants, and consider them Americans, as long as they had white skin.[100]

The years after World War II reinforced both the broad acceptance of the descendants of European immigrants, now known as white ethnics, and the centrality of their history to the Statue of Liberty as a national symbol of freedom and American identity. In 1956 Congress changed the name of the statue's site from Bedloe's Island to Liberty Island and began planning for a national museum of immigration.[101] In 1965 the federal government passed a new immigration law overturning the Johnson-Reed Act of 1924 and removing that law's racial and geographical restrictions. President Lyndon Johnson signed it into law on Liberty Island at the base of the Statue. During the early 1980s the statue underwent a massive facelift and cleaning, which included equipping it with electric lights, in preparation for its one hundredth anniversary in 1986. That year the Reagan administration orchestrated a huge four-day celebration, "Liberty Weekend," in honor of the centennial. The theme of immigration occupied pride of place during the ceremony, highlighted by Chief Supreme Court Justice Warren Burger's naturalization of sixteen thousand immigrants en masse.[102]

Some commentators at the time and since noted that these celebrations took place in a period when the United States was debating new restrictions on immigration, calling into question the symbolism of the statue as the Mother of Exiles. To charge such hypocrisy is, however, to miss the point, for in a very real sense the Statue of Liberty never

FIGURE 14. Arthur Poinier, "Americans All!" (1941). *Detroit Free Press*, June 19, 1941.

celebrated immigration. Rather, as the 1941 cartoon made clear, it honored the descendants of immigrants who had become Americans, not the immigrants themselves. The centennial apotheosis of the Statue of Liberty took place in a time when most immigrants were coming from Asia and Latin America, not Europe. The statue saluted those of European immigrant background who had achieved whiteness in America while at the same time turning a cold shoulder to those who had not. No one proposed building similar statues on the US-Mexico border, in Miami, or on Angel Island in San Francisco Bay, to mark these new waves of immigration, and certainly no one suggested building a similar memorial in Charleston, South Carolina, or other ports involved in the Middle Passage.[103] As a symbol of both liberty and European immigration, the Statue of Liberty has to this day remained perhaps America's leading icon of white freedom.

A Global Symbol

Probably only a minority of Americans today realize that the great monument in New York harbor is not the only Statue of Liberty in the world. There are in fact hundreds of replicas of the famous statue stationed throughout the United States and the world. Paris, the birthplace of the statue, has three, including the famous replica at the Pont de Grenelle in the middle of the Seine just downriver from the Eiffel Tower. Those arguing that the real Statue of Liberty is Black have at times pointed to the actual Black version in the Caribbean island of St. Martin. Statue of Liberty replicas frequently decorate commercial enterprises, most notably the New York-New York Hotel and Casino in Las Vegas, but more often serve as civic and public monuments. The Statue of Liberty, in some ways like the idea of freedom itself, is both an intensely American icon and a global symbol.[104]

One of the most interesting of these replicas was the *Goddess of Democracy*, which Chinese activists erected in Tiananmen Square during the democracy movement of the late twentieth century. As in Eastern Europe and the Soviet Union, the liberalization of the Chinese economy during the 1980s prompted a movement for political liberal democracy and the end of Communist Party rule. In April 1989 Chinese students began a series of demonstrations demanding freedom of speech, freedom of the press, and other reforms. The movement coalesced in Beijing's great Tiananmen Square, and from there spread throughout the nation.[105]

On May 27, 1989, in an effort to bolster support and create a rallying point for the pro-democracy movement, art students in Beijing began building a large statue they would call the *Goddess of Democracy*. Thirty-three feet high and made of papier-mâché, the statue bore a striking resemblance to the Statue of Liberty, even though its creators, in the interest of not appearing too pro-American, denied the connection.[106] On May 30 they erected it in Tiananmen Square, facing a large portrait of Mao Zedong. The *Goddess* proved an effective and memorable symbol, drawing large new crowds to the square and quickly attracting media attention from around the world. In a public statement its creators declared:

> At this grim moment, what we need most is to remain calm and united in a single purpose. We need a powerful cementing force to strengthen our resolve: That is the Goddess of Democracy. Democracy. . . . You are the symbol of every student in the Square, of the hearts of millions of people. . . . Today, here in the People's Square, the people's Goddess stands tall and announces to the whole world: A consciousness of democracy has awakened among the Chinese people! The new era has begun! . . . Chinese people, arise! Erect the statue of the Goddess of Democracy in your millions of hearts! Long live the people! Long live freedom! Long live democracy![107]

The *Goddess of Democracy* had a spectacular but very brief existence. Chinese authorities had waffled between attacking and trying to appease the students and their supporters, but ultimately decided to suppress the movement. In the first week of June the Chinese Army moved tanks into Tiananmen Square, killing thousands of demonstrators and smashing the movement for democracy. On the night of June 4 tanks knocked over the *Goddess of Democracy*, quickly reducing it to rubble as television reporters transmitted the images across the world.[108] It had stood in Tiananmen Square for only five days, and its fall symbolized the defeat of the pro-democracy movement in China. Supporters of the movement would build replicas of the *Goddess* in places as far apart as Hong Kong, San Francisco's Chinatown, and York Canada.[109]

The *Goddess of Democracy*, along with the destruction of the Berlin Wall, became one of the most prominent symbols of the global movement for liberal democracy and freedom in the late twentieth century. Like the Statue of Liberty itself, the *Goddess* also had an important racial dimension. The whiteness of the statue—not just the white color of the papier-mâché but more significantly the prominent European features of its face—contrasted sharply with the typical Communist statuary in China, including in Tiananmen Square itself.

More generally, the pro-democracy movement in China began with a wave of racist attacks against African students. Prejudice against Africans was nothing new in China, where many saw African students as unduly privileged (a criticism made much less often of other foreign students). In December 1988, a series of attacks and demonstrations against Africans broke out in several cities, most notably in Nanjing but also Hangzhou, Wuhan, and Beijing.[110] Resentment over African men dating Chinese women often provoked clashes, but many Chinese students also attacked the regime for importing and protecting the Africans. As Barry Sautman has noted, "Student 'democrats' did attach slogans about human rights and freedom to anti-Black exhortations and thus used the events to advance their own agenda by claiming that the regime failed to protect the rights of Chinese against the alleged depredations of Africans."[111] In China, as in other parts of the world, desire for freedom and racial prejudice were strange but close bedfellows. The *Goddess of Democracy* symbolized not just liberty but white freedom as well.

An exhaustive and systematic analysis of the politics of Statue of Liberty replicas scattered throughout the world lies beyond the scope of this study. The example of the *Goddess of Democracy* does nonetheless suggest that the link between the famous monument and the concept of white freedom is not limited to America or France. The Statue of Liberty has been replicated like perhaps no other monument since the Great Pyramids, and its repeated imitation testifies to the importance of freedom in the modern world. At the same time, the racialization of this icon highlights the global significance of racial difference and whiteness, and of the roles such concepts play in defining what it means to be free.

Conclusion

Nothing compares to the Statue of Liberty as a symbol of freedom in the modern world. In many different contexts, from the French struggle for republicanism to American debates about immigration, it has stood for human liberty and prosperity. Standing in New York harbor, at the gateway to the United States from Europe, it has become the quintessential representation of American national identity while equally exemplifying America's transnational and global presence. The Statue of Liberty has been instrumental in affirming the belief that liberty is the essence of America's national life as well as its promise to all the peoples of the world.

In this chapter I have argued that this promise is shaped by race and racial difference. The Statue of Liberty throughout its history has represented a white vision of freedom, one shaped by developments in France, the United States, and elsewhere. In France, Laboulaye's vision of the statue emphasized a rejection of revolutionary politics in favor of a moderate republicanism that largely excluded a racialized working class and embraced an imperial vision of the nation-state that created a massive new colonial empire structured by racial difference. In the United States the statue's roots in antislavery were largely hidden, and it became a symbol of European immigration when, and only when, the descendants of those immigrants had won acceptance as white Americans. In both countries the very idea of freedom had a racial component, one that helped shape its most monumental representation. In a sense, the Statue of Liberty's cold European facial features were no accident, expressing instead the racial aesthetics and politics of liberty in the modern world.

I contend, therefore, that the Statue of Liberty is the world's greatest representation of white freedom. In the rest of this study I will consider the roots of this ideological phenomenon and how it has developed and changed in the course of modern and contemporary history. The whiteness of the Statue of Liberty is the most prominent expression of an underlying theme in the history of human freedom, which the following chapters will explore from the eighteenth century to the present day.

PART 2

CHAPTER 3

Black Slavery, White Freedom

FREEDOM AND RACE IN THE ERA
OF LIBERAL REVOLUTION

Man is born free and everywhere he is in chains.

—JEAN-JACQUES ROUSSEAU, *THE SOCIAL CONTRACT*, 1762

What to the slave is the Fourth of July?

—FREDERICK DOUGLASS, JULY 5, 1852

On September 30, 1791, Mozart's final opera, *The Magic Flute*, premiered at the Freihaus-Theater auf der Wieden in Vienna. Inspired by Mozart's belief in the ideals of Freemasonry, championing brotherhood, enlightenment, and liberty, *The Magic Flute* portrays the triumph of light over darkness, the victory of the benevolent leader Sarastro over the evil Queen of the Night. The great opera, which was an immediate success and has remained popular ever since, is a prime example of Enlightenment popular culture, with its veiled attack on Austrian empress Maria Theresa and on despotism in general. Interestingly, this attack has an important racial dimension, and not just in the broader opposition between beneficent light and evil darkness. Pamina, the heroine of the opera and daughter of the Queen of the Night, is kidnapped by Sarastro's

FIGURE 15. "Monostatos, *The Magic Flute*." Photo by Richard Moran, www.richardmoran.co .uk. © 2007 Richard Moran. http://www.mvdaily.com/articles/2007/01/magic-flute1.htm.

Moorish slave Monostatos, who tries to rape her. Sarastro disavows him as a result, leading Monostatos to ally with the Queen of the Night after she promises Pamina to him. Sarastro's defeat of the Queen of the Night and of Monostatos thus represents the triumph of Enlightenment freedom over royal oppression and also the reassertion of white racial and sexual purity.[1]

While Mozart's singers performed this opera of racialized enlightenment in Vienna, a very different drama of race and freedom was playing out on the other side of the Atlantic. On the night of August 22, 1791, a month before the premiere of *The Magic Flute*, Black slaves in the French Caribbean colony of Saint-Domingue staged a massive uprising, which would soon become a full-fledged revolution against slavery and French rule and ultimately succeed in ending bondage and creating the free and independent nation of Haiti. While the slave revolt was inspired by the calls for liberty emanating from the French Revolution and its impact on the Caribbean, at the same time the rebel slaves often portrayed themselves as loyal to the nation's embattled King Louis XVI.[2] By the

FIGURE 16. Haitian Revolution. "Burning of the Plaine du Cap—Massacre of whites by the Blacks" (1833). FRANCE MILITAIRE: Histoire des Armes Françaises de Terre et de Mer.

time *The Magic Flute* opened, a slave army of several thousands attacked the leading port and economic center of Cap Français, killing two thousand whites and burning down much of the city before being repelled. They would return in 1793 to capture and destroy the center of French power in Saint-Domingue.[3] Was there a sense in which the Queen of the Night was not Austria's Maria Theresa but the French king Louis XVI? Denied in Vienna, the fury of Monostatos and his followers would triumph in the revolutionary Caribbean.

In no era of modern history does the issue of freedom loom larger than during the age of revolution at the end of the eighteenth century. The centrality of liberty in the ideas of Enlightenment intellectuals, and its role in the mass insurrections of the American and French Revolutions, made the struggle for freedom a dominant theme of the age and moreover laid the foundations for the ideal of political liberty in the modern world. Texts like the American Declaration of Independence and the French Declaration of the Rights of Man and the Citizen to this day constitute the essential statements of the centrality of freedom to

Western civilization.[4] At the same time, the era has often symbolized the contradictory nature of modern freedom, especially in the context of racial thinking and oppression. The century of the Enlightenment also saw the height of the Atlantic slave trade, and the American colonies' revolution for freedom from England preserved and reinforced Black slavery in the newly independent nation.[5] In recent years, historians of the era have emphasized the racialized character of freedom struggles at the origins of modern ideas of political liberty.[6]

In this chapter I plan to give an overview of the relationship between Black slavery and white freedom during what I choose to call the era of liberal revolution. At the same time, I wish to challenge the idea that this relationship constituted a contradiction. As in the book as a whole, I argue in this chapter that race and racial difference played a seminal role in the creation of modern concepts of liberty, that the dominant concepts of freedom that emerged from this era bore the unmistakable stamp of whiteness and white racial ideology. The era also, of course, witnessed widespread resistance to this concept of liberty in the Atlantic world, above all in the great revolution of Saint-Domingue, perhaps the greatest slave revolt in world history. Yet the fact that rebel slaves and others were able to elaborate more racially egalitarian concepts and practices of freedom does not gainsay the dominance of white freedom in this crucial era. For the age of revolution, all too often the face of freedom was white.

This chapter will focus on four seminal events during the age of revolution: the Enlightenment, the American Revolution, the French Revolution, and the revolution in Saint-Domingue. It will explore the ways in which the revolutionary idea of freedom was frequently cast in racialized terms. In particular, it will consider the relationship between freedom and African slavery.[7] The Atlantic slave trade was one of the great political and moral concerns (not to mention tragedies) of the age, and the relationship between slavery and ideas of race casts a revealing light on the intellectual and political struggles for freedom during this period. Many proponents of freedom strongly opposed slavery and the slave trade, and yet when the era came to an end both remained largely intact. More generally, in all four episodes the question of the racial character of freedom emerged time and again. The age of revolution, therefore, was perhaps the key era in the birth of white freedom.

The Enlightenment

Race, Slavery, and Freedom

The philosophy and political heritage of the Enlightenment remains at the heart of what we mean by Western civilization. Despite many challenges from both within and without, the philosophies that came together in Europe and America during the eighteenth century, emphasizing rationality, progress, and the struggle for freedom, continue to shape the ideals and fates of nations throughout the world.[8] In particular, ideas of freedom and popular sovereignty developed by Enlightenment thinkers fueled the great revolutions in America, France, and Saint-Domingue. As a result, the influence of the Enlightenment is inseparable from modern ideas of freedom.[9]

It is also inseparable from the less savory aspects of Western civilization. The Romantics who succeeded the Enlightenment in the early nineteenth century criticized it for an overreliance on rationality at the expense of emotion, and many subsequent critiques have returned to this theme.[10] In their famous study *The Dialectic of Enlightenment*, written during World War II, Max Horkheimer and Theodor Adorno argued that the Enlightenment tradition was fundamentally unstable and contradictory, implicating its influence in the rise of fascism and totalitarianism.[11] More recently scholars like Emmanuel Chukwudi Eze have challenged the idea that the Enlightenment was progressive, noting instead the frequency of racist stereotypes in key Enlightenment texts.[12] In general, many scholars have attacked Enlightenment universalism as normalizing the experiences of Western white men while suppressing those of women and peoples of color that did not fit into that paradigm.[13]

I hope in this chapter to contribute to this debate by considering not just Enlightenment ideas about race but more specifically their relationship to the movement's concepts of freedom. Without a doubt, the ideal of freedom lay at the heart of the Enlightenment project. Writers and thinkers like Diderot, Voltaire, Kant, Locke, Montesquieu, and Rousseau wrote extensively about the nature of human liberty and how to achieve it in the modern world. Their different ideas became the heart of liberal political philosophy, which itself made the question of liberty the central political issue of the age.[14] Enlightenment philosophers also wrote extensively about race and racial difference, drawing upon the movement's heritage from the Scientific Revolution to explore the natures of and relationships between different peoples past and present. The movement thus combined liberal political philosophy with racial (and frequently racist) ethnography. The two themes come together in Enlightenment considerations of slavery, which most saw as the antithesis of liberty. As we shall see, the often strident opposition of Enlightenment philosophers to slavery did not necessarily translate into a belief in or desire for racial equality. Instead, the intersection of these themes frequently produced a racially coded vision of freedom.

Enlightenment Freedom

No man has by nature been granted the right to command others. Liberty is a gift from heaven, and every member of the same species has the right to enjoy it as soon as he is possession of reason.

—DIDEROT, *ENCYCLOPÉDIE*[15]

The Enlightenment ideal of liberty had several key themes. One was the idea that freedom was grounded in natural law, that it was the inheritance of mankind that no ruler had the right to take away. For writers such as Locke, Montesquieu, Diderot, and especially Rousseau, the major question was how to preserve this intrinsic state of freedom in an era of increasingly powerful and complex states. They protested against restrictions on liberty, while at the same time recognizing that individual freedom was not absolute, that the freedom of all could be guaranteed only by a structure of laws, representative government, and respect for the rights of property.[16] Often Enlightenment philosophers seemed to focus on negative ideals of liberty, the issue of freedom *from* oppression. Their opposition to religious intolerance and the power of ecclesiastical authorities is well known, as is their opposition to authoritarian royal power: not for nothing did Diderot proclaim, "Man will only be free when the last king is strangled with the entrails of the last priest." This opposition arose from the Enlightenment thinkers' fierce advocacy of intellectual liberty, of the rights of all men to express themselves freely in speech and writing. Only when people could debate ideas honestly without fear of retribution could mankind use its natural gifts of reason to construct a rational and just society.[17]

Probably the greatest single Enlightenment statement about freedom is Jean-Jacques Rousseau's *The Social Contract*. Opening with the magnificent passage I have quoted at the beginning of this chapter, *The Social Contract* constitutes an extended meditation on the nature of freedom in the modern world as well as setting forth guidelines about how to achieve a free society. Like many other writers of his time, Rousseau believed that in a natural state the individual was free, but over historical time he (the individual) had given up freedom in exchange for the safety of belonging to a collective society. The key problem therefore was how to restore the native freedom of mankind in the modern world. For Rousseau, the answer lay in the social contract, the creation of a society based upon the mutual agreement and sovereignty of the governed. Only such a society, grounded in the general will of the population, could make modern man free.[18]

In *The Social Contract* Rousseau dwelt at length on the issue of slavery. Bondage in his view represented the antithesis of natural liberty, and men consented to it to ensure their safety in collective society. To live in a country ruled by a regime not based upon popular sovereignty was to be a slave; that is the essential meaning of the phrase "man is born free and he is everywhere in chains." Slavery in this sense is a metaphor for despotism and oppression of all kinds; Europeans who lack political freedom are in effect slaves. For Rousseau, becoming free meant not only adapting the natural state of liberty to the modern world, it also meant ceasing to be a slave. Moreover, slavery was the antithesis of humanity: slaves were not truly human, were not free men because they were neither free nor men: "Every man born in slavery is born for slavery: nothing is more certain. Slaves lose everything in their chains, even the desire to escape from them; they love their servitude as the companions of Ulysses loved their brutishness. If, then, there are slaves by nature, it is because there have been slaves contrary to nature. The first slaves were made by force; their cowardice kept them in bondage."[19]

Several historians have commented on the importance of slavery as a metaphor for the thinkers of the Enlightenment. As David Brion Davis has noted, "For eighteenth-century thinkers who contemplated the subject, slavery stood as the central metaphor for all the forces that debased the human spirit."[20] Time and time again, Enlightenment writers assailed the denial of basic human rights, the oppressive acts of church and state, and the general lack of freedom as the enslavement of modern man. The historical context of all this is fascinating, for the slave metaphor mixed a concern with absolute monarchy and religious intolerance on the one hand, together with the problem of the Atlantic slave trade and American Black slavery on the other.[21]

By the late eighteenth century the burgeoning plantation economies of the Caribbean as well as South and North America had made African slavery a central presence in the life of the contemporary Atlantic world. Historians have fiercely debated the role of slavery in the economic history of Europe and America ever since Eric Williams published his landmark study *Capitalism and Slavery*, in which he argued that the profits of the slave trade helped finance Britain's Industrial Revolution.[22] More recently scholars like Edward Baptiste and Sven Beckert have shown how slavery in America played a pivotal role in the rise of the American economy.[23] Historians of Europe have also considered the importance of profits from the slave trade in economic growth. Cities such as Liverpool and Bristol in England, Bordeaux and Nantes in France, profited tremendously from the slave trade, and their wealthy merchants built impressive town houses that bore witness to the riches it generated.[24] Historian Louis Sala-Molins has estimated that at least a third of all commercial activity in eighteenth-century France was related to the slave trade.[25] The economic prosperity of western Europe that made Enlightenment society and culture possible rested to an important extent on the backs of African slaves.

Given this, it makes sense that Enlightenment philosophers should so often turn to slavery as a metaphor for oppression. At times writers like Voltaire and especially Condorcet did address and attack the evils of African slavery: the famous passage in *Candide* where the eponymous hero comes across a miserable slave who mournfully informs him that "it is at this expense that you eat sugar in Europe" is one prominent example.[26] For the most part, however, when Enlightenment writers talked about the evils of slavery they did so only in a metaphorical rather than a literal sense. The symbolic enslavement of Europeans by religious and royal oppression rather than the actual enslavement of Africans in the Americas was far and away their primary concern. For example, as Sala-Molins has trenchantly observed, nowhere in *The Social Contract* does Rousseau mention the French Code Noir of 1685, in which the royal government formally codified slavery in its Caribbean colonies.[27] Voltaire was similarly much more interested in slavery as metaphor than in the actual plight of African slaves. In his 1736 play *Alzire, or the Americans*, set in sixteenth-century Peru, Voltaire condemns royal oppression and corruption but has little to say about Black slavery in that colony.[28] This tendency to privilege the metaphorical over the actual experience of slavery spread far beyond the elite circles of Enlightenment writers. As Susan Buck-Morss has noted, the fact that the Dutch in the early modern era profited tremendously from the slave trade did not stop them from bitterly complaining about their enslavement by the Spanish Monarchy and portraying their fight for independence as a struggle against slavery.[29] Simon Schama's landmark study *An Embarrassment of Riches* tends to replicate this dichotomy, largely ignoring the "embarrassing" fact that much of Dutch prosperity came from investments in African bondage.[30]

How can one explain this contrast between the Enlightenment's often militant opposition to slavery as a political metaphor and the lack of concern with the actual slaves during the eighteenth century? One reason could be that some of the movement's leading figures directly profited from the slave trade. John Locke, whose *Second Treatise on Government* remains a classic statement of political liberalism, was a major investor in the African slave trade through the Royal African

Company.[31] Others, such as David Hume and Voltaire, held investments that benefited from slavery even if they weren't directly tied to the slave trade. Such examples merely reaffirm the broad importance of slavery to European economies in the eighteenth century.

More significant is the relationship between Enlightenment attitudes to slavery and to race. As Emmanuel Chukwudi Eze has demonstrated, Enlightenment writers devoted significant attention to the study of race and racial difference, often in the context of ethnographic research and analysis. Immanuel Kant, for example, wrote extensively about the different races of mankind as an ethnographer. As noted earlier, this study of race arose out of the Enlightenment's heritage from the Scientific Revolution, in particular the desire to apply the same level of systematic classification to humanity that scientists had developed for the natural world. Increased European exploration of the broader world had also generated a variety of travel narratives and other first-person accounts that fueled the interest in the comparative study of different peoples. The Enlightenment thus occupied a seminal position in the birth of scientific racism.[32]

The comparative study of races generally ranked peoples from high to low in a hierarchical continuum. In 1684, French doctor François Bernier published one of the first modern books on racial theory, entitled *A New Division of the Earth, According to the Different Races of Men Who Inhabit It*. He argued that the world's population was divided into four or five races, each with its own physical and mental characteristics.[33] Several Enlightenment scholars followed Bernier's lead, considering how different peoples (usually Europeans, Asians, Africans, and "Americans," or Native Americans) resembled and differed from each other in physical appearance and levels of intellect. Invariably, such rankings placed white Europeans at the top of the hierarchy, emphasizing their intelligence and physical beauty, while Africans were usually placed at the bottom of the scale when evaluated with these characteristics. In comparing different races, Immanuel Kant had this to say about Africans: "The Negroes of Africa have by nature no feeling that rises above the trifling. Mr [David] Hume challenges anyone to cite a single example in which a Negro has shown talents, and asserts that

among the hundreds of thousands of Blacks who are transported elsewhere from their countries, although many of them have even been set
free, still not a single one was ever found who presented anything great
in art or science or any other praiseworthy quality."[34] While Enlightenment writers strove to go beyond a simple binary analysis of racial difference by their use of scientific observation and analysis, in many cases
they tended to replicate the traditional division between civilized
peoples and barbarians. Civilization and reason were therefore largely
a province of the white races of Europe. As Eze has argued, "the Enlightenment's declaration of itself as 'the Age of Reason' was predicated
upon precisely the assumption that reason could historically only come
to maturity in modern Europe."[35]

This point is crucial, because for many Enlightenment thinkers freedom and self-government were closely linked to the capability for reason and rational thought. The great importance placed upon education,
both intellectual and moral, by the movement illustrates this fact. Only
the enlightened could be truly free, so that if reason was racialized so
then was liberty. Consequently, even though many Enlightenment writers condemned slavery and argued for the more egalitarian treatment of
Blacks and other peoples of color, few supported the immediate emancipation of the slaves or imagined that they could rule themselves.

The marquis de Condorcet illustrates the Enlightenment's ambivalence about racial equality. Condorcet was one of the Enlightenment's
most impassioned opponents of African slavery. His *Reflections on Black
Slavery* (1781) systematically demolished pro-slavery arguments, and as
a member of the Société des Amis des Noirs he campaigned for abolition. He opposed immediate abolition, however, not only because he
feared the economic consequences for the Caribbean but also because
he judged the slaves not ready for freedom: "the slaves in the European
colonies have become incapable of carrying out normal human func-
tions. . . . Thus there are natural rights of which very young children are
deprived as are madmen and idiots."[36] Ultimately Condorcet foresaw
freedom coming to Blacks when they merged with and disappeared into
the white population through miscegenation; as Louis Sala-Molins has
caustically observed, "granting them political rights only when they

FIGURE 17. Portrait of Marie Jean Antoine Nicolas
Caritat, Marquis de Condorcet (1743–94). Heritage
Image Partnership Ltd./Alamy Stock Photo.

cease to be Negroes."[37] In this reading of Condorcet, and to an important extent of the Enlightenment in general, freedom belongs to the white races.

It is fitting to close this section on the Enlightenment, and transition to the next section of the chapter, with a brief discussion of Thomas Jefferson. One of America's most eminent Enlightenment intellectuals and eventually the third president of the United States, Jefferson both harshly criticized slavery and owned slaves. In his *Notes on the State of Virginia* Jefferson discussed at length the evil effects of human bondage, on the slave owners as well as the slaves themselves. Yet he at the same time echoed the perspective of Kant, Hume, and others on the intellectual inferiority of Blacks. Jefferson did support emancipation, at least in theory, but only by expelling Blacks from America's white society and

FIGURE 18. Rembrandt Peale, *Thomas Jefferson*, official
portrait (1800). http://www.whitehouseresearch.org
/assetbank-whha/action/viewHome.

giving them a land of their own. An America without Blacks would thus
be a land of the free.[38]

For many Enlightenment thinkers, therefore, freedom was shaped by
race. They viewed slavery as the polar opposite of freedom, and many
opposed it strenuously, but in general they emphasized the metaphorical enslavement of Europeans over the actual enslavement of Africans. In a sense, freedom was the privilege of white men, and therefore
reducing them to the level of Blacks by "enslaving" them was morally
and politically unacceptable. The omnipresence of African slavery in the
eighteenth-century world horrified many Enlightenment intellectuals,
but it also shaped their ideas of freedom. In this sense, therefore, slavery
and reason were not so much paradoxical as complementary and mutually reinforcing. The next section of this chapter will further clarify how
that could be so.

A War for Liberty and Slavery

Race and the American Revolution

When Britain's American colonies declared their independence from the mother country in 1776, using Enlightenment principles to shape their political goals in general and the Declaration of Independence in particular, the *philosophes* of the Enlightenment were thrilled. Denis Diderot saluted the birth of the United States of America, congratulating the revolutionaries for having buried their chains and rejected their enslavement by the British.[39] He did not mention that the colonists busily engaged in breaking imperial chains of bondage themselves owned hundreds of thousands of Black slaves, some twenty percent of the population of the new nation. Liberty for white Americans would mean continued, even expanded, slavery for Black Americans.

As Edmund S. Morgan argued in *American Slavery, American Freedom*, the fact that the revolutionaries who founded the new nation based on Enlightenment principles of freedom also championed, or at least tolerated, slavery is the central paradox of American history.[40] The ways in which American historians, and the American public as a whole, have dealt with this paradox have changed over time, moving from ignoring it entirely to regarding it as a regrettable but exceptional fact of history, to more recently seeing it as essential to the founding of the American republic. In recent years a number of American historians have written books that don't just look at the history of slavery in the American revolution but use it to explore and reinterpret America's early national history in general, so that it is hardly possible today for professional historians to consider the American Revolution without placing the question of slavery at its center.[41] What does it mean to say that the foundation of the American republic as a slave republic also witnessed not only massive numbers of escape attempts by slaves but even slave revolts, directed against the revolutionaries fighting for that republic?[42] Or, as Alfred and Ruth Blumrosen put it in *Slave Nation*, "How then should we view the Founding Fathers?" By extension, how should we view the American Revolution, and American history in general?[43]

Gerald Horne's *The Counter-Revolution of 1776* provides one of the most systematic analyses of slavery and the American Revolution. Horne places the revolution in the context of British colonial rule in the greater Caribbean, arguing that many American settlers had come to the North American mainland as refugees from the endemic slave revolts in islands like Antigua, Barbados, and Jamaica. He notes how for decades before the 1770s the American colonies had grown ever more committed to African slavery while in Britain abolitionist sentiment became more and more pronounced. This culminated with the 1772 Somerset decision (see below), which stoked colonial fears that London might abolish slavery throughout the empire. Three years later the American Revolution began, in large part as a reaction against the colonists' fears that Britain would arm the slaves against them. As Horne has put it,

> Suppressing African resistance became a crucial component of forging settler unity—and the solidifying identity that was "whiteness," which cut prodigiously across religious, ethnic, class, and gender lines. The forging of settler unity and the congealing identity that was "whiteness" also consolidated the developing connection between settlers' fear of alleged British enslavement, their own possession of Africans as chattel, and the fear that the relationship between master and slave could be reversed to their crushing detriment.[44]

In keeping with the basic theme of this book, I argue that the paradox of American slaveholders fighting for liberty is not a paradox at all if one considers the racial dimensions of the American idea of freedom during the revolutionary period (and after). Denying freedom to Black slaves was not a contradiction, because freedom was reserved for whites. The same principle helps explain how the American Revolution could further the conquest of Native American lands and the dispossession of America's indigenous peoples, who as nonwhites did not have the wherewithal to build and profit from a modern free society.[45] Key to the history of the American Revolution was the fact that freedom for whites meant slavery for Blacks and defeat and genocide for Native Americans. Only an ideology of freedom grounded in racial superiority could make this possible.

At the same time, white freedom during the American Revolution created a powerful counternarrative of freedom for all. Blacks quickly seized upon the irony of white slave owners condemning enslavement by the British to press their own demands for liberty. The tens of thousands of slaves who fled to British lines in response to royal offers of manumission, or the slaves who fought for Britain against their own masters, testified to the importance of an alternate narrative of freedom. This alternate narrative will reappear time and time again in this study, challenging the idea of white freedom to be more truly inclusive and universal.

The American Revolution was one of the greatest achievements of the Enlightenment, and the patriots who founded the new republic consciously looked to the movement for intellectual and political inspiration. The Declaration of Independence, most notably, drew inspiration from Enlightenment ideas of civil liberties and popular sovereignty.[46] The American patriots also drew heavily on another Enlightenment theme, the slave metaphor, in important respects taking the contradictory nature of that narrative to new heights. Supporters of American independence complained constantly about being enslaved by the British, and those who held slaves themselves were among the first to do so. In 1768 John Otis, the largest slave owner in Philadelphia, wrote what would become "The Liberty Song," including lyrics like "In freedom we're born and in freedom we'll live, not as *slaves* but as *freemen* our money we'll give" (emphases in the original).[47] George Washington, the father of American independence and a slave owner, warned that "the once happy and peaceful plains of America are either to be drenched with Blood, or inhabited by Slaves."[48] When Thomas Jefferson drafted the Declaration *of Independence,* arguing that all men are created equal and endowed by their Creator with the right to liberty, he owned more than one hundred slaves.

For many patriots, slavery meant essentially political oppression, the denial of political rights and representation to a people by a tyrannical government. Like the writers of the Enlightenment, American patriots protested against the denial of civil liberties by royal authorities and argued that they were illegitimate because they were not based in popular sovereignty. The Declaration of Independence provides a comprehensive list of the colonists' grievances against the king, accusing him of denying them their rights as free-born Englishmen. The idea that British subjects were traditionally more free than others was a powerful one in colonial America, and frequently it was linked to the importance of property. Imperial Britain of course had proudly proclaimed its freedom while it took the lead in the Atlantic slave trade, so in claiming their rights as Englishmen it made sense for the rebel colonists to include the right to slave property. Moreover, many colonists argued that having slaves gave them the economic independence necessary for free men; to take away their property was to take away their freedom. In an era (and a country) where slavery was so central, to deprive them of their property was in effect to reduce them to the status of slaves. As Edmund Burke observed, the horrors of enslavement were very real to those who lived surrounded by slaves.[49]

This rather bizarre spectacle of slave owners complaining about being enslaved did not go unchallenged at the time, either at home or abroad. As the great British writer Samuel Johnson noted, "How is it that we hear the loudest yelps for liberty among the drivers of negroes?"[50] Although most colonists supported or at least accepted slavery, colonial America had a substantial abolitionist movement, and many of them also challenged the paradox of a war for freedom and slavery. As the Baptist minister John Allen thundered in 1774:

Blush ye pretended votaries for freedom! Ye trifling patriots! Who are making a vain parade of being advocates for liberties of mankind, who are thus making a mockery of your profession by trampling on the sacred natural rights and privileges of Africans; for while you are fasting, praying, nonimporting, nonexporting, remonstrating, resolving, and pleading for a restoration of your charter rights, you at the same time are continuing this lawless, cruel, inhuman, and abominable practice of enslaving your fellow creatures.[51]

Most significantly, the paradox of white slave owners protesting their own enslavement was not lost upon African Americans themselves, who quickly seized upon the language of freedom and slavery to press for their own emancipation. Some slaves literally sued for their own freedom, consciously deploying the language against slavery as a violation of universal natural rights deployed by the patriots against the British. Others submitted petitions to state legislatures respectfully expressing the hope that the fight against slavery would extend to them too. In 1773 a group of slaves submitted a petition to the Massachusetts State Legislature explicitly making the connection between the patriots' struggle against slavery and their own liberation:

> The efforts made by the legislative of this province in their last sessions to free themselves from slavery gave us, who are in that deplorable state, a high degree of satisfaction. We expect great things from men who have made such a noble stand against the designs of their *fellow-men* to enslave them. We cannot but wish and hope Sir, that, you will have the same grand object, we mean civil and religious liberty, in view in your next session. The divine spirit of *freedom* seems to fire every breast on this continent.[52]

The concerns of America's rebel colonists about slavery went far beyond the metaphorical use of the concept to champion their own liberty. Like elites in most slave societies, whites in colonial America, especially in the plantation South, lived in constant fear of slave revolts.[53] The prospect of people who lived in close and peaceful proximity to white colonists suddenly rising up one night to slaughter their masters in their beds is a recurring theme of slave and colonial societies, and a dreadful one to contemplate. While such fears were usually exaggerated, they did not lack a basis in fact. On Sunday, September 9, 1739, a group of slaves in South Carolina took to the roads and killed more than forty white men, women, and children before being overcome and mostly slaughtered by armed whites. Stono's Rebellion, the largest slave revolt in colonial America, triggered both new repressive measures against slaves and some calls for ending slavery as a menace to the white population.[54] Similarly, on December 7, 1774, a group of slaves in St. Andrew

Parish, Georgia, attacked and killed or wounded several white slave owners and their families.[55] When white colonial subjects during the revolutionary era imagined that British rule undermined slavery as an institution, they considered this as a threat not just to their property but ultimately to their very lives.

In 1769 the Virginia merchant Charles Stewart moved to London with his household, including a slave named James Somerset. Two years later, with the help of British abolitionists like Granville Sharp, Somerset fled the Stewart household and petitioned the courts to grant him his freedom, based on the Freedom Principle, the idea that Britain was a free land and that therefore he could not be held in slavery there. On June 22, 1772, judge Lord Mansfield ruled in Somerset's favor, in the process striking a mortal blow against slavery in Britain. In making his judgment Mansfield tried to limit its implications to the issue of slaves brought to Britain itself, and it did nothing to limit the empire's extensive involvement in the slave trade or the expansion of colonial slavery. Nonetheless, for many in the North American colonies the Somerset decision posed a major potential threat to their interests and even called into question their continued loyalty to the empire. For Virginia and the other southern colonies in particular, Somerset, coming a few years after the Stamp Act, suggested a new level of British interference with their property rights and thus their freedom. It implied that if Americans wanted to preserve slavery, they would have to seek their own liberation from Britain.[56]

Although up until the mid-1770s the British had shown no real intention of interfering with American colonial slavery, the outbreak of hostilities in 1775 changed that dramatically. The spring of that year had brought the battles of Lexington and Concord in Massachusetts, followed by the British siege of Boston and the Battle of Bunker Hill in June. By the fall London had declared the American colonies to be in open revolt, and both sides began mobilizing their armies for what had become the American Revolutionary war. Slavery immediately emerged as a key issue in the conflict. Many white southerners assumed that the British would use the slaves to fight the rebellion; as Simon Schama has noted, "By the summer and early autumn of 1775 a full-scale panic about the imminence of a Black rising, armed and sustained by the British, was under way from tidewater Virginia to Georgia."[57] In July authorities in Wilmington, Delaware, broke up a conspiracy by slaves to stage an uprising and slaughter the local population.[58]

This wave of fear about slave revolts culminated in November 1775, thanks to actions by the British. During the fall of 1775 the British position in Virginia steadily worsened as the revolt in the colony gathered steam. By the beginning of November their position was untenable, and the royal authorities prepared to flee Virginia. In doing so, however, on November 7 Lord Dunmore, the royal governor of Virginia, issued a fateful proclamation that not only called upon colonists to reaffirm their loyalty to their king but also promised to free the slaves of the colonial rebels and called upon the slaves to join British forces in fighting against the rebellion.[59]

Virginia alone accounted for forty percent of all Black slaves in America, and Dunmore's proclamation resounded there like a thunderclap. He had hoped that it would intimidate local slave owners into resisting the lure of revolution, but it had the opposite effect. Like Mansfield, Dunmore had tried to limit the impact of his decision but soon found that events spiraled out of his control. For the slave-owning colonists of Virginia and the South in general, his proclamation represented a full-fledged call not only for emancipation but for a slave revolt, calling on Black slaves to rise up against their masters. Far from being intimidated they reacted with a fury, increasingly deciding to cast their lot with the rebellious colonists of New England. If the British intended to abolish slavery and promote slave revolts, then colonists had no option but independence. A phrase from the Declaration of Independence—"He has incited domestic insurrections against us"—refers directly to this fear and illustrates its importance for the patriot cause. The American war for liberty thus became equally a war for slavery.

As this chapter has shown, there were many reasons why America's rebel colonists would fight a war for two diametrically opposed concepts. The paradox was certainly not lost on them, as the case of Thomas Jefferson makes clear, and in many cases it proved untenable. Many Northern states moved to abolish slavery once independence had been achieved, for example. But the fact remains that the American Revolution was a war fought for the right to enslave others in the name of liberty. Such a position was tenable only to the extent that slavery was identified with race, and the broader issue of race with white superiority and Black inferiority. Many different systems of bondage had helped populate the American colonies, and not all had been identified with race. By the late eighteenth century, however, the practice of white indentured servitude had declined sharply, while at the same time the number of Black slaves had increased. Given that at the same time there were very few free Blacks in the American colonies, less than ten thousand total, Americans could justifiably assume that to be free meant to be white and vice versa.[60]

Above all, however, white views of Blacks as inferior meant they could not be free men because in a sense they were not men at all. Jefferson's critique of slavery in his *Notes on the State of Virginia* criticizes slavery for its impact on whites as well as on Blacks, and while regretting the oppression of Blacks, it is clear he considered them intellectually deficient and incapable of freedom. Not only slavery but also liberty was identified with race, so that a revolution for white freedom was firmly grounded in the social realities of colonial America.[61]

A crucial part of the story, and of the history of the American Revolution in general, is the impact Lord Dunmore's proclamation had upon African American slaves. As the news of the war and the royal offer to free the slaves spread, many simply took matters in their own hands and deserted their masters in an attempt to gain freedom by reaching the British lines. They did so in massive numbers: nearly 100,000 slaves, including a quarter of those in South Carolina and a third of those in Georgia, fled their plantations in their own personal quest for emancipation.[62] George Washington alone lost seventeen people, leading him to observe that all his slaves would escape if they got the chance, and other signatories of the Declaration of Independence suffered similar losses.[63] Some did succeed in reaching British lines, but many others simply disappeared into the countryside, some establishing maroon settlements in places like the swamps of South Carolina and the Savannah River in Georgia.

Others chose to fight for freedom. The beginnings of hostilities with the British in the spring of 1775 brought a wave of rumors about possible slave insurrections throughout the South, as many white southerners feared that the patriot call to fight for liberty would be taken all too literally by the slaves, and that the British would encourage them to do so. In North Carolina in early July authorities intercepted and suppressed a planned slave revolt: the organizers had called upon all slaves "to fall on and destroy the family where they lived, then to proceed from House to House [burning as they went] until they arrived in the Back Country where they were to be . . . settled in a free government of their own."[64] Shortly after Dunmore proclaimed his intention to free the slaves of the patriot rebels, several hundred Black slaves joined his forces as soldiers, forming what became known as the Ethiopian Regiment and took part in the Battle of Kemp's Landing, Virginia, against the Americans. The Ethiopians marched into battle with the words *Liberty to Slaves* embroidered on their uniforms. Dunmore had in fact hoped to raise a massive army of rebel slaves to crush the rebellion in the South, but he lost the Battle of Kemp's Landing and with it control over Virginia. Some of the Ethiopians went on to serve in other parts of the war, notably the occupation of New York City in 1776.[65] At times it seemed that in response to the patriots' rebellion the British might unleash exactly the slave insurrection the colonists had long feared. The combination of massive slave flight and slave participation in British armies made the American Revolution, second only to the Civil War, the nation's greatest slave revolt.

Black slaves fought for the British in other theaters of the war as well, sometimes doing battle with Blacks fighting for the rebels in a kind of African American civil war.[66] However, Dunmore's vision of a mass slave insurrection in favor of British rule never materialized, in part because, as soon became clear, Britain had no real interest in freeing the slaves en masse, so that Blacks might be risking their lives simply to exchange one form of slavery for another. Also, for slaves who fled their masters the dangers of recapture and punishment were very real, leading many to stay put. Finally, after much hesitation the American patriots did decide to enlist Black soldiers, both slave and free, and some five thousand fought for the revolution.[67] Both the service of Black soldiers, and abolitionist pressure on the paradox of a war for freedom and slavery, led to the decline of the "peculiar institution" in the North after the war. Several Northern states moved to emancipate their slave populations, and the number of free Blacks in the United States increased from 10,000 in 1776 to 200,000 by 1810.[68] For a time, it seemed white freedom and Black freedom might converge.

Yet Black slavery remained the law of the land in the new United States, and even though it declined in what had been the thirteen colonies, it expanded enormously in the new territories to the west of Georgia and the Carolinas. The Americans had succeeded in creating a republic that in many ways exemplified the principles of the Enlightenment, but it was a slave republic, and would remain so until a new revolution, the Civil War, shook the pillars of the established order. Until then slavery remained, and it remained based on race: Black freedom was the exception rather than the rule. In time Americans would come to venerate the memory of Crispus Attucks and other Blacks who fought for the Revolution.[69] In contrast, the story of Thomas Peters, a slave who served with the British army in New York before eventually like many other former American slaves being resettled in Nova Scotia, remains essentially unknown.[70] Both men fought for liberty, but since Peters's struggle did not fit comfortably into the narrative of white freedom that lay at the heart of the American Revolution, it has to this day remained obscure. The United States was born as a land of free white men, up to that point the greatest embodiment of the principle of white freedom the world had ever seen.

White Revolution, Black Revolution

Upheavals in France and Saint-Domingue

Possibly the most studied single event in world history, the French Revolution lies at the heart not only of the liberal revolution of the late eighteenth century but of the history of freedom in the modern world. Several of the key themes of modern freedom, including popular sovereignty, restrictions on religious authority, individual rights, and electoral democracy achieved prominence during the revolution, and became a template for ideas of liberty throughout the world.[71] During the nineteenth century symbols of the French Revolution, most notably "La Marseillaise," came to represent the struggle for freedom far beyond France's borders. In grounding the struggle for political freedom in Enlightenment ideas of the universal rights of man, the revolution embraced universalism as a key dimension of both its own national heritage and of world history. The message emanated from revolutionary Paris that all men had the right to be free.[72]

Well, maybe not all. In recent years historians of the French Revolution have taken an increasingly global approach to the subject, and in particular that has meant coming to terms with the impact and significance of the revolution in Saint-Domingue.[73] What was the relationship between the overthrow of royal absolutism in metropolitan France and the insurrection against slavery in the nation's greatest Caribbean colony? Ever since C.L.R. James, historians have considered the impact of the French Revolution on that in Haiti, and more recently they have begun to look at the reverse phenomenon, how events in Saint-Domingue influenced the revolutionary process in Paris. This has meant rejecting the idea of the two revolutions as separate phenomena, instead reconceptualizing them as different parts of a whole.[74] As historians of colonialism have emphasized, metropole and colony constitute a unified field and must be studied as such.[75]

This section of the chapter will follow that perspective by considering how the French and Haitian revolutions dealt with the issues of freedom and slavery. By 1789 the American Revolution had established the precedent of a war for liberty and slavery at the same time, creating a slave republic. Many of the same dynamics that caused this were present in revolutionary France as well, so that at least for the first few years the leaders of the revolution dealt with the question of slavery hesitantly, if at all. The big difference between America and France, of course, was the massive slave insurrection that broke out in Saint-Domingue in 1791. The slave revolt in the French Caribbean prompted, or forced, the revolutionary government in Paris to abolish slavery, thus placing both France and the French Empire including Saint-Domingue in the fore-front of the global struggle for freedom. It also created a powerful link between antislavery and radical republicanism reinforced both by Na-poleon's restoration of slavery in the empire and by its final abolition at the hands of the French Second Republic in 1848. During the revolu-tions in Haiti and France the old metaphor of absolutism as slavery became to an important extent a reality.

This section will introduce a theme I will explore in greater detail in the next chapter, the challenge to white freedom that at times came from radical and progressive forces, often those with a working-class social base. As we have seen so far, despite their denunciations of slavery liberal intellectual and political movements usually failed to challenge it effectively and take a frontal stand for freedom for all. This failure in large part arose from a resistance to challenging property rights, and slaves constituted one of the most valuable types of private property during the era of liberal revolution. Social and political movements that challenged the right to private property were in contrast more likely to embrace the idea of freedom for all. This was certainly not always true, but as the example of the French and Haitian Revolutions demonstrates, the impulse for universal freedom usually came from the Left.[76]

Perhaps the greatest slave revolt in world history, the Haitian Revolu-tion frontally challenged the idea of white freedom, using the language of liberty to demand the abolition of the greatest obstacle to it and claiming that Black slaves had as much right to freedom as anyone else. It represented the culmination of the struggle against slavery in the At-lantic world and, as some scholars have recently noted, the high point of the age of democratic revolution.[77] At the same time, however, the intensely hostile reaction to the revolution and the new Black republic it produced illustrated the ways in which the general idea of freedom continued to be racially circumscribed. Overall, the French and Haitian revolutions reinforced the idea that liberty in the modern world was and would continue to be white.

Slavery in France and the French Empire

One important peculiarity of the Atlantic world in the eighteenth century was the rise of political units divided into nations and empires, half free and half slave. In part this arose from the greater need of colonial plantations for slave labor, but it also had important legal, political, and ultimately racial dimensions. Britain's Somerset case showcased the increasing contrast between the decline of slavery in the metropole and its continued vibrancy in the colonies, and the triumph of the American Revolution brought an increased demarcation between a free North and a slave South. Even before 1789 this contrast had reached its greatest extent in France, and the French Revolution would bring it to the breaking point.

What would become known as the Freedom Principle has a long history in France, antedating the rise of Black colonial slavery in the early modern era.[78] In 1315 King Louis X proclaimed that France was a land of free men, and that any slave setting foot on French soil should be freed. Over the following centuries French authorities at times intervened to put this principle into practice. Historian Sue Peabody has documented several cases of Caribbean slaves brought to France in the eighteenth century by their masters successfully suing in the royal courts for their freedom, based on the argument that France constituted free soil. In 1571, for example, a merchant from Normandy was arrested for selling African slaves in France, and his slaves were freed.[79]

The paradox, of course, is that French authorities continued to maintain the principle of France as a land of freedom while French merchants were not only heavily engaged in the slave trade but also building the most profitable slave economy the world had ever seen. The colony of Saint-Domingue was the center of both the French Empire in the New World and of Atlantic slavery in general. Spain had been the first European nation to rule the island of Hispaniola and immediately resorted to slave labor, first using Native Americans and then African slaves. France took over the western part of the island in 1697, naming it Saint-Domingue, and massively expanded its new colony's slave economy. By 1789 Saint-Domingue had roughly 500,000 Black slaves, more than all the British Caribbean colonies combined and nearly half of all those in the New World. It was the wealthiest colony in the French Empire, indeed in the world, producing forty percent of all the sugar used in Europe. These immense riches came as a result of extreme brutality against the slaves: frequent punishments included all manner of tortures, including being fed to dogs and burned alive. As a result, slaves in Saint-Domingue had extremely high death rates, which necessitated them being constantly replaced by new captives from Africa.[80]

France in the late eighteenth century was thus a nation divided between a society of free men in Europe and an extremely rapacious (and profitable) slave society in the colonies. The same country whose intellectuals and merchants clamored for freedom sustained itself to an important extent with the profits from the slave trade. For the most part, the French were determined to keep this dichotomy in place. French courts did at times respond to the claims of Caribbean slaves in France by offering them emancipation based on the Freedom Principle, but at the same time tried to restrict the number of slaves brought to the metropole at all. Increasingly, the principle that there should be no slaves in France merged with the idea that there should be no Blacks in France. If the kingdom was to remain a land of free men, it would have to be a land of white men.[81]

The outbreak of the French Revolution brought this contradiction to a head. At least initially, the revolutionaries who gathered in Paris to form the new National Assembly showed little interest in Caribbean slavery and even less in emancipating the slaves. As historian Hugh Thomas has noted, "a delegation from the newly founded and revolutionary Armée Patriotique of Bordeaux reached Paris and told both the Jacobin Club and the Assembly that five million Frenchmen depended on the colonial commerce for their livelihood, and that both the slave trade and West Indian slavery were essential for the prosperity of France."[82] The National Assembly followed this logic, refusing to act against slavery because of the possible consequences for the economy.

Some revolutionaries took a different view. In 1788 a group of French intellectuals and activists had formed the Society for the Friends of the Blacks to fight against slavery and the slave trade. Led in the National Assembly by Count Mirabeau, in February 1790 they submitted a motion to the government to abolish, if not slavery, at least French participation in the slave trade. The motion is notable for its timidity: in a land clamoring for freedom as a universal right of mankind, it only asked ultimately for better treatment of French slaves:

> We are not asking you to restore to French Blacks those political rights which alone, nevertheless, attest to and maintain the dignity of man; we are not even asking for their liberty. No; slander, bought no doubt with the greed of the shipowners, ascribes that scheme to us and spreads it everywhere; they want to stir up everyone against us, provoke the planters and their numerous creditors, who take alarm even at gradual emancipation. They want to alarm all the French, to whom they depict the prosperity of the colonies as inseparable from the slave trade and the perpetuity of slavery.
>
> The immediate emancipation of the Blacks would not only be a fatal operation for the colonies; it would even be a deadly gift for the Blacks, in the state of abjection and incompetence to which cupidity has reduced them. It would be to abandon to themselves and without assistance children in the cradle or mutilated and impotent beings.
>
> It is therefore not yet time to demand that liberty; we ask only that one cease butchering thousands of Blacks regularly every year in order to take hundreds of captives; we ask that henceforth cease the prostitution, the profaning of the French name, used to authorize these thefts, these atrocious murders; we demand in a word the abolition of the slave trade.[83]

Strongly opposed by colonial lobbies like the Committee on the Colonies and the Massaic Club, the Society for the Friends of Blacks had no success in moving the French Revolution to embrace a vision of universal freedom that included Black slaves.[84]

Revolutionary Saint-Domingue

The debates over slavery in Paris were soon overtaken by events in Saint-Domingue. As in the metropole, the calling of the Estates General in the summer of 1789 led to debates and political organizing in the colony. In Saint-Domingue, however, only whites had political rights and the recognized ability to take part in the revolutionary process. This was a small population, some thirty thousand compared to the nearly half a million Black slaves on the island, so that the beginnings of the French Revolution in the colony were completely circumscribed by race. This racialized character, however, soon meant that the revolution would take a very different path than in the metropole.[85] Saint-Domingue also had the largest population of free people of color of any French colony, and this community soon insisted on making its desires heard. Almost as large as the white population, Saint-Domingue's free people of color were largely mixed-race descendants of white settlers. They were often affluent and many owned slaves themselves, yet unlike whites they suffered from many different types of discrimination and had no political rights.[86] Their intervention in the revolutionary process as it unfolded in 1789 and 1790 proved crucial to the subsequent course of events in Saint-Domingue.

It soon became clear the two groups had very different ideas about freedom at the start of the revolution. For the whites, liberty meant above all the right to keep their slaves. Fearful of the antislavery currents surfacing in Parisian political debates, they strongly supported the co-lonial lobby and threatened to imitate their North American neighbors and seek independence if their wishes weren't granted. The free people of color certainly did not oppose slavery, but their vision of freedom entailed civil and political equality with the white population, some-thing the latter adamantly refused to grant. As a result, both groups sent delegations to Paris to claim membership in the new National Assembly, but only the white delegation was seated. The increasingly bitter confrontation between whites and free people of color led the latter to stage a major revolt in the fall of 1790. Vincent Ogé, a leader of the community, returned from Paris in October to demand that the local government implement a decree passed by the National Assem-bly granting full civil rights to people of color. When the colonial gov-ernor refused, Ogé organized an armed uprising, fighting colonial troops for a month before being forced to surrender and eventually executed. The defeat of Ogé's revolt made it clear that, at least for the time being, in Saint-Domingue the French Revolution would be for whites only.[87]

Meanwhile, however, the Black slaves of Saint-Domingue had their own ideas about freedom, and these ideas were nourished by the revolutionary turmoil overtaking the colony in 1789 and 1790. In August 1789 rumors that the French king had abolished slavery inspired a brief slave revolt in the smaller Caribbean colony of Martinique.[88] Vincent Ogé's uprising in 1790, even though it did not challenge slavery, also exemplified resistance to the white plantocracy that controlled Saint-Domingue. The massive slave uprising that erupted in August 1791 and soon engulfed France's richest colony did not just draw inspiration from these precedents but fundamentally redefined the nature of the revolution for liberty. Far more than the Enlightenment or American Revolution, it insisted that freedom meant the abolition of slavery and the freeing of the slaves, and that all men had the right to be free. As one rebel soldier argued in 1793, "There are no more slaves in Saint-Domingue; all men of all colors are free and equal in their rights . . . all Frenchmen shudder at the word *king*, who you must know were never happy unless they were surrounded by slaves, and that since the twenty-first of January our motherland no longer has one and enjoys perfect happiness."[89] It thus constituted a fundamental challenge to the ideology of white freedom.

The slave revolt in Saint-Domingue preceded and in some ways foreshadowed the most radical phase of the revolution in metropolitan France. French revolutionaries continued to use the slave metaphor as had opponents of the regime during the Enlightenment before them, but as the Revolution intensified many on the left tended to portray not just royal despots but also aristocrats as the equivalent of slave masters, and peasants and workers as the metropolitan version of slaves.[90] The radical Jacobins played a key role in pushing for the abolition of slavery. On April 4, 1792, the National Assembly dominated by the Girondin faction of the Jacobins enacted full equality for all free men of color, and their leader Jacques-Pierre Brissot became one of the most prominent abolitionist voices.[91] The execution of the king and the shift to the revolutionary Terror led by the followers of Maximilien Robespierre brought about the full abolition of slavery in February 1794. Unlike the new United States, France would not be a slave republic, and the ideology of freedom would not, at least for a time, be for whites only.[92]

Napoleon's restoration of slavery in the French Empire, and his failed attempt to suppress the revolt in Saint-Domingue, reinforces this point. Just as the establishment of the republic in 1792 soon led to slave emancipation, the reestablishment of slavery in 1802 foreshadowed the overthrow of the republic in 1804.[93] Not for nothing did people call the oppressive regime that followed the fall of Robespierre the White Terror.[94] There are other parallels between the radical Jacobin republic in France and the regime of emancipated slaves in the Caribbean. Both sparked major counterrevolutionary emigrations, and both had to contend with overwhelming and bitter opposition from abroad. Both triumphed, at least for a time, through sheer popular determination and mass mobilization. As I will explore more fully in the next chapter, the ideal of universal freedom that transcended race and included those not considered white often came not just from peoples of color but from the radical left as well. At the same time, populist and lower-class movements for freedom and social justice were frequently racialized as nonwhite, a consequence of the increased racial thinking of the nineteenth century. The intertwined histories of the French and Haitian revolutions illustrate the interaction of ideas about race and class in the construction of modern ideas about liberty.

The reactions to both the radical revolution in France and the slave revolt in Saint-Domingue emphasize this. The classic image of the French *sans-culottes* was that of a bloodthirsty savage mob, motivated not by high principles of liberty but rather by hatred, envy, and a thirst for revenge against their social betters:

Savage. Let us explain this word. When these bristling men, who in the early days of the revolutionary chaos, tattered, howling, wild, with uplifted bludgeon, pike on high, hurled themselves upon ancient Paris in an uproar, what did they want? They wanted an end to oppression, an end to tyranny, an end to the sword, work for men, instruction for the child, social sweetness for the woman, liberty, equality, fraternity, bread for all, the idea for all, the Edenizing of the world. Progress; and that holy, sweet, and good thing, progress, they claimed in terrible wise, driven to extremities as they were, half naked, club in fist, a roar in their mouths. They were savages, yes; but the savages of civilization.[95]

Even in Victor Hugo's sympathetic reading, the radical desire for freedom constituted a reversion to primitive and racialized savagery.[96]

The slave revolt in Saint-Domingue and the establishment of the independent Black nation of Haiti encountered fierce opposition from much of the Atlantic world. Under Napoleon, France tried to reconquer the insurgent nation not once but twice, its inability to do so constituting the greatest military failure of the emperor's reign until the disastrous Russian campaign. Shortly after the Haitians proclaimed their independence on January 1, 1804, the new government proceeded to massacre much of the remaining white population of the island, an act of revenge against the former slaveholders and of defiance against the world that had supported them. The main Atlantic powers reacted to this, and more generally to the prospect of an independent Black nation in the Americas, by refusing to recognize the new state. The French government withheld recognition until 1825, only finally agreeing to normalize relations after the Haitian government agreed to pay a massive indemnity to Paris in compensation for the 1804 massacres.[97] Much of the rest of Europe followed France's lead, largely isolating Haiti after independence.[98]

Far from regarding the Haitian Revolution as a fraternal revolt against European colonialism, most white Americans considered it a dangerous slave revolt and, especially after the massacres of 1804, worried it might set an example for their own slaves. In 1804 President Thomas Jefferson imposed an embargo on Haiti, one that lasted until 1862, a year before America freed its own slaves. While many African Americans cheered the overthrow of slavery, whites viewed it as an example of anarchic violence and mob rule, not a struggle for freedom. Lurid tales about the "horrors of Santo Domingo" circulated widely in the early nineteenth century, convincing many white southerners in particular of the impossibility of freeing their own slaves without risking a bloodbath and the collapse of civilization. Freedom for Blacks meant annihilation for whites.[99]

The greatest slave revolt in modern history, and the most radical revolution of the Age of Revolutions, thus came to symbolize the racial parameters of freedom. Liberty for whites meant independence, order, and prosperity; for Blacks it meant massacre and lawlessness. To the extent that European revolutions, such as the Terror in revolutionary France, departed from this script, they risked being racialized in their own turn. In his magisterial *Silencing the Past*, Haitian anthropologist Michel-Rolph Trouillot has addressed the ways in which historians and the historical record have at times downplayed the importance of his country's revolution. Arguing that the Haitian Revolution constituted an "unthinkable history" because the idea that African slaves could conceive of, let alone fight for, freedom lay outside the norms of world history, he argued that "What happened in Haiti between 1791 and 1804 contradicted much of what happened elsewhere in the world before and since."[100] I would simply add to this that the struggle of Black slaves for emancipation was unthinkable at the time and for a long time since because it lay outside the bounds of *white* freedom, and therefore exposed the racialization of freedom as a concept already in place in the eighteenth century. The subsequent history of Haiti as the poorest nation in the Western Hemisphere was both created by and reaffirmed the idea that liberty and national independence without whites equaled poverty, misery, and dictatorship; that Black freedom consequently constituted a political and conceptual impossibility.

The revolutions that swept France and especially Haiti at the end of the eighteenth century pushed the concept of liberty to its most extreme extent, yet in the end they reinforced the idea of freedom as essentially white freedom. The radical republic in France upheld the principle of liberty for all men, but Napoleon destroyed it after a tumultuous decade and it would not reappear for generations. Haiti did achieve a level of freedom that included former slaves, but at the severe price of international ostracism, poverty, and exploitation for much of its history as an independent state.[101] Moreover, the radical regimes in both France and Haiti came to symbolize violence, anarchy, and lawlessness rather than liberal ideas of freedom. Far from representing its logical extension, universal liberty was redefined as Black freedom, and therefore the enemy of the dominant ideology of white freedom.

Conclusion

As the example of *The Magic Flute* reveals, ideas of liberty during the Age of Revolution often contained a significant racial component. The emphasis on freedom felt so powerfully in both intellectual and political life developed alongside the unprecedented expansion of African slavery in the New World, an expansion that provided tremendous economic benefits to Europe and to an important extent made the affluent society of the Enlightenment possible. Few Enlightenment texts dealt with it directly, however, preferring to view slavery as a metaphor for oppression of all kinds rather than a condition afflicting millions of human beings. Even those most opposed to African slavery, like Condorcet, hesitated to advocate complete freedom for Black men and women.

The revolutions that broke out in Europe, America, and the Caribbean illustrated the racialized character of freedom. That great Enlightenment document, the American Declaration of Independence, demanded freedom but only referred obliquely to slaves as a threat to free men, not people deserving liberty, and in general the American Revolution combined a determination to win freedom for whites with an equal determination to preserve slavery for Blacks.[102] The independent United States thus became what should have been a complete contradiction, a slave republic. In its most radical phase the French Revolution did abolish slavery, but less than a decade later Napoleon Bonaparte reversed that decision, shortly thereafter destroying the republic that had made it. The Age of Revolution did bring about the greatest slave revolt in world history, but independent Haiti was not only reduced to poverty and international isolation but also made an example of the dangers of too much freedom, i.e., freedom for Black slaves. The freedom of the late eighteenth century was thus freedom for white men.[103]

This was not entirely true, of course. Haiti may have been poor but it had still abolished slavery, and the number of free Blacks in the United

States grew significantly, although they remained a distinct minority among the African American population. In 1807 both Britain and the United States banned the slave trade, the beginnings of a new phase in the history of slave emancipation. Moreover, the Age of Revolution in general must be considered a work in progress, by no means triumphant by the early nineteenth century. By 1815 France had restored the monarchy overthrown by the revolution, and the Concert of Europe directed by Austria's Metternich directed a new wave of conservatism across Europe. Liberty remained to a large extent an insurgent idea, and the progress of that idea and the fight against slavery frequently went together.[104]

Nonetheless, the Age of Revolution had established an important principle and template, that ideals of universal liberty could be and would be circumscribed by racial difference. In the next chapter I will explore the ways in which new political forms, in particular liberal democracy and overseas empire, gave a new twist to the idea of white freedom. The expansion of the association between liberalism and liberty, which the era of enlightenment and revolution had pioneered, would give its own racial cast to the struggle for freedom in the age of mass democracy.

CHAPTER 4

Empire, Racial Citizenship, and Liberal Democracy

Was Heathcliff Black?

Emily Brontë's classic gothic novel *Wuthering Heights* (1847) has remained popular ever since its publication nearly two centuries ago, offering the reader a witches' brew of love, passion, revenge, wealth and poverty, and the supernatural. As a number of commentators have noted in recent years, the question of race also looms large in the novel, mostly centered around the identity of its central, Satanic hero, Heathcliff, the ultimate literary bad boy. The reader first encounters him as a foundling of mysterious origin on the streets of Liverpool, which at the start of the nineteenth century was the most prominent slave trading port in Europe.[1] The novel constantly refers to his darkness of aspect, exotic background, and semi-savage nature, at one point describing him as "a regular Black" and his eyes as "Black fiends, so deeply buried, who never open their windows boldly, but lurk glinting under them, like devil's spies."[2] Yet this was not just literary license. Not only did proximity to Liverpool suggest a certain Black influence in early-nineteenth-century Yorkshire, but historians have documented the presence of slaves there as well. The prominent Sills family of Yorkshire, a family acquainted with the Brontës, employed enslaved Africans on its estate during these years. The idea of a Black man, or at least one of ambiguous racial identity, living in Yorkshire is thus not so fanciful as once assumed.[3]

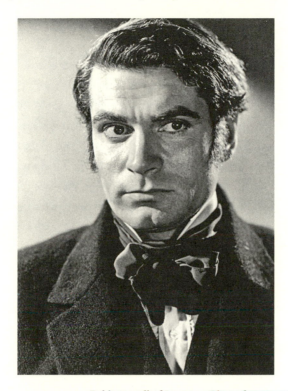

FIGURE 19. Publicity still of Laurence Olivier for
Wuthering Heights (1939). Samuel Goldwyn Pictures.

If the theme of race plays a role in *Wuthering Heights*, so does that of
freedom, in complex ways.[4] If Heathcliff symbolizes blackness in certain
ways, he also at times represents the slave owner. His departure from
Yorkshire as a poor youth and return several years later as a wealthy man
strongly suggests a fortune earned in the slave trade, the source of so
much nontraditional wealth in Georgian England.[5] Burning with a
thirst for revenge against the two genteel white families, the Earnshaws
and Lintons, who had denied him his soul mate Catherine, Heathcliff
time and time again uses his wealth to take members of the two families
prisoner, in effect enslaving them. He describes his first meeting with
his thirteen-year-old son, Linton Heathcliff, in the following terms: "I
feared I should have to come down and fetch my property myself.
You've brought it, have you? Let's see what we can make of it."[6] For the
mature Heathcliff freedom is power, power to exercise his will over

those who have denied him. It is a dark, if you will *Black* freedom, a revenge against white oppression.[7]

But this is not the only kind of freedom in the novel. As a youth, Heathcliff suffers abuse and scorn at the hands of the Earnshaw family, masters of the Wuthering Heights manor, but he also enjoys a measure of freedom that shapes his growing love of Catherine Earnshaw. Freedom in particular resides in the landscape of the Yorkshire moors, a countryside that is wild and beautiful, symbolizing a dark physical representation of liberty. The moors represent an escape from the civilized world, the world of adulthood and propriety. As the narrator observes of Heathcliff and Catherine early in *Wuthering Heights*, "They both promised fair to grow up as rude as savages, the young master being entirely negligent how they behaved . . . it was one of their chief amusements to run away to the moors in the morning and remain there all day, and the after punishment grew a mere thing to laugh at."[8]

For Heathcliff, therefore, freedom is a matter of childhood and nature; like that of the pirates and children discussed in chapter 2, it cannot survive the onset of civilization. On the contrary, the mature Heathcliff's vision of freedom is monstrous and brutal, not liberating. Ultimately the racial Other cannot bring liberty, which could survive only as part of white racial domination; Black freedom is no freedom at all. The beautiful Yorkshire moors will give way to the redbrick factory towns growing like weeds in the Britain of the Industrial Revolution. In the emerging liberal Britain of the nineteenth century neither the slave trade nor blackness has a place, and Heathcliff represents both. *Wuthering Heights* ends with Heathcliff's death, his demise the only way he could achieve his desire for his great love Catherine, and the reaffirmation of white control over the manor he had dominated so brutally. His successors, freed from his racially ambiguous legacy, can henceforth pursue their own white vision of liberty.

Emily Brontë published *Wuthering Heights* in 1847, during a period of social and political turmoil both in Britain and abroad. The Enlightenment and the Age of Revolution had made freedom the burning political issue of the modern world, and in Europe and America peoples and nations devoted much of the nineteenth century to working out how they could best achieve this goal. By the end of the century the tradi-

tional model of monarchical and aristocratic authority that had dominated Europe after the fall of Napoleon was clearly on the defensive, and
new social and political arrangements jostled for pride of place. The rise
of powerful nation-states made national citizenship the essence of not
only political authority but also freedom. Monarchies remained, such as
in Britain, Scandinavia, and the Low Countries, but they became increasingly constitutional, vesting ultimate state authority in the free consent
of the governed. In addition, mass-based socialist movements campaigned for the rights of workers as key to the liberation of mankind.[9]

Central to these new visions of political freedom was the rise of liberal democracy as a form of government. Over the course of the nineteenth century the Enlightenment ideal of freedom, emphasizing civil
liberties, religious tolerance, and property rights gradually merged with
the principles of popular sovereignty and democratic rule to constitute
a basic template for the governance of modern states. Liberal democracy could take different forms, such as republics in France and the
United States or constitutional monarchies in Britain, the Netherlands,
and to a certain extent Germany. But in general, liberal democracies
combined an orderly electoral procedure for channeling the popular
will into choosing political leaders with protections for individual liberties. The ability of citizens to vote for their own leaders became a key
symbol of political freedom, so that campaigns for electoral democracy
exemplified the struggle for liberty in the modern world. Closely tied
to this was the ability of peoples to form their own independent nations,
free from control by other nations or empires. The United States and
Haiti had blazed this trail during the Age of Revolution, and national
liberation became a central dimension of modern freedom.[10]

Here again we confront a paradox that, upon closer examination,
turns out not to be a paradox at all. A standard trope of the history of
the modern world is the gradual decline of multinational empires and
their replacement by independent nation-states. In Europe, the nineteenth century witnessed the increased importance of regimes grounded
in the principles of liberal democracy and the decline of traditional empires like Russia and Austria-Hungary.[11] This process was even more
dramatic in Latin America, where the collapse of the Spanish Empire
produced a range of new nation-states.[12] At the same time, however, the

nineteenth century gave rise to the greatest period of colonial expansion in world history. Moreover, two of the world's most advanced liberal democracies, France and Britain, also carved out the world's biggest empires. Far from being opposed to each other, liberal democracy and empire during the age of high imperialism were often strange bedfellows.[13]

The solution to this contradiction lay in the racialization of liberal democracy in the century after the French Revolution. Building upon the legacy from the Enlightenment and the Age of Revolution, liberal democracy in the nineteenth century developed as a political system for whites only. The great European empires created in Asia and Africa imposed authoritarian rule upon masses of brown and Black subjects, so that while aristocratic imperial politics were declining in Europe they enjoyed a new lease on life overseas. In the United States, the end of Reconstruction after the Civil War as well as the expansion of American imperial rule throughout the West and overseas gave the politics of white supremacy a new lease on life. During the late nineteenth century in particular, the racial science inherited from the Enlightenment both fed upon and justified the politics of racial democracy on a global scale. Liberal democracy thus became enmeshed with racial citizenship, so that even within the political boundaries of a single state the color of one's skin defined one's membership within a nation and the rights one derived from that membership. In the modern era the expansion of liberty went hand in hand with the racialization of liberty, so by the dawn of the twentieth century freedom was whiter than ever.

The Rise of Liberal Democracy

I think that democratic communities have a natural taste for freedom: left to themselves, they will seek it. . . . But for equality, their passion is ardent . . . they call for equality in freedom; and if they cannot obtain that, they still call for equality in slavery.

—ALEXIS DE TOCQUEVILLE[14]

In the modern world we are so used to thinking of liberal democracy as a unified entity, as a *thing*, that we frequently forget it consists of two different and to an important extent opposed principles, liberalism and democracy. The essence of liberalism, as developed by Enlightenment philosophers like Montesquieu and John Locke, emphasized the importance and rights of the individual. Liberals stressed the ability of individuals to speak and write freely without fear of censorship, to worship (or not) as they chose, and to possess private property. If liberalism focused on the individual, democracy stressed the prerogatives of the collectivity. Democracy meant above all the right of "the people," or at least a majority of them, to choose its own rulers and its political destiny. One protected the rights of the individual against society, the other championed the imperatives of society against the individual.[15]

Given this rather fundamental opposition, it is something of a political miracle that liberal democracy ever came into existence, much less became so widespread by the beginnings of the twentieth century. In the aftermath of the Age of Revolution many liberals were horrified at the prospect of democracy, equating it with terror, anarchy, and mob rule.[16] The specter of the Terror in the French Revolution, where liberal politicians were sent to the guillotine by crowds of "savage" *sans-culottes*, was a case study in the dangers of democracy, of vesting political power in the hands of the people. A number of leading intellectuals and politicians, including John Adams, Alexander Hamilton, Edmund Burke, and John Stuart Mill, inveighed against "the tyranny of the majority"; as Mill put it, "'the tyranny of the majority' is now generally included among the evils against which society requires to be on its guard."[17] Even if, especially if, the state reflected the desires and belief of the majority of the population, it could still threaten the right of the individual to her own ideas, much as the Church had done to heretics and nonbelievers. The concept of the tyranny of the majority has often been used to protect minority rights and communities, but it had its origins in fears of "excesses" of democracy.[18]

Perhaps most important, liberals feared that democracy could threaten one of the most cherished individual prerogatives, the right to private property. Since most people in early-nineteenth-century Europe and America had little or no property, majority rule meant giving power to the poor. If one did so, what then was to stop them from using their control of the state to expropriate the property of the wealthy? This was the essence of the idea of social revolution, of course, and the rise of industrial society in western Europe and America in the early nineteenth century, with its juxtaposition of extreme wealth and poverty, tended to conflate fears of democracy and social insurrection. As Britain's Lord Macaulay said in response to working-class demands for democracy in 1848:

> My firm conviction is that, in our country, universal suffrage is incompatible, not with this or that form of government, but with all forms of government, and with everything for the sake of which forms of government exist; that it is incompatible with property, and that it is consequently incompatible with civilisation. If it be admitted that on the institution of property the well-being of society depends, it follows surely that it would be madness to give supreme power in the state to a class which would not be likely to respect that institution.[19]

If possession of private property was the ultimate individual and liberal right, democracy could exist only if it did not endanger that right.[20]

This, then, was the key challenge for liberal democracy: to construct a state and society based upon the principle and practice of popular sovereignty that nonetheless did not endanger private property or other individual rights. As I noted in the previous chapter, the issue of property was central to the emergence of white freedom, so the fact that protecting individual property rights became a major issue for the construction of liberal democracy in the nineteenth century underscored its centrality to modern ideas of liberty. In order to stop freedom from turning into license and disorder, the people had to be prevented from succumbing to their own worst impulses: as James Madison, one of the framers of the Constitution of the United States put it, the role of government was "first to protect the people against their rulers [and] secondly to protect the people against the transient impressions into which they themselves might be led."[21]

Over the course of the nineteenth century politicians and state makers in Europe and America came up with several solutions to the problem of combining popular sovereignty and individual rights. One approach was to create bicameral legislatures, with the upper house dominated by the aristocracy and acting as a brake upon the democratic aspirations of the lower. The prototype for this was the British House of Lords, whose members came exclusively from the nobility and were not chosen by popular vote. As elections to the House of Commons became more democratic during the nineteenth century, the House of Lords loomed ever larger as a bulwark of aristocratic privilege. In 1910 a crisis erupted after the Lords defeated a proposal in the Commons to increase taxes on the aristocracy. Thanks to the support of King George V, the Commons was able to pass the Parliament Act of 1911, stripping the Lords of much of its power.[22] The American Senate, which was not elected by popular vote until 1913, constitutes another example of the ways in which bicameralism could restrain the popular will in liberal democracies.[23]

Another was to expand the franchise over time, starting with propertied elites and gradually allowing broader and broader classes of society to vote. Britain provides perhaps the most dramatic and extensive example of this. The history of elections for public office in England goes back to the thirteenth century, but only a tiny percentage of the adult population could vote. In the nineteenth century, however, a series of reform acts gradually extended the franchise to adult men, based upon property qualifications. In the aftermath of World War I, 1918's Representation of the People Act granted the vote to all adult men. It also, for the first time, extended the franchise to women, although this came with age and property restrictions. Not until 1928 could all adult Britons vote. France and the United States implemented universal manhood suffrage earlier, in 1848 and 1856 respectively, but there as well this was preceded by a period of limiting the franchise based upon property qualifications. Only in the era of World War I did universal suffrage for men and women become a reality in large parts of the world. The conflict between liberalism and democracy, so evident during the French Revolution, took more than a century to resolve in the Western world.[24]

The strategy of creating liberal democracy by gradually expanding the franchise over time depended heavily upon the idea of uplift, both political and moral, to train the population to be good and reliable citizens. The nineteenth century was in large consequence a golden era of mass education, which started with the struggle to teach men and women how to read and write. Literacy made significant strides during the century in Europe and America, due largely to the creation of free public schools.[25] A central concern of France's Third Republic after 1870 was developing a nationwide network of secular free public schools and making primary education compulsory for all French boys and girls. Public education would be above all for citizenship in the nation, enabling the people as a whole to engage in political life and justify the faith of the elites in liberal democracy.[26]

Throughout this period race played an important role in the development of liberal democracy, in several different respects. As I will discuss in more detail later in this chapter, universal manhood suffrage did not necessarily mean the vote for all men; like property, belonging to the right race was often an important qualification. Although Canada achieved near-universal suffrage by the end of World War I, some provinces, notably British Columbia, prevented people of Chinese, Japanese, or Native American descent from voting for another generation.[27] In the United States before the Civil War, most free Blacks were denied the right to vote; ironically, as America gradually increased the franchise for white men, it placed increasing limitations on the political rights of Black men.[28] As I will discuss later in this chapter, even the abolition of slavery during the nineteenth century did not necessarily give the new freedmen the right to vote.

At the same time, the class distinctions that posed such a challenge to the idea of liberal democracy were frequently racialized during the nineteenth century. Especially in Britain, the rise of vast new working-class populations in the aftermath of the Industrial Revolution led many social commentators to believe that the poor were not just unfortunate individuals but constituted a separate species. Languages of class and of race thus tended to overlap.[29] As Susan Thorne has shown, British missionaries in the early nineteenth century often compared local workers with foreign natives: she quotes the Reverend George Greatbatch, speaking of the working-class population in Lancashire: "I had little thought there was a station for me at home which so much resembled the ideas I had formed of an uncivilised heathen land."[30] Similarly in France, observers often portrayed the vast working-class suburbs outside Paris as the habitat of savages, barbarians lurking at the gates of civilization.[31]

The development of racial science highlighted the idea of both social and racial difference as key to modern life. Whereas during the Enlightenment commentators on race had tended to portray differences between populations as mutable, in the nineteenth century European scholars increasingly saw racial distinctions as fixed and unchanging.[32] This squared with a more pessimistic perspective on class, and indeed on the whole classic liberal project. As European laborers became increasingly de-skilled and distinct from the middle classes after the mid-nineteenth century, the working classes seemed more than ever a separate stratum of society, in fact a separate race.[33] The growing importance of nation-states and national cultures in nineteenth-century Europe also fed upon and contributed to increasing social polarization, for which race became the ultimate metaphor.[34] The view of nations as (antagonistic) races, a perspective that culminated in World War I, also testified to the salience of race thinking in the making of modern Europe.[35] H. G. Wells's 1895 science fiction novel *The Time Machine*, portraying future society as racially divided between the elite Eloi and the proletarian Morlocks, was a futurist projection of contemporary British anxieties about class and race.[36]

Moreover, much of the new racial science had deep roots in discourses about social class. In Britain, the "social Darwinism" of Herbert Spencer and others represented liberalism at its most muscular. Based on the presumption that the dominance of the strong was essential to progress and the rule of civilization, social Darwinism quickly acquired a racial component. European triumphs over natives in Africa and Asia clearly showed the superiority of the former over the latter, and justified colonial rule as a means of improving the human condition in general. At the same time, social Darwinism argued that British workers had only themselves to blame for their misery, portraying class stratification as the consequence of innate inequalities of ability.[37] In France, Count Arthur de Gobineau's *An Essay on the Origins of Inequality* was a pioneering text of the new scientific racism of the nineteenth century. Gobineau's fears of racial degeneracy and miscegenation reflected anxieties about the revolutionary Parisian mob and its proletarian heirs, thus racializing concerns about modern society in general and class conflict in particular.[38]

The development of increasingly class-stratified societies in Europe during the nineteenth century, societies that often expressed and conceived of this class stratification in racialized terms, posed a fundamental hurdle to the rise of liberal democracy. How could liberal society possibly survive when based in the sovereignty of populations so fundamentally Other? By the early twentieth century, however, liberal democracy had largely overcome this hurdle, after World War I becoming the dominant political form of the modern age. In spite of the threat posed by Marxism and organized labor, most European societies (Russia being of course the great exception after 1917) succeeded in integrating the working class into capitalist forms of liberal democracy that provided for popular representation through universal suffrage while at the same time preserving property rights.[39]

Part of this success has to do with the history of the Great War itself, to which I will turn in the next chapter. But a key factor was the rise of the "new imperialism" in the late nineteenth century, the European conquest and colonization of large parts of Asia and Africa. The campaign for empire fundamentally changed life not just in the colonized territories but in the colonizer nations as well. Especially in Britain and France, it created new types of racial divisions, between metropole and empire, that facilitated the rise of European liberal democracy in the late nineteenth and early twentieth centuries. As the next section of this chapter will argue, the rise of liberal democracy was deeply rooted in a racialized vision of the modern colonial encounter.

From Abolition to Empire

> Despotism is a legitimate mode of government in dealing with
> barbarians, provided the end be their improvement.
>
> —JOHN STUART MILL, ON LIBERTY

The struggle to abolish Atlantic slavery in the late eighteenth and nineteenth centuries was one of the great freedom sagas of the modern world. As noted in the previous chapter, African slavery constituted the ultimate denial of the world of liberal freedom and human rights envisaged by the activists and thinkers of the Enlightenment and Age of Revolution. During this era the struggles for freedom and against slavery had diverged to a significant degree, as in both America and Europe the idea of liberty developed an important racial character. In the half century after the fall of Napoleon, however, abolitionism became a much more powerful and determined movement, especially in Britain and the United States, and pushed for the complete overthrow of human bondage. Starting with the ban on the international slave trade in 1808, followed by the outlawing of slavery in the British Empire in 1832, and culminating with the Emancipation Proclamation of 1863 and the Union victory in the American Civil War, international abolitionism campaigned successfully for the principle that no man should be the slave of another.[40]

The universal struggle against slavery did not, however, bring universal freedom. During the nineteenth century the idea of freedom gradually shifted from not being a slave to having rights as a citizen of a liberal democratic and independent nation, and the two were by no means the same.[41] In particular the creation of massive overseas empires by the leading European states in the aftermath of the campaigns against colonial slavery illustrated the failure of the abolitionist movement to realize the liberal dream of freedom in the modern world. Why did the turbulent transition to the modern era bring about new forms of colonial control rather than making people free? How, more specifically, did ideas of freedom and empire coincide and how did they together contribute to the rise of liberal democracy?[42] The fact that this transition occurred primarily during the first half of the nineteenth century, and that the new imperial forms it involved adopted much of the ideology of democracy, suggests an important connection. In short, the centrality of liberalism to modern empire arose to a significant extent out of the cauldron of democratic revolution.

The abolitionist movement played a crucial role in the history of European liberalism in the early nineteenth century, especially in Britain. British liberalism defined itself in the struggle against human bondage.[43] During the wars against Napoleon, for example, the British Navy not only fought to ensure the safety of national shipping but to suppress the Atlantic slave trade.[44] The triumphs of liberalism at home went hand in hand with the struggles against slavery in colonies: as Emilia Viotti da Costa has shown in her history of Guyana's Demerara slave revolt of 1823, rebel slaves were both inspired by and in turn inspired the abolitionist faith of nonconformist missionaries.[45] The abolition of slavery in Britain's colonies ten years later inspired liberal organizations like the Anti-Corn Law League, whose battle against mercantilism would triumph during the next decade.[46]

In France as well, the movement against slavery and for a liberal society went closely together. Napoleon's overthrow of the revolutionary regime in France restored slavery in what remained of the French Caribbean, and it took another French revolution to abolish it once and for all. The combination of antislavery agitation in the metropole and the threat of slave insurrections in Martinique and Guadeloupe meant that once the revolution triumphed in 1848, the new provisional government speedily put an end to bondage in the colonies. In the same brief period, France abolished forever both the monarchy and slavery; universal suffrage and citizenship came both to the people of the metropole and to those of the "old colonies."[47]

Because the struggle against slavery was so central to nineteenth-century liberalism, it also played an important role in the rise of the new liberal imperialism. At the heart of the liberal imperial project, particularly in Britain and France, lay a concern with uplift and modernization, what the French would come to call *la mission civilisatrice* and Rudyard Kipling would immortalize as "the white man's burden."[48] This concern linked the antislavery of the era of democratic revolution with the aggressive expansionism of the New Imperialism. It was no accident that a major rationale for British and French conquests in sub-Saharan Africa was initially the effort to stamp out the slave trade by going upriver from the African coasts to root it out at its source in the interior of the continent.[49] Just as in Britain and France where liberal democracy required the creation of an educated populace integrated into the acceptance of a liberal worldview, so too in their colonies must the natives be "civilized" to make democracy possible—at least someday. This orientation justified both the subjection of native peoples and the violation of certain basic liberal principles of governance and justice. In both metropoles and colonies, liberal democracy was neither purely liberal nor purely democratic, but a complex mixture of the two ideals.[50]

In France the overthrow of slavery and the creation of a new liberal empire overlapped significantly, illustrating the important connections between the two. If the revolution of 1848 spelled the end of old forms of empire, the revolution of 1830 marked the beginning of the new.[51] In that year, French troops conquered Algeria, laying the cornerstone of the nation's new imperial expansion of the late nineteenth century. The Algerian campaign also had an important antimonarchical dimension: undertaken by the regime of Charles X in a futile effort to allay domestic discontent, in actual fact it facilitated the success of the 1830 revolution by removing large numbers of royal troops from Paris at a crucial time.[52] Yet three succeeding French regimes pursued the conquest of Algeria, which was not complete until the late 1850s, reflecting the growing embrace of imperialism by liberals in France.

For Alexis de Tocqueville, the conquest of Algeria was justified by the struggle against despotism: France would free the Arabs from Turkish rule and bring them into the civilized world. As he noted in 1837, "We need in Africa, just as in France, and even more than in France, essential guarantees to the individual living in society; nowhere is it more necessary to establish individual liberty, respect for property, and guarantees of all rights than in a colony."[53] A determined opponent of slavery, Tocqueville's support of empire in Algeria—in his own mind at least—confirmed rather than contradicted the support of liberty that would eventually lead him to champion the emancipation decree of 1848.

In 1851 Louis Napoleon, the nephew of Napoleon Bonaparte, overthrew the government of the French Second Republic, a year later appointing himself emperor of the new Second Empire. Fittingly, the new emperor devoted considerable attention to overseas expansion, taking up where his illustrious predecessor had left off. Under the Second Empire the French took colonial control of Tahiti and significantly expanded their presence in Indochina and sub-Saharan Africa. At the same time, however, the regime maintained the principle of universal manhood suffrage adopted by the Second Republic. It was a principle that was often violated in practice, but the principle nonetheless remained.[54]

Napoleon III's most infamous overseas adventure, his invasion of Mexico, also claimed to bring modernity and freedom to the Mexican people. After conquering the country in 1864 the emperor organized a national plebiscite of very dubious quality to prove that Mexicans had voted to make the Habsburg prince Maximilian their next emperor. Maximilian, another believer in the modernizing force of empire, gladly accepted the crown, proclaiming to his new subjects:

> Mexicans: You have desired my presence. Your noble nation, by a voluntary majority, has chosen me to watch henceforth over your destinies. I gladly respond to this call. Painful as it has been for me to bid farewell forever to my own, my native country, I have done so, being convinced that the Almighty has pointed out to me, through you, the mission of devoting all my strength and heart to a people who, tired of war and disastrous contests, sincerely wish for peace and prosperity; to a people who having gloriously obtained their independence, desire to reap the benefit of civilization and true progress.[55]

The French imperial venture in Mexico collapsed in 1866, four years before war and revolution overthrew the Second Empire in France itself.

Napoleon III was to be France's last emperor, yet his downfall did not bring to an end the nation's visions of imperial glory. The Third Republic that replaced him and would go on to be the longest-lived regime in modern French history, not only continued his pursuit of overseas empire but expanded it, and so, the regime that did more than any other to make republicanism and liberal democracy the political norm in France also created the greatest empire in the nation's history. By the beginnings of the twentieth century France had completed its conquest of Indochina and North Africa, as well as carving out vast new territorial possessions in west and central Africa. Only Britain could claim a

FIGURE 20. French Mission with Sultan Mulai Abd al-Aziz IV, in Fez, Morocco (1905). Front page of French newspaper *Le Petit Parisien*, January 29, 1905. Leemage/Universal Images Group/Getty Images.

mightier or more expansive empire. France thus became that oddest of political entities, a state that was simultaneously a republic and an empire, an imperial regime without an emperor.[56]

And, like that of Britain, France's great empire was to be an empire of freedom, rescuing the inferior races from the oppression of savagery and ignorance and bringing them into the light of civilization. The ideal of the civilizing mission, especially in the form of the doctrine of assimilation that guided French imperial policy for most of the nineteenth century, was to turn the natives into French men and woman by teaching them French culture; how to build modern roads, hospitals, schools; and other vectors of civilization. Once integrated into French civilization, they would therefore be prepared for citizenship as equal members of the political community of liberal democratic France. As Alice Conklin and other historians have pointed out, liberal ideas of enlightenment, modernity, and freedom were intrinsic to France's republican empire.[57]

This idea of uplifting the natives and preparing them for freedom has of course obvious parallels with the project of making the working classes in Europe ready for democracy; we shall also see it in attitudes toward the freedmen of the American South after the Civil War. Yet a key part of the story concerns an essential divergence. Whereas liberal democracy triumphed in imperial France, it did not in her colonies. Ultimately France concluded that her colonial subjects were fundamentally different from her metropolitan citizens, in ways that both recalled and diverged from notions of difference in their own societies. In his classic history *Peasants into Frenchmen*, Eugene Weber not only considered the attempts to integrate French peasants into republican liberal democracy but also mused about why this process of integration did not work for France's overseas colonies.[58] My concern is less why this did or did not work, but what this reveals about ideas of liberal democracy in France, and of white freedom in general. Ultimately the distinction between colonies and metropoles cuts to the heart of the history of modern liberal democracy.

Part of the story concerns changing beliefs about the possibilities of integrating colonial natives into liberal democracy, and indeed into Western civilization in general. By the end of the nineteenth century,

French theorists of colonialism were moving away from the doctrine of assimilation, which emphasized turning the natives into French citizens, to one of association, focusing on the "preservation" of native cultures and multiple routes to civilization. Association had the benefit of validating different ways of life, but in the colonial context it ultimately constituted the abandonment of the idea that the colonized had a place in the national community of France. In an era of democratic expansion, one might dream of civilizing the white savages of the provinces, but the overseas natives were by and large fated to remain essentially other.[59]

Equally important, however, was the increasing willingness of European nations to accept working people into the framework of liberal democracy, and in doing so, to reassess the image of them as racially different. This is not to say that workers in Britain, France, and elsewhere were fully integrated into bourgeois society. The rise of mass-based working-class socialist parties, at least in theory advocating the revolutionary overthrow of capitalism, continued to project a racialized image of class.[60] At the same time, however, working people were also integrated into popular nationalism through mass education, the rise of the popular press, and increased literacy; as 1914 would demonstrate, national identification to a large extent trumped class identity. Moreover, even socialist and labor union organizations, ostensibly devoted to class struggle, could help standardize working-class protest, rendering it more routine and less threatening. In his classic study of the German Social Democratic Party during the late nineteenth century, Guenther Roth coined the term *negative integration* to describe the ways in which the most powerful socialist party of the age gradually became a part of the system it protested against.[61] While not completely ceasing to be the racial Other, European workers in the late nineteenth century nonetheless became a part of liberal democratic society and politics.[62]

More generally, the idea of working men and women as revolutionary savages declined during the course of the century. The history of Irish migration to Britain in the nineteenth century is an excellent example of the interactions between metropolitan ideas of class and colonial ideas of race. In many respects Britain's original colony, Ireland also furnished one of the first major colonial migrations in the history of modern Europe.[63] Irish immigrants in early-nineteenth-century Britain—and the Irish in general—were frequently racialized as non-white, and caricatures of the times depicted them as sharing the negative qualities commonly ascribed to those of African descent.[64] Firmly placed at the bottom of the social hierarchy in Victorian London and other British cities, the Irish represented a colonial population adrift in the metropole, utterly foreign and inassimilable despite being the product of centuries of English rule.

At the same time, Irish immigrants, who were almost all working-class and poor, played a significant role in the formation of class consciousness in nineteenth-century Britain. Both directly and indirectly, Irish immigrants made important contributions to Chartism, often pushing it toward more radical and violent action;[65] half a century later, London's Irish figured prominently in the Great Dock Strike of 1889.[66] Participation in the strike was to win them new respectability for the social stratum to which they belonged, in effect helping to make them more "English"; thus, whereas during the early nineteenth century Irish working-class agitation was often viewed as analogous to that of up-rooted peasants or even rebel slaves, by the century's end one could make out a new vision of the Irish in Britain as increasingly acknowledged members of the British working class.

It is perhaps no accident that the integration of the Irish working class in Britain came at a time of imperial expansion in Africa and Asia. London's East End, the center of the 1889 dock strike and a symbol of both Irish and working-class poverty, was also the great port area that represented links with the overseas colonies. The rise of mass democracy in Britain and new imperial ambitions thus manifested themselves in the same urban setting; while, more broadly, the creation of a new colonial Other facilitated—if only to a certain degree—the increased acceptance of the old.[67]

The early history of France's Third Republic provides another example of the passage to working-class respectability in a colonial context. The new regime was born in the crisis of military defeat and revolution, dramatized above all by the fiery apocalypse of the Paris Commune, which represented the final major manifestation of the insurgent Parisian crowd that had haunted French politics since 1789. The bloody defeat of the Communards definitively exorcised this threat, rendering the creation of a viable liberal democracy possible in the last quarter of the nineteenth century.[68]

Conquest of the Commune by the forces of conservatism in 1871 was a victory for both liberal democracy and empire. The images of savagery that surrounded the Communards, most notably the portrayals of Communard women as incendiary Amazons, strongly suggested the triumph of civilization over barbarity.[69] It is worth noting that a leading punishment for those insurgents who survived the government's vicious repression was deportation to the colonies: more than four thousand were sent to New Caledonia alone. When in 1878 the indigenous peoples of the island staged a major revolt against the French, the bulk of the Communard exiles sided with the colonial authorities against the insurgents, some even taking up arms and joining the forces of order to suppress the Kanaks. As Alice Bullard has noted, in New Caledonia two visions of savagery, political and racial, confronted each other. A year later, the Communard veterans were allowed to return to France and the French state amnestied them in 1880. By abjuring their own insurgent traditions and taking up the cause of imperial authority, the former Communards symbolized the alliance of liberal democracy and empire that lay at the heart of the Third Republic.[70]

The rise of liberal democracy also developed new perspectives on the intersections between race and gender, especially in Britain. The nineteenth century brought the rise of the middle-class household with the increased relegation of men and women to separate (and usually unequal) spheres. Social and cultural norms relegated middle-class women to the home, where they were supposed to embrace the cult of domesticity, at the cost of taking them out of the workplace and depriving them of the ability to earn a living on their own. This emphasis on female dependency had important political implications. Those women, property owners and widows, who had been able to vote during the early nineteenth century lost that right in 1835. The inequality and powerlessness intrinsic to the middle-class image of women sparked the rise of the feminist movement in Britain. Beginning with Mary Wollstonecraft, who published *The Vindication of the Rights of Women* in 1792, by the late nineteenth century British feminism was focused on winning the right to vote for women, a campaign that did not fully succeed until 1928.

Just as new visions of race shaped discourses of social class in Britain, so did racial questions play an important role in discussions of gender. As in the United States, feminism in nineteenth-century Britain had deep roots in the movement to abolish slavery.[71] Many feminists had first become politically active in the struggle for abolition, and like labor activists they at times used slavery as a metaphor, portraying the oppression of women as a similar kind of bondage. Yet, as Claire Midgley has argued, feminists in the UK generally adopted the slave metaphor less than their activist sisters in the US. Instead, they tended to draw parallels between the abolitionist movement and efforts to improve the condition of native women in the British Empire.[72] In doing so, they often created and emphasized a dichotomy between free white British women and oppressed brown and Black women, the liberty of the West versus the oppression of the East. It therefore became the duty of British feminists to defend their colonial sisters against the brutality of their own husbands, fathers, and rulers by extending to them the benefits of imperial rule. This kind of "imperial maternalism" affirmed the racial superiority of British women, and the idea that freedom naturally belonged to those with white skin.[73]

This maternalist approach had classist as well as racial dimensions. For most of its history during the nineteenth century British feminism mobilized primarily middle-class women; the ultimate example of this was the willingness of suffragettes like Emmeline Pankhurst to accept the limitation of the 1918 law granting female suffrage to women of property.[74] British feminists often emphasized the uplift of the lower classes at home, notably in the temperance movement, and such perspectives frequently carried over to native women in the empire. For example, a leading British feminist, Josephine Butler, led a campaign in the 1870s and 1880s to repeal the nation's Contagious Diseases Act, which she and other activists attacked for burdening and humiliating prostitutes. After the 1886 triumph of this crusade in Britain, Butler promptly launched a similar campaign in India on behalf of native prostitutes there, challenging India, often in fiery terms, to improve its treatment of native women: "We, as women, desire to protest in the strongest and most solemn manner possible against the wrong done to our sisters and fellow subjects in India. At the same time we venture to warn you of the danger to our Indian rule in thus trifling with the best instincts of the people. We have reason to believe that the seeds of rebellion are being rapidly propagated. . . . Nothing so surely produces a spirit of rebellion as trampling on the womanhood of a subject race by its conquerors."[75] As this passage makes clear, British feminists like Butler defended native women while at the same time emphasizing their commitment to empire. Indeed, they viewed colonial rule as an important factor in their efforts to improve the lives of women of color. Their attempts to civilize both working women at home and native women abroad ultimately highlighted their own prestige and superiority as free white women.

By the end of the nineteenth century, a large portion of the globe was controlled by European nations committed to some form of liberal democracy at home. Their colonial possessions did not have legislatures or other democratic political structures for the most part, and few of their people had the right to vote or any ability to choose their rulers. In contrast, in the metropoles that controlled these colonies the principle of popular sovereignty was gradually becoming the norm, as was the idea that all adult men should have the right to vote. Moreover, nations like France and Britain that had made the most progress in developing liberal democracy at home had also created the largest overseas empires. The fact that metropole and empire were usually legally distinct served to mask the fact that they nonetheless constituted whole political units internally segregated by race. Within them, liberal democracy was largely for whites, while nonwhites were subject to authoritarian imperial rule.

In both the British and French empires, somewhat like in the United States, voting practices varied widely according to local traditions and legal customs. Often, however, whites could vote and "natives" could not, or if the latter could in some cases vote, their votes would not translate into any meaningful political power or self-rule. Electoral rights varied widely across the British Empire, but in most of its colonies the local privileges around racial distinctions meant that inhabitants could not vote, and frequently within the colonies the British designed electoral privileges around racial distinctions.[76] Many colonies, like Britain itself, based suffrage rights upon property, and that fact alone usually prevented most of the indigenous, nonwhite population from voting. In India, for example, only a tiny percentage of adult males could vote until after World War I.[77] In Jamaica, while Black and colored men could vote in the nineteenth century, property qualifications—especially for those who wanted to run for office—were high enough to keep a white oligarchy firmly in the saddle. As historian Thomas Holt has commented, "If, all things being equal, Black men should rule the island, then all things could not be equal."[78]

The racialized character of British imperial electoral democracy was most evident in the white settler colonies. Democracy was often much more advanced there than in the mother country; for example, New Zealand was one of the first modern nations to give women the vote. This liberality usually did not extend to indigenous or nonwhite populations. In Canada before 1867, British male subjects could vote, but not Catholics, Jews, or indigenous peoples. In both Australia and New Zealand, formal as well as informal restrictions kept most members of the indigenous populations away from the polls. Interestingly, South Africa represented one of the few cases where colonial Africans could vote in large numbers, a major factor in prompting white South Africans to seek independence. To an important extent, Britain's white colonies gave their white subjects all the rights of freeborn Englishmen, and in a colonial situation this traditional sense of rights increasingly translated into the right to vote.[79]

Although the French Empire was in general more centralized than that of the British, it also practiced various approaches to native enfranchisement. When the French abolished slavery in their Caribbean and Indian Ocean colonies in 1848, they made the former slaves citizens of France and gave the men of the "old colonies" the right to vote on an equal footing with French men in the metropole. That at least was the theory; the reality on the ground in Martinique, Guadeloupe, Réunion, and French Guiana was very different. The old colonies remained colonies, even though their inhabitants were citizens, a fact that circumscribed their political autonomy vis-à-vis France. Moreover, the white planters and former slaveholders continued to dominate the local economies, essentially based in the production of sugar. French ex-slaves could in fact vote, but their ability to do so did little to improve their conditions in the years after the abolition of slavery.[80]

Most of the inhabitants of the rest of the French Empire were subjects and therefore had no right to vote. It was possible for natives to become citizens by attaining the status of *évolués*, "evolved individuals," by giving proof of assimilation into French culture and law.[81] Since this meant not only obtaining French education in colonies with few schools but also renouncing other legal traditions, notably Islamic, it was a path open to and taken by only a few individuals.[82] In colonial Algeria, for example, the number of "evolved ones" amounted to only a few thousand out of several million people.[83] This practice not only benefited few people but also reinforced the idea that freedom was a European idea reserved for white Europeans.[84]

The rise of European empires thus reinscribed, on a global scale, the idea of white freedom that abolitionists had hoped would end with slavery. Imperial liberal democracy had a paradoxical cast—citizenship in the metropole, subjecthood in the colonies—and the difference was racial. The liberal idea of gradually educating colonial subjects for democracy and self-rule proved a nonstarter for the most part, in sharp contrast to the integration of the metropolitan working classes. Colonial education was in general woefully underfunded, and where it did exist was highly segregated racially and did not in general train students for citizenship.[85] As the idea of freedom became more closely tied to ideas of popular sovereignty and national independence, it became ever more distant for colonial subjects. Ironically, colonial expansion, which had been to an important extent, especially in Africa, inspired by the desire to eradicate slavery and liberate men from the shackles of superstition and ignorance continued to deny them freedom on the basis of race. The world of imperial liberal democracy was one that boasted of its advancement of human freedom, but where that freedom was essentially reserved for whites.

France and Britain had the largest overseas empires, but by the start of the twentieth century the United States had developed into the world's most powerful liberal democracy. Here also the abolition of African slavery did not bring about universal liberty. Instead, America became an example of how ideas of liberty continued to be racially circumscribed in the modern era. Under the lamp of the Statue of Liberty, America became one of the world's greatest examples of white freedom.

America, the White Light in the West

As the previous chapter showed, the United States was born out of a revolutionary struggle for white freedom. The American Revolution championed the right of white Americans to liberty and national independence, while at the same time preserving their right to own Black slaves. The flagrant hypocrisy of such a position did help create an alternative vision of universal freedom that would include African Americans, so that during the Revolutionary era the number of free Blacks increased dramatically and many of the new states moved to abolish slavery altogether. Yet this trend would prove temporary: not only would slavery gain a new dynamism in the South during the early nineteenth century, but it would in many ways remain a national institution. Only the Civil War would finally bring chattel slavery to an end in America, in the prophetic words of John Brown purging the sins of the guilty land in blood.

The history of the United States during the nineteenth century is important to this chapter not just because of the nation's character as a slave republic but also because of its importance to the history of liberal democracy. In an important sense America is the world's quintessential liberal democracy, a nation without a monarchy or titled nobility, born of a popular revolt for liberty and independence. Moreover, the founding structures and documents of the United States provided both for individual liberties and popular sovereignty, and have remained the basis of American law and politics ever since. The principle of universal manhood suffrage was widely cherished in the new nation, and by the middle of the century had essentially become the law of the land. As I will explore in detail below, the reality of the democratization of voting rights was more complicated. The federal structure of the United States meant that enfranchisement varied widely from state to state. Nonetheless, the right to vote gradually became seen during the nineteenth century as a key aspect of what made Americans a free people.[86]

Yet the very concept of Americans as a free people was grounded in a racialized definition of what it meant to be both free and American. The fact that most African Americans were slaves until the Civil War meant that liberal democracy had racial limits, but more generally the right to vote and participate in American life as a citizen of the republic had a strong racial character. Even after emancipation, moreover, the failure of Reconstruction and the creation of Jim Crow in the South meant that most Blacks still could not vote and that therefore democracy and freedom were a function of race in America. The disenfranchisement of African Americans was not, as it sometimes has been portrayed, merely an exception to a general narrative of democratic enfranchisement. On the contrary, it fit into a broader pattern of racialized liberal democracy throughout the nineteenth century and beyond that highlighted the central role played by white freedom in the modern history of the United States.[87]

One can trace interesting parallels between the American South after 1865 and the overseas empires of France and Britain: both were part of nations that considered themselves liberal democracies based on freedom, and in both, peoples of color could not vote nor had any right to popular sovereignty.[88] The other striking parallel between Europe and the United States in the nineteenth century is that between workers in the former and European immigrants in the latter. Like working-class Europeans, American immigrants from Ireland, Italy, eastern Europe, and elsewhere in the Old World had to struggle for acceptance as free and equal citizens in the United States, and yet ultimately the success of their struggle, and as a result of the fight to create mass-based liberal democracy in America, came down to their ability to claim whiteness and white identity. In both Europe and America, freedom by the dawn of the twentieth century would assume the political structure of white liberal democracy.

The Rise of White Democracy and the White to Vote

One key symbol and vector of freedom in American history has been the right to vote, the ability of a sovereign people to select its own leaders and thus govern itself, to choose freely its own destiny. Voting is mentioned more often in the Constitution than any other right of American citizens. Yet, as Eric Foner once noted, there has frequently been a tension in American history between "voting as a right and voting as something that only the right people should do."[89] Voting has never been a universal privilege in the United States: it has never been granted to legal minors, for example. The ability to elect one's leaders has been not only a right of free men (and men alone until 1920), but also a responsibility for the stewardship of the nation, one that only those worthy of freedom deserved to exercise. The character of the United States as a liberal democracy was central to the ideal of American freedom, but democracy did not necessarily mean voting rights, or freedom in general, for all.[90]

As historians like Alex Keyssar have shown, the popular image of the United States as democratic from birth is not quite accurate. America's federal political structure meant that individual states often decided their own rules about the franchise, which led to tremendous variations across the country. Not until the 1850s did universal manhood suffrage become the effective law of the land, and women would wait for another seventy years before they too could vote.[91] In this section I will consider the ways in which race shaped ideas about and practices of suffrage in nineteenth century America, arguing that to a very important extent whiteness was a key precondition of the right to vote. Racial restrictions on the franchise in America thus were another significant aspect of the interpretation of freedom as white in the nation that considered itself the cradle of liberty.

In colonial British North America suffrage was generally considered a privilege rather than a right, and the ability of colonists to vote varied widely from one colony to another. For the most part, however, voting was limited to white men of property. The emphasis on property, corresponding to the discussion above about wealth and civic responsibility, accentuated the conviction that only men who had both a stake in society and the independence that ownership granted should be entrusted with the ability to direct the affairs of state. Estimates as to how many British colonists could vote vary widely among historians, but many agree that at least half of adult white men were enfranchised, a proportion far higher than in Britain at the same time. The number of British colonists with suffrage rights was thus a small proportion of the total colonial population, but at the same time it was large enough to lay the foundations of a mass electoral political culture.[92]

The American Revolution's focus on white freedom meant challenging the restrictions that limited the franchise to men of property. Whereas conservative colonists still championed the importance of property qualifications, radicals like Thomas Paine argued forcefully that all men should enjoy the freedom to vote as a right. As Paine argued, "The right of voting for representatives is the primary right by which other rights are protected. To take away this right is to reduce a man to slavery, for slavery consists in being subject to the will of another, and he that has not a vote in the election of representatives is in this case."[93] As political participation spread beyond traditional colonial elites, more and more voices demanded the ability to vote as part of not only that participation but also their right as free men. In particular, the idea of voting as a natural right became more and more prominent, meshing with other natural rights that the revolution fought to guarantee. Notably, the insurgent colonists came to regard suffrage as a key component of the freedom they were fighting for. The result was a dramatic expansion of the franchise by the time the new nation achieved its independence. Pennsylvania took the lead, abolishing the property requirement in favor of taxpaying status. Vermont went furthest, allowing all men to vote regardless of financial status. In general, by the end of the war the majority of white adult men in most of the United States could vote. Seen in global context, this made the new nation the most inclusive democracy of its time.[94]

The expansion of voting rights as part of the revolutionary struggle for freedom and national liberation left a defining mark on the new nation. Between the Revolution and the Civil War Americans progressively expanded the franchise, realizing the goal of universal white male suffrage by the 1850s. This essentially progressed state by state, but the underlying general expansion of the right to vote was undeniable. In particular, the early nineteenth century saw the gradual abandonment of property requirements for voting. Change came in particular from the West: all of the new states admitted to the Union after 1783 permitted men to vote without regard to their wealth or property. The spirit of Jacksonian democracy, its emphasis on a populist vision of the United States, encouraged the idea that all free men, regardless of property qualification, should have the right to vote, or else they were not truly free. As a result, by the end of the 1850s property requirements for voting had essentially disappeared, and only a few states had a taxpaying requirement. The America that entered the Civil War did so as a populist democracy.[95]

It also did so as a nation in which democracy was circumscribed by gender and race. During the early nineteenth century gender remained the great determinant of who could or could not vote. After New Jersey abolished the right of women of property to vote in 1807, suffrage remained a masculine privilege until 1920.[96] The role played by race in shaping electoralism was less straightforward, but in some ways more interesting. Most African Americans were slaves, so there was no question of extending to them the right to vote. The United States also had a sizable population of free Blacks in the early nineteenth century; however, it was concentrated in the North, where slavery had largely disappeared as an institution after the War of Independence.[97] As noted in the previous chapter, the contradiction between a struggle for freedom waged by slaveholding colonies had created a vision of a nonracist ideal of liberty, one that seemed to offer the possibility of greater racial equality in the new United States. Some Americans, both Black and white, argued that slavery would gradually fade away in the free United States.

It was not to be, at least in the short term. Not only did slavery gain a new lease on life in the early nineteenth century, but even those Blacks who were not slaves found that was not the same as being free. The 1790 Naturalization Act that defined citizenship as the privilege of free white men became a template for imposing racial criteria on the idea of American freedom. Frequently states denied African Americans privileges, like equality before the law or the ability to attend public schools, that were routinely extended to whites. In particular, most free Blacks did not possess the right to vote. Moreover, the disenfranchisement of Blacks steadily *increased* during the early nineteenth century, at the same time as more and more white men obtained the right to vote. Until 1800 free Blacks could vote in all Northern states, but in the next few decades New Jersey, Maryland, Connecticut, and New York either drastically curtailed or abolished altogether African American suffrage. Of equal significance, with the exception of Maine, every state that entered the Union after 1800 banned free Blacks from voting. By the eve of the Civil War only New England (minus Connecticut) granted voting rights to free Blacks.[98]

Most fascinating here is thus not just the denial of voting rights to free Blacks but the fact that it occurred at the same time as the progressive enfranchisement of white men without regard to wealth or property qualifications. What explains such a curious parallel history? The emancipation of slaves in the Northern states was by no means universally popular, and even those opposed to slavery did not necessarily believe in or accept Black equality. As the free Black population grew, the possibility that they could not only vote but play a decisive role in elections became a more threatening prospect. Moreover, property qualifications had traditionally prevented most free Blacks from voting. As those declined, the possibility of a racially egalitarian democracy in America became more real, so that the racial order they had helped to guarantee had to be protected in more explicit ways. Some whites also feared that giving Blacks the vote would attract a flood of runaway slaves from the South.[99]

Above all, by the mid-nineteenth century most white Americans regarded Blacks as not really Americans, and certainly not citizens. In 1857 the Supreme Court's *Dred Scott* decision wrote this into federal law, defining Blacks as not white and therefore not citizens.[100] Opponents of African American suffrage freely and stridently expressed racist attitudes toward Blacks, regarding them as unfit intellectually and morally to participate in political life. In 1860 Theophilus C. Callicot, Democratic assemblyman from Brooklyn, spoke against Black suffrage, contending that "the proposition to put negroes on a footing of political equality with the white men is repugnant to the sense of the American people. . . . Americans would never consent to share the proud title of 'American Citizen' with an inferior and abject race."[101] In spite of frequent protests by Black activists and their white allies, by the time of the Civil War voting, and with it the definition of freedom in America, had become largely a function of race. The right to vote had become the white to vote.

The history of voting rights among other racialized groups in American society both affirms and to a certain extent nuances this perspective. To an important degree, the enfranchisement of Native Americans and Mexican Americans before the Civil War rested upon the extent to which they were defined as white, or could claim white identity. Unlike African Americans, who were always considered the negative referent of whiteness, members of these groups could sometimes claim white identity in principle, even if that claim was often rejected in practice. Their right (and usually more important, their *ability*) to vote often hinged on the extent to which they could claim whiteness culturally and politically as well as legally. To be, in Laura Gomez's memorable phrase, "off-white," was to push up against the racialized limits of suffrage, and freedom in general, in antebellum America.[102]

Like free Blacks, Native Americans had largely been banned from voting in colonial America. After independence their enfranchisement varied from state to state, determined primarily by two factors. The most important rested upon definitions of their racial status. In states that considered them white they could vote; Michigan, for example, decided they were white simply because they were not Black. In contrast, states that considered them nonwhite generally banned them from voting. The other factor was their status as members of tribes, in theory sovereign entities which in effect made them foreigners. The ambiguous national and legal status of Native Americans frequently served as a pretext for disenfranchising them, although some authorities argued those that left their tribes (especially those that surrendered title to tribal lands) and assimilated into American life could become citizens. As a result, few Native Americans could vote before the Civil War.[103]

The situation of Mexican Americans was similarly ambiguous. The United States waged war against Mexico from 1846 to 1848, and as a result of its victory annexed the northern half of the country, including notably Texas and California. This gave America for the first time in its history a sizable Mexican American population, some 100,000 strong.[104] The Treaty of Guadalupe Hidalgo, which ended the war, gave this population both American citizenship and legal status as whites. However, as would often be the case in American history, this legal status did not translate into political and social rights, particularly in Texas, home to perhaps the largest Mexican American population. The independent Republic of Texas established before the American war had banned all Mexican Americans from voting or citizenship rights.[105] Even after annexation by the United States, although they had the legal right to vote few succeeded in exercising it thanks to racist pressure from the white population. The inability to vote in effect helped to racialize a population that sought unsuccessfully to claim the white status guaranteed it by law.

During the early nineteenth century, therefore, the right to vote in the United States was closely entangled with race. Not only was suffrage extended to virtually all white men by the eve of the Civil War, thus breaking down traditional restrictions based on property and class, it was also and at the same time increasingly denied to those who were not white men. The early years of America as a free and independent nation were thus a period when voting was more and more defined in racial terms. The idea that voting rights were gradually expanded to ever more Americans does not fit the facts of the early nineteenth century, which instead saw the franchise both broadened and restricted, along racial lines, at the same time. The white to vote consequently illustrated how the growth of freedom in America was in reality the growth of white freedom. The political culture of the American republic was grounded in whiteness, a fact that, as we shall see in the next section, even the greatest conflict in American history would not change.

From Jubilee to Jim Crow

The Rise and Fall of Black Freedom

As He died to make men holy, let us die to make men free.

—JULIA WARD HOWE, *THE BATTLE HYMN OF THE REPUBLIC*, 1862

Slavery is not abolished until the Black man has the ballot.

—FREDERICK DOUGLASS, 1865[106]

More than perhaps any other time in American history, during the Civil War and the Reconstruction that followed it the meaning of freedom specifically included, even embraced, the nation's Black population. Although that was not its initial goal, ultimately America's bloodiest conflict achieved the destruction of slavery, and three amendments to the Constitution made all men free citizens of the United States with the right to vote in its elections. In the aftermath of the Union's great victory, made possible to an important extent by the determination of African Americans to fight and die in what they called "the freedom war," white freedom seemed as though it might fade into the nation's past in the face of a new vision of racial equality.[107]

That did not happen. As African Americans would learn to their bitter disappointment, the nation's commitment to abolishing slavery did not necessarily mean freeing the slaves themselves. The dominance of the Radical Republicans, who embraced a fervent desire not just for the abolition of slavery but also for Black equality and empowerment, proved fleeting, and by the end of the 1870s the Reconstruction dream of racial equality in the former Confederacy had largely faded away. In particular, the enfranchisement of the freedmen was increasingly challenged by the kind of white terror symbolized by the Ku Klux Klan, so that by the end of the century the ability of African Americans to exercise their right to vote in the South, where the overwhelming majority of America's Black population lived, had effectively ceased to exist. In the United States as a whole, therefore, whiteness continued to define freedom.

The Civil War began not when the states of the South seceded from the Union but when the federal government and the Northern states decided to force them to remain. A desire to liberate the slaves had little to do with this initial decision. Whereas for Blacks and abolitionists the war against the insurgent South was clearly a war for freedom and the overthrow of slavery, most Northerners viewed the conflict as a struggle to preserve the Union, not one to free the slaves. In an 1861 address to Congress President Lincoln stated he had "no purpose, directly or indirectly, to interfere with slavery in the States where it exists."[108] In response both the House and Senate passed resolutions the same month affirming that the struggle to preserve the Union had nothing to do with any desire to free the slaves. In the first year of the war even the abolitionists muted their demands for the overthrow of slavery, feeling correctly that public opinion in the North strongly opposed them.

In fact, not the North but the South saw the conflict as a war for liberty. Southerners often portrayed themselves as the true heirs of 1776, like their forefathers fighting for freedom against tyranny. This freedom included the right to own property, notably slaves. As one Southerner argued, "We are fighting for our liberty against tyrants of the North ... who are determined to destroy slavery."[109] Or, as Jefferson Davis put it, "Will you be slaves or will [you] be independent? ... Will you consent to be robbed of your property [or] strike bravely for liberty, property, honor and life?"[110] Even for the majority of whites who owned no slaves, secession was a war for freedom because it alone could preserve white supremacy and prevent Southerners from falling under the domination of "Black Republicans." More than ever, during the Civil War the American South defined freedom in racial terms.

Given this, how did the Civil War come to adopt emancipation as its guiding principle and eventually abolish slavery? Much credit, of course,

goes to African Americans themselves. North and South, free and enslaved, Blacks in America viewed the war as a crusade for liberty. In the
North free Blacks held meetings and organized to pressure politicians
to turn the war into a struggle against slavery. In the South slaves clan-
destinely followed the progress of the Union armies as they approached,
and often as soon as the opportunity presented itself fled their plantations to gain the northern lines and freedom. Entire families and communities took to the roads. The idea of moving from one place to another in search of a better life has been a classic theme in American
history, but at no time was it more poignant than during the Civil War
as the slaves sought to emancipate themselves by following the northern
star.[111]

Had the North quickly won the Civil War the institution of slavery
might well have survived, but instead the Union armies floundered at
first, only very gradually gaining an upper hand in the conflict. As the
war dragged on it became increasingly clear that the Confederacy depended on the mobilization of slave labor to sustain its war effort, and
depriving it of that labor could weaken and ultimately destroy it. Northern abolitionists pushed this argument with ever greater determination,
with the result that by the end of 1861 the Union armies began welcoming escaped slaves as "contrabands," underscoring the link between freedom and property.[112]

There was also the British position to consider. English cotton mills,
and thus industrial society in general, depended heavily on Southern
cotton, and the Union blockade of the South caused widespread hard-
ship in the country. Yet the cause of antislavery, linked to the powerful
social and political forces of liberalism and Methodism, was extremely
popular in Britain (*Uncle Tom's Cabin* was one of the best-selling books
there in the nineteenth century). Making the war a crusade against slavery, abolitionists argued, would render British intervention on the side
of the Confederacy politically impossible.[113]

Ultimately the South was caught in an untenable situation: it could
not at the same time suppress over one-third of its population and fight
a war against a larger, stronger power. As W.E.B. DuBois put it in *Black
Reconstruction in America*:

It was not the Abolitionist alone who freed the slaves. The Abolitionists never had a real majority of the people of the United States back
of them. Freedom for the slave was the logical result of a crazy attempt to wage war in the midst of four million Black slaves, and trying the while sublimely to ignore the interests of the slaves in the
outcome of the fighting. Yet, these slaves had enormous power in
their hands. Simply by stopping work, they could threaten the Confederacy with starvation. By walking into the Federal camps, they
showed to doubting Northerners the easy possibility of using them
as workers, and as servants, as farmers, and as spies, and finally, as
fighting soldiers. And not only using them thus, but by the same ges-
ture, depriving their enemies of their use in just these fields. It was
the fugitive slave who made the slaveholders face the alternative of
surrendering to the North, or to the Negroes.[114]

To an important extent, therefore, the Black slaves of the South used the
trauma of civil war to free themselves.

Lincoln resisted the idea of emancipation throughout much of 1862,
fearing the presence of free Blacks on American soil, yet events soon
overtook his reluctance. In September 1862 Lincoln issued the Prelimi-
nary Emancipation Proclamation, stating that he intended to free the
slaves unless the Confederacy surrendered by the end of the year. This
was not a politically popular stance, as the sharp losses of Lincoln's Republican Party in the 1862 elections made clear. Nonetheless, on January 1, 1863, the federal government officially enacted the Emancipation
Proclamation, granting freedom to the over 3 million slaves of the Confederacy. In spite of its limitations (for example, it did not apply to slaves
in slaveholding states that, like Maryland, had remained in the Union),
its promulgation sparked massive celebrations by Blacks and abolitionists throughout the North. In Boston thousands packed into the city's
Tremont Temple on New Year's Day to wait for the official word from
Washington. When it came by telegraph the crowd exploded in jubila-
tion, joining Frederick Douglass in singing the spiritual "Blow Ye the
Trumpet Blow." As word of the decision spread throughout the South
the slaves celebrated and began making plans for their own liberation.

FIGURE 21. "The Emancipation of the Negroes, January 1863—The Past and the Future." Drawn by Thomas Nast. From *Harper's Weekly*, January 24, 1863.

A few months later escaping slaves on a riverboat in the Mississippi River sang of the new day:

> Oh, praise an' tanks De Lord he come
> To set de people free;
> An' massa tink it day ob doom,
> An' we ob jubilee.
> De Lord dat heap de Red Sea waves,
> He jes' as strong as den;
> He say de word: we las' night slaves,
> To-day de Lord's free men.[115]

Freedom did not come at once, of course, but the Emancipation Proclamation turned the war of the Union armies into a crusade for liberation. Wherever the soldiers in blue went they freed the slaves, and their progress gradually brought the last throes of the peculiar institution. General Sherman's famous march across Georgia to the sea in 1864, remembered by Southern whites as a scorched earth campaign of brutal destruction, seemed a victory parade to the many former slaves who followed in his train.[116] Nearly 200,000 African American men joined the Union armies, a third of them making the ultimate sacrifice for freedom. By June 19, 1865, when federal troops formally occupied Texas and decreed the emancipation of its slaves, the Civil War had ended with the triumph of Black freedom.[117]

But what did such freedom mean, apart from the absence of slavery? This was the central question of the post-Emancipation era, or Reconstruction.[118] The former slaves certainly had their own ideas. Freedom meant the ability to reunite with family members, to travel and choose where they wanted to live, to be paid for their labor and have the right to turn down work they did not want, to not be subjected to imprisonment, physical punishment, and abuse. Freedom did not just mean individual rights, however, but also the ability to form free communities, to create institutions like churches and schools. In effect, freedom meant not having a master, being in control of one's own destiny.[119]

For the former slaves, the right to obtain an education was a central aspect of their new freedom. Throughout the former Confederacy Blacks flocked to the new schools. From the many elementary schools that taught both young and old how to read and write, to the nation's first Black universities like Fisk and Howard, the thirst for learning consumed the freedmen and -women.[120] The other great desire was land. In a largely rural society where land ownership lay at the very heart of social and political independence, those who had until recently been property hungered to own property themselves. Many felt that they were entitled to the plantations they had suffered on as slaves: as one group of South Carolina freedmen told their former master, "We ain' gwine nowhar. . . . We gwine wuk right here on de lan' whar we wuz bo'n an' whar belongs tuh us."[121] At the same time, for many, land ownership— the ability to earn one's own living independently—seemed like the only viable alternative to continuing to work for whites on their plantations, which was justifiably considered simply a new version of slavery. The demand for forty acres and a mule was the ultimate concrete statement of the freedmen's desire for liberty, and the decision not to redistribute land to the former slaves a powerful indication of its limitations.[122]

Finally, freedom for the former slaves meant the right to vote. Immediately after the end of the war Blacks began organizing to demand suffrage for all men regardless of race. For them, voting, like land ownership, was important both as a practical guarantee and as a symbol of their newly free status. This desire for the political franchise was supported by the Radical branch of the Republican party, which for a decade after Appomattox largely controlled the national government. In 1866 the Republicans passed the Fourteenth Amendment to the Constitution, which made all former slaves US citizens, and a year later followed it with the Reconstruction Act, requiring Southern states to ratify the amendment and allow Blacks to vote as a condition of their readmission to the Union. The result was a political revolution in the South, as the former slaves streamed to the polls in overwhelming numbers, with their white allies electing a series of progressive state governments across the region. This expansion of the franchise reached its zenith in 1870 when the Fifteenth Amendment, granting the right to vote to men of all races, became the law of the land.[123]

Most white Southerners viewed these changes with horror and moved to limit the impact of emancipation as much as possible. In 1865 and 1866 several Southern states passed Black codes that forced freedmen to provide proof of employment, usually by signing contracts to work on plantations. They became one way of "getting things back as near to slavery as possible."[124] More ominously, Southern whites initiated a campaign of violence and terror against local Republicans, both Black and white. At the end of 1865 Confederate veterans in Tennessee founded the Ku Klux Klan, which over the next few years murdered hundreds of Blacks and their white supporters. The Klan targeted in particular Republican politicians in a violent attempt to disenfranchise the Black population and maintain white supremacy. This reign of terror continued until 1872, when President Grant suppressed it with federal troops.[125]

The suppression of the Klan showed that the key to Black freedom lay in the North; only as long as the Radical Republicans held power would they enforce the right of Southern Blacks to vote. By the early 1870s the signs were not encouraging. As we have seen, Black suffrage was not popular in the North before the war, and even after 1865 proposals to enfranchise African Americans were voted down in most Northern states. By the early 1870s many Northern whites were more interested in reconciliation with the South than with protecting Black rights there. The Democratic Party scored a major election victory in 1874, winning control of the House of Representatives, signaling that the reformist approach to the former Confederacy had lost much of its steam.

White Southerners soon drew their own conclusions from these signals, and in 1875 renewed their violent campaign against Reconstruction. In Mississippi, armed vigilantes murdered Republican politicians and terrorized their supporters from voting, enabling the Democrats to win the state by a landslide. The same happened in South Carolina in 1876, by which time Democrats and their terrorist allies had overthrown all the Reconstruction state governments in the South. Unlike in 1872, the federal government refused to intervene. Instead, in 1877 the new presidential administration of Rutherford B. Hayes agreed, in exchange for Southern support in the disputed election of the previous year, to withdraw all federal troops from the South and recognize the legitimacy of its Democratic state governments. The so-called Bargain or Compromise of 1877 effectively ended the Reconstruction of the South, and with it hopes for Black freedom.[126]

The next two decades witnessed the rebirth of white supremacy in the South. During the last quarter of the nineteenth century Southern states passed a series of laws to keep their Black populations separate and inferior. Collectively known as Jim Crow, these measures rigidly segregated Blacks in all major spheres of life, from hospitals, schools, and public parks down to telephone booths and drinking fountains. Facilities available for Blacks were invariably inferior in quality, highlighting their exclusion from the mainstream of Southern life. Jim Crow was not just a Southern phenomenon, however; public racial segregation existed throughout the North and West, and the Supreme Court's 1896 *Plessy v. Ferguson* decision upholding the doctrine of "separate but equal" made it in effect national policy.[127]

The main thrust and goal of the post-Reconstruction reaction, however, was the disenfranchisement of the Black population. Starting in earnest in 1890, Southern states began enacting a variety of measures to keep African Americans from voting. These included residency requirements, literacy tests, and poll taxes requiring people to pay a fee for the right to vote. As a result of these and other restrictions and of the racist terror that continued to threaten those Blacks who attempted to exercise their franchise, Black electoral participation dropped precipitously in the South. By 1910 only four percent of all Black men in Georgia had registered to vote, whereas for the South in general less than ten percent of eligible African Americans routinely came out for elections. The right to vote had once again become the white to vote, and the effective elimination of the Black franchise and Black political power illustrated the racialized nature of democracy. Since the overwhelming majority of African Americans lived in the South, their disenfranchisement essentially limited voting to whites in general. The Civil War and Reconstruction thus ended in a ringing reaffirmation of white supremacy and white freedom.[128]

On January 29, 1901, congressman George Henry White of North Carolina gave his final speech in the US House of Representatives. The last of the Black politicians elected during Reconstruction, Representative White had lost his battle for reelection thanks to the disenfranchisement of most of his African American constituents. In the speech that marked the end of Black freedom in America, congressman White declared:

Now, Mr. Chairman, before concluding my remarks I want to submit a brief recipe for the solution of the so-called American negro problem. He asks no special favors, but simply demands that he be given the same chance for existence, for earning a livelihood, for raising himself in the scales of manhood and womanhood that are accorded to kindred nationalities. . . . This, Mr. Chairman, is perhaps the negroes' temporary farewell to the American Congress; but let me say, Phoenix-like he will rise up some day and come again. These parting words are in behalf of an outraged, heart-broken, bruised, and bleeding, but God-fearing people, faithful, industrious, loyal people—rising people, full of potential force.[129]

The implementation of Jim Crow throughout the South by the dawn of the twentieth century underscored the durability of slavery and the racial nature of liberty in America as a whole. The defeat of the greatest challenge to white freedom in the nation's history would play a key role in shaping the character of American democracy in the modern era.

Immigration and Whiteness in Turn of the Century America

> The Jewish emigrant for the first time in his life rejoices. . . . He is on his way to a country that greets all new arrivals with a gigantic statue of liberty. . . . To some extent, the reality *does* correspond to the symbol. Not because they really are all that serious about liberty in the new country, but because they have people who are more Jewish than the Jews, which is to say the Negroes. Of course Jews are still Jews. But here, significantly, they are first and foremost whites. For the first time a Jew's race is actually to his advantage.
>
> —JOSEPH ROTH, *THE WANDERING JEWS*[130]

In the summer of 1863 one of the largest race riots, indeed civil disturbances of any kind, in American history broke out in the city of New York. Afraid that the Emancipation Proclamation would flood the city with Black competitors for jobs and incensed by the new national draft, which had been decreed in March, thousands of working-class whites went on a rampage against people and property in Manhattan for three bloody days. Largely but not exclusively composed of Irish immigrants, the mobs targeted not only symbols of Republican Party authority but also African American men, women, and children. The rioters burned the Colored Orphanage on Fifth Avenue to the ground and lynched several Black men unlucky enough to fall into their hands. They were not the only victims; as one observer noted, "A child of 3 years of age was thrown from a 4th story window and instantly killed. . . . Children were torn from their mother's embrace and their brains blown out."[131]

FIGURE 22. "The Riots in New York: The mob lynching a negro in Clarkson Street."
New York Draft Riots (c. 1863). Fotosearch/Getty Images.

Having for years reserved work on the New York docks for white men, the insurgents fought to apply the same standard to life in the city as a whole. They had some success: hundreds of Blacks fled the city, which by the end of the year had its smallest African American population since 1820.[132]

The story of the New York draft riots belongs to the histories of both American racism and American immigration, illustrating some of the complex connections between the two. The half century from the Civil War to World War I witnessed both the rise and fall of Black freedom, as we have seen above, and one of the greatest periods of foreign immigration in American history. For a long time, historians of the United States tended to treat the two as separate phenomena. Whereas immigrants came mostly to the burgeoning cities of the industrial North and East, African Americans remained largely in the post-Emancipation South. To the extent that they placed the two histories in comparative context, it was often to portray them as similar examples of nativist hostility and racism toward outsiders.

Whiteness studies has offered a radical departure from this perspective. Created by David Roediger, Matthew Frye Jacobsen, Alexander Saxton, and others, whiteness studies in a nutshell argue that being white is a social and political rather than a biological category, that dominance in racially segmented societies is as much achieved as given. Conceptualizing America in particular as a "white republic," whiteness scholars have considered the ways in which foreign immigrants were (or were not) integrated and accepted into national life by both embracing and being granted white identity.[133] This has brought to the study of immigration a new focus on race as a vital part of that history. Moreover, because the flip side of being white is not being Black, it has prompted new perspectives on the relationship between immigrants and African Americans. The field of whiteness studies has given rise to new questions about the history of European immigration in particular: What did white identity mean to them, and how did it intersect with desires for Americanization? Did the achievement of whiteness happen gradually in America, as scholars Noel Ignatiev and Karen Brodkin have argued, or were European immigrants, in the words of Thomas Gugliemo, "white on arrival"? Above all, how does one square the systematic and pervasive discrimination against foreign immigrants in the nineteenth and early twentieth centuries with the idea that they nonetheless were able to achieve some version of white privilege?[134]

In answering these questions, one must distinguish between different waves of immigration before World War I. Most Americans came from immigrant stock, of course, primarily from Britain, and those easily fit into a predominantly Anglo-Saxon culture. During the early nineteenth century the other major waves of immigration came from two places, Ireland and Germany. The primarily Protestant German population, while often remaining culturally distinct, nonetheless was generally accepted into American life.[135] The Irish were another matter. Between 1830 and 1860, especially after the Great Famine of the 1840s devastated their island, nearly 2 million Irish immigrated to the United States. They crowded into big cities and towns in the East and Midwest, usually living in squalid conditions and working in low-wage casual labor. Stigmatized for both their poverty and their Catholicism, Irish immigrants were scorned and discriminated against by the dominant society. In particular, they were seen as so degraded that they were often analogized to Blacks, as "niggers turned inside out."[136]

For the most part, the Irish reacted to this victimization by seeking to assimilate into American society and win acceptance as American citizens, and to an important extent this meant embracing racism so as to distinguish themselves from African Americans. The rivalry over labor on the New York docks mentioned above formed part of a broader process of excluding Black competition from the low-wage jobs on which the Irish depended, and doing so by proclaiming the privilege of white labor. At the same time Irish immigrants allied themselves with the Democratic party, and the latter's opposition to abolition both attracted the Irish and further reinforced their hostility to Blacks. Both Noel Ignatiev and Angela F. Murphy have commented on the visit of Daniel O'Connell, one of Ireland's great fighters for equality and justice, to the United States in 1841. O'Connell appealed to Irish immigrants to join the cause of antislavery, only to be firmly rebuffed. Prejudice against Blacks, combined with a reluctance to be singled out as immigrants, led the Irish in America to reject the call for abolition, even when it came from a venerated national leader.[137] As Frederick Douglass observed in 1853, "The Irish, who, at home, readily sympathize with the oppressed everywhere, are instantly taught when they step upon our soil to hate and despise the Negro."[138]

Over time, Irish immigrants were able to mobilize and deploy their whiteness to win acceptance in American society. For a useful counterpoint, one can compare their history in the nineteenth century with that of another group of immigrants, the Chinese. The two populations that would meet in 1869 at Promontory Point, Utah, completing the construction of the transnational railroad that would make America a global economic power had very different receptions in their new country.[139] The California gold rush first prompted significant numbers of Chinese to immigrate to America, and the overwhelming majority settled on the Pacific coast. By the early 1880s more than 100,000 Chinese nationals lived in the United States. Mostly single men, they worked not only on the railroads but also in agriculture, manufacturing, laundry work, and restaurants. Starting in the 1850s "Chinatowns" became distinctive characteristics of San Francisco and other West Coast cities.[140]

Like the Irish, Chinese immigrants encountered hostility and discrimination from their American hosts, but because unlike the Irish they could not take refuge in whiteness, this hostility took a much more dramatic and tragic turn. Although prejudice against Asians was certainly not new in the United States, starting in the 1870s whites began organized campaigns to discriminate against the Chinese and eventually to exclude them from America altogether. In particular working-class whites in California, many of them immigrants from Ireland and other parts of Europe, took the lead in anti-Chinese agitation. In July 1877, a two-day pogrom against the Chinese in San Francisco spurred the growth of the new Workingmen's Party of the United States, founded by anti-Chinese activists. Soon led by Irish immigrant Denis Kearney, the party would go on to take control of the California state legislature and launch a national campaign against the Chinese.[141] It achieved a resounding success when in 1882 the federal government passed the Chinese Exclusion Act banning Chinese nationals from immigrating to the United States. It was not a complete racial ban: it did not expel those Chinese already living in America, and in 1894 a Supreme Court decision ruled that Chinese born in the US were American citizens. But the Chinese Exclusion Act nonetheless proved very popular, and by the early twentieth century was applied to virtually all Asians with the exception of the Japanese.[142]

The 1882 Chinese Exclusion Act was the first American law since the 1790 Alien Naturalization Act to ban immigrants solely on the basis of race or national origin. As historians like Andrew Gyory and especially Najia Aarim-Heriot have pointed out, the timing of Chinese exclusion was no accident, but bore close relationship to the end of Reconstruction and the reimposition of racial rule in the South.[143] The gradual decline of Radical Republicanism which led to the end of Reconstruction also facilitated racist legislation against the Chinese. Moreover, the ability of California's anti-Chinese activists to succeed on a national level was due in large part to the support they received from white Southerners. Not only did anti-Chinese sentiments frequently draw upon the language of antiblack racism but, as Andrew Gyory has pointed out, with the decline of Reconstruction Southern elites no longer feared they would need Chinese workers to replace a truculent Black population.[144] A year after the Act, in a major decision, the *Civil Rights Cases* of 1883, the Supreme Court significantly weakened legal protections for African Americans against discrimination.[145] The two events thus reaffirmed the key importance of whiteness in determining who was an American.

This atmosphere of white privilege and racial exclusion established the context in which massive numbers of immigrants from southern and eastern Europe came to the United States starting in the 1890s. As I noted in chapter 2, these new Americans faced significant hostility that often took on racist overtones. The rise of a powerful nativist movement, culminating in the Immigration Act of 1924, known as the Johnson-Reed Act, that sharply limited foreign immigration, was only the most dramatic indication of the widespread belief that the new European immigrants constituted an inferior species of humanity. For example, Italians, the largest group of Europeans, were routinely subjected to Jim Crow laws in the South, and eleven perished in an 1891 race riot in New Orleans. In 1912 members of Congress held a debate about whether Italians were "full-blooded Caucasians."[146]

At the same time, however, Americans generally viewed the new European immigrants as white, if sometimes not quite. The fact that Judah P. Benjamin was a Jew did not prevent him from serving as Secretary of State for the Confederacy, a regime devoted to whiteness if there ever was one.[147] Whether they realized it or not, for European immigrants white skin had its privileges. Most notably, unlike the Chinese they were granted free and unrestricted entry into the United States; until 1924 no laws barred them from America's shores. European immigrants also found it much easier to win American citizenship, since the nation's courts still looked to the 1790 law as grounding the right to naturalization in whiteness. Time and time again, they ruled that Europeans seeking naturalization were white and thus entitled to it.[148] Thanks in part to the battles waged by the Irish against Black labor, the new immigrants could find acceptance in industries and unions largely closed to African Americans and other peoples of color. Moreover, European immigrants experienced nothing comparable to the systematic campaign of racist terror directed against Blacks in the South. As a letter to the *Chicago Defender* in 1942 pointed out, "The immigrants had all the advantages of coming to the open American white freedom while Negroes had to continue in bondage."[149]

As was the case in the Jim Crow South, the ability to vote provided a key determinant of white privilege. Whatever the challenges they faced, Irish and German immigrants quickly became voters in both local and national elections during the nineteenth century, and American politicians competed for their favor. Until the late nineteenth century resident aliens could vote in many parts of the United States, and even when those privileges were overturned it often remained possible to naturalize the new immigrants quickly so as to grant them electoral rights. One result of immigrant voting was the rise of urban political machines like Tammany Hall in New York, which mobilized immigrants to vote by providing access to employment and social services in exchange. American nativists quickly seized upon "boss rule" as an example of the corruption enabled by immigrant voting, and by the end of the nineteenth century were actively campaigning to impose formal voter registration procedures and literacy tests to restrict the franchise of immigrants and new Americans.[150]

Such efforts had only a limited impact, however, especially as more and more immigrants (and their native-born children) became American citizens. In electoral rights, as in so many other spheres of American life, whiteness became a key litmus test of citizenship. The widespread enfranchisement of white immigrants combined with the disenfranchisement of virtually all African Americans by the end of the nineteenth century emphasized this crucial distinction. As Alex Keyssar has noted, "In New York and Massachusetts, an illiterate immigrant could gain the franchise by learning to read; for a Black man in Alabama, education was beside the point, whatever the law said."[151] To vote in America, to exercise political power as a member of a democratic polity, one essentially had to be white. As the twentieth century dawned in the United States, the nation remained committed to a racialized vision of citizen, one stressing the fact that the key to freedom in the land of the free was white skin.

Conclusion

At the dawn of the twentieth century three major features characterized the world as a whole. First, more than ever before it was a world as a whole, united not only by economic and commercial networks but to an unprecedented degree by administrative and political ones as well. The rise to global prominence of European empires, above all those of Britain and France, as well as the dynamism of the United States and other nations of European origin, had knit the world together like never before. Second, this global unity had a central racial component, as white European elites ruled over nonwhite masses and natives. Even when those nonwhites had citizenship, as in the United States, a variety of customs and practices prevented them from exercising it. Finally, the world was in many ways more free than it had ever been. Notably, abolitionist activists had pressured liberal governments into effectively eradicating the ancient scourge of chattel slavery. In addition, the most powerful nations had largely adopted liberal democracy as a central approach to governance, an approach that the challenges of the new century would only reinforce.

The combination of these features produced a world dominated by the principles of white freedom as never before. Significantly, as the global political order became more wedded to principles of liberalism and liberal democracy, racial distinctions within that order became more, not less, salient. The rise of white manhood suffrage along with Black disenfranchisement in the United States exemplified this theme, as did the coterminous expansion of liberal democracy and authoritarian colonial rule in Britain and France. As freedom became increasingly central to white masculine identity in Europe and America, as it increasingly belonged not to elites but to the masses of white people, it seemingly had to be denied to those who were not white.

In 1900 W.E.B. DuBois proclaimed that the color line would be the central issue for the new twentieth century. In the chapters that follow, this study will explore how ideas of whiteness and freedom intersected to shape the contemporary era.

PART 3

CHAPTER 5

Fighting for Whose Liberty?

FREEDOM AND RACE IN THE
ERA OF TOTAL WAR

On Sunday, March 26, 1944, several white men abducted the Reverend Isaac Simmons, a sixty-six-year-old African American minister, from his home in Liberty, Mississippi. Rumors had spread that there was oil under Simmons's land, and the men demanded to be shown the property line. Calling Simmons and his son Eldridge "smart niggers" for having had the foresight to hire a lawyer, they forced him and his son into their car and drove them a short distance. They beat the son mercilessly while ordering the minister to get out of the car, firing at him with a shotgun as he ran for his life. When Eldridge finally found his father after being released, the man was dead with numerous gunshot wounds in his back, teeth broken, and his tongue cut out. The murderers were never held accountable for the crime, and Eldridge Simmons was forced to flee the area.

A few months later, African Americans confronted another example of the gap between the ideal and the reality of freedom. By the summer of 1944, wartime labor shortages threatened to bring the mass transportation system in Philadelphia to a halt. Feeling they had no choice, the directors of the Philadelphia Transportation Company decided to do the unthinkable: hire eight Black men into positions traditionally reserved for whites. This caused an uproar; more than four thousand white transit workers promptly went on strike, and fights between

Blacks and whites broke out throughout the city. These events prompted one Black armory worker, Charles White, to storm into Independence Hall and throw a quartz paperweight at the Liberty Bell. "Liberty Bell? Liberty Bell?" White shouted. "That's a lot of bunk. There is no justice."[1]

In both situations Black men confronted the conflict between freedom and race. One spoke to a long tradition of racist attacks, the other to the angry response such racism provoked. One looked to the past, the other to the future. Out in the wider world beyond Mississippi and Philadelphia, American troops besieged German forces at Monte Cassino in Italy, while to the east Soviet armies steadily pushed the Wehrmacht back into Belorussia. Millions were fighting and dying for freedom, but for one Black southern minister and one Black munitions worker, at least, the word *liberty* meant only hypocrisy and ultimately murder.[2]

In 1900 the United States and much of Europe enjoyed not just unparalleled prosperity and world dominance but also a belief that such progress and security would continue unabated for the foreseeable future. It was not to be. Instead, the first half of the twentieth century was dominated by two wars of destruction on a scope and level unprecedented in human history. World Wars I and II knit the planet together as never before, shattering the confidence and global dominance of Western Europe while propelling America to the center of world affairs and power. Overthrowing old regimes and giving birth to new ones, destroying entire cities, and above all killing tens of millions of people, the two world wars brutally transformed the planet and set the tone for life in the contemporary era.[3]

Both freedom and race often loom large as themes in military conflicts generally, and they played a central role in the history of the two world wars. Virtually every war in the modern era has been portrayed as a struggle for liberty; the list of military history books with the word *freedom* in the title seems endless.[4] This is especially true of the wars of the twentieth century, not just the world wars but also the anticolonial wars and struggles for national liberation after 1945.[5] As freedom became nationalized in the modern era, a property of independent nation-states, so did the art of war as practiced by nations increasingly garb it-self in the language of liberty. World War I and World War II in particular took the form of struggles for freedom against despotism, above all but not only in the case of the war against fascism. Freedom became mixed up with defense of homeland and nation, and as such the one value for which millions were willing to, and did, give their lives.[6]

While representing freedom struggles, the wars of the twentieth century have also been race wars, conflicts in which racial difference loomed large. Such massive struggles of life and death tended to create an image of the enemy as the Other, a brute whose racialized character symbolized not opposed interests but absolute evil. If nation-states truly represented their peoples, then the peoples of enemy nation-states must be not only malevolent but fundamentally different, even nonhu-man. In the era of powerful nation-states, therefore, national wars be-came, in part at least, wars about race.[7] The fight against the racialized enemy thus contributed to the idea of national defense as a struggle for white freedom. At the same time the world wars took place in, and con-tributed powerfully to, a context of unprecedented ethnic and racial diversity. The mobilization for the war effort of peoples of color, such as European colonial subjects and American racial minorities, called into question but also reaffirmed ideas of liberty as racially coded.[8] Moreover, the rise of racialized totalitarianism, most notably in the case of Nazi Germany, at the same time reinforced and challenged the as-sociation between whiteness and freedom.

This chapter will consider the ways in which the great world wars of the early twentieth century shaped, contested, and in some ways reaf-firmed ideologies of white freedom. To what extent could racialized ideas of liberty survive in a world where literally tens of millions of people, of many different races and nations, fought for freedom, and if they did survive, what new forms would they take? In answering this seminal question, I will explore how the great wars changed ideas of both race and freedom, and the extent to which new ideas of white free-dom arose from these changes. White freedom certainly survived the era of the great wars and remained a key determinant of social and po-litical power and prestige on a global scale. At the same time, however, the world wars generated major challenges to that ideology that this study will consider in the next chapter, on the postwar world.

Freedom and Race in an Era of Total War

Writing in Brazilian exile during World War II, shortly before he took his own life, the Viennese Jewish writer Stefan Zweig described the world of his youth before World War I, trying to convey the unimaginable to younger generations who had only known war, suffering, and displacement:

> Forty years of peace had strengthened the economic organism of the nations, technical science had given wings to the rhythm of life, and scientific discoveries had made the spirit of that generation proud; there was sudden upsurge which could be felt in almost identical measure in all the countries of Europe. . . . The streets became broader and more showy, the public buildings more impressive, the shops more luxurious and tasteful. Everything manifested the increase and spread of wealth. . . . There was progress everywhere. Whoever ventured, won. . . . Never had Europe been stronger, richer, more beautiful, or more confident of an even better future.[9]

One may justifiably object that such a perspective says much more about the trauma of World War II and the Holocaust than would a realistic description of the prewar world. Nonetheless, during the Belle Époque between the turn of the twentieth century and the outbreak of World War I, European nations could claim an unprecedented level of affluence and power. Europe dominated the world economy, which had become integrated as never before: decisions by investors in the stock markets of London, Paris, and other European financial capitals decided the fates of anonymous millions around the globe. European empires controlled the majority of the world's land surface and population, their resources and markets making an important contribution to European prosperity. As Zweig noted, warfare had disappeared from the European continent since the Franco-Prussian war, having been successfully exiled to the colonial world.[10]

If one global challenge to European hegemony loomed large, it was certainly the increasing power and wealth of the United States of America. By 1914 America could boast not only of the world's most productive economy, the source of more than one-third of the planet's entire industrial output, but also of some of the highest standards of living. Its national population dwarfed that of any European nation. Moreover, while it had relatively few colonies, in the twenty years before World War I it had begun to create an overseas empire, expanding especially into the Caribbean and the Pacific. America had become a world power, and like those of Europe, its national leaders exuded optimism and confidence in the future.[11]

For many citizens of Europe and America at the dawn of the twentieth century, freedom seemed a key aspect of their exceptional well-being. Although most of Europe was still ruled by monarchies and empires, in more and more countries not just middle-class but also working-class citizens played an important role in national politics. By the turn of the century the leading European nations either had universal manhood suffrage or were close to it, whereas in the United States it had been in place since before the Civil War, at least for white men. America and the most advanced and powerful European countries also had well-organized political parties, including major liberal and socialist movements, that sought and sometimes achieved national political leadership. While certainly not omnipresent, liberal democracy seemed not only the wave of the future but a major characteristic of the world's most powerful nations.[12] For many, the faith in progress was a belief in a future when men (and for increasing numbers, women) would be ever more free.

Freedom was not just a matter of individual rights or even liberal democracy, however. As the discussion above suggests, it also became increasingly connected to the idea of citizenship, especially citizenship in a powerful nation-state. Such a connection did not happen automatically, of course, and even today parts of it remain quite controversial. To many political conservatives, for example, the nation-state, or at least aspects of it ("big government") represents the enemy of individual freedom, not its advocate.[13] As nation-states developed their own powerful political cultures in the modern era, however, the idea of free-dom often loomed large in them. Even as early as the seventeenth century, John Lilburne's idea of "the freeborn Englishman" served both to describe and rally the foot soldiers of Britain's Puritan revolution.[14] E. P. Thompson's classic *The Making of the English Working Class* fa-mously deals with both class consciousness and national identity, and the relationships between the two.[15] The essence of modern French political culture is often summed up in the famous phrase *"liberty, equal-ity, fraternity,"* with liberty taking pride of place.[16] Definitions of the term *Americanism* almost always allude to freedom as a key value shared by the peoples of the United States.[17] In particular, it has usually domi-nated popular immigration narratives, the idea that foreigners come to America not for material advantage but above all to achieve freedom.[18] To be free, therefore, was increasingly defined as enjoying citizenship in a free nation.

But what did it mean for a nation to be free? More specifically, was a free nation one that provided civil liberties and/or electoral democracy to its citizens, or was it a nation free from domination and control by other nations? Historians have written extensively about the rise of a new, more aggressive spirit of nationalism, expressed in particular by the British term *jingoism*, in Europe during the late nineteenth century. Part of the growth of mass society in general, the new nationalism had roots both in popular imperialism and imperial rivalries as well as in the development of broader social polities, engaging not just elites but also middle- and working-class Europeans.[19] One classic narrative of the origins of World War I argues that, beyond the diplomatic intricacies and problems of the alliance system, popular nationalism pushed the different European governments into the conflict; the tremendous dem-onstrations that greeted the outbreak of war in August 1914 seemed to prove this.[20]

Such nationalism, in the tradition of popular democracy in general, was less concerned about individual freedom and much more focused on national survival, the survival of the people as a whole. Regimes went to war to protect not personal liberty but the freedom of their nations from invasion and occupation by others. The fact that during wartime all democratic belligerent nations severely restricted civil liberties, and to a certain extent even electoral democracy in general, illustrates this point.[21] Moreover, the fact that most nations resorted to conscription, a kind of temporary indentured servitude of millions of young men, to mount their armies and pursue their military goals further illustrates this.[22] In order to be free, a nation first had to survive, and generally for most (but not all) of its citizens this was worth the sacrifice of individual liberties.

As this section (and this chapter in general) will also show, freedom in wartime was very much a racial issue, in several respects. As the previous chapter demonstrated, freedom easily coexisted with slavery and empire in nineteenth-century Europe and America, as long as it was defined in racial terms, as white freedom. The vaunted supremacy of the Western world at the dawn of the twentieth century was in fact white supremacy, symbolized above all by the massive empires that ruled much of Asia and Africa. The era of the great world wars would both challenge and in some ways bolster that supremacy. World War I brought an unprecedented mixture of peoples on a global scale, so that tens of thousands of Asians and Africans traveled to Europe, while at the same time masses of African Americans were moving from south to north during the Great Migration. For these peoples, wartime offered new opportunities but also frequently illustrated and reinforced their racially subordinate status. The realities of racial discrimination coexisted with the alluring prospect of an egalitarian multiracial freedom.

At the same time the wars fostered and intensified both official and popular cultural narratives that racialized the enemy, portraying him or her as a member of a different, hostile, and inferior race. Achieving national freedom and survival came to mean defeating other nations increasingly viewed as racially different. From the national propaganda campaigns of World War I to the racialized genocide of World War II, resistance to and destruction of the national enemy all too often took the form of race war. As a result, the era of the world wars powerfully reinforced ideas of white freedom, and on a global scale. At the same time, however, by promoting the ideal of national freedom it cleared the way for the massive challenges to white freedom in the postwar era of decolonization, which will be the subject of this book's next chapter. In the early twentieth century, race, war, and freedom were strange bedfellows, but exploring their interaction is crucial to understanding the history of the modern age.

The War to Begin All Wars

The conflict of races is now about to start openly within nations and between nations. . . . I am convinced that in the next century people will slaughter each other by the million because of a difference of a degree or two in the cephalic index.

—GEORGES VACHER DE LAPOUGE, 1899[23]

World War I was in important respects a race war.[24] It took place in the context of an international political climate of increased national rivalries and popular tensions, where public commentators frequently portrayed one country's gain as another's loss. Moreover, it broke out in a climate of racialized nationalism in general. Scholars and popular writers often characterized nations as races, so that people spoke of the Latin race, the Teutonic race, the Slavic race, and so on.[25] At the same time the war brought hundreds of thousands of people of color onto the European continent, the center of the conflict. Many Europeans had the experience of meeting someone with dark skin for the first time in their lives. In both respects, World War I increased official and popular consciousness of racial difference, making it a significant aspect of the belligerent nations' struggles for freedom.[26]

World War I was also a war for empire. The war that broke out in Europe in the late summer of 1914 had, as many historians have pointed out, its roots in imperial rivalries both overseas and on the European continent itself.[27] The two great imperial democracies, Britain and France, had established prosperous and free societies to an important extent on the basis of colonial mastery and exploitation, thus laying out a template for national success in the modern world. They saw the war as an opportunity to increase their colonial holdings and world dominance. At the beginning of 1916 they drew up the secret Sykes-Picot

Agreement, which divided the Ottoman Empire between them. From the perspective of London and Paris, the war would not only increase their own power but that of imperial democracy in general.[28]

By contrast, imperial Germany, which by the early twentieth century outmatched its European rivals in population and economy, suffered (in the minds of its leaders and many of its citizens) from a lack of colonial possessions. Like the United States, it was a global powerhouse that had gotten into the rush for empire relatively late in the game; the partition of Samoa between the two nations in 1899 highlighted both their imperial ambitions and their latecomer status. Unlike the United States, however, which ever since the Monroe Doctrine of 1823 had laid exclusive claim to the vast region of Latin America, Germany's Second Reich had relatively limited overseas colonial opportunities.[29]

As a consequence, it focused on the commercial and ultimately military domination of eastern Europe. German settlers and invaders had traditionally dominated the Slavic peoples of the East, and the renewal of such dominance would be crucial to the nation's greatness. What would ultimately become policies of racial conquest, exploitation, and extermination achieved their apogee in World War II, but they began in the early years of the twentieth century.

The fact that Germany cast its imperial vision in racial terms exemplified the entanglement of empire and race in World War I.[30] On October 4, 1914, a group of prominent German intellectuals published the "Manifesto of the 93" defending Germany's invasion of Belgium and conduct during the war in general. This spirited defense at times took on racialized imagery: "[I]n *the east* the earth is saturated with the blood of women and children *unmercifully butchered* by the wild Russian troops, and in the west *dumdum bullets* mutilate the breasts of our soldiers. Those who have allied themselves with *Russians* and *Serbians*, and present such a shameful scene to the world as that of inciting Mongolians and negroes against the white race, have no right whatever to call themselves upholders of civilization" (emphases in the original).[31] The manifesto used the language of race in defense of Germany's struggle to defend its freedom, a vision of freedom that was thus essentially white.

Germany was hardly the only nation to express the struggle for national defense and freedom in racialized terms during World War I. Allied, especially British, propaganda frequently demonized the enemy as the Hun, portrayed as a bloodthirsty inhuman beast. The British seized in particular upon the German invasion of Belgium at the start of the war as an example of bestial cruelty, not stopping at images of Belgian babies being spitted on German spike helmets.[32] One of the most striking racialized images of the enemy was published by the United States Army in 1918. Entitled "Destroy This Mad Brute!," it featured a growling gorilla wearing a German spiked helmet. In one hand he held a club labeled "Kultur," in the other arm he grasped a prostrate white woman.[33] Clearly grounded in American fears of miscegenation and rape, the poster portrayed the Germans as a racial enemy. During the war, therefore, both sides deployed racialized images of each other, illustrating the absolutist character of the conflict. In a climate of total war, the enemy had to be dehumanized and treated as the racial Other.[34]

The racialization of enemy European nations as savages occurred concurrently with the mobilization of nonwhite populations for the war effort and their introduction onto European soil. World War I was an imperial war, during which the leading nations mobilized their colonial resources in service to the national effort. As the masters of the largest empires, the British and French took the lead in imperial mobilization. One of the most important of these resources was labor: ever since the era of African slavery colonial workers had been a key source of wealth for European empires, but the labor shortages caused by the mobilization of millions of European men into the military made this a critical need.

Colonial subjects served the war effort both on the front lines as soldiers and in wartime factories and fields as laborers. More than 100,000 Indian soldiers fought for the British Army on the Western Front in 1914. Britain also mobilized soldiers from the Caribbean and brought in Blacks from South Africa to work in industry.[35] France, however, made the most extensive use of colonial manpower during the war. France had a long tradition of employing colonial soldiers, going back to Napoleon's invasion of Egypt in 1798, and during the nineteenth century the

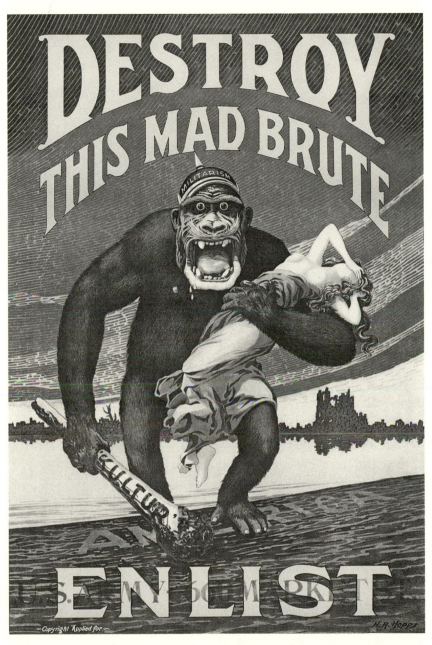

FIGURE 23. Harry R. Hopps, "Destroy this Mad Brute" (1917). American World War I poster. Library of Congress Prints and Photographs Division. Digital ID ds.03216.

FIGURE 24. Indian troops at a crossroads on the Fricourt-Mametz Road, Somme, France (1916). John Warwick Brooke/Imperial War Museums (IWM Q 3983.jpg).

Armée d'Afrique had played a major role in the conquest and rule of North Africa. In his 1910 book *La Force Noire*, General Charles Mangin had argued strenuously for the use of Black African soldiers as a way to counter the Germany's greater population.[36]

World War I represented, however, the first time France deployed colonial soldiers on French soil. Faced with invasion and national disaster, the French government did not hesitate to recruit soldiers from all over the empire to take part in the defense of the nation. During the course of the war it brought some 500,000 colonial subjects, from North Africa, Black Africa, Indochina, and the Caribbean, to fight the Germans. They fought extensively on the Western Front, notably in the bloody battle of the Chemin des Dames in 1917, rendering important service to the nation's war effort. The smiling African soldiers featured in the famous "Y'a Bon!" posters for Banania (a popular chocolate drink) illustrated the new wartime presence of nonwhites in the French metropole.[37]

Colonial subjects came to France to work as well as fight. Confronted with a massive labor shortage, France began actively recruiting foreigners, bringing in more than 200,000 from European Italy and Spain, for example. When these proved insufficient, the government turned to colonial labor. The French imported some 300,000 nonwhite workers, not only colonial subjects but also Chinese nationals, to work in wartime industry and agriculture. The mobilization of young French men had left the national economy bereft of labor at a time when industrial production was more important than ever, so that national authorities rushed to bring in "exotic labor."[38]

Colonial soldiers and workers were an important source of manpower for the Allied war effort during World War I, but many looked askance at the prospect of bringing large numbers of nonwhite men to the European continent. British authorities removed most colonial soldiers from the Western Front by 1915, sending them to fight in the Middle East instead.[39] The prospect of arming colonial subjects and telling them to shoot white people gave some British authorities pause. France, ten percent of which was occupied by the Germans, proved more accepting of colonial soldiers. Consequently, colonial regiments often received warm welcomes in French villages and towns.[40]

Colonial workers were another matter. As the conflict dragged on and antiwar sentiment mounted in France many French workers came to resent them, not only for taking "their" jobs but also for freeing them up to be slaughtered at the front. Then there was the issue of relations with French women. In order to deal with the shortage of wartime labor the French government and leading industries made extensive use of female workers, who often ended up working side by side with foreign and colonial workers. French authorities were greatly concerned by the prospect of interracial *liaisons*, in particular because they considered them a threat to the sexual and racial political order in the colonies to which the workers would return after the war. They tried to prevent them by keeping colonial workers in separate barracks and closely monitoring their correspondence for any signs of interracial intimacies. For many French male workers the prospect of nonwhite men taking both their jobs and their women was an outrage, so that by the spring of 1917 a series of race riots against colonial workers erupted in France. In this case, and in many others during the war, questions of race, class, and gender intersected.[41]

Nonwhite soldiers and workers also came to the World War I battlefields of France from the United States. Roughly 200,000 African American soldiers saw military service on the French Front during the war, representing the first time in history a large number of Black Americans had traveled overseas. Most worked as longshoremen in French ports, unloading the endless amounts of military supplies and war materiel shipped from American factories across the Atlantic. About twenty percent, however, served as soldiers, taking part in a number of battles during 1918. The American Army was more than a little suspicious of the idea of Blacks as soldiers and while they were in France assigned them over to French army units rather than integrating them into the US military. This proved fortunate for the Black soldiers, who were often amazed to see that white officials could treat them with kindness, and helped to create the myth of France as a color-blind nation. During the war, therefore, France became the place where the fates of colonial subjects from European empires and men of color from the United States briefly intertwined.[42]

What motivated colonial and African American men to fight and work for freedom in a foreign land? Many, of course, had no choice. British and French military authorities generally conscripted native soldiers, just as they did their own citizens. French colonial laborers were volunteers in theory, but many in effect came to France under duress; in Indochina, for example, village mandarins would frequently choose young men for service and "volunteer" them. Their service to their nations thus often reflected not their embrace of white freedom but their exclusion from it and raised the question of why they would accept it and fight for countries that wouldn't fight for them. A German propaganda leaflet dropped over African American lines in 1918 made this point in stark terms:

Hello, boys, what are you doing over here? Fighting the Germans? Why? Have they ever done you any harm? Of course some white folks and the lying English-American papers told you that the Germans ought to be wiped out for the sake of humanity and Democracy. What is Democracy? Personal freedom; all citizens enjoying the same rights socially and before the law. Do you enjoy the same rights as the white people do in America, the land of freedom and Democracy, or are you not rather treated over there as second class citizens?[43]

The Germans had a case, since most Blacks in the US military worked in conditions little different from the chain gang. Yet most African Americans rejected such arguments, and not just because they came from the enemy. The great majority of Blacks who served were drafted, however, the African American community overwhelmingly embraced the war effort; in several southern states more Blacks signed up for the army than whites. In memoirs of their wartime experiences many French African veterans spoke warmly of their times in France and of their love for the *patrie*.[44] Perhaps the most striking example of this kind of colonial loyalty during World War I was the extensive Irish support for the British war effort. More than 200,000 Irishmen fought in the war, with the widespread support of both Protestant and Catholic society. Only a small minority of radical nationalists opposed Irish participation, going on to mount the Easter Rebellion against British rule in 1916.[45]

For colonial and racial minority groups, the war represented an opportunity to increase their own integration and acceptance into their national communities. By fighting for the national cause, they would prove to their fellow citizens and colonial masters their worth as equal citizens. The struggle for freedom overseas would bring freedom at home. In July 1918 W.E.B. DuBois published an editorial entitled "Close Ranks." Calling the war "a crisis of the world," he argued that:

We of the colored race have no ordinary interest in the outcome. That which the German power represents today spells death to the aspirations of Negroes and all darker races for equality, freedom and democracy. Let us not hesitate. Let us, while this war lasts, forget our special grievances and close our ranks shoulder to shoulder without our own white fellow citizens and the allied nations that are fighting for democracy. We make no ordinary sacrifice, but we make it gladly and willingly without eyes lifted to the hills.[46]

Millions of people around the world hoped that the great war would bring a future world of both national freedom and racial equality. The settlements that structured the transition from war to peace in 1919 would show the futility of that hope.

White Freedom and the Peace of Paris

World War I had begun as a classic war between Europe's major powers, but the spring of 1917 dramatically changed the significance of the conflict. Two great events, the overthrow of the czarist regime in Russia and America's decision to enter the war, fundamentally transformed the nature of the conflict into a struggle for liberty against despotism on a global scale. The triumph of the Bolshevik Revolution at the end of the year and the dramatic calls for world revolution issuing from the new Soviet Union reaffirmed the transformational character of the war.[47] With the collapse of Germany and the end of the war in November 1918 the world seemed set for a new era of peace and freedom unparalleled in the modern era. It soon became clear, however, that the racialized liberty of the nineteenth century would not only endure but dominate the new era.

More than any other individual, American president Woodrow Wilson would symbolize the search for a postwar settlement emphasizing freedom and democracy. He would also represent the importance of racist ideas of liberty. Born in Virginia to a slave-owning family that had supported the Confederacy, Woodrow Wilson was the first southerner elected president since the Civil War.[48] As a scholar he supported the Dunning School's "Lost Cause" narrative of the Civil War, emphasizing the nobility of the Southern struggle for independence, and at times wrote approvingly of the Ku Klux Klan.[49] More concretely, as president he implemented widespread racial segregation of the federal administration, reinforcing white supremacy and privilege at the heart of national life.[50]

This was the man who would emerge as the leader of the free world in 1918–19. At the same time that he supported segregation, Woodrow Wilson embraced progressivism. As president, he enacted new regulations for worker safety and child labor and established the Department

FIGURE 25. Council of Four at the WWI Paris peace conference, May 27, 1919. (L—R) Prime Minister David Lloyd George (Great Britain); Premier Vittorio Orlando, Italy; Premier Georges Clemenceau, France; President Woodrow Wilson, USA. Edward N. Jackson (US Army Signal Corps).

of Labor. Both progressive and racist ideas informed his approach to making peace at the end of World War I.[51] As leader of the most power-ful victorious nation in 1918, he championed the idea of peace without annexations or indemnities, rejecting the idea that the Central Powers must be punished and instead viewing the peace treaty as a way to create a new, more harmonious world. In a speech to Congress on January 8, 1918, President Wilson outlined what became known as the Fourteen Points, a plan for the peace treaty and the postwar settlement that em-phasized democracy, self-determination, and the rights of national mi-norities, as well as freedom of the seas and of trade. This vision of a peace that would bury the hatreds of a long and bitter war made Wilson tremendously popular, so that when he traveled to Paris in Decem-ber 1918 to take part in the peace talks, massive crowds hailed him as a conquering hero.[52]

The results of the Paris peace talks, embodied in the peace treaty signed at Versailles on June 28, 1919, reaffirmed Wilson's racist tendencies and the general idea that freedom should be reserved for whites. Perhaps the most significant result of the peace treaty was the creation of new nations in Europe out of the ruins of the Austro-Hungarian, Russian, and Ottoman empires. To a significant extent the treaty simply recognized the realities on the ground created by insurgent national groups as those empires collapsed, but in doing so it recognized and gave a stamp of approval to new international realities. Moreover, these new nations took the form of democratic republics; whereas there had been only three republics on the European continent in 1914, there were thirteen by the end of 1918.[53] Revolution had overthrown the Russian and German empires and replaced them with nation-states, and across central and eastern Europe national minorities clamored for democratic representation, leading to the creation of composite nations such as Czechoslovakia and Yugoslavia. Although it would not last, in 1919 Europe presented an image of national liberty and self-determination.

The perspective from the colonial world was very different. The Fourteen Points had stated that the future of the colonies should be decided both by the imperial powers and by the residents of the colonies themselves. During the first half of 1919 delegations from different parts of the colonial world traveled to Paris to plead for national self-determination. In essence these pleas fell upon deaf ears. Unlike the situation in Europe, where the collapse of empires had led to the creation of free nations, the British and French empires had not only survived but won the war, and their leaders were in no mood to surrender power over any of their territories.[54]

There remained the question of what should happen to the colonies of the defeated Central Powers in Africa, the Middle East, and the Pacific. Whereas European former colonies such as Poland and the Czech lands became free and independent nations, the victorious powers decided that those outside Europe were "not ready" for self-government. Instead they developed the mandate system: created as a part of the new

League of Nations established to maintain peace, the mandates were former German and Ottoman colonies placed under British and French rule, with the idea that they would be prepared for eventual independence. The system represented an unsavory compromise between Wilsonian ideals of self-determination and the determination of the other allies to profit from their victory. As skeptics noted, these were simply colonies under a new name, and the mandate system in the Middle East in particular simply fulfilled the goals of the Sykes-Picot Agreement.[55]

More broadly, however, the contrast between successful national self-determination in Europe and the perpetuation of colonialism in the imperial world bolsters an interpretation of the Paris peace of 1919 as a key moment in the history of white freedom. In the global outline for the new twentieth century that the peace treaty intended to provide, white nations could be free, but nonwhite colonial territories would remain dependent on European empires, at least for the foreseeable future. The lofty idealism that Wilson brought to the negotiations, and that informed much of the peace treaty, was thus firmly tied to whiteness and white privilege. The decision of the Allies to reject Japan's proposal to include a statement affirming racial equality in the constitution of the League of Nations illustrates this basic fact, as does its refusal to pay serious attention to the pleas of the delegates to the Pan-African Congress that met in Paris in February 1919.[56]

Historians and other commentators have often portrayed the 1919 peace treaty as a compromise between the idealism and belief in self-determination of Woodrow Wilson and the cynicism and realpolitik of European leaders such as Georges Clemenceau and David Lloyd George. When it came to issues of race and whiteness, however, the eventual shape of the treaty, and of the world it created in the early twentieth century, perfectly replicated Wilson's own commitments to both progressive ideals and white privilege. If only briefly, freedom triumphed at the end of World War I, but that freedom was white.

Making a World Safe for Whiteness

We *return*. We *return from fighting*. We return *fighting*. Make way for Democracy!

—w.e.b. dubois, *the crisis*, may 1919

Workers of the world, unite and fight for a white South Africa.

—south africa industrial federation, 1922

The years immediately after the Armistice, what the Italians call the *biennio rosso*, the "red two years," were notable for extreme levels of political conflict and mobilization. Throughout much of the world revolution loomed on the horizon, or at least seemed to. The transition from world war to global peace brought about a range of revolutionary political activism striking not only in its intensity but equally in its scope and breadth. From the Seattle general strike in February to the Amritsar, India, massacre in April, popular radicalism seemed poised to overthrow the established order. At the heart of the turbulence lay the defeated empires of Europe and Euro-Asia. The Russian revolutions of 1917 had made the new Soviet Union the world's revolutionary center, not only fighting its own civil war against conservative forces but also loudly calling for and trying to mobilize world revolution. In the chaos following the collapse of the German, Austro-Hungarian, and Ottoman empires at the end of 1918, different national and political constituencies struggled to create new regimes based on popular sovereignty. At the same time the dominant Allied powers, both during and after the Paris peace talks, sought to contain the forces pushing for a new world in the established structures of imperial power. During 1919 and 1920 in particular, the relationship between popular freedom and imperial hegemony seemed to hang in the balance.[57]

One particularly important aspect of new ideas of freedom in the postwar era was the new acceptance of women's suffrage. Women had played an active role in the war industries and public service of most belligerent nations, and in many they campaigned successfully for female suffrage after the war. From 1917 onward a large number of countries, including not only the United States and Britain but Russia, Germany, Hungary, Poland, Sweden, Canada, the Netherlands, and New Zealand, all voted to grant women the vote in one form or another. Among Western nations France was the main holdout, not finally enfranchising women until after World War II. While granting women the vote certainly did not bring about full gender equality, it effectively doubled the number of active citizens in many nations and gave the idea of freedom a much more universal quality than before the war.[58]

At the same time, women's suffrage tended to reinforce white freedom. The new female suffrage movement applied almost entirely to white women in Western countries and had no impact on the situation of colonized women. African American women, like African American men, remained essentially disenfranchised after World War I. It is also important to note that in several countries, such as Britain, female enfranchisement was at least limited to women of property, only later being extended to working-class women. The great wave of women's suffrage after World War I thus both expanded popular ideas of freedom and equally demonstrated the racial limits of that ideal.[59]

As we have seen above, the new emphasis on national freedom reflected in the Treaty of Versailles had a significant racial component, promoting democratic nationalism in Europe while firmly shunting it aside in Africa and Asia. This contradiction did not pass unnoticed by many colonial subjects. As a result, 1919 in particular saw an eruption of anticolonial revolts. In Korea, students inspired by President Wilson's Fourteen Points speech began organizing to demand the right of self-determination and independence from Japanese colonial rule. On March 1, millions of Koreans demonstrated throughout the country against imperial control, only to be met with brutal repression by Japanese authorities, resulting in the deaths of thousands.[60] Similar violence erupted in India a month later. After a British crackdown on civil liberties triggered a massive protest movement throughout the country, Indians gathered in the Punjabi town of Amritsar to defy colonial repression. Colonial troops led by General Reginald Dyer responded by closing off the gathering and raking the crowd with machine gun fire, killing at least several hundred individuals.[61]

Events in Egypt and Ireland formed a partial exception to the rule of white freedom after World War I. In Egypt, popular expectations that Egyptian representatives would be able to attend the Paris peace conference provoked a conflict with the ruling British authorities. The movement soon began demanding the end of the British protectorate over Egypt and the Sudan. Led by the Wafd party (*Wafd* means "delegation" in Arabic), a series of massive demonstrations broke out in March, resulting in the deaths of hundreds of protestors at the hands of colonial troops. The movement continued into the summer, leading the British to appoint a commission, which eventually recommended the end of colonial rule. In 1922 Egypt achieved semi-independence, limited by Britain's continuing right to maintain a military presence in the country and control of the Suez Canal.[62]

In Ireland, the centuries-old struggle against British colonial rule came to a head in the years after World War I. British repression of the Easter Rising in 1916 had only increased Irish popular support for self-rule. In December 1918 the nationalist party, Sinn Féin, won an overwhelming victory during a national election, and the following month proclaimed independence for the island. Shortly thereafter the newly formed Irish Republican Army began a campaign of guerrilla warfare against British soldiers and institutions in the island. Britain responded in force, sending in the troops known as the Black and Tans, and for the next two years Ireland descended into violence and chaos. By 1921 the British concluded they could not win the war, and after extensive negotiations in 1922 the Irish Free State formally gained its independence.[63]

Again, the examples of Egypt and Ireland complicate and also ultimately reinforce the importance of whiteness to national freedom in the aftermath of World War I. Unlike most of the imperial world, both were colonies that gained independence. For the Egyptians, however, this independence came with important limits, as would become clear during World War II, when the British essentially assumed control of the country. Irish independence was much more real, even though Ulster remained a part of the United Kingdom. When Ireland achieved independence it did so as a white European nation, similar to Poland and the other new nations of Eastern Europe. As the previous chapter dem-

onstrated, by the late nineteenth century Irish immigrants in both Britain and the US had largely achieved white status. The independence of
the Irish nation in 1922 thus represented the culmination of that achievement in the home island itself. White Ireland could finally leave its colonial past behind, whereas brown Egypt could not.

The renewed emphasis on whiteness after World War I also took
place within several Western nations. As we have seen, the war itself had
brought large numbers of men of color to Europe, especially France, and
in the United States had fueled the first Great Migration of African
Americans to the North.[64] The end of the war brought a powerful rejection of this wartime multiculturalism and a reassertion of whiteness, at
times in conjunction with radical and revolutionary labor movements.
The ultimate example of this came in 1922, when striking South African
miners adopted the slogan *Workers of the world unite and fight for a white
South Africa*, but this was not an isolated incident.[65] The year 1919 in
particular saw intense labor and revolutionary struggles as well as widespread race riots. From January to August of that year, for example, a
series of riots erupted in Britain's port cities, as white sailors and longshoremen attacked men from the Caribbean, Africa, and South Asia and
the Middle East. In a climate of postwar economic downturn, white
port workers and their unions attacked nonwhites for "taking" their
jobs, often successfully expelling them from increasingly white work-
places on the docks of Liverpool, Bristol, London, and other cities. This
took place in a climate of radical working-class politics in general, so that
in Glasgow Scottish workers seemed to threaten revolution.[66]

The situation was more extreme in France. During the war France
had brought in more than 300,000 workers from its colonies and China
to labor in its factories and fields. With the end of the war, tensions increased between industry, the government, and the unions over the role
of labor in the postwar period. Dazzled by the specter of the Russian
Revolution, many French workers moved sharply to the left, leading to
the creation of the French Communist Party at the end of 1920.[67] At the
same time, however, France needed labor more than ever. Roughly 1.6
million Frenchmen had died in the war, and many more had returned
wounded and unable to work. Moreover, the nation had one of the

lowest birth rates in Europe and would soon achieve negative population growth in the interwar years, while at the same time it needed more workers to rebuild the country and repair the destruction caused by the war.[68]

In this revolutionary climate, however, the one thing all the major parties could agree on was the need to get rid of colonial workers. By the end of 1919 French authorities had rounded up and repatriated 90 percent of the "exotic" workers in the country. At the same time, it made new arrangements to bring foreign workers from Southern and Eastern Europe, whose numbers would swell to the millions in the 1920s. In making the argument for European over colonial labor, French authorities made clear their desire to reverse the multiracial immigration that had begun during the war, saying "[It is necessary] To call upon labor of European origin, in preference to colonial or exotic labor, because of the social and ethnic difficulties which could arise from the presence upon French soil of ethnographic elements too clearly distinct from the rest of the population."[69] The choice of European over "exotic" workers was a clear statement of the importance of whiteness to the character of the nation, and it paralleled the contrast between the extension of liberal democracy in postwar Europe and the continuation of imperial rule in postwar Asia and Africa.[70]

Britain and France had emerged victorious from a war that, especially toward its end, emphasized the struggle for national freedom against German barbarism. At the same time, they remained the largest colonial powers in the world. This contradiction between freedom at home and racialized empire overseas remained more salient than ever in the years after the Armistice. The war itself had undermined that contradiction to a certain extent by bringing colonial subjects to Europe as both soldiers and workers, and it was vital to the racial politics of empire to reverse that phenomenon, to keep metropole and colony separate. European nations could remain free only if the colonial lack of liberty was not allowed to intrude into their political spaces, and the repression and exclusion of colonial labor (who, unlike colonial soldiers, had a reason to stay in Europe once the fighting stopped) played an important role in that process. In order to survive in Europe at the end of the war, freedom had to be white freedom.

A similar process unfolded in the United States at the end of the war. As noted above, the war had brought an unprecedented mobilization of African Americans, in two respects. Not only did nearly 400,000 Black Americans serve in the armed forces, but roughly half a million Black southerners joined the Great Migration to the North between 1914 and 1920. In both cases, these movements out of the South (where ninety percent of the Black population lived at the time) brought new experiences of freedom and new levels of confidence. As the above quotation from W.E.B. DuBois in the magazine *The Crisis*[71] makes clear, Blacks sent overseas to fight for freedom and democracy wanted to enjoy them at home as well.

White American society responded to this new sense of Black empowerment harshly, emphasizing the importance of maintaining and reaffirming the color bar in America. Many whites were particularly outraged by reports of egalitarian treatment of Blacks by the French and were determined to remind Blacks who had become "spoiled" by such magnanimity of their subordinate position in the United States. Senator James K. Vardaman of Mississippi warned against the danger that "French women-ruined negro soldiers" posed to white women and girls.[72] Some also saw newly returned and more assertive Black veterans as a political threat, in the revolutionary context of 1919. Woodrow Wilson himself at one point declared "the American Negro returning from abroad would be our greatest medium in conveying Bolshevism to America."[73] The result was an unprecedented wave of lynchings of Black men. More African American men, nearly one hundred, were lynched in 1919 than in any other year of American history, and many of them were ex-soldiers in military uniform.[74]

The use of violence to restore the prewar racial order targeted not just Black individuals but entire communities. As we have seen, during the war hundreds of thousands of southern Blacks had moved north in search of both jobs and relief from racism, and at times took jobs formerly held by whites. This had already led to riots against Black communities in the summer of 1917, in East St. Louis, Illinois, and in Houston, Texas. The end of the war brought both an economic downturn and the return of millions of white veterans seeking jobs and finding Blacks employed where they had not worked before. The fact that Black workers had sometimes been used to break strikes by whites in 1917 further increased racial tensions in American cities.[75]

This was the context that produced what Blacks called the Red Summer, a name that reflected the toxic mixture of political fears and racial violence. During the summer and fall of 1919, rioting between Blacks and whites broke out across the country, usually triggered by white invasions of Black communities.[76] Hundreds of people died, mostly Blacks, in what became the worst single wave of race riots in American history. Although the great riots in northern cities like Chicago and Washington, DC, attracted the most attention, probably the majority occurred in the South, including in New Orleans and Tuscaloosa, Alabama. The worst single example took place in Elaine, Arkansas, and it exemplified the volatile combination of political and racial fears. In the majority-Black region whites responded with deadly violence to Black attempts to organize a sharecroppers' union. The resulting conflict took the lives of five whites and at least one hundred African Americans, probably many more.[77] Moreover, the violence continued after 1919. In May and June of 1921 white rioters attacked the prosperous Black community known as "the Black Wall Street" of Tulsa, Oklahoma, literally bombing it from the air and killing at least thirty-nine people. The early 1920s also saw a rebirth of the Ku Klux Klan, this time not just in the South but the North as well.[78]

African Americans were not the only ones affected by the racial backlash in the United States after World War I. Those concerned with preserving whiteness in America also targeted immigrants, especially those from southern and eastern Europe and from Asia. As we saw in the previous chapter, American racism had targeted a variety of different peoples, in different ways. Italian immigrants might have privileges that African Americans and Chinese did not, but they were still not considered equal to native Americans, nor fully white. In 1916 Madison Grant published *The Passing of the Great Race*, which argued that new immigrants would destroy American civilization.[79] Together, racial animosities and fears of revolution proved a potent combination. The Palmer Raids of 1919 (see below) targeted immigrants in particular as dangerous radicals, deporting hundreds. In 1920 police in Massachusetts arrested two Italian immigrants, Nicola Sacco and Bartolomeo Vanzetti, on suspicion of taking part in a bank robbery, but their real crime for many was being anarchists and Italian immigrants. As Vanzetti wrote from prison, "I am suffering because I am a radical and indeed I am a radical; I have suffered because I was an Italian, and indeed I am an Italian."[80]

The increasing hostility to immigrants culminated in the passage of new restrictions on immigration in 1924. During the 1920s American legislators passed laws to redefine the racial character of citizenship. For example, in 1924 Congress granted US citizenship to all Native Americans, breaking a pattern that had existed since the American Revolution. In the same year, however, it passed the Johnson-Reed Act, which sharply limited immigration from southern and eastern Europe, including Jewish immigration. The Act also extended the 1882 Chinese Exclusion Act to virtually all Asians, except Filipinos, targeting in particular Japanese immigrants, and it established a complex series of national quotas that heavily favored immigrants from Northern Europe and cut immigration from the rest of Europe and Asia to a trickle over the next few decades.[81]

In some respects the new legislation did not necessarily privilege whiteness: not only did Native Americans gain citizenship but Black Africans were exempted from the restrictions, for example, and many employers were willing to forgo European immigrants because they had started using African American labor. The law also continued to permit essentially unrestricted immigration from Latin America. But by favoring northern over southern and eastern Europeans it reinforced the image of the latter as racially suspect, even nonwhite. In particular, racial concerns together with fears of radicalism combined to reverse the acceptance of large numbers of European immigrants. Whiteness gained a new, political character as postwar immigrant legislation reflected the nexus of race and class.

In the years immediately after the Armistice concerns about both race and class spread throughout Europe and America. The prospect of red revolution fanning out from Moscow to engulf the world terrified not just capitalist elites but broad sectors of society throughout the

West.[82] The idea of revolution frequently took on racial implications, however, not just in racialized images of the Bolsheviks as the new barbarians from the east, but more generally in fears that unrest among native populations in the colonial world and racial minorities and immigrants in the United States represented both a political and a racial threat to the established order.[83] The fact that the Bolsheviks spoke out forcefully against both racism and European colonialism, such as during the Congress of the Peoples of the East held in Baku, Azerbaijan, in 1920, only underscored this connection.[84] Keeping the world safe for white democracy meant defeating red revolution, both in the colonies and in Europe and America. Tensions of race and class thus gave a new political dimension to white freedom in the early twentieth century.

"Freedom for the Wolves Means Death for the Sheep": Fascism and White Freedom

What we must fight for is to safeguard the existence and reproduction of our race and our people, the sustenance of our children and the purity of our blood, the freedom and independence of our fatherland.

—ADOLF HITLER, *MEIN KAMPF*[85]

Arbeit Macht Frei [Labor Makes One Free]

—SIGN AT THE ENTRANCE TO AUSCHWITZ

As we have seen, 1919 was a year of both revolution and counterrevolution. The Bolshevik seizure of power in 1917 had sparked a civil war with a range of anticommunist forces ranging from reactionary to liberal and moderate socialist, and the resulting conflict did not end until 1922. Radical attempts to seize power elsewhere, such as in Germany and Hungary, prompted a frequently reactionary response: in Berlin Spartacus was crushed by the Freikorps, for example. Similarly, colonial uprisings in Egypt, Korea, and India brought an often brutal response from imperial powers. Sometimes the assertion of establishment power occurred in response not to actual revolution or social upheaval but to the threat of it. In the United States, in response to a major strike in the steel industry and to the threat of revolution overseas, the federal government unleashed a wave of repression against radical organizations. Under the direction of US Attorney General A. Mitchell Palmer, from November 1919 to January 1920 federal authorities raided the offices of radical organizations, arrested more than five thousand people, and deported hundreds of immigrants (including noted anarchist leader Emma Goldman).[86]

Such acts of repression for the most part sought to defend the liberal democratic order, even if (as in the colonies) those principles were not consistently exercised. But 1919 also saw the birth of another, much more radical, form of counterrevolution. On March 23, 1919, a small group of Italian war veterans and political activists came together in Milan to create a new political movement. Led by veteran, former Socialist, and nationalist agitator Benito Mussolini, the group founded the Fasci Italiani di Combattimento, which began a terrorist campaign against the Italian Left.[87] Two years later it would formally reconstitute itself as the Italian Fascist Party. Earlier the same year, on January 5, a German locksmith and nationalist activist named Anton Drexler led a small group of activists in creating the new German Workers Party, dedicated to German populist nationalism, racial anti-Semitism, and anti-Communism. The small new party attracted the attention of a war veteran named Adolf Hitler, who joined and in February 1920 helped give it a new name, the National Socialist German Workers Party. Mussolini and his Fascists would take over the Italian government in 1922, creating the world's first fascist state. It would take the Nazis another decade to destroy the wobbly Weimar republic, but by the beginning of 1933 Hitler and his followers established a powerful fascist regime in the heart of Europe.[88]

On the face of it, discussing ideals of freedom in the history of fascism would seem not only ridiculous but obscene. Fascist Italy and Nazi Germany overthrew democratic regimes and the rule of law, assassinated their political opponents and destroyed civil liberties, and ultimately murdered millions of innocent people. Even the prosperity the Nazis brought to Germany came at the expense of political repression and self-censorship, so that individual Germans quickly learned the limits of what they could safely say and do. The Nazis in particular turned much of Europe into a charnel house of unimaginable human suffering, whose ultimate symbol was the concentration camp. The only freedom they brought to millions was the freedom that comes with death.[89]

And yet, as the quotation above from *Mein Kampf* suggests, ideas of freedom did play a significant role in the ideology of fascism. As I noted earlier in this chapter, by World War I, Western ideas of freedom had come to emphasize national self-determination and independence, not so much opposed to individual liberty as the necessary precondition for it. Interwar fascism, usually viewed as a rejection of Western traditions of freedom and democracy, in some ways represented the culmination of such an approach, the fulfillment of individual freedom through membership in a national community. As Benito Mussolini argued in 1932:

> Anti-individualistic, the Fascist conception of life stresses the importance of the State and accepts the individual only in so far as his interests coincide with those of the State, which stands for the conscience and the universal, will of man as a historic entity. It is opposed to classical liberalism which arose as a reaction to absolutism and exhausted its historical function when the State became the expression of the conscience and will of the people. Liberalism denied the State in the name of the individual; Fascism reasserts the rights of the State as expressing the real essence of the individual. *And if liberty is to be the attribute of living men and not of abstract dummies invented by individualistic liberalism, then Fascism stands for liberty, and for the only liberty worth having, the liberty of the State and of the individual within the State.* The Fascist conception of the State is all embracing; outside of it no human or spiritual values can exist, much less have value. Thus understood, Fascism, is totalitarian, and the Fascist State—a synthesis and a unit inclusive of all values—interprets, develops, and potentates the whole life of a people [emphasis added].[90]

Freedom was thus the freedom of a nation, and only through national freedom could the individual citizen find his or her own liberation. Unlike liberal democracy, fascism viewed the nation-state as a goal rather than a means to an end, but to an important extent both considered freedom inseparable from citizenship and membership in the national community.[91]

The question therefore became, how did one define the nation, and it is through this perspective on national freedom and survival that race became so important. Race, as some scholars have argued, is not necessarily key to fascist ideology in general. Fascist Italy, for example, had no significant racial legislation until 1938, nearly a generation after the establishment of the fascist state.[92] However, as Aaron Gillette has shown, not only were racial scientific theories widespread in Italy at the beginnings of the twentieth century but they had an important influence on Mussolini and other Italian fascists.[93] Ideas of "the Italian race," while often vague and contradictory, nonetheless permeated fascist discourse: as Mussolini informed an audience in 1927, "We need to be seriously vigilant in regard to the destiny of the race; we need to take care of the race."[94]

To a far greater extent than in Italian fascism, racial definitions of the nation, and its enemies, lay at the heart of German national socialism. Historians have examined roots of Nazi racism in the historical genealogy of racism in modern Europe, starting with the Enlightenment and proceeding through the rise of racial anti-Semitism in the late nineteenth century to the rise of the Nazi racial state.[95] Racism, and a racialized vision of the German nation, formed the core of Nazi ideology from the beginnings of the movement. In Mein Kampf Hitler identified the German people as a racial group, the "Aryan" race, arguing that it not only had the right to dominate inferior races but that such domination was the motor of human progress. He elaborated a typology of human races, ranging from the superior Aryans down to Latins, Slavs, and ultimately nonwhites, arguing, "If we were to divide mankind into three groups, the founders of culture, the bearers of culture, the destroyers of culture, only the Aryan could be considered as the representative of the first group."[96] Aryan Germany was thus both a nation and a race, and its freedom was white freedom, a function of its racial supremacy and dominance.

Although Nazi racism constituted a worldview in which many different peoples found their place in a racialized hierarchy of mankind, racialized anti-Semitism and hatred of the Jews lay at its heart. Nazi anti-Semitism was a rather bizarre compendium of theories and prejudices, but above all it emphasized race over religion: the Jews were a race, not a spiritual or religious community.[97] Some leading themes drew from traditional anti-Semitism, such as the Jew as capitalist exploiter of others, which went back to medieval stereotypes of Jews as usurers. Others were more modern, such as the idea of the Jew as dangerous radical and Bolshevik, and an important part of the work of Nazi anti-Semitism lay in its amalgamation of such different and often contradictory stereotypes. Ultimately, many of the aspects of modern life attacked by the Nazis, such as capitalism, socialism, liberal democracy, and modernist culture, became personified in the figure of the Jew.[98]

Two aspects of Nazi anti-Semitism in particular are important to the argument of this book. First, the Nazis believed that not only were the Jews a race but an alien race, one that was not European and did not belong in Europe. As the Nazi Party's 25-Point Program of 1920 put it, "Only a member of the race can be a citizen. A member of the race can only be one who is of German blood, without consideration of creed. Consequently, no Jew can be a member of the race."[99] The Jews came from Asia, from the Levant, and therefore could not be considered Aryan, European, or ultimately white. They were therefore racially inferior, lacking true culture or creativity. To an important extent Nazi anti-Semitism existed as part of a worldview based on white supremacy.[100]

But another important difference gave Nazi anti-Semitism a particularly vicious character. Second, and more crucial, the Jews were not just an inferior race, they were also an evil and an enemy race, one whose existence and machinations constituted a mortal danger to the Aryan people. Nazi propaganda constantly harped upon the Jews' manipulations of German institutions, politics, and culture in their efforts to destroy Aryan civilization and achieve world domination. This theme frequently blended anti-Semitism with anti-Marxism, portraying the Russian Revolution as the seizure of power by the Jews.[101] Ultimately, with the German invasion of the Soviet Union in 1941, the wars against communism and against the Jews would become one. For Germany to be free, therefore, and even to survive, it must shake off the stranglehold of Jewish power, which it could only accomplish by destroying the Jews. As Adolf Hitler declared in 1939: "The struggle for world domination will be fought entirely between us, between Germans and Jews. All else is facade and illusion. Behind England stands Israel, and behind France, and behind the United States. Even when we have driven the Jew out of Germany, he remains our world enemy."[102] In Nazi Germany, freedom was inextricably entangled with the struggle against the racial enemy. The road to genocide was built upon the ideological paving stones of white freedom.

As noted above, historians George Mosse and Leon Poliakov among others have explored the intellectual roots of Nazi anti-Semitism and the Final Solution in the history of modern Europe, in particular the counterreaction to the Enlightenment and modernity. They have portrayed the rise of *völkisch* ideology in the late nineteenth century, coupled with the devastating economic and political impact of World War I on not only Germany but much of central and eastern Europe, as the essential preconditions for fascism in interwar Europe. In particular, scholars in this tradition have focused on the shift from religious to racial anti-Semitism as a product of increased social tensions generated by the modernization of European societies, producing anxieties that crystallized around the figure of the Jew as symbol of all the ills of the modern world.[103]

Other scholars have taken a different approach to the history of fascism and the Holocaust. One key issue has been the relationship between Nazi genocide in Europe and European colonialism overseas, with several intellectuals arguing for a close link between the two, that in fact the latter was a main precursor of the former. No one is more closely associated with this perspective than the great German Jewish émigré philosopher Hannah Arendt. In 1951 Arendt published her celebrated and controversial study *The Origins of Totalitarianism*.[104] A comparative analysis of Nazism and communism as examples of totalitarian political movements, *The Origins* examined among other things the rise of modern imperialism and its role in creating scientific racism. Arendt thus argued that the Nazi racism which brought about the Holocaust had substantial roots in the history of European overseas colonialism. Arendt referred to this as the "boomerang effect," noting that "African colonial possessions became the most fertile soil for the flowering of what was later to become the Nazi elite. Here they had seen with their own eyes how peoples could be converted into races and how, simply by taking the initiative in this process, one might push one's own people into the position of the master race."[105]

Arendt was the most famous but far from the only writer to make the analogy between colonialism and fascism. W.E.B. DuBois made the same point a few years earlier, arguing that "There was no Nazi atrocity—concentration camps, wholesale maiming and murder, defilement of women or ghastly blasphemy of childhood—which the Christian civilization of Europe had not long been practicing against colored folk in all parts of the world in the name of and for the defense of a Superior Race born to rule the world."[106] The Black French intellectuals Aimé Césaire and Frantz Fanon made similar arguments, contending that Europe had been racist long before the Holocaust, and that what made the Final Solution singular was its application to other whites. A survey of the modern historical record can find numerous points of overlap between colonialism and fascism, ranging from the numerous examples of colonial genocide like the Belgian Congo or the German devastation of the Herero peoples in Southwest Africa to Hitler's admiration of (and hopes to emulate) the British Empire. As I will discuss in greater detail later in this chapter, from this perspective Nazi racism and genocide arose from the implementation of colonial rule over other whites in Europe itself.

If European colonialism provided one model for Nazi anti-Semitism, American racism was the source of another. Historians have long debated the extent to which Hitler and the Nazis drew inspiration from racially discriminatory ideology and practices in the United States. The fact that America proclaimed itself a white nation from its birth and inscribed Black slavery into its Constitution did not pass unnoticed in the Third Reich. In *Mein Kampf*, written right after the passage of the Johnson-Reed Act, Hitler praised America's racial approach to immigration: "There is today one state in which at least weak beginnings toward a better conception are noticeable. Of course, it is not our model German Republic, but the American Union, in which an effort is made to consult reason at least partially. By refusing immigration on principle to elements in poor health, by simply excluding certain races from naturalization, it professes in slow beginnings a view which is peculiar to the folkish state concept."[107]

In his recent study *Hitler's American Model: The United States and the Making of Nazi Race Law*, James Q. Whitman methodically illustrates the links between American and Nazi racism, specifically the ways in which the Third Reich used the racial legislation of the United States as a model. Challenging historians who have argued that references to American racism were merely propaganda, he explores how such parallels appeared repeatedly in internal party debates and literature. In particular, he shows how a variety of Nazi theorists closely studied American race laws, using them as a template for the Nuremberg Laws of 1934–35. He also points out that at times the Nazis considered American ideas of race, notably the one-drop rule of Black identity, too extreme and not relevant to Germany.[108]

America's policies toward Native Americans also attracted a lot of attention in Nazi Germany. The Nazis often made parallels between America's westward expansion and their *Drang nach Osten*, especially during the beginnings of the invasion of the Soviet Union: Hitler at one point claimed that the Volga would be the German Mississippi; "Europe—and not America—will be the land of unlimited possibilities."[109] For Germany, eastward expansion and ultimately racial purification would offer the same advantages America had gained from its conquest of the West. Carroll Kakel and Edward B. Westermann have looked at the relationship between the extermination of America's Native population and the Holocaust, exploring both the similarities and differences between the two.[110] Kakel in particular takes pains to demonstrate that there was more than a little similarity between the concepts of Manifest Destiny and *Lebensraum*. As one American settler in Oregon during the 1850s wrote, "Extermination, however unchristianlike it may appear, seems to be the only resort left for the protection of life and property."[111]

Such considerations do not constitute a study in comparative genocide, and certainly not a judgment about the relative horror of each. The
point is that Nazi racism took place in a larger context of white racist
ideology and practices developed throughout Europe and America,
often by nations that viewed themselves as paragons of freedom, and
that the Nazis were fully aware of this context and learned from it. What
differentiated fascism in general most from liberal democracy was not
the presence or absence of racism but rather the view of freedom as
something belonging to the state and the collective people as a whole
rather than to the individual, and even this distinction was not absolute.
The fact that Hitler and Mussolini defined freedom differently from the
liberal West does not, however, gainsay the fact that both defined freedom in racial terms.

Starting in 1938 with the *Anschluss* (annexation) of Austria, Nazi Germany proceeded to build a continental empire that by the end of 1941
rivaled that of Napoleon as the greatest in European history. The next
section of this chapter will explore the relationship between the Nazi
empire and the overseas empires of the European colonial powers, in
particular considering the relationship between race and freedom in
both. In its own peculiar way, imperial Nazism would write a new chapter in the history of white freedom.

Empire of Race in Europe

As noted above, historians have long debated the relationship between
colonialism and fascism, and in recent years that debate has intensified.[112] One reason for this has been the rise of postcolonial studies,
with its emphasis on the ways in which European colonial encounters
have shaped life in Europe itself. Picking up on the "boomerang" thesis
of Arendt and others, such scholars have tended to view the history of
fascism through a colonial lens, often arguing that colonialism shaped
not just fascism but liberal democracy and other European political practices. They tend to support the idea that Nazi imperialism and the Holocaust represented the application of colonial methods and atrocities to
Europeans, and that much of the horror associated with them arises from

the idea of colonial rule over white people. In the words of Robert Young, fascism was simply "European colonialism brought home to Europe."[113]

One aspect of this new perspective on empire and fascism has been the rise of a new historiography of German colonialism, also a response to the new emphasis on imperialism in the historiographies of Britain and France. Lora Wildenthal and George Steinmetz have challenged the traditional neglect of German colonialism with studies that emphasize its importance to the history of Germany's rise as a modern nation. Especially in the context of not only colonial but the new transnational historiography, studies of German colonialism advance a vision of Germany as a global nation, both influencing and shaped by trends in the wider world beyond Europe.[114]

Underlying much of this research has been the so-called "continuity" thesis, the exploration of the relationship between German colonialism and Nazi practices of empire and genocide.[115] In general, during its military campaigns to establish colonial rule in Africa, the German army adopted a policy of extreme brutality and destruction, shooting Africans *en masse* and destroying entire villages. The only way to defeat the enemy was to annihilate him. For example, Carl Peters, a major colonizer and founder of the German East Africa company, led a brutal war against the Masai in the late 1880s and would go on to frequent anti-Semitic circles in Germany, seeing both their ideas and the killing of Africans as germane to his *völkisch* ideas.[116]

In particular, historians have pointed to Germany's brutal suppression of the Herero and Nama peoples in German Southwest Africa. Prompted by a revolt against German attempts to expropriate tribal lands in favor of their own settlers, starting in 1904 the German army began a brutal war of aggression against the Herero and Nama, one that forced many into concentration camps and starved hundreds of thousands to death. Scholars have estimated that a majority, at least sixty percent, of Herero and Nama peoples died during the conflict.[117] In 2005 George Steinmetz published an article about the catastrophe titled "The First Genocide of the Twentieth Century and its Postcolonial Afterlives: Germany and the Namibian Ovaherero," portraying the war as not just colonial conquest but deliberate genocide and thus as a model for other genocides of the modern age.[118] In general, while some advocates of the continuity thesis have argued for a direct link between German imperialism and the Holocaust, the majority view tends to emphasize connections that are not necessarily causal but nonetheless significant.

Historians have also considered the relationship between colonialism and fascism in the case of Fascist Italy. Unlike Germany, which had been stripped of its African colonies after World War I and never regained them, Italy did combine fascism and overseas colonialism. One of Mussolini's greatest achievements was the conquest of Ethiopia in 1935 and 1936. Before the mid-1930s the attitude of the Italian Fascists to racism had been ambivalent, to say the least: Nordic racism in particular often used as a way of arguing for Italian inferiority, especially after the Nazi seizure of power, had relatively little appeal. At the same time, however, some fascist theorists, notably Enrico Corradini and Giuseppe Sergi, promoted the image of Italy as a nation of the Mediterranean race, with its own racial gifts and characteristics.[119]

Erasing the shame of Italy's defeat at Adowa in 1896 and demonstrating that fascism was able to succeed where liberal democracy had failed, Italy's victory over the Ethiopians and its new role as a colonial power in Africa both illustrated and fostered the racist dimensions of fascist ideology.[120] The occupation of Ethiopia intensified anti-African prejudice among Italian Fascists, and in particular spurred fears of racial mixing and therefore racial degeneration. In August 1936 the Italian government began to enact measures strictly segregating whites and Blacks in Ethiopia—not merely to preserve the biological sanctity of the Italian race but also to promote racial consciousness in Italy. As Mussolini argued,

> Naturally, when a people becomes conscious of its own racial identity, it does so in relation to all the races, not of one alone. We became racially conscious only in the face of the Hamites, that is to say, the Africans. This is why the racial laws of the empire will be rigorously observed and that all who sin against them will be expelled, punished, imprisoned. Because for the empire to be preserved the natives must be clearly and forcefully aware of our superiority.[121]

A series of other racial laws followed in colonial Africa, foreshadowing the rise of racial legislation in Italy itself. For example, in 1936 the Fascist regime proposed forcing Jews to move from Italian cities to a region of Ethiopia that had traditionally been the home of the Falasha Jews, where they would create a Jewish state controlled by Italy.[122] Further racial legislation for the African colonies followed in 1937. In July 1938 Fascists published the "Manifesto of Race," proclaiming that Italians were an Aryan race to which Africans and Jews did not belong. This set the stage for the laws of November 1938, the first major Italian laws targeting the Jews as a race, the beginnings of systematic anti-Semitic exclusion and persecution in Italy. Widely seen as modeled on Germany's Nuremberg Laws, it is clear they had an important colonial dimension as well. Historians have long debated the reasons for Mussolini's striking turn toward anti-Semitism in the late 1930s after having long argued in favor of Italy's Jews, but one answer lay overseas. In Fascist Italy, the rise of overseas empire and colonial racism marched in sync with the development of fascist anti-Semitism and ultimately the Holocaust.[123]

Finally, one cannot adequately discuss fascist racism and imperial expansion without considering the place of the Slavic peoples in Nazi ideology and the creation of the Nazi empire in Europe. Unlike Fascist Italy, Nazi Germany did not devote much energy to restoring the overseas empire it had lost after World War I. Instead, following traditions of eastward expansion that dated back to the Middle Ages, it decided to establish its empire in eastern Europe. As Hitler argued in *Mein Kampf*: "For Germany, consequently, the only possibility for carrying out a healthy territorial policy lay in the acquisition of new land in Europe itself. Colonies cannot serve this purpose unless they seem in large part suited for settlement by Europeans . . . such a colonial policy could only have been carried out by means of a hard struggle which, however, would have been carried on to much better purpose, not for territories outside of Europe, but for land on the home continent itself."[124]

The concept of *Lebensraum* formed the key template for the idea of creating a racially based German empire in the East. Lebensraum as an idea first arose in the late nineteenth century in Germany, but it received new attention in the aftermath of World War I. Basically, the concept argued that for Germany to survive and prosper it must expand eastward, seeking new resources as well as new lands for agricultural exploitation and on which to settle its growing population. In one sense the idea, or at least the practice, was nothing new; during the Middle Ages groups including the Hanseatic League and the Teutonic Knights promoted what became known as the *Ostsiedlung*.[125]

Lebensraum built upon this (at times legendary) history, but with some modern twists. First, it reinterpreted the move to the East as an expansion of the German *state*, a state that was defined racially. As the 1938 occupation of Czechoslovakia's Sudetenland demonstrated dramatically, ethnic Germans throughout eastern Europe were to be a part of the Reich, and their presence would both facilitate and justify Germany's domination of the East.[126] Second, during the interwar years lebensraum developed in a world in which Germany had been stripped of its overseas empire. Colonialism in eastern Europe was not only more desirable but also seemed to be the only real option for a renewed German empire.[127]

Lebensraum envisaged the mass settlement of German colonists in the empty lands of the East, forming a dynamic new population of robust farmers and their families that would not only form thriving new communities but also by their example help revive the vitality of Germany itself. The problem, of course, was that these lands were not empty. As a result, from its beginnings the idea of lebensraum had contained a strong racial component. Its proponents argued that the rich lands of the East were wasted on the inferior Slavs, who must make way for the new, superior German population. The Third Reich adopted such ideas enthusiastically and built upon them once the war began. Nazi views of the Slavs (like much else in Nazi ideology) had always been vague and somewhat contradictory: Hitler himself distinguished between different populations, regarding the Czechs more highly than the Poles, for example, and some Nazis saw them capable of assimilating into the German *Volk*. In general, however, the Nazis viewed and all too often treated the Slavs as subhumans, people to be displaced at best, eliminated at worst. Moreover, the fact that Soviet Russia, the Bolshevik enemy, was a Slavic country only highlighted and intensified Nazi disdain for the Slavs.[128]

The result, with the German invasions of first Poland and then the Soviet Union, was a bloodbath. The brutality and massacres created by the Nazi armies in eastern Europe had no parallel in the occupied West, home to populations viewed as racially superior. Massive racist war crimes ranging from the murder of much of the Polish intelligentsia to the deliberate starving to death of 3 million Soviet prisoners of war testified to the brutal character of what was in effect a race war against the Slavs. Indications are, moreover, that had Nazi Germany triumphed in its campaign for lebensraum in the East it would have gone further. Between 1939 and 1942 officials in the SS developed what was known as the *Generalplan Ost*, or Master Plan for the East. This plan would have realized the idea of lebensraum by clearing the Slavic population out of eastern Europe entirely, either by deporting them into Siberia or by starving them to death. Timothy Snyder has estimated that, if the plan had gone into effect, up to 45 million inhabitants of Poland, Czechoslovakia, the Ukraine, and other Slavic lands would have died to make room for the new German settler population.[129]

The ultimate bloodbath in eastern Europe, of course, was Hitler's war against the Jews, and it was not just theoretical but all too real. The German invasion of the Soviet Union in June 1941 brought together the crusades against Bolshevism and against the Jews in a savage war of annihilation. Led by the *Einsatzgruppen*, paramilitary death squads unleashed on Jews and other enemies of the Reich, the invading Nazi armies made the brutal elimination of the racial Other one of their priorities. Many Soviet Jews succeeded in escaping eastward ahead of the Nazi armies, but those who did not rarely survived. In September Germans murdered more than 33,000 Kievan Jews in the infamous Babi Yar massacre, and a month later killed 50,000 in Odessa. Between the invasion of Russia in June 1941 and the Wannsee Conference in January 1942, before the development of the death camps and the implementation of systematic mass murder, German forces executed some 900,000 Soviet Jews.[130]

As noted above, lebensraum, in both its earlier theoretical and in its ultimate Nazi variations, drew heavily upon the model of America's

FIGURE 26. German concentration camp, Auschwitz, Poland. Taken May 22, 2010.
Xiquinhosilva (https://www.flickr.com/photos/xiquinho/16380127035/). CC BY 4.0.

westward expansion and the idea of Manifest Destiny.[131] Manifest Destiny not only proclaimed white American racial superiority but resulted in the devastation of indigenous peoples in the territories it claimed. From the Nazi perspective, this then constituted a template for the replication of American power and prosperity on the European continent. The Nazi belief that the Slavs were an inferior people who must give way to the Germans as the avatars of civilization and progress directly replicated American arguments about Native Americans.[132] More generally, the racism displayed by German colonists in Africa as well as eastern Europe prompted analogies with American racial practices. As Hitler himself noted, "Who remembers the Red Indians?"[133] Even the victims of Hitler's policies sometimes made these links; as a Ukrainian woman mused in 1941 after the German invasion, "We are like slaves. Often the book *Uncle Tom's Cabin* comes to mind. Once we shed tears over those Negroes, now obviously we ourselves are experiencing the same thing."[134]

One must note, however, that the idea of Manifest Destiny represented not just American empowerment in particular but equally the progress of freedom and democracy in general. Lebensraum, especially in its Nazi interpretation, saw the conquest and settlement of the East as a key component of German national and racial progress, and thus of German freedom. As we have seen, for fascism in general freedom was the property of the nation-state rather than the individual, and in Nazi Germany in particular it was defined as a racialized concept, an aspect of the triumph of the race. Like America with its Manifest Destiny, Nazi Germany had to grow or die, had to develop an empire or perish. The struggle for lebensraum was thus not just for "freedom" but for the very survival of the German people.

This chapter has explored the many important colonialist roots of fascist and Nazi ideology and empire building in Europe. There is, however, a major difference here from the history of European overseas imperialism, and it proved crucial. Unlike the establishment of Iberian empires in the Americas or western European colonies in Asia and Africa, Nazi Germany in particular built its empire in the throes of the greatest global conflict the world has ever known. The racist crimes of the Nazi regime were also frequently war crimes, and in general the Holocaust and the many other massacres of subject populations took place in the context of a *guerre à outrance*, a war to the death.[135] Both racial discrimination and even exterminism existed in European overseas empires, but the context of total war gave them an unprecedented urgency for the Nazi regime. In order for Germany to be free it must conquer, and in the end it could conquer only by exterminating its enemies, defined as racial enemies. As Joseph Goebbels declared in 1942, "this is not the Second World War, this is the Great Racial War. The meaning of this war . . . is to decide whether the German and Aryan will prevail or if the Jew will rule the world."[136] The identification of freedom as a national, racial characteristic led inexorably to the elimination of those defined as nonwhite and thus incapable of true freedom.

Questions of the relationship between race and freedom also lay at the heart of the global struggle against fascism. As we have seen, World War I reinforced the idea that freedom was the natural, even exclusive, province of white peoples. Such perspectives certainly remained powerful among the coalition that ultimately destroyed the Nazi empire in World War II. At the same time, however, the great antifascist mobilization strained and exposed the contradictions of white freedom to an unprecedented degree. The final section of this chapter will explore the ways in which the struggle against Nazi racism and fascism in general both shook and in some ways reinforced the racial assumptions at the heart of ideals of liberty.

Race and Freedom in the Great Antifascist War

Paris! Paris outraged! Paris broken! Paris martyred! But Paris liberated! Liberated by itself, liberated by its people with the help of the French armies, with the support and the help of all France, of the France that fights, of the only France, of the real France, of the eternal France!

—CHARLES DE GAULLE, PARIS, AUGUST 25, 1944[137]

I venture to think that the Allied Declaration that the Allies are fighting to make the world safe for freedom of the individual and for democracy seems hollow, so long as India, and for that matter Africa, are exploited by Great Britain, and America has the Negro problem in her own home.

—LETTER FROM MAHATMA GANDHI TO
FRANKLIN D. ROOSEVELT, JULY 1, 1942[138]

Few if any wars of the modern era have made freedom more central to their cause than World War II, in particular the great struggle waged by the Western powers and their dependents against Nazi Germany. From the Spanish Civil War and the antifascist movements of the prewar era to the titanic armed struggles of the war itself, first small groups of political activists then ultimately the Allied powers together held up freedom as a banner and a rallying cry. In Europe and East Asia subject peoples fought for the liberation of their nations from German and Japanese occupation. In America government leaders and opinion makers in general constantly trumpeted the idea of the war as a struggle to protect their free society and to destroy fascist authoritarianism. Throughout the world millions took up arms to die to make men free, in the words of "The Battle Hymn of the Republic."[139]

It was readily apparent, however, both at the time and in historical perspective, that this crusade for freedom had its own contradictions.

The fact that one of the leading, in some senses *the* leading, antifascist powers, the Soviet Union, was a brutal dictatorship that had executed millions of its own people during the 1930s, and that the ultimate military struggle of the war in Europe which finally crushed fascism was a battle between dictators, complicated the idea of a war against tyranny.[140] As many in eastern Europe would learn after the war, liberation did not necessarily bring freedom. It was also true, as the quotation above from Gandhi illustrates, that the Western powers had their own complex relationship to the idea and practice of liberty. To an important extent Britain and France fought the war against fascism both for national freedom and for empire, and the contradiction between these two aims did not trouble many. The United States waged the war in Europe and the Pacific with segregated armed forces, so that the army units which disembarked in Vichy-controlled North Africa in 1942 carrying copies of the Atlantic Charter were divided between Blacks and whites. In the fight for freedom and against Nazi racism it did not hesitate to imprison its own citizens, at least in part because of the color of their skin. Rather than accuse the Allies of hypocrisy, one must emphasize the fact, as this study has taken pains to do, that the idea of freedom was a complicated affair. Never did these complications stand out in sharper relief than during the war against fascism.

As noted at the beginning of this chapter, during the early twentieth century the idea of freedom became in effect nationalized, emphasizing the integrity of the nation rather than (and in some cases over that of) the individual. For the Allies that came together in the grand alliance to destroy fascism, the war was above all one of national salvation, and the victory one of national triumph. It is worth noting in this context that the two major Allied powers, the United States and the Soviet Union, entered the war only when they were physically attacked by the Axis. In 1939 the Soviets turned their backs on the antifascist crusade in order to protect the Russian state, and when war did come to them officials promptly labeled it the Great Patriotic War, a defense of the homeland rather than a war against fascism.[141] Similarly, in spite of its hostility to both Germany and Japan as well as its creeping alliance with the British, the American government did not enter the war until forced to do so by the Japanese attack on Pearl Harbor. Moreover, only when Nazi Germany declared war on the US did Washington respond in kind and pledge itself to fight in the European theater, at that point making the conflict a true world war.[142] In the case of both great powers, but especially the Soviet Union, the antifascist fight for freedom merged with and was dominated by the struggle for national survival.

The final section of this chapter will first consider the ways in which white freedom manifested itself in the world war against fascism, examining how the salient contradictions of waging a racist war against Nazi racism forced a reappraisal of Western ideas of freedom and how its racial underlying logic in many ways endured. It will then move on to explore the movements for a more expansive vision of freedom mounted by subaltern groups in both America and Europe's colonies.[143] This exploration will set the stage for the last chapter of this book, a study of white freedom in the era of civil rights and decolonization.

A War on Two Fronts

I'm just a Negro soldier
    Fighting for "Democracy,"
A thing I've often heard of
    But very seldom see . . .
To hell with a war perpetuated by greed
    While the hungry masses cry
But to win complete equality
    I'd gladly fight and die.

—BILL HORTON, "JUST A NEGRO SOLDIER"[144]

I joined the Army of Liberation as a volunteer, and I die within inches of Victory and the final goal. I wish for happiness for all those who will survive and taste the sweetness of the freedom and peace of tomorrow. I'm sure that the French people, and all those who fight for freedom, will know how to honor our memory with dignity.

—MISSAK MANOUCHIAN, ARMENIAN MEMBER OF THE
FRENCH RESISTANCE, EXECUTED BY THE GERMANS
IN FEBRUARY 1944[145]

On June 4, 1940, facing a desperate struggle against the triumphant Third Reich, Winston Churchill gave perhaps the finest and most famous speech of his political career. Defiantly avowing before Parliament and the British people the continued resistance to Nazi aggression, he said, "and if, which I do not for a moment believe, this island or a large part of it were subjugated and starving, then our Empire beyond the seas, armed and guarded by the British Fleet, would carry on the struggle."[146] In this bold declaration Churchill emphasized a basic truism, that the United Kingdom was bigger that Britain and Northern Ireland, and that its colonies were central to the realm.

Far more than in World War I, Europe's overseas colonies played a key role in World War II. In part, this was because war came directly to the colonies. In World War II the Axis forces had a much greater global reach than did the Central Powers in the first world war, so that the Western Allies battled the Germans in North Africa, and the Japanese not only overran British Malaya, French Indochina, and the Dutch East Indies but at times threatened to invade India and Australia. Colonial forces did not just defend their home turfs, however. National governments also mobilized imperial personnel and material resources in the desperate struggle against the Axis in Europe itself. For the second time in the twentieth century, imperial governments called upon and mobilized in the defense of national freedom populations that were not free.

In 1939 the British Empire constituted the biggest political unit in the world, and in human history, encompassing twenty-five percent of the world's population and thirty percent of its landmass.[147] A crazy quilt of dominions, crown colonies, and other territories, its complexity was to a significant extent organized along racial lines. The dominions, or British Commonwealth, consisting of Canada, Australia, New Zealand, and South Africa, were former white settler colonies that by the outbreak of the war functioned in effect as independent nations. Not just between the metropole and the colonies but even within the British Empire, the principle of white freedom largely held sway. The response of the dominions to London's call to arms was immediate (all four declared war on Germany within a week after Britain did, Australia and New Zealand on the same day) and dramatic. The dominions sent hundreds of thousands of soldiers to participate in all the theaters of war, ranging from flying fighter planes during the Battle of Britain to fighting against the Germans in North Africa and the Japanese in East Asia. By the end of the war Canada had the third-largest navy in the world.[148]

The response of the nonwhite colonies to the imperial war effort was more ambiguous, and for good reason. They had contributed generously during the First World War, but hopes that this support would be rewarded with greater freedom or even independence had largely come to naught. In India, for example, many were painfully aware that Britain had rewarded their wartime service to the Empire with the Amritsar massacre.[149] As we shall see below, the British call for support during World War II met a large amount of ambivalence and even resistance. Nonetheless, some 2 million Indians served in the British armed forces during the war, as did 500,000 subjects from Britain's African colonies. The colonies also furnished massive amounts of war materiel as well as military bases and port facilities. All told, the majority of British troops in the World War II came from the Empire.

Imperial resources played an even more important role in France during the war. Unlike for the British, the nightmare scenario outlined in Churchill's speech quoted above actually came true for France in June 1940 with defeat and conquest by the Germans. While the French government capitulated to Hitler's forces and set up a collaborationist regime in Vichy, Charles De Gaulle, the youngest general in the French Army, refused to accept defeat and fled to London. There on June 18 he issued a famous call for continued French resistance, one that, like Churchill's speech two weeks before, emphasized imperial themes: "For, remember this, France does not stand alone. She is not isolated. Behind her is a vast empire, and she can make common cause with the British Empire, which commands the seas and is continuing the struggle."[150]

De Gaulle's London speech in effect created the French resistance, and right from the start it became clear that the empire would play a central role in the movement for a free France. In effect, the struggle against the collaborationist Vichy state began in the colonies: although most colonial administrators rallied to Vichy as the legitimate government of France, in Chad, Félix Éboué, the only Black governor of a

French colony, declared for De Gaulle and Free France in August. Éboué's troops went on the offensive against Vichy forces in Africa, and by October had conquered most of French Equatorial Africa, although meeting defeat in French West Africa.[151] By the end of the year New Caledonia and Tahiti had also rallied to De Gaulle, and Brazzaville in Chad became the first capital of Free France. The Allied invasion of North Africa at the end of 1942, followed by revolts against Vichy in the Caribbean islands of Martinique and Guadeloupe in 1943, would spell the end of the collaborationist regime in the colonies. The first Free French troops were Black Africans, and during the war as a whole the majority of De Gaulle's soldiers came from the colonies. If, as De Gaulle claimed, France to a significant extent liberated itself during World War II, this liberation came from the empire.[152] Colonial France *was* Free France, and yet its subjects were not free men and women.

While the forces of Free France fought outside the country, a powerful series of resistance movements arose within occupied France. Similar to the colonial subjects who played a central role in the armies of Free France, many partisans of the French resistance were also outsiders. In recent years historians have devoted more attention to the contribution of foreigners and Jews to the resistance in France. On the eve of the war France, and Paris in particular, had been a haven for refugees from all over Europe, people who had nowhere to go once the Germans marched in.[153] As a result, foreigners, including antifascist Germans, Italians, and Poles, exiled Spanish Republicans, and others, started resistance movements of their own and gradually merged with the French Resistance in general. The French Communist Party in particular took the lead in organizing immigrants after the invasion of the Soviet Union, forming the MOI (*Main-d'Oeuvre Immigré*, Immigrant Labor Section) of its resistance army.[154]

The role of French and especially foreign Jews in the Resistance deserves special mention. As anti-Semitic legislation and harassment increased in France, culminating with the roundup of thirteen thousand Parisian Jews at the Vélodrome d'Hiver (known as the "Vél d'Hiv") in July 1942, many foreign Jews felt they had no choice but to go underground.[155] Jews fought both as members of French resistance organizations and in their own networks. Jewish Communists in particular built up a series of important networks, and Zionist Jews also organized resistance. Many of these organizations specialized in saving Jews, especially Jewish children, by hiding them or smuggling them over the frontiers into Switzerland or Spain. Jews also formed the majority of several MOI groups, notably the Manouchian network, which operated in Paris for a few months during 1943.[156] Annie Kriegel, a young Jewish girl who joined the group after her family fled Paris, and eventually became a distinguished historian of France, described its appeal.

> To understand it is necessary to start from one basic fact: the brutal collapse for them of all those systems of protection, even if sometimes oppressive, which an individual acquires from belonging to a regulated society. Homeland, name, family, house, school, neighborhood, work, everything which provides a point of fixity, and definition of self, had been swallowed up in nothingness. . . . Thus the resistance provided membership of a group, a narrow group, but one which was tightly structured and hierarchical, the reconstitution of a network of interpersonal relations where the survival of each depended on the solidarity of all the others. [It] once again peopled the days with faces and gave them back a savour and a value, an existence freighted with both fear and hope.[157]

This group became famous for daring attacks against German soldiers, even succeeding in assassinating an SS General. For many Jewish partisans, resistance work was a way of creating and integrating themselves into the France of their dreams, a land of freedom and justice for all.[158]

Whether France deserved such loyalty was another question entirely. The roundup at the Vél d'Hiv was organized by French police, not German troops, and in general foreign Jews (the majority of the Jewish population in wartime France) were in danger not just because of the Nazi occupation but also because the Vichy government made a deal with German authorities to round up and deport them if the Germans spared Jews with French citizenship.[159] Thanks in part to this arrangement three-quarters of Jews in France survived the war, but it also represented a betrayal of the French universalist principle that freedom should extend to all and underscored the idea that freedom came from citizenship.

This pattern of people fighting for national freedom denied to them as racial outsiders characterized much of the experience of Allied colonial subjects in general during the war. In spite of widespread opposition from Indian politicians, the British government of colonial India declared that questions of self-rule and independence would have to wait until after the war was over. The British also used the war to reassert imperial authority in the Middle East, overthrowing the government of Iraq in 1941 and the Egyptian regime in 1942.[160] The clear message was that, at least until the defeat of the Axis, colonialism would remain firmly in place. The fact that imperial and Commonwealth soldiers fought for Britain also did not shield them from British racism. Black soldiers in particular received lower pay, worse rations, and far fewer chances for advancement than their white counterparts. The British military generally refused (as in World War I), to deploy them in Europe; they also tried to prevent contacts between them and African American soldiers for fear that the antiracist attitudes of the latter would undermine the empire.[161]

The French situation was different, since colonial troops did not enter France until the Liberation. Yet the Gaullist argument that Free France represented France as a whole tended to mask the diversity of both the Free French and the Resistance. In arranging for French troops to liberate Paris in 1944, for example, De Gaulle bowed to American demands for the exclusion of Black colonial soldiers, so that the LeClerc Division, which entered the French capital on August 25, 1944, consisted largely of Spanish Republican exiles. The liberation of Paris must be a white liberation.[162]

The United States during the war also mobilized people of color to an unprecedented degree while at the same time stubbornly retaining traditional racial standards. World War II represented the greatest overseas war effort the nation had ever seen, the first time America (or any nation) had waged such a massive struggle on two oceans at the same time. Over 16 million Americans served in the armed forces during World War II, more than any other war effort before or since. Moreover, the tremendous mobilization of production that made the United States the "Arsenal of Democracy" required vast labor resources, prompting the migration of millions to new jobs and transforming the nation's industrial landscape.[163] This massive military and economic mobilization took place in a new political context, for America had changed significantly since World War I. The New Deal represented one of the most progressive regimes, and political cultures, in US history, and Franklin Delano Roosevelt's attitudes toward race were far removed from those of Woodrow Wilson.[164]

The result was a multicultural war effort that dwarfed that of the First World War. More than 1 million African Americans served in the armed forces, compared to fewer than 400,000 during World War I, and hundreds of thousands more left the South on "liberty trains" to find work in the war plants of the Midwest and California.[165] In August 1942 the US and Mexican governments signed the Mexican Farm Labor Agreement, the beginnings of the *bracero* programs that would bring tens of thousands of Mexicans a year (and hundreds of thousands after the war) to work in America's fields.[166] Hundreds of thousands of Mexican Americans served in the US military during the war, as did 25,000 Native Americans.[167] In 1943 the US government finally repealed the Chinese Exclusion Act, and some 13,000 Chinese Americans also fought for their country during World War II.[168]

One notable aspect of the war on American race relations was the changing view of European immigrants and those of immigrant heritage. As noted in chapter 1, the decline of immigration and the maturation of an assimilated second generation of Americans of eastern and southern European origin had led to increasing acceptance of European immigrants as white during the interwar years. The New Deal mobilized support from immigrants and appointed several to high-level positions in Roosevelt's cabinet. In 1933 New York elected Fiorello LaGuardia as its first Italian American mayor.[169] Emma Lazarus's poem "The New World Colossus" on the Statue of Liberty had been largely ignored for decades, but by the end of the 1930s it began to receive new attention as a symbol not just of immigration but of Americanism in general.[170] By June 1941 the *Detroit Free Press* could portray a smiling

Statue of Liberty welcoming young people of European descent as "my children."[171]

World War II marked a major step forward in the assimilation of European immigrants and their descendants into the mainstream of American life. Hollywood movies about the American armed forces, such as *Air Force* (1943) and *Lifeboat* (1944) frequently featured a wide variety of white characters of different ethnic backgrounds, all fighting together for America.[172] This process was not complete: thousands of German and Italian Americans were interned as threats to national security during the war.[173] Nonetheless, World War II marked a major stage in the transformation of European immigrants from foreigners into white ethnics.

More generally, World War II did mark some important achievements in America's struggle for racial equality. For example, Franklin D. Roosevelt became the first president in American history to denounce lynching as a crime. During the 1940 presidential campaign Roosevelt's Republican opponent Wendell Willkie ran on a civil rights platform, pledging to integrate the armed forces and the federal government if elected. After Black labor leader A. Philip Randolph threatened a massive march on Washington to protest segregation in the defense industry, in June 1941 Roosevelt issued Executive Order 8802 banning racial discrimination in war plants and creating the Fair Employment Practices Commission (FEPC) to enforce it.[174] Although the FEPC had little power, the prospect of a federal agency actually devoted to fighting racial discrimination had great symbolic weight and did help Blacks and other minorities gain access to jobs in the burgeoning war industry.

In general, however, racial discrimination and segregation persisted in America during World War II. Whatever his personal feelings, Roosevelt's New Deal coalition depended upon the support of white southern legislators, who remained adamantly opposed to policies promoting racial equality. Roosevelt may have denounced lynching, but the US government never enacted federal anti-lynching legislation. During the 1930s many New Deal social programs, such as the Federal Housing Authority, discriminated against Blacks, and this pattern continued during the war.[175] Most notably, in spite of some Democratic promises to the contrary, America's armed forces remained segregated for the duration of the conflict. As in World War I but to an even greater extent, the US military fought around the world for white freedom.[176]

Racism in World War II was not just a matter of government policy. During the war race riots erupted in American cities, usually involving white attacks on Blacks and other peoples of color. In June 1943 the so-called Zoot Suit Riots (named after a clothing style made popular by Black jazz musicians and embraced by minority youth) broke out in Los Angeles, involving attacks by thousands of white soldiers and sailors primarily against Latino young men.[177] A scant two weeks later Detroit experienced its own major race riot, prompted by attempts to integrate the city's housing and defense industries.[178] Public transportation and other facilities remained largely segregated, and not just in the South. At times this went so far as to require Black soldiers in uniform to give up seats on trains to German prisoners of war.

The most egregious example of racial discrimination in America during World War II was the internment of Japanese Americans. At the beginning of the war the Japanese American community in America numbered around a quarter of a million individuals, most of whom lived on the West Coast and in Hawaii. As noted in the previous chapter, California in particular had a long history of anti-Asian racism, directed mostly against Chinese immigrants, which culminated in the Chinese Exclusion Act of 1882. Imperial Japan's attack on Pearl Harbor revived such sentiments and now targeted the Japanese American community. As historian John Dower has demonstrated, the Pacific war between the United States and Japan was to an important extent a race war. For many Americans, it made no sense to wage war against "Japs" abroad while at the same time tolerating them at home.[179]

Spontaneous rioting against Japanese Americans broke out right after Pearl Harbor. By the beginnings of 1942 many whites, especially in the West, claimed that Japanese Americans were a potential (or actual) fifth column, threatening national security. In response to this pressure, in March 1942 President Roosevelt signed Executive Order 9066, expelling all Japanese Americans from the West Coast and placing them in internment camps. More than 110,000 men, women, and children—two-thirds of them American citizens—were forced out of their homes, many losing everything they owned. This policy contrasted markedly with the treatment of German and Italian Americans, only a few of whom were interned. Also deeply ironic was the fact that it mostly did not affect Japanese Americans living in Hawaii, who constituted nearly forty percent of the territory's population, even though the attack on Pearl Harbor had targeted those islands rather than California.[180]

The internment of Japanese Americans speaks both to the racism that continued to mark American life during the war and to the mobilization of communities of color in service of the national war effort. More than eighteen thousand Japanese Americans served in the US military during World War II. Most came from Hawaii, but some, whose relatives were often in internment camps, were from the West Coast. They served primarily in the famed 442nd Infantry Regiment. Deployed in North Africa and Europe (the army refused to use them in the Pacific war), the unit helped liberate the Dachau concentration camp and in general became the most highly decorated unit in American military history. Japanese American servicemen and -women thus provided another example of people fighting abroad for freedom that was denied them at home.[181]

Many have at times viewed the sordid history of Japanese American internment as an exceptional moment in the prosecution of America's "good war." In fact, it represented rather an extreme example of the overarching theme of white freedom and how that ideal persisted during World War II. Contradictions between not only the battle for freedom but also the rejection of fascist racism, on the one hand, and the survival and even reinforcement of the color line among the Allied powers, on the other hand, were a key characteristic of the greatest war in human history. As we have seen, European colonial subjects and American peoples of color often dealt with these contradictions by focusing on supporting the national effort in hopes of a better day after the war. At the same time, however, some chose either not to accept continued racial subordination or searched for ways to combine the struggles against fascism and for racial justice.

FIGURE 27. Japanese American soldier in France, World War II. A Company F,
442nd Regimental Combat Team squad leader, November 1944. Courtesy of U.S. Army.

For Jews in Britain and America the choice was clear. Both nations
had a history of anti-Semitism that did not disappear during the Second
World War. In both countries, fascist movements had been active during
the 1930s, preaching anti-Semitic propaganda. In America, Catholic
priest Father Coughlin attracted millions of listeners with radio broad-
casts supporting fascism and vilifying Jews.[182] In Britain, Oswald Mosley's British Union of Fascists staged street battles with Jewish groups
in London.[183] Both nations also proved reluctant to admit Jewish refugees after 1933. Nonetheless, for Jews in America and Britain, the advent
of the war meant their concerns for their people and their loyalties to

their nations became one. In both countries Jews, many of European refugee origin, joined the armed forces in numbers greater than their percentage of the national population. One example was Max Fuchs, a New York Jew born in Poland who took part in the Normandy invasion and in October 1944 led the first public Jewish religious service in Germany since the beginning of the war.[184]

How to deal with America's call to arms soon became a poignant issue for African Americans. African American newspapers constantly made analogies between Nazi and American racism, for example, portraying both as the enemy of Black people. On January 31, 1942, the *Pittsburgh Courier*, the most popular Black newspaper in America, published a letter to the editor from James G. Thompson of Wichita, Kansas, entitled "Should I Sacrifice to Live 'Half American'?" Thompson's letter squarely posed the dilemma felt by many African Americans as their nation went to war:

> Being an American of dark complexion ... these questions flash through my mind: "Should I sacrifice my life to live half American?" ... "Would it be demanding too much to demand full citizenship rights in exchange for the sacrificing of my life? Is the kind of America I know worth defending? Will America be a true and pure democracy after this war?" ...
>
> I suggest that while we keep defense and victory in the forefront that we don't lose sight of our fight for democracy at home. ...
>
> The V for victory sign is being displayed prominently in all so-called democratic countries which are fighting for victory over aggression, slavery and tyranny. If this V sign means that to those now engaged in this great conflict, then let we colored Americans adopt the double VV for a double victory. The first V for Victory over our enemies from without, the second V for victory over our enemies from within. For surely those who perpetrate these ugly prejudices here are seeking to destroy our democratic form of government just as surely as the Axis forces.[185]

The *Courier* embraced Thompson's suggestion, polling its readers, who responded overwhelmingly in favor of the idea. An editorial two weeks later pledged the paper's full support of the new campaign, arguing,

"Thus in our fight for freedom we wage a two-pronged attack against our enslavers at home and those abroad who would enslave us. WE HAVE A STAKE IN THIS FIGHT . . . WE ARE AMERICANS TOO!"[186]

So was born the Double V campaign. Appropriately enough, in a nation that was waging a two-front war, African Americans fought their own struggle on two fronts. The campaign spread throughout America's Black population, and beyond, with the speed of a prairie fire. The *Courier* ran Double V articles in every issue for the next year, encouraging the formation of Double V clubs. Supporters wore Double V pins and created Double V gardens. There was even a Double V hairstyle, the "Doubler." The campaign won support not only from leading Black politicians and celebrities but also whites, including Wendell Willkie. Although many in the federal government feared that the campaign, and the Black press in general, might undermine the war effort, African Americans overwhelmingly supported it. For Black Americans the Double V was in reality one campaign, for a vision of liberty that transcended white freedom to embrace all peoples.[187]

Fighting both fascism and Western racism during World War II was also a key issue for the colonial subjects of European empires. This was especially true of those in Asia, confronted by the threat (or reality) of Japanese invasion and occupation. More than in the case of the Allied struggles against Nazi Germany and Vichy in North Africa, Imperial Japan's approach to the war made this a very complex question. On the one hand, Japan's war effort, especially against China, was motivated by its own racial prejudices. Japanese troops frequently looked down on the Chinese as dogs, and such attitudes helped facilitate widespread massacres against the civilian population.[188] On the other hand, the Japanese portrayed the war in the Pacific as a pan-Asian campaign against Western imperialism and their conquest of colonies like the Dutch East Indies and the Philippines as wars of liberation. Japan certainly had its own colonies, notably Korea and Taiwan, but it nonetheless saw itself as a force for Asian racial deliverance and freedom. During the Paris Peace Conference of 1919 Japan had supported a resolution for racial equality that was defeated by the Western powers, and many Japanese saw the Pacific war as merely a new phase in this struggle for racial equality.

In August 1940 Japan formally announced the creation of the Greater East Asia Co-Prosperity Sphere.[189] Heralded with slogans like *Asia for the Asiatics*, the Sphere proclaimed its intention to bring all the peoples of East Asia together in opposition to Western imperialism and racism. For the most part, the Sphere merely masked Japanese interests in the occupied Asian nations; the Japanese nationalists in power clearly saw the nation's empire as a source for raw materials and other benefits for the imperial war economy. Nonetheless, Japan continued to use it to argue for racial solidarity in the region. In November 1943, as the tide of the Pacific war was clearly turning against Tokyo, Japan hosted a Greater East Asia Conference. Attended by delegates from several Asian countries, it proclaimed their intention to fight against the racist imperialism of the West. There the ambassador to Japan from the Philippines declared, "the time has come for the Filipinos to discard Anglo-Saxon civilization . . . and to recapture their charm and original virtues as an oriental people."[190]

This stance prompted a variety of different reactions throughout colonial Asia. It had perhaps the greatest success in the Dutch East Indies, a vast territory prized by the Japanese for its oil resources. During its occupation of the colony Japan both destroyed the Dutch colonial infrastructure and encouraged Indonesian nationalism; as a result the nationalist parties declared the independence of Indonesia two days after the Japanese surrender in August 1945.[191] The situation in the Philippines was very different. The American government had granted the islands semi-independent Commonwealth status in 1935, with the expectation of full independence to follow. The Japanese occupation interrupted this process, leading the Filipino government to go into exile and prompting a major resistance movement against Japan in the islands. After the liberation, the Philippines achieved full independence in 1946.[192]

The situation in India was more ambiguous. Many Indians had bitter memories of Britain's unfilled promises for more autonomy during World War I, and in spite of the fact that by early 1942 the Japanese had conquered Burma and were threatening to invade, India was less than enthusiastic about supporting the British war effort a second time. The Indian National Congress denounced Nazi Germany and temporarily suspended its activities during the Battle of Britain. Nonetheless, when the war with Japan broke out it responded with the Quit India Movement. In August 1942, the congress announced its refusal to cooperate with the British war effort until the crown granted Indian independence. On August 8, Mahatma Gandhi gave a major speech supporting the Quit India Movement and calling for nonviolent resistance against the Japanese.[193]

The movement shocked the British, and the colonial government responded harshly, throwing much of the Congress leadership in prison for the duration of the war. Many other Indian political parties and factions rejected the movement, notably the Muslim League, the colony's largest Muslim political organization. As we have seen, some 2 million Indian soldiers fought for the British during the war.[194] Nonetheless, the fact that the colony's largest political party refused to support the war effort unless Indians were treated as an equal sovereign people illustrated the limits to white freedom in the colonial era in general.

Wartime Vietnam presented one of the most noteworthy examples of the relationship between antifascism and anticolonialism. When France surrendered to Nazi Germany in June 1940, the new Vichy government moved to consolidate control over the nation's overseas colonies. It replaced the Third Republic's regime in French Indochina with its own governor, Jean Decoux, assuming effective control of the colony. Over the next few months Decoux pursued a complicated series of negotiations with both Vichy and Tokyo until Japan invaded and took over the colony in September. The Japanese left the Vichy regime largely undisturbed, however, even encouraging its repression of anticolonial forces.[195]

The effective unity between Japanese fascism and French colonialism prompted the Vietnamese resistance to oppose both. French Indochina had a long and vigorous history of anticolonialism dating back to the early years of the twentieth century, and in 1930 both Communist and non-Communist groups had staged major uprisings against French rule.

In the winter of 1941, Communist leader Ho Chi Minh returned from exile in the Soviet Union to Vietnam and that spring led the founding of a new Communist resistance movement, the Viet Minh. Right from the beginning the Viet Minh called for resistance to both French and Japanese rule, like Communist resistance movements in Europe downplaying its Marxism for the sake of a broad-based struggle against fascism and for national independence. Like the Double V campaign in America, it waged a struggle on two fronts, for a postwar world of national freedom and the end of colonial white privilege.[196]

Peoples of color around the world played a massive role in the struggle against fascism and for freedom during World War II. To a much greater extent than during World War I, many asked what kind of freedom would victory bring and, more pointedly, whether that freedom would extend to them. The war thus brought the practice of white freedom to the breaking point, on a global scale. As the defeat of the Axis loomed, questions about the relationship between race and freedom became ever more pressing. As we shall see in the next chapter, these questions would in significant ways dominate the postwar era.

Conclusion

The great wars of the early twentieth century brought the diverse peoples of the planet together as never before in history. The 1919 Peace of Paris was the first truly global political settlement the world had ever seen, and World War II in particular coordinated military struggles and strategic objectives across the globe to an unprecedented degree. In such a globalized reality, ideas of both freedom and race took on new meanings and dimensions. As we have seen, the rise of the nation-state, brutally accelerated by the needs of total war, came to dominate ideas of freedom. To be free meant more than ever before belonging to an independent nation, even if that national independence came at the cost of individual liberties. Ideas of race also became nationalized to an important degree, so that conflicts between nations at times assumed the character of race wars. In the case of Nazi Germany above all, nation and race were indistinguishable, and thus the struggle for the survival of the Aryan race and German nation necessitated the subjugation and even extermination of rival and hostile races.

World War II ended with the complete defeat of the fascist model of freedom through race war, and the revelations about the Holocaust made that model not just a military failure but morally completely beyond the pale. Yet it did not put an end to the idea of white freedom, of which fascism was merely one variant. Although the Soviet Union ultimately played the key role in the destruction of Nazi Germany, the liberal democracies of Britain and the United States also emerged victorious in the struggle with fascism, and they did so as representatives of a different kind of white freedom. It was certainly less deadly than the Nazi version, but nonetheless to an important extent based on the idea and practice that one must be white to be free.

At the same time, the era of the great wars challenged the idea of white freedom like never before. From the Korean and Egyptian revolutions of 1919 to the Quit India and Double V movements of World War II, peoples of color throughout the wartime world asserted a radically different vision of human liberty, which was not grounded in racial superiority. The war years, especially World War II, illustrated but ultimately did not resolve the contradictory nature of white freedom, in part because of the common need to overcome the fascist menace. With the surrender of Germany and Japan in 1945, however, the challenges to white freedom that had begun during the world wars became more urgent than ever, as we shall see in the final chapter of this book.

CHAPTER 6

Freedom Now?

THE FALL AND RISE OF WHITE FREEDOM
DURING THE COLD WAR

On May 8, 1945, spontaneous celebrations broke out in cities across the world as Nazi Germany formally and unconditionally surrendered to the Allied powers, ending World War II in Europe. In the city of Sétif on the coast of Algeria a crowd of several thousands gathered both to celebrate the victory and also to protest French colonial rule. Demonstrators marched through the city's streets with banners calling for a Free Algeria and the release of nationalist leader Messali Hadj. Scuffles broke out between the demonstrators and the French police, leading the latter to fire upon the crowd. Armed Algerians responded over the next few days, killing roughly one hundred French settlers (*pieds noirs*). This led the French military to crack down in force, along with *pieds noirs* vigilantes summarily executing hundreds of Algerian Muslims. By the time the violence ended, between 1,000 and 45,000 Algerians had perished. The full-fledged armed struggle to liberate Algeria from the French would not break out for another nine years, but the Sétif massacre marked the beginning of the end of colonial rule. On the day the war in Europe ended the war against European colonialism began.[1]

World War II brought an unprecedented series of challenges to the idea and practice of white freedom, exposing its weaknesses and inconsistencies as never before. In Europe in particular, it took the shape of a war for freedom and against racism. The contradiction of nations like the United States and Britain fighting against Nazi bigotry and for racially segregated and oppressive societies was not lost on most observers, especially their own citizens and subjects who belonged to those subordinate groups. As we saw in the previous chapter, the view of the war as a struggle for freedom and justice on many fronts engaged millions around the world, suggesting that victory should bring not just the defeat of fascism but a fundamentally new and more just world order.

The postwar challenge to white freedom took two primary forms. Most dramatically, after the war European nations relinquished most of their colonial possessions as peoples throughout the world struggled for national independence. The great wave of decolonization during the 1950s and 1960s fundamentally transformed the politics of the globe, creating a host of new independent nations in Asia and Africa and highlighting the diminished power of white Europeans in the postwar era. At the same time, the civil rights movement in the United States exposed and challenged the contradiction between the American ideal of liberty and the American practice of racial discrimination, not only addressing the grievances of African Americans but also serving as a model for other movements for racial and social justice. The movements for colonial liberation and for civil rights both grew directly out of the wartime experience, and together they posited and demanded a vision of freedom that would be truly egalitarian and postracial.

To a very important extent, these movements transformed both the nature of freedom and the world in general in the decades after 1945. A generation after the dropping of the atomic bomb on Hiroshima, President Lyndon Johnson signed into law the Civil Rights Act of 1964 banning racial discrimination in America. By that year virtually all the former European colonies had achieved independence, so that Black, brown, and Asian national leaders sat next to their white colleagues at the United Nations as peers and equals. In sharp contrast to the League of Nations in 1919, the 1945 United Nations Charter linked freedom and racial equality, stating its belief in "promoting and encouraging respect for human rights and for *fundamental freedoms* for all without distinction as to race, sex, language, or religion" (emphasis added).[2] The idea that all men (and, increasingly, women) deserved to be free became a staple of political discourse after 1945.

And yet the idea and especially the practice of white freedom survived and even prospered in the late twentieth century. By the time of the election of Margaret Thatcher in 1979 and Ronald Reagan in 1980, racial difference had reasserted itself as a major factor in European and American political life. The rise of a new conservative movement that emphasized the freedom of the individual against the demands of the welfare state went hand in hand with a "whitelash" against minorities as privileged recipients and symbols of that new political order. Many former colonies became authoritarian regimes after independence, thus introducing a new global contrast between the freedom of whites and the oppression of nonwhites. In a world where colonial liberation all too often turned into a postcolonial impoverished reality, migrants from Asia and Africa sought a better life in Europe's former imperial powers, introducing new complications of race and politics there. As humanity approached the dawn of the twenty-first century, freedom and whiteness in many respects still went together.

This final chapter will explore the postwar struggle against white freedom, making note of its many victories as well as the fact that racialized ideas and realities of liberty remained a potent force at the end of the twentieth century. The survival of white freedom illustrated just how deeply rooted it was in global political culture, so that even powerful mass movements did not dislodge it completely. Dominant political ideologies might proclaim the importance of both racial equality and human freedom, but white identity and white privilege nonetheless remain significant determinants of the ability to be free.

The Fight for a Free World

Liberty and Race in the Cold War Era

In 1942 Twentieth Century-Fox released the documentary film *Prelude to War*, part of the Why We Fight series directed by Frank Capra. The documentary, an analysis of the rise of fascism and a clarion call for

America's entry into the struggle against it, centered around the portrayal of two planets, one white and one Black, one free and one slave. It quoted Henry Wallace's statement that "This is a fight between a free world and a slave world." At the end of the film the white planet literally eclipses and destroys the Black planet as the narrator dramatically proclaims, "Two worlds stand against each other. One must die, one must live." In *Prelude to War* the struggle for freedom was a struggle for whiteness.[3]

The idea of the free world, based in a Manichean struggle between light and dark, may have originated in World War II, but it became a defining characteristic of the cold war.[4] In March 1947, President Harry Truman delivered a speech before Congress that proclaimed what came to be known as the Truman doctrine of resistance to global communism. In the context of a struggle between a Western-oriented authoritarian regime and Communist insurgents in Greece, Truman declared:

> We shall not realize our objectives, however, unless we are willing to help free peoples to maintain their free institutions and their national integrity against aggressive movements that seek to impose upon them totalitarian regimes. . . . At the present moment in world history nearly every nation must choose between alternative ways of life. The choice is too often not a free one. One way of life is based upon the will of the majority, and is distinguished by free institutions, representative government, free elections, guarantees of individual liberty, freedom of speech and religion, and freedom from political oppression. The second way of life is based upon the will of a minority forcibly imposed upon the majority. It relies upon terror and oppression, a controlled press and radio; fixed elections, and the suppression of personal freedoms.[5]

A year earlier Winston Churchill had delivered his famous speech in Fulton, Missouri, warning against the existence of an Iron Curtain dividing Europe in the aftermath of World War II.[6] The two leaders thus established a world divided between free and unfree, between light and darkness.

The concept of the free world clearly referred to the United States and the liberal democracies of Western Europe, whereas the Soviet Union and its Communist satellite states in Eastern Europe constituted the unfree world of captive nations. At the end of World War I, as we saw in the previous chapter, the Peace of Paris had effectively consti- tuted Europe as a free space, giving its blessing to the establishment of newly independent and democratic European states east of the Rhine River while tolerating the persistence of colonial rule elsewhere. This had broken down partially during the interwar years, with most of the new Eastern European states falling into authoritarian rule but nonethe- less remaining independent. From the perspective of the Western allies, they had gone to war to free occupied Europe from Nazi rule, only to see the eastern half of the continent subjected to a new authoritarianism— communist dictatorship—after 1945. The fact that freedom remained alien to large parts of the European continent seemed a violation of the world order established by the victorious powers in 1919, of the idea that Europe should be free.

It is easy enough to point out the contradictions inherent in the cold war concept of the free world. It included a number of nations, for ex- ample Spain and Portugal, ruled by anti-Communist dictatorships. No one seemed quite sure how to classify Yugoslavia, after 1945 a Commu- nist authoritarian state but nonaligned and the recipient of significant American aid.[7] Most notably for the purposes of this study, however, the concept of the free world during the cold war had an ambivalent relationship to Europe's colonies in Asia and Africa. In his Iron Curtain speech, for example, Winston Churchill stated, "We cannot be blind to the fact that the liberties enjoyed by individual citizens throughout the British Empire are not valid in a considerable number of countries, some of which are very powerful."[8] Yet these colonies did not generally enjoy rights like representative institutions and civil liberties character- istic of the free world, and as a result were usually ignored in discussions of it. The free world thus included a lot of people who were not free.

Revisionist historians of the cold war have responded to this para- dox by accusing the West of hypocrisy. The real issue, many have ar- gued, was less freedom than capitalism, and as long as regimes accepted the capitalist global order they were therefore part of the "free" world.[9] As William Appleman Williams has argued:

> Beginning with the rise of Jacksonian Democracy during the 1820s, moreover, Americans steadily deepened their commitment to the idea that democracy was inextricably connected with individualism, private property, and a capitalist market economy. . . . Seen in historical perspective, therefore, what we are accustomed to call the Cold War . . . is in reality only the most recent phase of a more general conflict between the established system of western capitalism and its internal and external opponents.[10]

There is much truth to this, of course, but I'd like to propose an alternate perspective, namely that the concept of the free world centered around ideas of freedom as whiteness. In particular, Western cold warriors were outraged by the denial of freedom and independence to the white nations of Eastern Europe, an outrage that certainly did not extend to the absence of self-determination for the peoples of the colonial world. White people must be free, and any political order that denied this freedom, be it either fascist or communist, was simply beyond the pale.

Let us consider, for example, the idea of "captive nations," widely applied to the Communist satellite states of Eastern Europe during the cold war.[11] During the early 1950s natives from several Eastern European countries exiled in America formed the Assembly of Captive European Nations, and for the next several years organized to raise awareness among both government officials and the American public as a whole of the plight of their homelands.[12] In 1959 President Dwight Eisenhower proclaimed "Captive Nations Week" in support of their efforts to publicize and ultimately overthrow the authoritarian regimes of Communist Eastern Europe. The US Congress passed a supporting resolution, stating that:

> Whereas the enslavement of a substantial part of the world's population by Communist imperialism makes a mockery of the idea of peaceful coexistence between nations and constitutes a detriment to the natural bonds of understanding between the people of the United States and other peoples; and

Whereas the imperialistic policies of Communist Russia have led, through direct and indirect aggression, to the subjugation of the national independence of Poland, Hungary, Lithuania, Ukraine, Czechoslovakia, Latvia, Estonia, White Ruthenia, Rumania, East Germany, Bulgaria, mainland China, Armenia, Azerbaijan, Georgia, North Korea, Albania, Idel-Ural, Tibet, Cossackia, Turkestan, North Viet-Nam, and others;

Now, therefore, be it resolved by the Senate and House of Representatives of the United States of America in Congress assembled,

That the President of the United States is authorized and requested to issue a proclamation designating the third week in July 1959 as "Captive Nations Week" and inviting the people of the United States to observe such week with appropriate ceremonies and activities.[13]

Not all in the West during the cold war approved of the idea of captive nations. Some Soviet exiles, for example, argued that it neglected the absence of freedom in Russia itself, and others considered it too provocative, committing the American government to the overthrow of foreign governments.[14] What is interesting here is the attack on Communist rule as imperialistic, at a time when the US government had backed away from its earlier opposition to European colonialism. The list of captive nations in the resolution is predominantly European, with some exceptions. Even though the resolution began by emphasizing America's commitment to racial equality, signaling the impact of both decolonization and the civil rights movement (which this chapter will address below in depth), in effect it highlights the idea that imperialism and enslavement were especially egregious when applied to white people. No one referred to British and French colonies in Africa and Asia as "captive nations," or for that matter as nations at all. The idea that countries like Poland and Hungary had been sovereign and independent, only to be occupied by a foreign power, lay at the heart of the idea of captive nations. But because this idea applied primarily to Eastern Europe, it had an important racial dimension. Captive nations were those denied the privilege of white freedom.

This emphasis on white freedom in the cold war included a view of the conflict as the opposition between liberty and slavery. In April 1950, officials of the US Department of State drew up a secret memo for President Truman entitled "United States Objectives and Programs for National Security." One of the most forthright statements of the American view of the cold war, what became known as NSC-68 dramatically portrayed a world divided between Western freedom and Communist slavery, a total conflict that only one side could win.

> The antipathy of slavery to freedom explains the iron curtain, the isolation, the autarchy of the society whose end is absolute power. The existence and persistence of the idea of freedom is a permanent and continuous threat to the foundation of the slave society; and it therefore regards as intolerable the long continued existence of freedom in the world. What is new, what makes the continuing crisis, is the polarization of power which now inescapably confronts the slave society with the free.[15]

NSC-68 conceived of freedom as a progressive ideal; the document praised diversity as one of the key strengths of a free society, and it explicitly condemned colonialism as well. Planners wrote it in the aftermath of the shock produced by the Communist victory in China and focused on the threat to the Eurasian continent as a whole. Nonetheless, the heavy emphasis on the opposed tropes of freedom and slavery inevitably recalled the polarity between white and Black, between white freedom and Black slavery. The focus of this document, and of American cold war ideology generally, on the enslaved nature of the Soviet Union's Eastern European satellites reinforced the perspective that something was wrong with a world in which white people lived in bondage. The struggle against communism was thus a struggle for their liberation, and for white freedom in general.[16]

The idea of freedom that powered the anticommunist perspective during the cold war emphasized the classic liberal tenets of liberty: freedom of expression, individual freedom, freedom from political oppression; in short, freedom *from*. But this was not the only interpretation of freedom to emerge from the cauldron of World War II, and especially from the struggles against fascism. For many, the defeat of the fascist dictators represented not just a victory for individual liberty but equally the triumph of a more just and socially egalitarian society. This vision, often distinctly anticapitalist if not necessarily revolutionary, felt the postwar world should not simply restore that of the prewar era but rather create social democracies, regimes that guaranteed adequate standards of living for all as well as individual liberties.[17] It was this interpretation of freedom that made Britain's Beveridge Report, a white paper that advocated national health care and social services, a runaway best seller in 1942.[18]

In March 1944, the French National Resistance Council published a charter outlining its vision for France after the Liberation. It devoted several sections to the idea of national freedom, first political, then social and economic. Political freedoms included freedom of speech, assembly, and of the press; economic and social freedoms received more attention, including "the establishment of a true economic and social democracy," and "guarantees of wage levels that would assure each worker and his family security, dignity, and the possibility of a truly human life."[19] Significantly, as we shall shortly see, the document ended with a vague statement about guaranteeing the rights of natives and colonized populations.

Even in the United States the idea that social and economic prosperity and justice were central to freedom played an important role. In 1943 American artist Norman Rockwell painted his famous Four Freedoms series of oil paintings. One of the four scenes, *Freedom from Want*, showed a Thanksgiving table laden with food, a scene that spoke not only to the privations of the Depression but to the idea that freedom without a decent life for everyone was incomplete.[20] Whereas the Truman Doctrine of 1947 called for an armed struggle against Soviet subversion, the Marshall Plan of 1948 provided billions of dollars to help rebuild the economies of Western Europe in the belief that prosperity was democracy's best safeguard against communism.[21] Although the United States remained firmly committed to classic liberalism, after World War II it became clear that freedom must have an important social component.

Both concepts of freedom represented a reaction to the privations of World War II, to the oppressive authoritarianism of fascism, and to the social conditions that allowed fascist movements to thrive and take power. They represented a vision of a new, prosperous, and peaceful world that the Allied victory was supposed to bring. The fact that this did not happen in a large portion of the European continent meant that in effect victory was incomplete, that the cold war represented the continuation of the wartime struggle for liberty. The very idea of the cold war betrayed the Eurocentric bias of this perspective, because if the conflict between America and Russia did not bring armed conflict to Europe, the same was not true in other parts of the world. The battle between the two world views produced "hot" wars in Asia, especially Korea and Vietnam, so that whereas the cold war represented a campaign for white freedom, its actual military victims were mostly nonwhite.[22]

This happened largely because the rivalry between communism and the West soon intersected with the struggle against empire and for colonial independence. Ultimately, both interpretations of freedom in the postwar West had to wrestle with the challenge to imperialism. The movements for both decolonization and civil rights occurred during the cold war era, and both movements traced their origins to the Second World War. Above all, both centered around the idea of freedom, and their interactions highlighted the multiple forms this ideology could take. In particular, the contrast between anticommunist and anti-imperialist struggles was not only geographical but also racial. Their interplay would highlight both the struggle against white freedom and the reasons for its continued importance.

The Struggle for Freedom and the End of Empire

Not so very long ago, the earth numbered two thousand million inhabitants: five hundred million men, and one thousand five hundred million natives.

—JEAN-PAUL SARTRE[23]

I have not become the King's First Minister in order to preside over the liquidation of the British Empire.

—WINSTON CHURCHILL, 1942[24]

The collapse of formal European empires in the twenty years after the end of World War II was one of the most dramatic series of events in modern world history. In that generation Britain, France, and other European nations granted independence, willingly or not, to most of their colonial possessions. In much of the Asian continent and virtually all of Africa, colonies became independent nations, with their own flags, legislatures, and armies. The United Nations grew from 55 member states in 1946 to 117 in 1965, and most of the new members were former colonies in Africa, Asia, and the Caribbean. For the first time in history, the modern nation-state expanded beyond Europe and the Americas to embrace all the peoples of the world.[25]

For most political activists in the colonies, the struggle against colonialism was above all a struggle for freedom. In 1940, for example, the Indian National Congress passed a resolution demanding freedom and independence for India from the British Empire.

> The Congress hereby declares again that nothing short of complete independence can be accepted by the people of India. Indian freedom cannot exist within the orbit of imperialism, and dominion status, or any other status within the imperial structure is wholly inapplicable to India, is not in keeping with the dignity of a great nation, and would bind India in many ways to British policies and economic structure. The people of India alone can properly shape their own constitution and determine their relations to the other countries of the world, through a Constituent Assembly elected on the basis of adult suffrage.[26]

During the 1950s and 1960s many other anticolonial activists clothed their struggles against empire in the language of freedom. Kwame Nkrumah, leader of the Gold Coast's anticolonial movement and first president of the independent nation of Ghana, wrote several books and essays on the topic of colonial freedom and the anti-imperialist movement to achieve it. In *I Speak of Freedom*, for example, he wrote: "People listening to my speeches throughout the years could not have failed to notice two recurrent themes. The first is freedom of the individual. The second is political independence, not just for Ghana or West Africa, but for all Africa. I do not know how anyone can refuse to acknowledge the right of men to be free."[27]

Other leaders of the colonial struggle for independence after World War II spoke and wrote extensively about their movement as a freedom struggle and commented on the different aspects of that freedom. Julius Nyerere, the first president of independent Tanzania, wrote some six separate books with the word *freedom* in the title.[28] His classic essay, "Freedom and Development," began with a concise definition of the meaning of freedom for the people of newly independent Tanzania:

> For what do we mean when we talk of freedom? First, there is national freedom; that is, the ability of the citizens of Tanzania to determine their own future and to govern themselves without interference from non-Tanzanians. Second, there is freedom from hunger, disease, and poverty. And third, there is personal freedom for the individual; that is, his right to live in dignity and equality with all others, his right to freedom of speech, freedom to participate in the making of all decisions which affect his life, and freedom from arbitrary arrest because he happens to annoy someone in authority—and so on. All these things are aspects of freedom, and the citizens of Tanzania cannot be said to be truly free until all of them are assured.[29]

The passages quoted above delineate multiple meanings of freedom, but two stand out: freedom for the individual and freedom for the nation.[30] Postwar anticolonial struggles focused on national independence as both the ultimate goal and as a necessary precondition for personal freedom. Only through independence from the colonial overlord could the colonized peoples realize the freedom of the individual. For many anticolonial activists and proponents, a key aspect of personal freedom that could come only with the end of colonial rule was racial equality, the ability of all members of society to be treated the same regardless of their race. As many historians and other scholars have argued, racism formed a central aspect of colonial societies during the modern era.[31] Not only was the general structure of colonialism rule by a minority of white Europeans over masses of nonwhites in Asia, Africa, and the Caribbean, but a complex range of legal, social, and cultural practices established racial difference and discrimination as key aspects of the colonial order. Racist practices were perhaps worst in white settler colonies, such as Rhodesia and Algeria, but throughout the colonial world white privilege was the norm.[32] In his autobiography, *Freedom and After*, Tom Mboya, a trade unionist who later became one of the leaders of Kenyan independence, described having to negotiate racial boundaries in colonial Kenya:

> But there were a good many . . . racial incidents. I was put under a European inspector to gain experience, and the two of us went around Nairobi together several times in the course of our work. I was surprised to find that from time to time he expected me to sit in the car when he went to inspect premises. I refused to do this and we had some heated words. He drove back to City Hall and said we could never work together again.
>
> A number of times I was thrown out of premises I had gone to inspect by Europeans who insisted they wanted a European, not an African, to do the job . . . even inside the department there was discrimination. African inspectors were paid only one-fifth of the salary which a European inspector received for doing the same job.[33]

As Mboya's comments suggest, colonial racism had a particular impact upon native elites, one that increased over time. As colonial societies grew more complex under imperial rule, it became necessary to promote educated native subjects to positions of some responsibility, even if always under the supervision and control of Europeans. These individuals, like Mboya, often found themselves in situations where they were doing the same work and had the same qualifications as Europeans, but with significantly less authority. Moreover, they were often consigned to live in segregated "native" quarters even when they could afford to live in nicer areas that were reserved solely for Europeans. For many, consequently, colonial oppression was a matter of racial discrimination pure and simple.[34] The well-known example of Mohandas Gandhi's expulsion from a South African train in 1893, because he was riding in a first-class compartment ostensibly reserved for whites, exemplified the impact of racism on colonial elites. Gandhi, a young lawyer at the time, was inspired by the incident to stay in South Africa and fight for the rights of Indians, developing the techniques of nonviolent resistance that would ultimately go on to transform colonial India (and earn him the honorific title of Mahatma).[35] Among other things, his example would decades later be a model for another transformative act of resistance to segregation on public transportation, that of Rosa Parks.[36]

Especially in the early years of the struggles against empire, social elites dominated many anticolonial movements. The founding members of the Indian National Congress, for example, were educated men, mostly lawyers and journalists.[37] Some historians and other scholars have argued that social and intellectual elites often led struggles against colonial rule because they had the economic and cultural resources necessary to do so.[38] But I would also argue that these elites came together first to pursue racial justice in the colonial context. As the slim possibility of this became increasingly clear, they began to demand national independence as the only way of guaranteeing racial equality. Even when they grew into mass movements, anticolonial campaigns emphasized freedom for all, without regard to race.[39] As Kwame Nkrumah put it in *Freedom Now*: "Many of the advocates of colonialism claimed in the past—as some of them do now—they were racially superior and had a special mission to colonise and rule other people. This we reject. We repudiate and condemn all forms of racialism, for racialism not only injures those people against whom it is used but warps and perverts the very people who preach and protect it."[40] The anticolonial freedom struggle was thus a struggle against white freedom, in which national liberation from European rule would bring liberty for peoples of every race and heritage.[41]

The social elites that fought for colonial liberation were also usually male elites, a fact that calls for an analysis of the role played by gender

in the history of decolonization. Women engaged in anticolonial struggles in a variety of ways, ranging from critiques of the masculine leadership of the movement to active participation of many different kinds.
Feminist scholars have long critiqued and debated Frantz Fanon's attitudes to gender, notably in his important essay "Algeria Unveiled."[42]
Women played an instrumental role in the fight for the independence
of India and Pakistan, for example, not just as family members of male
movement leaders but as leaders in their own right.[43] Throughout the
colonial world women also took up arms for freedom, ranging from the
Algerian women who planted bombs in the European quarter during
the Battle of Algiers to the women of Zimbabwe who fought in guerilla
armies against the British.[44] The struggle against white freedom thus
developed as a struggle for the liberty of all.

Movements for colonial freedom and independence took many different forms, ranging from the peaceful and orderly turnover of power
to violent conflicts and cataclysmic wars. Studies of decolonization for
a long time contrasted the relatively peaceful end of the British Empire
with the violent anticolonial struggles that consumed France, and to a
lesser extent the Netherlands and Belgium.[45] Yet even the end of British
rule over the Indian subcontinent in 1947 led to the deaths of hundreds
of thousands of people in intercommunal violence as India and Pakistan
established themselves as independent nations.[46] At the same time the
British withdrawal from Palestine produced bitter warfare between Is-
raelis and Palestinian Arabs, a war that over seventy years later has yet
to end.[47] Not for nothing has Frantz Fanon's *The Wretched of the Earth*,
which is among other things an extended meditation on the poetics of
violence, become the classic text of the decolonization era.[48]

In short, violence was endemic to the end of European empire after
World War II, and although it took many different forms, race frequently
played a key role in the carnage. This was especially true of the great
wars of decolonization, such as in Kenya, Indochina, and above all Algeria.[49] These military conflicts between anticolonial militants fighting
for independence and the forces of order committed to maintaining
imperial rule often took on the character of race wars. In particular, in
colonies that, like Algeria and Kenya, combined major insurgencies

with a large European settler population, the conflicts over independence derived much of their brutality from racial conflict. Fanon considered race central to colonialism and anticolonial violence merely a reaction to the racial violence of the imperial order. In his chapter "On Violence" he argued: "Looking at the immediacies of the colonial context, it is clear that what divides this world is first and foremost what species, what race one belongs to. In the colonies the economic infrastructure is also a superstructure. The cause is effect: You are rich because you are white, you are white because you are rich."[50] During the insurgencies in both Kenya and Algeria, guerrillas and imperial troops massacred civilians indiscriminately, largely because of their racial identities. The British in Kenya placed virtually the entire Kikuyu Nation under administrative detainment, during which thousands of people died from abuse.[51] In Algeria, the French military responded to FLN attacks against white settlers by slaughtering hundreds of thousands of Arab civilians, as during the Philippeville massacre of 1955.[52] This racial violence extended to metropolitan France, most notably during the police riot of October 17, 1961, which killed up to two hundred Algerians in the heart of central Paris.[53]

The violence of decolonization reaffirmed the relationship between freedom and race, and the challenge to white freedom, in the decades after World War II. All too often imperial authorities responded to colonial movements for liberation by racially informed repression, in effect reinforcing the reality that to be nonwhite was to be unfree.[54] More generally, the resistance to decolonization, even if it involved reforms and more liberal visions of colonial life, fundamentally rested upon the conviction that white elites had not only a monopoly on freedom but the right to rule nonwhite populations around the world. Decolonization ultimately destroyed that conviction, at least in theory, and so upended traditional parallels between whiteness and freedom.

In doing so, decolonization did not affect just the colonies. As a generation of Europeanist historians has argued, the end of empire reshaped life in the metropoles as much as it did in their colonial possessions.[55] Especially for Britain and France, decolonization and the retreat from empire had a major impact on how those nations saw themselves and their relationships to the wider world. In an era of superpowers, the attempt to maintain imperial power represented both their efforts to cling to great power status and, to a significant extent, their failure to do so. As Kristin Ross has argued for France, the loss of the colonies also implied Europeans' new status as colonies of the United States.[56]

Just as the creation of European colonial empires in the nineteenth century went together with the rise of liberal democracy, so too did decolonization coincide with the turn toward social democracy in Europe after World War II. Facing the need to rebuild from the devastation of the war, many Europeans saw themselves confronted with a choice between fighting to retain their empires and investing in physical and social reconstruction at home. The parallel was closest in Britain, where the first majority-based Labour government, elected in 1945, presided over the granting of independence to India and Pakistan at the same time as it implemented a major expansion of welfare state policies.[57] In France as well the retreat from formal empire under the Fourth Republic took place at the same time as the dramatic growth of *l'état providence*.[58] Social democracy, which blended the mass character of liberal democracy with the socialist commitment to social equality, or at least the guarantee of basic living standards, arose inexorably from the trauma of the Second World War, as did widespread decolonization.

As noted at the beginning of this chapter, social democracy rose out of a new conceptualization of freedom that emphasized not just individual liberties but also social justice and mass well-being. The fact that the rise of the welfare state in Europe took place at the same time as the collapse of colonialism raises the question of the relationship between the two: why was jettisoning the empire integral to the creation of freer, more democratic European societies? Such a formulation shows how far postwar Europe had come from the social imperialism of Cecil Rhodes and others at the beginning of the century, the belief that colonial exploitation would guarantee higher living standards in the metropole. In Britain in particular, many saw the cost of empire as outweighing its benefits after 1945 and argued that ensuring the prosperity and freedom of the metropole meant getting rid of the colonies.[59] France managed to create the structures of social democracy while at the same time fighting two ruinous colonial wars, but by the end of the 1950s much of the French nation had come to the same conclusion, that empire wasn't worth it.[60]

The turn against empire in postwar Europe was not only economic, however, but also had a significant racial component. Decolonization was not the only alternative to imperialism in the years after 1945. One could also transcend the colonial past by granting the colonies not independence but equality in the national framework.[61] In 1950, for example, Léopold Senghor developed the idea of *Eurafrique* as a nation in which Africans and metropolitan French would enjoy equal rights and status.[62] The constitution of France's Fourth Republic, promulgated in 1946, had abolished the legal distinction between metropolitan citizens and colonial subjects, yet it still fell far short of Senghor's egalitarian idea. Ultimately the vision of a truly multicultural France, the majority of whose population would be non-European and nonwhite, was simply not feasible. Ideas of the equality of all members of the national community, not just in principle but in fact as well, could not accommodate the radical, and racialized, inequality between colonizer and colonized. Given a choice between making the natives equal or setting them free, the logic of decolonization led inexorably to the latter.[63] Granting the colonies national independence might create new multiracial ideas of liberty, but it would at the same time preserve the European metropoles as a space for white freedom.

The actions and attitudes of the United States constituted a final important aspect of the history of race and freedom in the process of decolonization. In 1945 America was not only the most powerful nation in the world but was also widely acknowledged as the global standard bearer of freedom. During the war the US government had made its disapproval of European colonialism clear; for President Roosevelt, for example, the Atlantic Charter of 1942 was meant to apply to all peoples, not just those occupied by the Axis powers.[64] The Americans also practiced what they preached with their own empire. Having agreed in 1934 to grant independence to the Philippines after a ten-year waiting period, in 1946 the US formally ended colonial control over that nation.[65] A little over a decade later America implemented Senghor's alternative route of postcolonial equality by making Hawaii a full-fledged state, the only state with a majority nonwhite population.[66]

After victory was assured, America took steps to prevent the restoration of the European empires.[67] In particular, Washington was concerned they would hurt free trade or, in essence, America's ability to dominate the global economy, so it tailored its financial aid to its former allies to prevent that from happening. The most prominent example of this was the Anglo-American Loan Agreement of 1946. Under its terms America loaned an economically prostrate Britain 3.75 billion pounds, at extremely low interest rates, to help it rebuild. However, one important term of the loan was that the pound be made convertible to the dollar within twelve months. The impact of this was in effect to force London to choose between its welfare state programs and its overseas commitments, and the political climate forced it to choose the former. As William Roger Louis and Ronald Robinson put it, "The imperial economy, in effect, was to be dismantled."[68]

By the end of the 1940s, however, American opposition to European imperialism had diminished significantly. As the cold war intensified, many American policymakers began to rethink their support for anticolonialism, particularly anticolonial insurgencies led by (or perceived to be led by) communists.[69] This was especially true as the cold war became a major concern in Asia, and above all with the Communist victory in China and the Korean war. The fact that both Maoist China and North Korea saw themselves as very much a part of the global revolt against European imperialism led many in Washington to see anticolonial revolutions in general as primarily communist movements dedicated to the suppression of freedom rather than popular struggles for liberty.[70] By the beginning of the 1950s, therefore, the US government had in effect committed itself to propping up the European empires as a bulwark against communism.

The most notable example of this was the French war in Indochina.[71] During World War II the United States had supported the Viet Minh in its struggle against the Japanese occupation of Vietnam. The French decision in 1946 to reoccupy Indochina by force in 1946, and its bombardment of Haiphong Harbor and landing of troops in the North in

FIGURE 28. Captured French soldiers, escorted by Vietnamese troops, walk to a prisoner-of-war camp in Dien Bien Phu (1954). http://www.ibtimes.co.uk/vietnam-celebrates-60th-anniversary-battle-dien-bien-phu-victory-1447556.

November, forced the US to reassess its position. America's primary concern was the threat of communism in Europe, and in France, French Communist support for the Viet Minh was not only one of the party's key commitments but also one of the major factors in the collapse of the Tripartite coalition with the Socialist Party.[72] The logic of anticommunism in Europe thus led the US inexorably to support the French war in Indochina against the Communist Viet Minh, so that in effect the war in Southeast Asia became a kind of proxy for the cold war in France. By the end of the war in 1954 the US government was shouldering the lion's share of the financial burden for the French war and would of course go on to pursue its own disastrous conflict in Vietnam. America would fight for the freedom of the natives from Communist rule, even if it meant supporting colonial and racist rule. Political freedom was important, but ultimately must not conflict with white freedom.[73]

The history of the first Indochina war illustrates the fact that postwar decolonization took place in the context of the cold war. For America in particular, the struggle against communism was a global phenomenon and also had a significant racial dimension. Preserving free Europe from Soviet rule generally took priority, even if the rise of communism in China and elsewhere in Asia led it to wage war there to forestall its spread. The fact that America's anticommunist wars in Asia had their own colonial and racial dimension affirmed the place of white freedom in its cold war crusade.[74] At the same time, the fact that American society was hardly immune from racial prejudice had its own implications for American anticommunism. The next section of this chapter will explore the significance of the challenge to white freedom posed by the civil rights movement for the relationship between race and liberty both in the United States and on a global scale.

The Struggle for Black Freedom in the Land of Liberty

Oh, freedom!
Oh, freedom!
Oh, freedom over me!
And before I'd be a slave
I'll be buried in my grave
And go home to my Lord and be free.

—AFRICAN AMERICAN SPIRITUAL

When we allow freedom to ring . . . we will be able to speed up that day when all of God's children, Black men and white men, Jews and Gentiles, Protestants and Catholics, will be able to join hands and sing in the words of the old Negro spiritual, "Free at last, Free at last, Great God a-mighty, We are free at last."

—DR. MARTIN LUTHER KING JR., "I HAVE A DREAM,"
MARCH ON WASHINGTON, 1963

On March 5, 1957, the people of Ghana celebrated the end of British rule and the independence of their new nation. One of Kwame Nkrumah's invited guests was Martin Luther King Jr., experiencing his first moments in the international limelight after the triumph of the Montgomery bus boycott the year before. At one point he commented to another American guest, Vice President Richard M. Nixon, that "I'm very glad to meet you here, but I want you to come visit us down in Alabama, where we are seeking the same kind of freedom Ghana is celebrating."[75]

At the end of World War II the United States was not only the wealthiest and most powerful nation on earth but also prided itself on being the most free. Whereas the great industrial powers of Germany and Japan were dominated by bombed-out cities and shattered factories, America produced half of the world's manufactured goods in 1945. The Soviet Union might have a larger army, but the US alone had the atomic bomb. Moreover, unlike most other wartime belligerents, America's population had actually grown between 1939 and 1945. Not for nothing did *Time* publisher Henry Luce proclaim the dawn of the American Century at the end of the war.[76]

Yet at least as important for many Americans was not just their nation's military and economic prowess but its freedom. From being the ultimate refuge for refugees from Nazism during the 1930s to leading the global military crusade against fascism in both Asia and Europe during the 1940s, Americans prided themselves on their commitment to freedom for all of humanity. With the onset of the cold war the American struggle for liberty assumed a new form, the fight against world communism, but this shift only reemphasized the importance of freedom to American life and the centrality of America to the global fight for liberty.[77]

One must approach the history of the postwar civil rights movement from the perspective of this broader context, the general history of freedom in America. For example, Martin Luther King Jr.'s "I Have a Dream" speech focused on the phrase *Let freedom ring*, a line drawn directly from the famous patriotic song "My Country 'Tis of Thee." As historians Brenda Gayle Plummer, Penny Von Eschen, and Mary Dudziak have demonstrated, the history of the civil rights movement is intimately connected with that of the cold war: American policymakers constantly had to confront, when preaching alliances to peoples overseas, the contradiction between America as the land of freedom and its oppression of its Black population. One could not convincingly champion freedom globally while denying it locally.[78]

The issue of freedom was thus central to the civil rights movement, and also made that movement central to American history. Historians have debated how to draw the boundaries of the movement, both geographically and chronologically.[79] From looking at the movement's relationship to US foreign policy to considering how peoples around the world reacted to it, studies have considered the ways in which the struggle for Black liberation went far beyond the borders of the US South.[80] At the same time, scholars such as Adrienne Lentz-Smith and Chad Williams have argued for a direct connection between the Black experience in World War I and the beginnings of the movement, for example, and many now point to efforts like the Double V campaign as ways in which World War II generated the struggle for civil rights.[81]

In one sense, of course, the fight for Black freedom in America began when the first African slave set foot on what was to become the United States some four hundred years ago. Nonetheless, for the purposes of this study it makes sense to focus on a narrow interpretation of the civil rights movement, ranging in time from the *Brown v. Board of Education of Topeka* Supreme Court decision in 1954 to the passage of the Voting Rights Act in 1965. Several reasons recommend this approach. In this era the movement had a geographical and thematic unity that tended to dissipate in later years. To a greater extent than in later years, it both appealed to and attracted significant white support by portraying the oppression of Blacks in America as a fundamental contradiction to the ideals of the republic. Frequently referred to as the Second Reconstruction, it explicitly linked itself to earlier struggles for racial justice. Moreover, focusing on these specific years highlights the movement's strong parallels with decolonization in Africa and Asia, parallels evident at the time and commented upon ever since.[82]

Above all, the civil rights movement of the 1950s and 1960s saw itself as a movement for freedom, making the idea of liberation from racism the essence of what it strove to achieve. Like decolonization, but perhaps to an even greater extent, the civil rights movement argued that all peoples should be free, no matter what the color of their skins. Phrases like *freedom rides, freedom schools, freedom trains, freedom marches,* and *freedom summer* summed up its central ideas. The number of books about the movement, both memoirs and histories, that contain the word *freedom* in their titles is almost too numerous to count.[83] As Martin Luther King Jr. argued in his "Letter from Birmingham Jail," freedom was the ultimate goal of the worldwide struggle against racism:

> Oppressed people cannot remain oppressed forever. The urge for freedom will eventually come. This is what has happened to the American Negro. Something within has reminded him of his birthright of freedom; something without has reminded him that he can gain it. Consciously and unconsciously, he has been swept in by what the Germans call the Zeitgeist, and with his Black brothers of Africa and his brown and yellow brothers of Asia, South America, and the Caribbean, he is moving with a sense of cosmic urgency toward the promised land of racial justice.[84]

The movement thus challenged white freedom as a contradiction, and like the battles for colonial liberation sought to move beyond it to a world where freedom had no color.

The emphasis on freedom went far beyond Martin Luther King Jr., of course. For African Americans living in the South, freedom meant above all the final realization of the abolition of slavery. It meant dismantling the entire apparatus of Jim Crow built up by the white Southern establishment to keep the former slaves dependent and subordinate. Not for nothing did the Black press hail *Brown v. Board of Education* as a "second Emancipation Proclamation."[85] Not for nothing did the Black church, the one institution in African American life that had given enslaved Blacks a glimpse of self-determination, frequently assume the leadership of the movement.[86] Not for nothing did the Black Muslims take new names (or non-names like X) to replace those inherited from the slave era. Within this broader context the civil rights movement struggled for many specific examples of freedom. As Eric Foner has put it: "[Freedom] meant enjoying the political rights and economic opportunities taken for granted by whites. It required eradicating historic wrongs such as segregation, disenfranchisement, confinement to low wage jobs, and the ever-present threat of violence. It meant the right to be served at lunch counters and downtown department stores . . . and to be addressed as 'Mr.,' 'Miss,' and 'Mrs.,' rather than 'boy' and 'auntie.'"[87] At its heart, however, the struggle for freedom waged by the civil rights movement took up the unfinished business of America's long battle over Black slavery. It meant risking (and suffering) beatings, imprisonment, even death, simply because in the end one would rather die a free man or woman than live as a slave. In 1901 George Henry White, the last of the Black Reconstruction-era congressmen from the South, had predicted that his people would rise again (see chapter 4). Some fifty-odd years later, his prophecy seemed about to come true.

Like Reconstruction, the history of the civil rights movement was dominated by two main issues: education and voting rights. Education would give Blacks the knowledge and understanding of how to protect their freedom, and voting rights would give them the ability to put that knowledge into practice. The two great bookends of the movement, *Brown v. Board of Education* in 1954 and the Voting Rights Act in 1965, illustrated the centrality of these issues to the new movement for Black freedom. They also highlighted its connection with the old: the freedom schools recalled those established by the Freedmen's Bureau for ex-slaves after the Civil War, and the emphasis on voting rights constituted a direct response to the overthrow of Reconstruction. In its struggle around these issues, the Second Reconstruction would succeed where the first had failed in finally abolishing slavery.

The movement to desegregate southern schools not only struck at the heart of American racism but also took place in a context of a new attention to education in general. America had long been a global leader in providing education for the masses, but this became even more important during the economic boom years after World War II, and it was especially true of higher education. In 1944 Congress passed the Servicemen's Readjustment Act, or GI Bill, which sent millions of veterans to college on the government dime, providing an unprecedented new model for mass higher education.[88] Public universities expanded impressively in the decades after World War II: to take one example, the University of California grew from two undergraduate campuses in 1943 to eight by 1965.[89] Leaders of government and industry argued that America must make this investment to secure the benefits of both economic prosperity and political liberty: as President Eisenhower argued, "No man flying a warplane, no man with a defensive gun in his hand, can possibly be more important than a teacher."[90] Mass higher education thus became a particularly American condition of freedom.

This was just part of a broader emphasis on education and schools in general. The "baby boom" between 1945 and 1964 brought an enormous new school-age population into American society, and many communities desperately scrambled to build new schools just to keep up.[91] The Soviet launch of the Sputnik satellite in October 1957 prompted massive government investment in public education, especially science education, in response to fears that America might lose its edge in science, technology, and defense-related knowledge in general.[92] The idea that a free populace must be an educated populace had deep roots in American culture, but never did this idea appear more important than in the era of the cold war.[93]

This emphasis on education as a key to liberty made the yawning gaps between the schooling of Blacks and whites more egregious than ever. First, America spent much more to educate white children than Black children at the start of the civil rights movement. This was especially true in the South: in 1945, southern states spent twice as much per white child as per Black child. Second, this went hand in hand with the overwhelming segregation of schools. In 1954, the year of the *Brown* decision, seventeen southern states *required* the racial segregation of schools, and four others permitted it.[94] The schools of the nation's capital had been segregated since the Civil War. Although most salient in the South, this was a national problem. School segregation in the North arose from segregated neighborhoods, but as Richard Rothstein has conclusively demonstrated in *The Color of Law*, neighborhood segregation itself arose from government policies.[95] School segregation both promoted racial inequality and made it manifestly clear: in 1940, for example, Mississippi's expenditures on Black schools were only fifteen percent of its expenditures on white schools. *Plessy v. Ferguson*, the 1896 Supreme Court decision that had upheld school segregation, had based its decision on the principle of "separate but equal."[96] Even a cursory glance at American public education after World War II, however, made it clear that segregated education was inherently unequal and racially discriminatory.

This was the essence not only of *Brown* but of the civil rights movement in general.[97] The *Brown* decision gave it a focus on the battle against segregation, one that embraced both the movement's legal and activist strategies. The struggle for school integration in particular became a central part of the movement, especially as the white Southern political establishment made it clear it would fight attempts to integrate Southern schools by any and all means necessary. When Black students tried to attend white schools and universities, they were frequently met with violence. In 1956 a mob prevented a Black woman, Autherine Lucy, from enrolling as a student at the University of Alabama. Five years later Alabama governor and segregationist firebrand George Wallace would literally stand in the doorway of the entrance to the university to prevent Black students from attending. In 1957 Arkansas governor Orval Faubus deployed the National Guard to stop nine Black students from enrolling in Little Rock's Central High School, only to be overruled by federal troops, who patrolled the school for a year. In 1962 James Meredith became the first Black student ever to enroll in the University of Mississippi, only after winning victories in the federal courts and in the face of white student riots.[98]

Inspired by *Brown*, the civil rights movement of the 1950s and early 1960s embraced the struggle against segregation in many different facets of American life. The movement's first mass campaign, the Montgomery Alabama bus boycott of 1955–56, demanded the right of Blacks to have the same access to the city's buses as whites, to sit anywhere on the bus no matter their race.[99] In February 1960, Black students in Greensboro, North Carolina, staged a sit-in in a Woolworth's lunch counter demanding the right to be served in an area reserved for whites. The sit-in movement spread rapidly throughout the South, mobilizing tens of thousands by the end of 1960 who campaigned for the integration of restaurants, swimming pools, movie theaters, and other public and commercial facilities.[100] These were followed by the freedom rides of 1961, in which integrated groups of passengers would ride buses throughout the South, defying local segregationist practices.[101]

But school segregation remained the most egregious, and most enduring, example of racial discrimination and white freedom during the civil rights movement. In theory, for example, the segregation of the Montgomery city buses did not have to be discriminatory: people on the front and back of the bus got to their destinations at the same time. This in essence was the logic of *Plessy v. Ferguson*. In reality, however, as the situation of the public schools so graphically demonstrated, segregation meant white privilege and Black inferiority. This simple reality explained both the mass mobilization of southern Blacks, in spite of the apparatus of white terror that all too often confronted them, and the fierce resistance of southern whites. Racial segregation in the South (and, as we shall see, in America generally) was the bulwark, the front line of defense of the whole apparatus of white freedom, now under assault as it had not been since Reconstruction.

The other main theme of the civil rights movement was the right to vote: if *Brown* marked the beginnings of the movement in 1954, the Voting Rights Act signaled its culmination in 1965. As we saw in chapter 4, the entire edifice of Jim Crow rested on the massive disenfranchisement of Black freedmen throughout the South after Reconstruction. Because few African Americans could vote, white local governments were free to implement a range of segregationist and racist legislation. At the national level as well, Southern congressmen and senators fought effectively against any challenges to the racist hierarchies in their home districts. As Frederick Douglass had recognized a century early, the right and ability of Blacks to vote was the essential requirement for the final destruction of slavery and thus the precondition for Black freedom. The integration of Southern society depended on the ability of Blacks to exercise political power, and by the early 1960s the struggle to register African Americans to vote had become the heart of the civil rights movement.

The campaign for Black enfranchisement in the South was led by SNCC, the Student Nonviolent Coordinating Committee. Formed by Black students in April 1960 under the sponsorship of major civil rights organizations like the Southern Christian Leadership Conference, SNCC cut its teeth in the freedom rides and sit-ins but soon developed

FIGURE 29. March on Washington for Jobs and Freedom (photographer unknown). August 28, 1963. U.S. National Archives and Records Administration (NAID 542003). Still Picture Records Section, Special Media Services Division (NWCS-S).

its own independent perspective on the movement.[102] Starting in the fall of 1961, under the leadership of activist Bob Moses, SNCC began a project to register Black voters in McComb County, Mississippi.[103] Local whites responded with violence, including the murder of a local Black man, and most of the SNCC volunteers saw jail time by the end of the year. Voter registration work was painstakingly difficult and extremely dangerous: not only did organizers risk violence but they also put their local Black hosts in peril. On several occasions, racist vigilantes firebombed the homes of Blacks who hosted civil rights workers. Yet SNCC persisted, seeing voting as the key to the overthrow of Jim Crow. It adopted the campaign slogan *One man, one vote* and stepped up its efforts. As Bob Moses argued, "[Blacks in Mississippi] want to learn. They want to vote. They feel that for once they have a chance at bettering their conditions."[104]

Perhaps the most dramatic example of the campaign for voter registration was what SNCC called Freedom Summer. The successful March on Washington in 1963 had brought national attention and goodwill to the civil rights movement, but the white South still violently resisted attempts to enfranchise Blacks or overthrow Jim Crow. The fight for desegregation in Birmingham, Alabama, during which the chief of police, Eugene "Bull" Connor, attacked Black children with dogs and high-pressure fire hoses in the spring of 1963, made that abundantly clear. In response, SNCC and other civil rights organizations decided to launch a major voter registration drive in Mississippi during the summer of 1964. Freedom Summer built upon SNCC's local grassroots organizing in the state during 1963, including the organization of a mock vote that mobilized thousands. In February 1964 SNCC organizers began touring northern college campuses, recruiting white students to spend their summer in Mississippi registering Blacks to vote. In June volunteers underwent a week's training on a college campus in Oxford, Ohio, before heading south to enfranchise Black voters.[105]

In Mississippi they found the epicenter of American racism. Mississippi had a greater percentage of African Americans than any other state in the Union, and one of the smallest percentages of Black voters, less than seven percent of the Black population. It also had a record of lynchings of Black men unmatched anywhere else in America.[106] During the ten weeks of the project Black and white volunteers worked to register Blacks to vote as well as organizing freedom schools to teach subversive subjects like Black history and constitutional rights. Activists also organized the Mississippi Freedom Democratic Party, a parallel political organization that ran its own elections and went on to challenge the regular state party at the Democratic National Convention in August.

Freedom Summer volunteers did this in the face of considerable violent resistance. More than one thousand volunteers were arrested, eighty were beaten, and more than thirty Black churches and homes were firebombed during Freedom Summer. On the first day of Freedom Summer, local whites kidnapped three activists, James Chaney, Andrew Goodman, and Michael Schwerner, unleashing a massive manhunt that culminated with the discovery of their bodies six weeks later. The murder of the three civil rights volunteers, especially the fact that two of them were white, served to focus national attention on the situation of Blacks in Mississippi like never before.[107] Freedom Summer did not succeed in gaining the right to vote for most Blacks in the state, yet the campaign marked the beginning of the end for Jim Crow, not just in Mississippi but nationally. On July 2, President Johnson signed the Civil Rights Act of 1964, banning racial discrimination in public facilities and federal projects.[108] This was a major step forward, yet the new law's safeguards for voting rights were relatively weak. Clearly more was needed.

The groundwork for Black voting rights laid by Mississippi's Freedom Summer in 1964 came to fruition in 1965. In the early months of that year the campaign shifted to Selma, Alabama, where SNCC had been organizing Blacks to vote since 1963. On October 7, 1963, for example, it had declared "Freedom Day" in Selma, lining up hundreds of Blacks to register to vote: most were denied their rights by the local authorities. In early 1965 local activists invited Martin Luther King and the SCLC to Selma to lend their weight to the movement. King took part in several marches in Selma, and after one demonstrator was murdered by local police he and others organized a march from Selma to the state capital of Montgomery for voting rights. On March 7 the march left Selma only to be attacked by mounted police wielding whips, billy clubs, and other weapons. The images of "Bloody Sunday," with peaceful demonstrators being beaten by armed police for seeking to vote, were broadcast on television worldwide and shocked the nation. Hundreds of people from throughout America responded to the call to join a second march a week later while sympathy protests broke out across the country, including the first-ever sit-in at the White House itself.[109]

The violence led President Lyndon B. Johnson to speak up more forcefully than ever before in support of the civil rights movement and voting rights for Southern Blacks. Shortly after Bloody Sunday he gave a televised address to the nation, calling on all Americans to support the movement and using its own language to claim that "we shall overcome." In late March, the Johnson administration sent the draft of the Voting Rights Act to Congress for approval. The violence in Selma helped convince both the House of Representatives and the Senate to pass the bill by overwhelming majorities, and on August 6, 1965, President Johnson signed the Voting Rights Act into law. The new law outlined discriminatory practices like literacy tests designed to prevent Blacks from voting and deployed federal marshals throughout the South to enfranchise citizens of all races. It had an immediate and dramatic impact: by the end of 1965, sixty percent of eligible Blacks in Mississippi had registered to vote, and within two years a majority of Black adults in most of the former Confederacy had registered.[110] Southern states fought the new law tooth and nail, but by the end of the 1960s it was clear that a revolution had occurred in the old land of slavery. For once at least, the slogan *Freedom now* seemed to accurately describe not only the desires but the achievements of the civil rights movement, and it was freedom for all, not the white freedom that had so long dominated the region and the United States in general.

The Civil Rights Act of 1964 and the Voting Rights Act of 1965 paralleled the work of the Fourteenth and Fifteenth Amendments a century earlier. Both sets of laws had challenged the ideas of white freedom and Black slavery, and the fact that legislators had to reaffirm the legislation of the Reconstruction era one hundred years later showed just how pernicious and enduring those ideas were in American history. With the Voting Rights Act in particular the Second Reconstruction had triumphed, but how complete the triumph was, and whether one day a third Reconstruction would be necessary, remained to be seen.

White Freedom

Continuities and Rebirth, 1965–89

To an important degree, the year 1965 seemed to represent the definitive death of white freedom on a global scale. South Africa might still embrace apartheid and white Rhodesia declare its independence as a racial state, but most of the formerly colonial world had shaken off imperial rule for good. Moreover, Europe in general seemed to have definitively turned its back on empire; by the late 1960s Portugal, the one remaining European colonial power (and one of the poorest nations on the continent) futilely fought African wars of independence that would triumph within a decade. Increasingly the membership of the United Nations consisted of the nonwhite representatives of former colonies, now independent nations. In America, the Voting Rights Act marked the triumph of the classic phase of the civil rights movement.

I want to stress this point. So far, this book's tale has recounted the development of freedom and racism at the same time in the modern world, continually interacting to produce ideas and practices of liberty that depended on racial difference. The rise of racially defined empire on a global scale, followed by the antiliberal and genocidal racism of the Nazi era, dramatically weakened the idea of white freedom, and the antiracist and anticolonial insurgencies in America, Africa, and Asia after 1945 seemed to deal it a death blow. A generation after the end of World War II few peoples, political movements, or states throughout the world made the explicit argument that liberty depended on whiteness, or that only whites deserved to be free. Those that did, like South Africa, increasingly became international pariahs, out of step with modern visions of progress and justice. One could argue, therefore, that after 1965 white freedom became increasingly anachronistic, that in a sense this book should end here.

As we shall see in the rest of this chapter, however, there is more to the story. The late twentieth century witnessed the rise of new variants of white freedom, as the attempt to make freedom color-blind not only faltered in practice but also gave birth to new ways of linking liberty and racial hierarchies. Many peoples in the colonized world found it was a lot easier to raise the flag of independent new nations than to bring the many relations of dependency with the formal colonial powers to an end. In the United States, the civil rights movement fragmented as it moved from challenging legal segregation and white terror in the South to the broader structures of racial inequality in America, and this evolution provoked widespread opposition that embraced whiteness as an aspect of color-blind ideology. In both Europe and America, new powerful waves of immigration from the nonwhite Third World brought new racial distinctions and conflicts, making the contrast between white affluence and nonwhite poverty local as well as global. Finally,

the collapse of Soviet Communism in Eastern Europe and Russia signaled a major new era of freedom centered for the most part in Europe.
Looking at the world on the eve of the twenty-first century, whiteness
and freedom thus still seemed closely linked.

The final section of this chapter will therefore consider new forms of
white freedom that arose in the aftermath of, and to an important extent
in reaction to, the massive rejection of racism after 1945. It will explore
both their continuities with earlier forms of racialized liberty and the
ways in which they broke new ground. Freedom remained as important
a goal as ever on the eve of the twenty-first century, and for all too many
people across the world whiteness continued to be a crucial aspect of
their ability to be free.

Independence without Freedom

You know, Ali, it's hard enough to start a revolution, even harder to
sustain it, and hardest of all to win it. But it's only afterwards, once
we've won, that the real difficulties begin.

—GILLO PONTECORVO, *THE BATTLE OF ALGIERS*, 1966

On July 5, 1960, Émile Janssens, the commander of the Force Pub-
lique, Belgium's colonial army in the Congo, called a meeting of his officers to discuss the rapidly changing political situation. Although anti-
imperialist movements had come late to the Belgian Congo, they had
burst into full flower the year before, prompting a panicked administration in Brussels to accede to nationalist desires for the end of colonial
rule. A week earlier, on June 30, Belgium had formally granted independence to the new Congolese government. In convening his officers,
however, Janssens emphasized the continuity of military power, and
colonial rule in general. As he told them, "Independence brings changes
to politicians and to civilians. But for you, nothing will be changed . . .
none of your new masters can change the structure of an army which,
throughout its history, has been the most organized, the most victorious
in Africa." To emphasize his point, he wrote on the blackboard, "Before
independence = After independence."[111]

Give the devil his due. Congolese soldiers reacted to Janssens's speech with outrage, that night launching a revolt which soon spread all over the country and triggered Belgian military intervention a few days later. By the end of the year the newly independent nation was involved in a full-fledged civil war that threatened to mesh with the global cold war as rival factions appealed to both the United States and the Soviet Union for military aid. The Congo crisis came to an end only with the definitive seizure of power by Colonel Joseph-Désiré Mobutu, who established a military dictatorship over the country that endured until his overthrow in 1997. Mobutu's military regime harshly suppressed any political dissent while trading influence for economic favors with a series of foreign nations and companies. The dreams of freedom that powered the movement for independence in the Belgian Congo during the late 1950s bore bitter fruit in subsequent decades.[112]

A key theme in the study of postcolonial Asia and Africa has been the extent to which the end of formal empire did or did not bring about true independence and freedom for the formerly colonized. In 1965 Kwame Nkrumah published *Neo-Colonialism: The Highest Stage of Imperialism*, a ringing denunciation and analysis of the former colonial powers' continued influence on African and non-Western affairs. In *Neo-Colonialism* Nkrumah made it clear that national independence was only the beginning of a long struggle for true colonial liberation, that even without formal colonial rule the structures of imperialist domination remained largely intact. In Nkrumah's Marxist analysis the ultimate world struggle took place between rich and poor countries, which represented a much more insidious form of colonialism: "The neo-colonialism of Today represents imperialism in its final and perhaps most dangerous stage . . . The essence of neo-colonialism is that the State which is subject to it is, in theory, independent and has all the outward trappings of international sovereignty. In reality its economic system and thus its political policy is directed from outside . . . Investment under neo-colonialism increases rather than decreases the gap between the rich and the poor countries of the world."[113] As Nkrumah and many others realized, the struggle to make viable, independent nations free of outside control, especially control by international capital and the former colonial powers, went far beyond raising a new national flag.

In practice, the former colonial powers continued to wield significant economic and military influence over their former colonies, especially in Africa, after granting them formal independence. In the Congo, for example, Belgian firms retained control of the bulk of the country's lucrative mining industry well after the end of that nation's crisis of independence.[114] In the postwar era, Britain became noteworthy for peacefully granting its former colonies national independence, but this often went along with economic dominance of the new national economies by British financial institutions and multinational companies. During the 1950s and 1960s Britain's Commonwealth of Nations helped link the economies of the former colonies to London, and after Britain joined the European Union in 1972 it continued to retain special economic ties to its former empire. Such ties were often subtle, and for the most part the British did not intervene militarily in Anglophone Africa after independence. Nonetheless, they ensured a continued British presence in its former colonies that transcended the granting of formal sovereignty to the empire.[115]

France played a much more direct and powerful role in its former colonies after the mid-1960s. In 1958, in the context of the crisis produced by the Algerian war and the collapse of the Fourth Republic, France held a referendum in its African colonies offering them either continued association with (and aid from) France or immediate independence. With the signal exception of Guinea, all the colonial subjects voted for the former.[116] Two years later, however, faced with increasing African demands for independence, the government of Charles De Gaulle decided that the days of direct colonial rule in Africa had come to an end. In 1960, as a result, France granted independence to no less than fourteen colonies in sub-Saharan Africa. French officials shuttled from one colonial capital to another, lowering the French flag and hoisting that of the new nation. By the time Algeria achieved its freedom in 1962, the French Empire in Africa was no more.[117]

That hardly spelled the end of French economic and political influence on the continent, however. Even more than Britain, France retained considerable influence over the new governments of its former

African colonies, a phenomenon often referred to as *Françafrique*.[118] In 1960 De Gaulle appointed Jacques Foccart, a veteran of the Gaullist resistance during World War II, special adviser to the president in African affairs. Foccart constructed a special office in the Élysée Palace, removed from parliamentary oversight or control, and used it for most of the rest of the twentieth century to direct French involvement in African affairs.[119] Foccart's office directed covert payments to African leaders to ensure their loyalty and compliance, and also financed secret wars against insurgent forces that threatened French interests. For example, French forces waged a secret war in Cameroon, overthrowing Marxist insurgents and ensuring the establishment of a compliant independent regime in 1960.[120] More generally, France included its former African colonies in a financial union called the franc zone, opening them to investment by French companies and in effect subsidizing France's economy. France also signed agreements for technical, cultural, and military cooperation with most Francophone African states and sent technical advisers, teachers, and other experts to Africa to promote French culture and politics.

Perhaps most strikingly, France intervened militarily time and time again in Francophone Africa. The French retained garrisons with thousands of soldiers in its former African colonies and used them to prevent challenges to French interests. Throughout the late twentieth century France maintained large military garrisons in Francophone Africa, frequently deploying their troops across the region. Between 1960 and 1995 France intervened thirty-five times in African conflicts, usually to prevent challenges to allied regimes. For example, in 1964 French paratroopers landed in Libreville, the capital of Gabon, to defeat an attempted overthrow of that regime. French interventions sometimes took place outside Francophone Africa. In 1977 and 1978 France intervened in the Congo to protect dictator Mobutu Sese Seko, a strong defender of Western interests in Africa. The fact that these interventions usually occurred at the invitation of a local ruler did not contradict the fact that as a general phenomenon they challenged the reality of Francophone African independence, independence which seemingly had to be defended time and time again by a white man's army.[121]

The particular issue of French military intervention in Francophone Africa relates to a broader question, that of the relationship between independence and democracy in the postcolonial world during the late twentieth century. As this study has shown, most colonial territories in Asia and Africa had been controlled by democratic European states, and many of them had inherited the structures of formal parliamentary democracy from their imperial masters, structures that in many cases the colonized used in the struggles for independence. Frequently, however, these structures did not endure into the postcolonial era. Instead, all too often colonial rule gave way to military dictatorship. This was especially true in Africa; as we have already seen, the independence of the Belgian Congo led quickly to the overthrow and assassination of democratically elected Patrice Lumumba and the dictatorship of Colonel Mobutu. In February 1966 Kwame Nkrumah, perhaps Africa's greatest independence leader, was overthrown by a military coup d'état widely rumored to have been facilitated by the American CIA.[122] When Algeria became independent in 1962, FLN leader Ahmed Ben Bella established an authoritarian regime, only to be overthrown by the army three years later.[123] By the end of the 1960s virtually all of the newly created African states had become military dictatorships.

Although this pattern occurred most noticeably in Africa, other parts of what had become known as the Third World were certainly not immune. Although the Middle East had been a major pioneer in the revolt against colonialism after World War II, the area soon fell under the control of a mixture of monarchies and military regimes. Latin America, which had largely freed itself from colonial rule in the early nineteenth century, remained dominated by military dictatorships in the late twentieth century, often aided by the neocolonial influence of the United States. The armed forces seized power in Brazil in 1964, in Argentina in 1966, and in Chile in 1973, among other examples, and in general, whether or not it was actually in power, the military remained a powerful political force throughout the region.[124] The main alternative to military rule in the postcolonial Third World was not liberal democracy but rather Marxism. Communist regimes in Vietnam, Cuba, and above all China, for example, had often successfully challenged the monumental problems of poverty and land reform in the postcolonial world, without making freedom a priority.[125]

There were of course some exceptions, notably India, which by the second half of the twentieth century could justifiably claim to be the world's largest democracy. India, however, had assets rare elsewhere in the postcolonial world, including a large educated middle class and a tradition of parliamentary and political activism that went back to the founding of the Indian National Congress in 1885.[126] These were exceptional, and so in general was the presence of liberal democracy in Africa, Asia, and Latin America. If one glanced at the global political order in the last quarter of the twentieth century, therefore, one would see a world where political regimes that championed liberty largely existed in Western Europe and North America. Although there were major exceptions like India and Eastern Europe, these were exceptions to a general rule that freedom was essentially white.

After Civil Rights

Busing and White Backlash in America

On April 5, 1976, Ted Landsmark, an African American attorney, was walking to work in downtown Boston. At the time, the Massachusetts capital was reeling from the racial tensions and violence resulting from the plan to integrate the city's schools, while at the same time preparing for the celebration that summer of the bicentennial of the American Revolution. A year and a half earlier another Black man, Andre Yvon Jean-Louis, had been pulled from his car and nearly murdered by a white mob in broad daylight while driving through South Boston. A month earlier, during the Massachusetts presidential primary, Boston had given a majority of its votes to the arch-segregationist governor of Alabama, George Wallace.[127] As Landsmark walked down the street he was suddenly set upon by a group of white teenagers. One of them attacked him with an American flag, severely beating him and producing a famous photograph that later won the Pulitzer Prize. In a city long known as America's cradle of liberty, on one spring day freedom took the form of racist violence.[128]

FIGURE 30. "The Soiling of Old Glory." Photo of Ted Landsmark by Stanley Forman, StanleyForman.photos.com. © Stanley Forman. "That's me in the picture: Ted Landsmark is assaulted in Boston, at an 'anti-bussing' protest, 5 April 1976," by Abigail Radnor, *The Guardian*, April 17, 2015. https://www.theguardian.com/artanddesign/2015 /apr/17/thats-me-in-picture-ted-landsmark-boston-anti-busing.

The period from the high-water mark of the civil rights movement in 1965 to the end of the 1980s illustrated both the revolutionary impact of the struggle for racial equality in modern America and the limits of that struggle. One of the great triumphs of the campaign for Black freedom was a permanent shift in American racial discourse. After the early 1960s most Americans no longer accepted racist language or appeals to racial bigotry. The idea that all men are created equal, enshrined in the founding documents of the Republic, now extended to men (and increasingly women) of all colors. Those who continued to harbor racist sentiments had to express them in veiled form or risk both condemnation and irrelevance. By the 1970s, Senator Strom Thurmond of South Carolina, a die-hard foe of integration and founder of the Dixiecrat Party in 1948, had denounced racism publicly and begun to work with African American leaders in his home state.[129] After the mid-1960s writers, politicians, and other public figures agreed, at least in theory, that overt racism had no place in American life.

The civil rights movement reshaped American life far beyond the concerns of African Americans. The movement sparked a crucial change in American immigration law. The landmark Immigration and Naturalization Act of 1965 overturned the Johnson-McCarran Act of 1924 by removing racial qualifications for foreigners desiring to settle in the United States. Passed the year after the Civil Rights Act, the overwhelmingly majority of Congress that voted for the new immigration law clearly drew inspiration from the movement's ideal of racial equality; as Attorney General Robert Kennedy noted, "Everywhere else in our national life, we have eliminated discrimination based on national origins. Yet this system is still the foundation of our immigration law."[130] The authors and proponents of the law predicted in 1965 that it would not have much of an impact on American life, but they were wrong. From 1965 to 2000, ninety percent of new immigrants to the United States came from outside Europe, a sharp break from the past. For the first time in history, most Americans accepted the idea that to be American did not necessarily mean to be white.[131]

The civil rights movement also inspired a number of other struggles for social equality during the 1960s in particular. The rise of the massive baby boom generation to young adulthood and the resultant student and New Left movements often drew direct inspiration from the campaign for Black equality; veterans of Mississippi's Freedom Summer played a key role in the first major student uprising, Berkeley's Free Speech Movement in the fall of 1964.[132] The rise of second wave feminism took place in the context of the struggle for civil rights, much as the movement for women's suffrage in the nineteenth century arose out of the abolitionist movement.[133] Civil rights activism provided both a positive example of the mass mobilization of women and men as well as at times a negative example of patriarchy and gendered hierarchies.[134]

The rebirth of feminist activism in the context of the civil rights movement led in particular to new multicultural visions of women's struggles for equality. Black feminism has a long history in America, going back to antislavery activists Harriet Tubman and Sojourner Truth. African American women played a seminal role in the civil rights movement: not only Rosa Parks but many others had powered the Montgomery bus boycott, for example.[135] During the 1960s, motivated by what they considered exclusion from the dominant narratives of both the civil rights and feminist movements, Black women spoke up and organized to highlight the confluence of gender and racial equality. In a similar fashion, Chicana feminism grew out of Chicano social and political movements, asserting the centrality of women's efforts in the racial struggle for inclusion in American society. During the 1960s and after, multicultural feminists not only demanded new attention to the challenges faced by women of color but also transformed feminism itself. The critique of "white feminism," of feminism as a movement for white, middle-class women, became increasingly central to the movement during the late twentieth century as the struggle for women's rights struggled to include and define itself as a movement for all women.[136]

Other groups in American society also began asserting their rights to full and equal citizenship. Latinos, who for so long had constituted much of the underclass that fueled the American dream in the West, especially California, began organizing to improve their condition both as workers and as Americans of color. In 1962 activists César Chavez and Dolores Huerta founded the United Farm Workers, organizing primarily Mexican American agricultural laborers to fight for better conditions and at the same time mobilizing the fast-growing Latinx population.[137] American Indians began calling themselves Native Americans and launched the Red Power movement. In 1969 activists occupied Alcatraz Island in San Francisco bay to draw attention to America's seizure of native lands.[138] That same year a police raid on the Stonewall Inn, a bar in New York's Greenwich Village frequented by homosexuals, prompted patrons and others to fight back, triggering three days of riots and beginning the modern movement for gay rights.[139] All of these movements had their own distinct histories that predated the civil rights struggle, but the fact that one of the most despised and oppressed groups in American society was now demanding equality reinforced the importance of their own causes. At the heart of the phenomenon that became known as "the Sixties" lay a universal vision of freedom, uncircumscribed by race, ethnicity, gender, sexuality, or identity in general.[140]

The civil rights movement thus helped spark a broader series of popular struggles that dealt a body blow to the idea and practice of white freedom. Yet white freedom hardly disappeared from American life; instead it assumed new forms that during the next twenty years produced a powerful renaissance of the idea. Some of this had to do with the history of the civil rights movement after the Civil Rights and Voting Rights acts. These were of course major accomplishments, helping to transform African American life in the South in particular, but they did not achieve the ultimate goal of making Blacks equal partners in American life. As the movement began to target issues beyond public segregation, like housing and economic inequality, and as it expanded into the North and West, it encountered new types of resistance. In 1966 the SCLC started a campaign to integrate housing in Chicago, a campaign that met with violent resistance from many whites in the city.[141] At the same time, many African Americans became disillusioned with the slow pace of peaceful change, turning instead to the Black Power movement against racism. In the same year as the Chicago campaign, Black activists Bobby Seale and Huey Newton founded the Black Panther party, organizing heavily armed citizen patrols to shadow the police in Oakland, California. Within a few years chapters of the militant organization had spread throughout the country, a symbol of the new assertiveness and the turn away from nonviolence of Black protest.[142]

By the last quarter of the twentieth century, although in many ways Black life had improved enormously compared to the heyday of Jim Crow, it was nonetheless clear that white freedom had not disappeared, that race remained a major determinant of American quality of life. The issue of school integration was one major example. As we have seen, the battle against educational segregation had not only given the civil rights movement its first signal victory, *Brown v. Board of Education*, but had in general served as a key rallying cry for Black activists and their allies. It also scored some notable successes: for example, the percentage of Black students in the South attending majority white schools rose from two in 1964 to thirty-five in 1971.[143] That, and the sharp rise of Black elected officials in southern states, were the civil rights movement's most tangible achievements.

As the struggle for school integration became nationwide, however, it encountered new forms of resistance. In February 1964 ten thousand white parents marched across the Brooklyn Bridge from Brooklyn to New York City Hall in Manhattan in protest against plans to desegregate the city's public schools, plans fueled by a massive school boycott of Black and Puerto Rican parents a month earlier.[144] This and other protests in New York had a direct impact on the 1964 Civil Rights Act, by helping to enshrine an ultimately rather specious distinction between *de jure* and *de facto* segregation. The argument that northern schools were segregated by accident, rather than by deliberate government policies as in the South, generally did not hold water when one considered policies like the segregation of public housing, federal mortgage redlining, and the tendency of school boards to site new schools so they would not be integrated; as James Baldwin archly noted in 1965, "De Facto segregation means Negroes are segregated, but nobody did it."[145] Nonetheless, in spite of the protests by Southern senators against the rank hypocrisy of such a move, the 1964 Civil Rights Act did not challenge the issue of de facto segregation of public schools, which applied essentially to schools in the North.[146]

In particular, the Act contained provisions banning the busing of students to counteract de facto segregation, and the struggle over "forced busing" would redefine the movement for school integration during the next decades.[147] In 1971 the Supreme Court decided, in the case of *Swann v. Charlotte-Mecklenburg*, that in cases where school authorities had consciously created segregated schools, busing was one acceptable means of achieving the integration mandated by *Brown* and the Fourteenth Amendment. Subsequent decisions by lower courts ordering busing put paid to the idea of de facto segregation, because in every case they found evidence that public authorities had intentionally violated the law.[148] This reality was largely lost in the firestorm of white public outrage and protest that greeted school busing programs for integration. Opponents portrayed busing as an attack on neighborhood

schools, or as a physical and health burden for small children. This outrage ignored some basic facts, like the fact that millions of (mostly rural)
schoolchildren were bused to school every day across America without
controversy, or the fact that no one seemed to object when Black
children were bused past white schools nearby to Black schools farther
away. The Reverend Theodore Hesburgh, civil rights activist and later
president of Notre Dame University, once noted, "I remember Medgar
Evers saying that his first recollection of busing was the new school
buses passing him and other Black children [walking] on the way to
school . . . splashing them with mud as the white children on their way
to a good school yelled out the window, 'Nigger! Nigger!' No objections
to busing then."[149] As Black civil rights activists observed during the
busing crisis of the early 1970s, "It's not the bus, it's us."[150]

There can thus be no doubt that, at bottom, the mass movement
against busing strove to preserve white privilege and Black inequality.
As Matthew Delmont has pointed out, the campaign against "busing"
was really a campaign against school integration, waged by whites who
did not want their children attending school with Black kids. The focus
on "busing" rather than integration allowed whites to argue that their
protest had nothing to do with race, but rather with a desire to preserve
schools and neighborhoods that just happened to be overwhelmingly
white. Even many white liberals, who would have been horrified at
being called racist, came to sympathize with what they regard as a
working-class populist movement against elite social engineers; casting
the movement as a struggle against busing rather than against integration made this possible. Joseph Biden, then a young senator from Delaware, was a case in point. Initially a supporter of busing, he turned
against it after getting an earful from white constituents, ultimately
going on to sponsor congressional antibusing legislation in alliance with
arch-segregationist Senator Jesse Helms of North Carolina.[151] As he
made clear, the problem was not "busing" but integration in general.

> The new integration plans being offered are really just quota systems
> to assure a certain number of Blacks, Chicanos, or whatever in each
> school. That, to me, is the most racist concept you can come up

with. . . . What it says is, "In order for your child with curly Black hair, brown eyes, and dark skin to be able to learn anything, he needs to sit next to my blond-haired, blue-eyed son." That's racist! Who the hell do we think we are, that the only way a Black man or woman can learn is if they rub shoulders with my white child?[152]

For those who believed segregation and racism were a Southern phenomenon, the antibusing movement of the 1970s came as a rude shock; as Malcolm X had observed a few years earlier, "As long as you south of the Canadian border, you South."[153]

The resistance to integration, north and south, also took on the guise of a freedom struggle. In March 1956, ninety-six southern congressional representatives issued the "Southern Manifesto," denouncing *Brown* as a violation of individual rights. They argued that "parents should not be deprived by Government of the right to direct the lives and education of their own children."[154] In the South, thousands of whites resisted integration by creating and enrolling their children in "segregation academies," all-white private schools. The number of white students in such schools in Mississippi tripled between 1968 and 1970, for example.[155] They were widely known as "freedom of choice schools" and in the 1970s would serve as one of the inspirations for the charter school movement.[156] In the North as well, opponents of integration draped themselves in the language of choice and freedom. The main antibusing organization in Boston took the name ROAR (Restore Our Alienated Rights) and condemned busing as an attack on parental and community rights.[157] Irene McCabe, leader of the antibusing movement in Pontiac, Michigan, organized a protest march in September 1971 that featured signs like "Bury the Bus, Keep Freedom Alive." Notably, antibusing activists often drew upon the organizational and rhetorical model of the civil rights movement. McCabe proclaimed that "Martin Luther King walked all over and got a lot of things done. This is our civil rights movement."[158] Just as the civil rights movement represented a struggle for Black freedom, so was resistance to integration a campaign for white freedom.

The most dramatic resistance to busing took place in Boston, when federal judge Arthur W. Garrity concluded that the Boston School Board had deliberately segregated the city's public schools and consequently ordered school busing to start in the fall of 1974. The massive antibusing movement that resulted highlights some of contradictions explored in this study.[159] Boston was of course famed as America's Cradle of Liberty, the city that had led the resistance against royal absolutism and the founding of the United States as the land of the free. Just two years earlier it had led Massachusetts into being the only state that voted for liberal Democrat George McGovern for president, and during the early 1970s it was preparing to celebrate the Bicentennial of the American Revolution. Yet Boston also had a reputation as one of the most segregated and racist cities in America, and during the busing crisis that racism came out in full force.[160] The beating of Ted Landsmark was merely one example among many: whites greeted Black students in South with signs like "Niggers Go Home!," and when police arrived to escort Black students from South Boston High School back home one day after a racial stabbing incident, crowds surrounded the bus shouting, "Bus 'em back to Africa!"[161] The combination of white racism and freedom even permeated the celebrations of the Bicentennial: in 1975 ROAR members marched in a celebration of the 205th anniversary of the Boston Massacre carrying signs like "Boston Mourns its Lost Freedom."[162]

By the 1980s the antibusing forces had clearly won, defeating not only school busing for integration but integration in general. In the 1974 *Milliken v. Bradley* case, the Supreme Court ruled against a school desegregation plan between Detroit and its suburbs. This meant that the courts would do nothing to stop white flight to evade integration, a body blow to efforts to integrate metropolitan schools, which became increasingly divided between minority inner cities and white suburbia.[163] The massive and violent nature of antibusing movements in Boston and other areas, and the willingness of both conservative and liberal politicians to support those movements against integration, dramatically weakened the resolve of the courts to enforce school desegregation. In particular, the strident opposition of President Reagan to busing during the 1980s, and his success in appointing hundreds of conservatives to the federal judiciary, increasingly stalled the process of desegregation in both North and South. The fact that study after study showed that Black students, indeed all students, benefited from desegregation made no difference.[164]

Busing for school integration effectively ended in Boston in 1988, a year that represented the high-water mark of American school integration in general. A series of Supreme Court cases in the 1990s released most major cities from court-ordered busing programs, and more generally facilitated the resegregation of the nation's schools. By the time America commemorated the fiftieth anniversary of *Brown* in 2004 that process was racing ahead, so that seventy percent of Black students in America attended majority-minority schools.[165]

Roughly a century after George Henry White left Congress, signaling the end of the Reconstruction, the decline of school integration in America most clearly heralded the defeat of the Second Reconstruction. Obviously, much divides the two historical eras, but this is nonetheless a parallel worth noting, because it speaks to the survival, the resiliency of white freedom in America. The resegregation of American schools was not just about education; it had a profoundly political dimension. The mobilization of whites against Black demands for liberty would play a major role in the rise of a new conservative movement which would transform the politics of the United States during the last quarter of the twentieth century. The birth and triumph of the New Right would write a new chapter in the history of white freedom in the United States.

The New White

Race and Conservatism in the Reagan Era

You start out in 1954 by saying, "Nigger, nigger, nigger." By 1968 you can't say "nigger"—that hurts you, backfires. So you say stuff like, uh, forced busing, states' rights, and all that stuff, and you're getting so abstract. Now, you're talking about cutting taxes, and all these things you're talking about are totally economic things and a byproduct of them is, Blacks get hurt worse than whites. . . . "We want to cut this," is much more abstract than even the busing thing, uh, and a hell of a lot more abstract than "Nigger, nigger."

—REPUBLICAN PARTY STRATEGIST LEE ATWATER, 1981[166]

America in the 1960s experienced not only a wave of liberal and leftist activism but also the birth of a new conservative political movement. Starting with the founding of Young Americans for Freedom in 1960, a diverse group of conservatives built a powerful right-wing coalition that would triumph in 1980 with the election of Ronald Reagan as president of the United States. To an important extent the New Right, by embracing the ideal of individual liberty as opposed to collectivist government, represented a strong reaction not only against the welfare state policies of the 1960s but even Franklin Delano Roosevelt's New Deal. At the same time, it drew heavily on white resentment of the civil rights movement and of minorities in general. For America's "suburban warriors," to use Lisa McGirr's term, the freedom they so cherished meant freedom from government interference in their lives, in particular government interference to promote the interests of other races at the expense of whites. Personal liberty was therefore, as the popular struggles against school integration showed, to a very important extent racial liberty.[167]

During the 1950s and early 1960s the new conservative movement began to come together, focusing on fusing traditional conservatism and libertarianism and emphasizing freedom as the core of their ideology. In 1955 William F. Buckley Jr. founded *The National Review*, which would become the intellectual leader of the movement.[168] In 1962 University of Chicago economist Milton Friedman published *Capitalism and Freedom*, which argued that economic freedom and the free market in particular are essential to political freedom and harshly attacked what would soon become known as "big government."[169] In September 1960, a group of young intellectuals convened at Buckley's house in Connecticut to found a new conservative organization, the Young Americans for Freedom.[170] At this meeting the newly formed YAF adopted a statement of principles, the "Sharon Statement," which clearly stated its members' views on the nature and importance of freedom.

> We, as young conservatives, believe:
> That foremost among the transcendent values is the individual's use of his God-given free will, whence derives his right to be free from the restrictions of arbitrary force;

That liberty is indivisible, and that political freedom cannot long
  exist without economic freedom;
That the purpose of government is to protect those freedoms
  through the preservation of internal order, the provision of
  national defense, and the administration of justice;
That when government ventures beyond these rightful func-
  tions, it accumulates power, which tends to diminish order
  and liberty. . . . [171]

The path from the "Sharon Statement" to the electoral triumph of the
New Right a generation later was by no means straightforward; going
from a small meeting of conservative young people to a mass-based
political movement took time. The libertarianism that inspired the YAF
could look left as well as right, toward either conservatism or anarchism,
and the party experienced a major split in 1969. The New Right not only
endured but ultimately conquered, and its success derived from two
primary factors. First, starting in the 1950s the new conservatism embraced traditional moral values as well as individual liberty, bringing
together two very disparate perspectives in a new doctrine called fusionism.[172] From this perspective government programs like the welfare
state were bad not just because they denied individual liberty but
equally because as materialist programs they undermined human dignity based in spiritual values. As the leading conservative thinker Frank
Meyer argued, American political culture combined "the acceptance of
the authority of an organic moral order together with a fierce concern
for the freedom of the individual person."[173] In particular, conservatives
emphasized the importance of religion and spirituality; in sharp contrast to Ayn Rand and other atheist libertarians, they argued that freedom without a moral compass and set of values was meaningless.

This last point is crucial, because one of the key factors in the rise of
the New Right as a mass political movement was the emergence of the
new evangelical Christian right during the late 1970s. Although conservative Christians had long been active in politics, they had not played a
major role in election campaigns for the most part; in 1976 Jimmy Carter, a Democrat but also a southerner and self-proclaimed born-again

Christian, won the majority of the evangelical vote. By then, however, conservative white evangelicals had begun mobilizing around two main issues: abortion and the denial of tax-exempt status to Christian schools. In 1979 conservative minister Jerry Falwell founded the Moral Majority political action committee. Fueled by the growth of evangelical mega-churches and a savvy use of televised religious programs, the Christian Right mobilized millions of believers to vote for conservative positions and candidates.[174]

Race and racial conflict also contributed to building a mass base for the New Right. To an important extent it played a role in the rise of the Christian Right, which remained an overwhelmingly white movement in spite of the fact that many African Americans followed similar evangelical traditions. The decision by the federal government to strip tax-exempt status from all-white Christian schools enraged white evangelicals and helped turn them to politics.[175] More generally, conservatives opposed *Brown* and federal desegregation efforts in general in the name of individual liberty, i.e., the right of all parents to send their children wherever they saw fit. At times conservatives went beyond a defense of individualism; writing in *The National Review* in 1957, William F. Buckley argued, "The central question that emerges is whether the White community in the South is entitled to take such measures as are necessary to prevail, politically and culturally, in the areas in which it does not predominate numerically. The sobering answer is *Yes* . . . because, for the time being, it is the advanced race. . . . The *National Review* believes that the South's premises are correct. If the majority wills what is socially atavistic, then to thwart the majority may be, though undemocratic, enlightened."[176] Although in the past conservatives had rejected the racism of organizations like the John Birch Society and the American Nazi Party, right from the beginning the movement opposed the civil rights movement's campaign for racial equality.

During the 1960s questions of race became a central issue in American politics, and the New Right used this to help transform itself into a mass movement. In 1960 Richard Nixon won the Republican nomination for president as a representative of the party's moderate faction, and his moderation included strong support for civil rights. This incensed the party's conservative wing, which after his defeat began organizing to win control of the GOP. Years of effort bore fruit in 1964 when they succeeded winning the nomination for Barry Goldwater, senator from Arizona.[177] Goldwater had established a strong reputation as an opponent of civil rights: in 1962, for example, he had denounced the use of federal troops to enforce the integration of the University of Mississippi. He had concluded by 1964 that Nixon lost to Kennedy in 1960 because he failed to mobilize southern opposition to desegregation, and therefore whatever his personal views on race he was determined not to make the same mistake. In voting against the 1964 Civil Rights Act, Goldwater called it a threat to individual liberty: "To give genuine effect to the prohibitions of this bill will require the creation of a federal police of mammoth proportions. . . . These . . . are the hallmarks of the police state in the destruction of a free society."[178] Goldwater's opposition to civil rights led conservatives to flock to his banner, enabling them to take control of the Republican Party and enlist it solidly in the struggle for white freedom.[179]

During the 1964 presidential campaign Goldwater made the famous remark that, given the impossibility of winning a large share of the Black vote, Republicans needed to "go hunting where the ducks are." This statement was a key moment in the elaboration of what became known as the "Southern Strategy," the GOP's political conquest of the South as a route to national power. To understand how revolutionary a moment this was in American politics, one needs to revisit the history of the "Solid South." Thanks largely to the fact that the Republican Party was born as an antislavery movement and led the conquest of the Confederacy during the Civil War and Reconstruction, ever since the 1870s Southern voters (which, given the violent disenfranchisement of Blacks meant white southern voters) had cast their ballots overwhelmingly for Democrats. For decades the Democratic Party won large regional majorities in presidential elections and controlled virtually every national and local elected office.[180]

Southern loyalty to the Democrats began to erode during the later years of the New Deal as President Roosevelt made some hesitant nods to opposing racial discrimination, and it suffered a major setback during the presidential campaign of 1948, when the Democratic Convention passed a resolution in favor of civil rights. This triggered a walkout by Southern Democrats who went on to form their own party, the "Dixiecrats," and nominated Senator Strom Thurmond of South Carolina for president, winning four southern states in the general election that November.[181]

Historians disagree about exactly when the Republicans' Southern Strategy began, but all agree that the civil rights movement played a key role.[182] When President Johnson signed the 1964 Civil Rights Act he reportedly commented to an aide, "I think we just delivered the South to the Republican party for a long time to come."[183] Even though Republicans as well as Democrats had supported the Act, the future would prove him right. Although Barry Goldwater lost the 1964 presidential election in a landslide, he managed to win most of the Deep South. In 1968 Alabama Governor George Wallace ran for president as an Independent. He repeated the success of the Dixiecrats in 1948, winning five southern states. The death knell of Democratic Party influence below the Mason-Dixon Line was sounded in 1964 and 1968; the Solid South was no more.[184]

Increasingly, moreover, racial politics was not just a southern phenomenon. Between 1964 and 1968 the growing militancy of the civil rights movement and the birth of Black Power not only gave racial politics a new dimension in America but also took it beyond the South to the North and West, making it a nationwide question. Starting in New York City's Harlem in 1964, northern cities experienced a series of race riots every summer, culminating in the Detroit uprising of 1967. These "long hot summers" testified to Black frustration at the slow march of racial equality, shocking many white onlookers with the spectacle of widespread death and destruction, of urban neighborhoods occupied by uniformed soldiers and armored vehicles. As the furor over busing and school integration in northern cities would soon demonstrate, racial hostility and racialized politics were a national issue.[185]

The issue of race played a central role in facilitating the conservative takeover of the Republican Party, at the same time giving that party a new dominance in American political life more generally. In 1969 Kevin

Phillips, a political strategist who had advised Richard Nixon's successful presidential campaign the year earlier, published *The Emerging Republican Majority*. At the heart of Phillips's classic study lay the idea that Republicans could use white backlash against the civil rights movement to win not just the South but the nation as a whole. In a meticulous analysis of the 1968 election results, Phillips argued that the nation was undergoing a political sea-change, fueled largely by racial politics, that would ensure Republican electoral dominance for some time to come. As he observed,

> The presidential election of 1968 marked a historic first occasion— the Negrophobe Deep South and modern Outer South *simultaneously* abandoned the Democratic Party. And before long, the conservative cycle thus begun ought to witness movement of congressional, state and local Southern Democrats into the ascending Republican Party.
>
> Considerable historical and theoretical evidence supports the thesis that a liberal Democratic era has ended and that a new era of consolidationist Republicanism has begun.[186]

The presidential election of 1972 dramatically confirmed the validity of Phillips's analysis. That year the Republican Party won one of the greatest electoral victories in its history, winning more than sixty percent of the popular vote and carrying every state except Massachusetts. In earlier times Nixon had shown some sympathy for civil rights and the victims of racial oppression; in 1969, for example, he sponsored the Philadelphia Plan, one of the nation's first major affirmative action programs.[187] This changed in 1972, as the Republicans successfully campaigned to win over those voters who had supported George Wallace in 1968. In particular, Nixon took a strong stand against busing, opposing the Supreme Court's 1971 *Swann v. Charlotte-Mecklenburg* decision. As a result, Nixon not only won most of Wallace's former supporters but also performed extremely well with working-class whites in the North. The Southern Strategy had become a reality, producing the Republican majority Phillips had predicted three years earlier.

In many ways Richard Nixon was a transitional figure, one who never completely embraced, let alone won the trust of, the New Right. His resignation in disgrace as a result of the Watergate scandal, and the election of Democrat Jimmy Carter to the presidency in 1976, cast some doubt on the validity of the Southern Strategy. Carter, a white southern born-again Christian, swept the South in 1976, becoming the last Democratic presidential candidate to do so.[188] Yet the late 1970s also witnessed important developments that would enable the New Right to seize power in 1980. One, already mentioned above, was the organization of the religious Right. Another was the new support for conservative thought and politics by corporate America, as reflected in the growth of think tanks such as the American Enterprise Institute.[189] The rise of the neoconservative movement, composed of former liberals including Norman Podhoretz and Jeane Kirkpatrick who rejected the New Left and embraced a strongly anticommunist foreign policy, constituted a third factor.[190] At the same time, the end of postwar prosperity and the prolonged economic downturn of the 1970s weakened the Carter administration, as did the seizure of American hostages by Iran's revolutionary Islamic regime in 1979.[191]

The 1980 presidential election brought the political triumph of the New Right and the Southern Strategy. Republican candidate Ronald Reagan handily defeated sitting president Jimmy Carter and swept the South, with the sole exception of Georgia, Carter's home state. Conservatives were jubilant: Kevin Phillips hailed Reagan's win as "the greatest victory for conservatism since the American Revolution."[192] Moreover, the remaking of the Solid South as a Republican fiefdom proved enduring. The GOP swept the region again during the presidential elections of 1984 and 1988, and even popular southern Democrat Bill Clinton was able to make only partial inroads in the region during the elections of 1992 and 1996. Moreover, the Republican Party increasingly monopolized other elected offices throughout the South, ranging from city councils to senators and governors. Like many other parts of southern life, politics became ever more segregated as local Democrats became more and more dependent on Black support. The part of America that more than any other stood for white racism thus became the center of the new conservative movement for political freedom.

Ronald Reagan became one of the most popular and dynamic American presidents of the twentieth century, and the Reagan Revolution brought the New Right to power.[193] He also thoroughly represented the movement's emphasis on white freedom. Reagan's own personal views on race were complex: he counted numerous nonwhite friends and allies, for example, and reacted with fury whenever he was (frequently) accused of racism.[194] Yet he often took positions that opposed the movement for Black equality. Following Barry Goldwater, whom he supported, Reagan rejected the Civil Rights Act of 1964, arguing, "You can't guarantee someone's freedom by opposing someone else's."[195] He campaigned for governor of California in 1966 pledging to repeal the state's Fair Housing Act, saying individual property owners should have the right to rent to whomever they wanted. Reagan launched his 1980 campaign for president in Neshoba, Mississippi, a small town a few miles from the place where the civil rights workers Schwerner, Chaney, and Goodman had been murdered, and there proclaimed his belief in "states' rights," a well-known racist code-phrase in the South.[196] As president, Reagan appointed few Blacks to his cabinet, moved to weaken busing and affirmative action, and used racial stereotypes like that of the "cheating welfare queen." As Black *New York Times* columnist Bob Herbert put it, "Reagan may have been blessed with a Hollywood smile and an avuncular delivery, but he was elbow deep in the same old race-baiting Southern strategy of Goldwater and Nixon."[197]

During the last third of the twentieth century, conservative intellectuals joined forces with political evangelism and opponents of the civil rights movement to create the New Right, a blend of racism and individual liberty. This was not always an easy marriage; some libertarians looked askance at the religious right's focus on fighting abortion, a focus opposed by liberals who proclaimed a woman's individual right to choose. Nonetheless, by opposing the struggle for racial equality in the name of individual freedom, traditional conservatism was able to make common cause with those seeking to preserve white privilege in (and well beyond) the South, creating a mass base for the movement and enabling it to dominate American politics after 1980. American conservatives thus responded to the civil rights movement's challenge to white freedom by blending ideas of white privilege and liberty into a powerful new version of that ideology. The movement's impressive success clearly demonstrated that, in spite of the important gains for racial justice achieved by the civil rights movement, white freedom remained a force to be reckoned with in America.

1989: The Triumph of Freedom in Europe

On Friday, June 12, 1987, President Ronald Reagan arrived in West Berlin for a formal state visit. It was not without controversy: fifty thousand Berliners demonstrated against him and large parts of the city were cordoned off for both political and security reasons, while many of his advisers considered the trip an unfortunate provocation of the Soviets. None of this deterred the American president. That afternoon, standing in front of the Brandenburg Gate at the Berlin Wall, Reagan delivered a direct challenge to the new reformist Soviet leader, Mikhail Gorbachev, to make good on his promises of change.

> We welcome change and openness; for we believe that freedom and security go together, that the advance of human liberty can only strengthen the cause of world peace. There is one sign the Soviets can make that would be unmistakable, that would advance dramatically the cause of freedom and peace. General Secretary Gorbachev, if you seek peace, if you seek prosperity for the Soviet Union and Eastern Europe, if you seek liberalization: Come here to this gate! Mr. Gorbachev, open this gate! Mr. Gorbachev, tear down this wall![198]

Less than three years later Reagan's visionary request became a reality. While diplomats and historians have debated whether or not the president's remarks made a difference, it is nonetheless true that, after Gorbachev refused to support repressive policies by the East German authorities, Berliners themselves tore down the wall. By doing so they not only demolished the great symbol of the postwar division of Europe but set in motion events that would ultimately destroy the Soviet Union itself.[199]

FIGURE 31. Ronald Reagan speaking in front of the Brandenburg Gate and the
Berlin Wall, June 12, 1987. Ronald Reagan Presidential Library/White House
Photographic Office (ID C41244–9).

The year 1989 has gone down in history as not only the year that ended
the cold war in Europe but also as one of the great years of freedom in
modern world history. The Berlin Wall fell two hundred years after the
seizure of the Bastille touched off the French Revolution, and 1989, like
1789, brought unforeseen changes to the world as a whole.[200] Frederik
de Klerk assumed the leadership of South Africa and began the process
of dismantling apartheid in that country, while a powerful pro-democracy
movement arose in China.[201] The events of that momentous year would
inspire Stanford University Press to establish a book series, The Making
of Modern Freedom, that would eventually publish fifteen titles.[202]

At the heart of this era was the collapse of communism throughout
Eastern Europe that toppled regime after regime until it culminated
with the overthrow of the Soviet Union two years later.[203] The fact that
peaceful mass uprisings, not war and destruction, brought about these
changes was especially noteworthy. The photos and video images of
cheering crowds tearing down monuments and images of the commu-

nist era circulated around the globe, affirming the power of peoples to change their world for the better. For conservatives in particular, including members of America's New Right, the revolutions of 1989–91 illustrated the unity of liberty and capitalism, the idea that economic and political freedom, the free market and democracy, could not be separated.[204]

How should one read this history from the perspective of the relationship between freedom and race, and how do the revolutions of 1989–91 express the changing nature of white freedom in the postwar era? In answering these questions, one can start by considering the centrality of Europe to the freedom crusades of the late twentieth century. The overthrow of communist regimes in this period happened in the whitest, most "European" part of the world, one barely touched by the history of European overseas colonialism or non-European immigration. In a modern world where in general whiteness had equaled not only freedom but prosperity, the relative backwardness and authoritarianism of Eastern Europe had stood out as an anomaly. The revolutions of 1989–91 erased this exception and, to a greater extent than ever, highlighted the relationship between liberty and whiteness.

One must note that the collapse of communist rule in Eastern Europe was part of a broader historical pattern, one that brought economic development and political liberty to the continent as a whole. Until the late 1970s, for example, much of Mediterranean Europe had been ruled by authoritarian, illiberal regimes. Dictatorships had governed Spain and Portugal since the interwar years, and Greece experienced a seizure of power by the military in 1967, which lasted until 1974. Like Eastern Europe, the continent's Mediterranean region had been traditionally impoverished and dominated by peasant smallholders. Prosperity after World War II had modernized local and national economies, bolstering those social and political forces in favor of liberal democracy and greater freedom. In April 1974 Portuguese military officers, frustrated by the nation's hapless struggle to suppress anticolonial revolts in its African empire, overthrew the authoritarian regime in Lisbon, then ceded power to a new democratic government headed by moderate socialists. In July of the same year the Greek junta collapsed, fatally weakened by its failed attempts to liberalize the national economy and its mishandling of a crisis with Turkey over Cyprus. Venerable Spanish dictator Francisco Franco died in November 1975, leaving power to King Juan Carlos. The king oversaw Spain's transition to parliamentary democratic rule, the new regime surviving a military coup attempt by discontented officers in 1981.[205]

Moreover, liberalization and the challenge to dictatorship went well beyond Europe during the 1980s. The collapse of apartheid in South Africa was the most dramatic example of this, but not the only one. Latin America, a region dominated by military dictatorships (usually supported and facilitated by the US government) during much of the twentieth century, witnessed a flowering of democracy during the decade and after. Whereas the region only had three democratic governments in 1978, the next decade and a half brought a massive wave of liberalization, so that by 1995 only Cuba and Haiti remained under authoritarian rule.[206] In his comprehensive study *The Third Wave: Democratization in the Late Twentieth Century*, eminent political scientist Samuel P. Huntington argued that the collapse of the Portuguese dictatorship in 1974 unleashed a worldwide process of democratization: "During the following fifteen years this democratic wave became global in scope; about thirty countries shifted from authoritarianism to democracy, and at least a score of other countries were affected by the democratic wave."[207]

One must therefore view the revolutions of 1989–91 in Eastern Europe as the culmination of a larger movement toward freedom in general on the European continent and well beyond. As the 1990s would show, these new freedoms were not an unmixed blessing. Throughout the region the end of communism brought the collapse of censorship and the police state, and the revival of a free press and freedom of speech. Especially in Poland, Hungary, and Czechoslovakia, all countries with a long history of resistance to the postwar Soviet order, the transition to liberal democratic capitalism proceeded relatively well. Elsewhere, however, building postcommunist societies proved more difficult. The end of communism unleashed a massive process of privatization of former state assets, a process often exploited by the old political elites and directed by foreign authorities like the International Monetary Fund and the World Bank. Privatization also meant the abandonment of the social security net provided by the communist regimes. This was especially true of the former Soviet Union, where millions fell into desperate poverty; the lifespan of the average Soviet male declined from sixty-nine in 1991 to fifty-eight in 1996.[208] In post-Communist Eastern Europe, all might be free, but some were freer than others.[209]

The end of Communism also brought a revival of nationalism and racism to the former Soviet bloc.[210] Even one of the most successful post-Soviet states, Czechoslovakia, in 1993 peacefully split into the separate nations of Slovakia and the Czech Republic. The most extreme example of national breakdown came with the collapse of another hybrid state, Yugoslavia, into a brutal civil war in 1991. During the war Yugoslavia, which many had considered a model multiethnic state under the independent Communist rule of Marshall Tito, descended into a frenzy of ethnic cleansing and genocide not seen in Europe since the Nazi era.[211] The war in Bosnia, pitting ethnic Serbs against Bosnian Muslims, saw the worst horrors; in July 1995 Serb soldiers massacred several thousand Muslim civilians in the town of Srebrenica.[212]

Elsewhere in Eastern Europe nationalist and racial tensions also increased after 1989. The Roma, or "Gypsies," whose communities had lived in Europe for centuries and had been massacred during the Holocaust, faced pogroms and other forms of racial persecution throughout Europe after the fall of Communism.[213] The reunification of Germany saw a revival of far-right political organizations, some with ties to neo-Nazis, and waves of violence against foreigners. In September 1991, racist riots engulfed the East German city of Hoyerswerda as right-wing mobs attacked foreigners from Vietnam and Mozambique whom the former government had brought to the city as guest workers.[214] One can hardly argue that no racism existed under the former Communist regimes, but the end of censorship and official antiracist ideologies gave space for the open expression of racism against foreigners. Many in the former Soviet Bloc desired above all to become united with Europe as a whole, and for some that meant conceiving of Europe as a "white" space and therefore rejecting those who were not white.

As we saw in chapter 2 with the pro-democracy movement in China during the same years, mass protests against Communism and for freedom could spill over into racist social movements. The irony for Eastern Europe, of course, was that their racial images of Europe did not reflect the realities of life in the capitalist West. After reunification, for example, the residents of former East Berlin found themselves part of a city with a huge Turkish minority.[215] By the 1980s and 1990s, Western Europe was experiencing its own challenges with multiculturalism. Decolonization had not completely separated white metropoles from nonwhite empires, as the postwar economic boom brought increasingly large waves of postcolonial migrants to the former mother countries. By the 1980s large nonwhite communities had taken root in and around European cities, such as Kreuzberg in West Berlin, Brixton and Southall in London, and the *banlieues* (suburbs) surrounding Paris.[216] Their growth had been accompanied by the rise of increasingly strident and powerful racist parties, such as the National Fronts of both Britain and France.[217] Increased protests by the so-called "second generation immigrants"[218] often benefited more mainstream politicians, notably Margaret Thatcher in Britain, just as Nixon and Reagan had exploited the reaction against the civil rights movement in America.[219] Their challenges to postwar social democracy and the welfare state often went hand in hand with increasing hostility to immigrants, usually seen as nonwhite immigrants. For many Europeans, East and West, at the end of the twentieth century the preservation of whiteness and of freedom went hand in hand.

The liberalization of Mediterranean Europe and the collapse of the Soviet sphere in the late twentieth century created a new vision of the continent united around liberal democracy and freedom. It was also, to an important extent, a vision of white freedom. Europe, the paradigmatic white continent, was entirely free after 1989 and could claim freedom in ways that no other part of the world could, with the exception of predominantly white North America. The survival of Communist regimes in Asia reinforced that point. Even China, which combined continued Communist rule with spectacularly successful economic liberalization during the 1990s, reinforced the maxim that political freedom existed primarily in white countries.[220]

A central irony of this perspective is the fact that, compared to a half century earlier, both parts of Europe, not to mention the United States, were less "white" than ever. Both regions not only possessed growing nonwhite populations but to an unprecedented extent embraced an image of themselves as multicultural and multiracial societies. Such images could not claim universal or even majority acceptance, however, as the history of the New Right in both Europe and America demonstrated. Indeed, I argue that precisely the threat of demographic change spurred many to claim white identity and to point to events like the collapse of the Soviet Bloc as evidence of the essential whiteness of liberty. Eastern Europe might continue to struggle with creating and maintaining liberal democracy in the decades after 1989, but its embrace of freedom in the revolutions of that year reaffirmed the general observation that to be white was to be free, and to be free was to be white.

Conclusion

The Second World War challenged racism and white freedom to an unprecedented degree in modern history, and to a very important extent that challenge succeeded in crafting and implementing a vision of liberty that applied to all men and women. The roughly forty-five years of the cold war era brought dramatic changes to the relationship between freedom and racial difference, changes that promised a new era of universal liberty. A generation after the conquest of Nazi Germany and Imperial Japan, the era of formal European empire had essentially come to an end, thanks both to the efforts of the colonized themselves as well as to the increasing inability and reluctance of the imperial powers to maintain their rule. In the United States African Americans built upon the lessons of wartime's Double V campaign to organize a powerful movement for racial justice. The civil rights movement transformed America, making the equality of all peoples a central national principle as never before. The challenge to white freedom reached a crescendo in these years, one that fundamentally changed the nature of race and liberty in the contemporary world.

Yet as the second half of the cold war era showed, it was one thing to proclaim freedom, another to make it a reality. In the former colonial world, it gradually became clear that national independence did not necessarily bring individual freedom, and that all too often relationships of economic and military dependence on former colonial powers survived the hoisting of the national flag. In America, the civil rights movement gave way to a powerful New Right that blended an emphasis on individual freedom with white racial backlash. Postcolonial migration into Western Europe brought new racial tensions to Britain and France, as well as new right-wing political movements that embraced ideologies of white freedom. The collapse of the Soviet empire in Eastern Europe, and ultimately the Soviet Union itself, marked the culmination of freedom in the European continent as a whole. A general overview of the state of the world in the early 1990s revealed free white nations struggling to integrate their nonwhite minorities while nonwhite former colonies still struggled to free themselves from poverty and dependence.

None of this contradicts the argument that white freedom was never the same after 1945, that the emphasis on liberty as a universal right became and remained dominant in the contemporary world. It shows, however, how difficult it was and has remained to put that ideal into practice. The tremendous historical legacy of white freedom could not be shaken off easily; going beyond it remains a key task for the twenty-first century.

CONCLUSION

White Freedom and Freedom from Whiteness

Americans are asking "Why do they hate us?" . . . They hate our freedoms: our freedom of religion, our freedom of speech, our freedom to vote and assemble and disagree with each other.

—PRESIDENT GEORGE W. BUSH, AFTER THE ATTACKS OF
SEPTEMBER 11, 2001[1]

In 1987, as noted in chapter 6, President Ronald Reagan called upon the leaders of the Soviet Union to tear down the Berlin Wall, an appeal that became reality two years later. Roughly thirty years after Reagan's famous speech, another American Republican president, Donald Trump, called on the leaders of Mexico to pay for the construction of a wall along the border between the US and Mexico. During his successful 2016 presidential campaign, Trump repeatedly announced his intentions to build a wall, and five days after he assumed office in January 2017 he signed Executive Order 13767 to begin its construction. To reinforce his determination to build the wall, at the end of 2018 President Trump triggered a partial government shutdown, lasting more than a month, because he refused to sign any federal spending bill that did not include funding for the wall.[2]

During the struggle over the wall on the US-Mexico border, some of Trump's strongest support came from the House Freedom Caucus. Founded in 2015 by nine mostly white and male right-wing Republican members of the House of Representatives, the Freedom Caucus organized opposition against not only America's first Black president[3] but also against moderate Republican leaders like John Boehner.[4] Freedom Caucus members soon came to see President Trump as an ally, enthusiastically backing his promise to build a wall on America's border with Mexico. During the crisis caused by the government shutdown in December 2018 Caucus Chairman Mark Meadows made this support explicit, declaring, "I'm here with a number of my colleagues tonight to say we're ready to fight on behalf of all the freedom-loving Americans to make sure we have secure borders and that never again do we have to worry about terrorist and drug traffickers coming across our southern border."[5]

Two Republican American presidents, two walls, two visions of liberty. One proposed destroying a wall in the name of freedom, the other demanded building a wall in the name of freedom. Of course, the point of a wall is not the edifice itself, but rather what it seeks to keep out, or keep in. Reagan and other conservatives condemned the Berlin Wall because it prevented East Germans and other Eastern Europeans from moving to a free society, and ultimately from emulating at home the freedom they sought. That wall was thus offensive not only because it restricted freedom of mobility but equally because it divided the white peoples of Europe from each other. Trump's border wall, in contrast, sought to preserve American freedom by keeping out those racial Others whose very presence on the soil of the United States would endanger it. As one conservative commentator put it, "The communists built the Berlin Wall to limit freedom by trapping good people in. President Trump wants to expand America's border wall to protect our freedom by keeping bad people out. The difference between the two walls couldn't be greater."[6] For both presidents, therefore, walls brought together the free and divided them from those not free, perceiving both categories in racialized terms. One had to destroy the Berlin Wall to promote white freedom, just as one had to build the US-Mexico border wall to preserve and protect it.

This example illustrates the idea that, where white freedom is concerned, William Faulkner's aphorism, "The past is never dead. It's not even past," is very much to the point.[7] In this conclusion to *White Freedom* I would like to sum up some of its major arguments and findings, then explore some of its broader implications for the study of modern history as well as the present condition and future prospects of the relationship between race and liberty. This is a work of history, certainly not one of contemporary political analysis and most definitely not an attempt to predict the future. Nonetheless, a history that does not address Faulkner's point stated above has not completely fulfilled its mission and its obligations to its readers. To what extent, therefore, does the racialized character of liberty analyzed in *White Freedom*, and the conditions that produced it, offer us lessons for the present day and for the generations that will follow us? Hopefully, a final review and summary of the history contained in these pages will offer some insights into this question.

White Freedom Past (with apologies to Charles Dickens)

The central argument in this study, as stated in the introduction, is the idea that during much of the modern world both popular and theoretical concepts of liberty have had an important racial dimension; so much so that in many ways to be white meant to be free, and to be free meant to be white. In approaching the topic, the two chapters in part 1 provided a general thematic approach to the topic, both general and specific. Parts 2 and 3 proceeded chronologically, starting with the discussion of the Enlightenment and the Age of Revolution in chapter 3 and ending with the analysis of the late twentieth century in chapter 6. As noted in the introduction, while the book has a certain focus on the histories of France and the United States, it takes a generally global approach to the rise of white freedom in the modern era.

And what have we learned from this history? In general, *White Free-dom* shows how since the eighteenth century the importance of free-dom has grown in the world, that struggles for freedom have trans-formed the political landscape of entire nations and ultimately continents. At the same time, the expansion of freedom has coincided with a growth of racial distinctions and racialized consciousness; in short, liberty and whiteness have grown not only at the same time but in a manner that has frequently been mutually reinforcing. The great revolutions of the late eighteenth century, for example, took place in a context of white privilege and also reinforced and expanded that con-text. The rise of liberal democracy took place at the same time, and in intimate relation to, the expansion of national and imperial polities with white citizens and nonwhite subjects. As I have argued throughout this study, the paradox between liberty and racism was no paradox at all; instead, racial distinctions played a key role in the rise of modern ideas of freedom and cannot be separated from those ideas.

Although the book focuses primarily on this theoretical and histori-cal relationship, it also considers the resistance to white freedom, the attempts to make liberty a truly universal value and practice. Chap-ter 6 in particular considers this issue, exploring how anticolonial move-ments in European empires and the struggle for civil rights in America posed a frontal challenge to the racialization of liberty. It shows how formidable coalitions arose to fight for universal freedom, and it details both the nature and the limitations of their successes. In the end, it ar-gues that white freedom remained a powerful political and ideological force in the world on the eve of the twenty-first century. I will consider what this means for the future later in this conclusion.

Ultimately, *White Freedom* represents an exploration of the possibili-ties and results from placing race at the center of modern history. Most recent general studies and textbooks about American and world history discuss slavery, colonialism, and racial discrimination, often in great detail. Many tend, however, to portray them as either relatively periph-eral to a dominant narrative of progress and liberation, or see them as key examples of the barriers to liberation, barriers ultimately over-thrown or at least fundamentally challenged by the forward march of humanity. I have argued, in contrast, that racism was part and parcel of this forward march, that it played a central role in shaping our ideas of and movements for freedom. Such a narrative is inspired by and hopefully contributes to other attempts by historians to question standard representations of the center and the margins of history, ranging from the new colonial historiography that contends colonialism lies at the center of European history to the work of scholars of slavery who show how it was central to the economic and social history of modern America.[8] To conflate a seemingly universal value such as liberty with such a generally suspect idea as race is to call into question the moral dimensions of modern history, to explore how our notions of good and evil, and the relationship between them, changed over the course of centuries.

White Freedom Present

If, as some historians contend, the short twentieth century ended with the collapse of state communism in Eastern Europe, the twenty-first began with Al Qaeda's destruction of New York's World Trade Center on September 11, 2001.[9] Both of these epochal events spoke to the relationship between freedom and whiteness in the contemporary era. The end of the Soviet Union seemed to usher in an unprecedented new era of peace and prosperity in the West and beyond during the 1990s: 1989 brought not only the fall of the Berlin Wall but also the invention of the World Wide Web and the birth of the popular Internet, and during the 1990s the number of free countries, as measured by Freedom House, rose from sixty-five to eighty-five.[10]

For a while sub-Saharan Africa seemed to exemplify new hopes for democratization. As we have seen, military strongmen ruled most African nations during the postcolonial era, but this began to change in the early 1990s, in part sparked by the democratization of South Africa. In February 1990 popular protests in Benin ousted the dictatorial government and led to its replacement by a democratic regime. Ghana embraced democratization more gradually: strongman Jerry Rawlings accepted multiparty elections in 1992, but not until 2000 did a democratic regime take power.[11] New parliamentary structures remained imperfect, not always fully corresponding to popular rule, but nonetheless led many to believe that the world would only grow more free in the new century.[12] In general, the end of apartheid in South Africa, and the increasing democratization of Black Africa and Latin America, part of what Samuel Huntington characterized in 1991 as the "third wave" of democratization, made liberal democracy the global norm of politics as never before.[13] The new levels of freedom as well as the impressive economic prosperity of the 1990s seemed poised to complete the work of the anticolonial and civil rights movements in making liberty the property of all peoples.

September 11 shattered this fond hope. If many had hoped that the end of the cold war would bring a new era of global peace and cooperation, that belief collapsed in the ashes of the World Trade Center. As Americans in particular struggled to understand how such an horrendous attack could happen, and what motivated such hatred of their country, many took some comfort in a simple answer; paraphrasing George Bush above, "they hate us for our freedom." Increasingly, the "they" in this response became racialized. The fact that Bush's address to Congress specifically and forcefully rejected blaming Muslims or Arabs in general for the terrorist attack tended to get lost in the shuffle as many Americans and Europeans focused on Islamic fundamentalism as the enemy, the equivalent of the Soviet Union during the cold war. The crusade against the Red peril gave way in the early twentieth century to the crusade against the Green menace.

This new crusade had an important racial dimension. Prejudice against Muslims has a long history in Europe and America, but the events of September 11, widely seen as an unprovoked attack against a free people, gave it a major new impetus. Scholars and journalists described the rise of Islamophobia in the United States as the number of attacks against Muslim and Arab Americans skyrocketed after 2001. Islamophobia targeted a particular religion, but it also had a strong racist component, frequently portraying Arabs and Muslims in identically negative terms. Like anti-Semitism, Islamophobia had both racial and religious dimensions, and during the first decade of the twenty-first century constituted a logical corollary to the idea that the white Christian West was engaged in a death struggle with the Muslim world. The war on terror that has in effect become a permanent feature of global politics ever since 9/11 has been a war against radical Islam and for freedom, but it has also been a race war.[14]

The Islamophobia that has arisen in Europe has roots that go back far beyond 2001, all the way to the Crusades, the Spanish *Reconquista*, and the Ottoman conquest of the Balkans. But it also became commingled, to a much greater extent than in America, with the question of immigration. Many of the immigrants into Western Europe after World War II had come from Muslim countries, such as North Africans in France, Pakistanis in Britain, and Turks in Germany. The sharp economic downturn of the 1970s had led to sharp anti-immigrant hostility as conservatives blamed them for high unemployment among European workers. Increasingly, however, anti-immigrant prejudice focused not just on economic but also cultural differences, on the idea that entire areas in European cities and towns had been taken over by "foreigners." Far from diminishing, this sense of cultural difference and estrangement only grew with the rise of new generations born in Europe to immigrant parents: in France people labeled them "second-generation immigrants," implying they were not really French. Meanwhile, 9/11 and the American invasions of Afghanistan and Iraq increased not only the general antagonism to Islam but also the suspicion that Muslim neighborhoods in Europe constituted a kind of fifth column in the war against terror, leading one conservative American newspaper to label the polyglot Paris suburbs "Falluja-sur-Seine."[15]

The rise of the National Front in France provided a powerful example of the new hostility to immigrants. Founded in 1972 by Jean-Marie LePen, a veteran of France's war in Algeria, the party has grown from a small right-wing sect to one of the most popular in France. From the beginning it emphasized hostility to immigrants, especially Muslim immigrants, rejecting their right to French citizenship and frequently calling for their deportation, as well as limits to immigration from former colonies like Algeria and Tunisia. Currently, under the leadership of LePen's daughter Marine LePen, the party (considered neofascist by many on the Left) has moderated its image somewhat but still frequently links Muslim immigration to Islamic terrorism and considers

Islam a danger to the national character of France. As Marine LePen declared in a newspaper interview in 2010, "The progressive Islamisation of our country and the increase in political-religious demands are calling into question the survival of our civilisation."[16] Today the National Front (in 2018 renamed the Rassemblement National, the National Rally) is one of the largest political parties in France, and it is not inconceivable that it could win the presidency in the near future.[17]

The recent growth of the National Front in France highlights one of the most remarkable global political developments of the twenty-first century, the rise of authoritarian populism. This is in many ways a global phenomenon, as the electoral victories of Narendra Modi in India, Benjamin Netanyahu in Israel, and Jair Bolsonaro in Brazil in one twelve-month span, 2018–19, illustrate. But it has had a particular impact in Europe and America. Since 2000 a number of charismatic right-wing leaders, for example, Viktor Orban in Hungary, Silvio Berlusconi in Italy, and Vladimir Putin in Russia, have taken power. The populist Right has overwhelmed the Far Left and is increasingly drawing support from the Center Right. In 2016 a small right-wing British political party pushed the country into the Brexit referendum, in which a popular majority approved the secession of the United Kingdom from the European Union. A few months later Donald Trump overpowered both the establishment in his own Republican Party and the Democratic opposition to win election as president of the United States.[18]

The new authoritarian populism is a complex affair, blending hostility to global elites, resentment at cultural change, and anger at working-class economic stagnation. But there can be no doubt that covert and overt appeals to racism and anti-immigrant hostility form a major part of its appeal. Trump himself has been especially outrageous in this regard, from characterizing Mexicans as "drug dealers, criminals, and rapists" to saying that there were fine people on both sides of a battle in Charlottesville, Virginia, between neo-Nazis and their opponents, but he is not alone in this regard. As a report noted in 2018, "Both Donald Trump's campaign and right-wing authoritarian populists in Europe have tended to exploit anxieties related to such demographic change. Trump's electoral base—as well as the base of the Republican Party—is overwhelmingly white. The Trump campaign took advantage of anxieties around immigration, race, and Islam, leaning into white identity politics with explicitly racist appeals."[19] Hostility to immigrants, foreigners, Muslims, and racially defined Others in general has thus been a key driver of contemporary authoritarian populism.

At the same time, many populists see themselves as engaged in a movement for freedom, in particular a movement to defend their nations against oppression by an alliance of global elites and the racial minorities and immigrants they exploit for their own ends. In a London pro-Brexit protest a demonstrator costumed as a hoplite of ancient Greece claimed, "I am here fighting for freedom. . . . The Brexit vote is a mass rebellion by the working class of this country, and I don't frigging blame them, because they have not been listened to by any of the parties for years."[20] As noted earlier in this study, freedom in the modern era has been closely identified with the defense of the nation-state; today's authoritarian populists see national cultures as threatened by globalization. In June 2015 representatives of several Far Right parties, including the French National Front, formed a rightist bloc in the European Parliament with the name of Europe of Nations and Freedom. Geert Wilders, head of the Dutch Freedom party, hailed it as an historic occasion, saying "Today is the beginning of our liberation, our D-Day," and arguing that the new bloc would defend national sovereignty against the European Union and the threat of Islamization.[21]

The dynamism of authoritarian populism in today's world shows that white freedom remains alive and well in the twenty-first century. As with the New Right in the late twentieth century, the movement blends a rejection of liberal democratic orthodoxies with appeals to white identity. I will conclude this study by considering what this portends for the times ahead.

White Freedom Yet to Come

As I noted earlier in this chapter, historians are not seers, and I certainly have neither the obligation nor the ability to predict the future. Rather, in this final section I would like to speculate on possible implications of

White Freedom for the world we live in today and tomorrow. This book has addressed and explored a major question in the modern world, the relationship between liberty and race, and I wish to conclude with some thoughts about how people might continue to approach (or not) this relationship. The fact that this question has come up time and time again over the last two hundred years suggests, to me at least, that it will continue to do so for some time to come.

We inhabit a world that is, at least formally, committed to racial equality as part of the democratic ideal. One should immediately note that modern societies frequently betray or fail to meet this standard, and the continued existence of white freedom as a social and political reality is an important part of that failure. Nonetheless, the idea that freedom is a universal value transcending race is now the default standard in modern societies, and it is hard to imagine that changing anytime soon. The powerful movements described in chapter 6 against white freedom did not succeed completely, and they provoked a powerful counterreaction that is still in evidence today. They did, however, permanently shift the goalposts of the game, a great accomplishment that we must never forget. Thanks to them, and to many others over the years who have struggled for racial equality, the primary question surrounding the relationship between race and freedom today is not so much how to challenge white freedom as how to make the reality of universal liberty live up to the ideal.

I would also observe that, except perhaps for some believers in libertarianism and anarchism, freedom has generally not been an end in and of itself. Rather, freedom enables us to do and enjoy things that all peoples value: live in security and peace, have adequate food and shelter, enjoy our friends and families, raise our children with confidence for their futures. I say this to make the point that the politics of white freedom has never been just about race, but it advocates racial distinction and white privilege as a way of achieving those ends. The rise of the New Right in the late twentieth century and of authoritarian populism today certainly has a major racial dimension, but is not just about race: many supporters of Trump and Brexit (including many nonwhite supporters) did not cast their votes in favor of bigotry. Today the push for white freedom is in many ways a response to the inability of modern societies to provide those achievements listed above that freedom was supposed to ensure, and as long as that remains the case, racialized visions of liberty will retain their ability to inspire and motivate those searching for a better life.

For me, therefore, the ultimate question is not so much whether racism will disappear and the universal vision of freedom triumph. Rather, it is whether future societies will overcome the need for white freedom by assuring a good life for all their members. Will the conditions that drive many to embrace a racialized vision of liberty melt away as a result? In a world that embraces racial equality in theory, whiteness is ultimately untenable, a burden as well as a privilege. In the last analysis, will we find a way to free our societies from the need for whiteness? A utopian vision, perhaps, but so much that has been considered utopian in the present has become reality in the future. The clarion call of the French Revolution for liberty, equality, and fraternity still rings true, especially if we consider not just these values in general but the relationship between them in particular.

I hope that historians of the future will be able to answer these questions, but it won't be until long after we are gone. At that point, they will then doubtless come up with new questions that we can't imagine. In the present, we must therefore content ourselves with posing them, with measuring how far we have come and considering the possible shapes of the road ahead. The history of white freedom considers the best and the worst of the human experience, its highs and lows, and the relationship between them. It is both a sobering tale and one full of hope, and if the past is a guide I consider myself justified in believing that hope will prevail in the future.

NOTES

Introduction

1. William C. Allen, "History of Slave Laborers in the Construction of the United States Capitol," June 1, 2005, 1.

2. *The Washington Post*, June 15, 2007. Jesse Jackson Jr. was an African American congressman from Chicago 1995–2012 and is the son of the famous Black civil rights leader Jesse Jackson.

3. *The New Pittsburgh Courier*, June 30, 2010.

4. Justin Roberts, *Slavery and the Enlightenment in the British Atlantic, 1750–1807* (New York: Cambridge University Press, 2013); Louis Sala-Molins, *Dark Side of the Light: Slavery and the French Enlightenment* (Minneapolis: University of Minnesota Press, 2006).

5. Among many, many works, see Ibram X. Kendi, *Stamped from the Beginning: The Definitive History of Racist Ideas in America* (New York: Perseus, 2016); Nell Irvin Painter, *The History of White People* (New York: W. W. Norton, 2010); Audrey Smedley, *Race in North America: Origin and Evolution of a World View* (Boulder: Westview Press, 2007); James Horn, *1619: Jamestown and the Forging of American Democracy* (New York: Basic Books, 2018).

6. See, for example, Edmund Morgan, *American Slavery, American Freedom: The Ordeal of Colonial Virginia* (New York: W. W. Norton, 2005); David Brion Davis, *The Problem of Slavery in the Age of Revolution, 1770–1823* (New York: Oxford University Press, 1999); Simon Schama, *Rough Crossings: Britain, the Slaves, and the American Revolution* (New York: Harper Collins, 2006); David Waldstreicher, *Runaway America: Benjamin Franklin, Slavery, and the American Revolution* (New York: Hill and Wang, 2004); Patricia Bradley, *Slavery, Propaganda, and the American Revolution* (Jackson: University Press of Mississippi, 1998).

7. Garry Wills, *Negro President: Thomas Jefferson and the Slave Power* (Boston: Houghton-Mifflin, 2003); Annette Gordon-Reed, *Thomas Jefferson and Sally Hemings: An American Controversy* (Charlottesville: University Press of Virginia, 1997).

8. See, for example, Alyssa Goldstein Sepinwall, *The Abbé Grégoire and the Making of the French Revolution* (Berkeley: University of California Press, 2005); David Patrick Geggus, *The Impact of the Haitian Revolution in the Atlantic World* (Columbia: University of South Carolina Press, 2001); David Barry Gaspar and David Patrick Geggus, eds., *A Turbulent Time: The French Revolution and the Greater Caribbean* (Bloomington: Indiana University Press, 1997).

9. Rick Atkinson, "Why We Still Care About America's Founders," *The New York Times*, May 11, 2019, https://www.nytimes.com/2019/05/11/opinion/sunday/history-americas-founders.html

10. Malcolm X, "The Ballot or the Bullet," April 1964. Speech delivered April 3, 1964, Cleveland, OH.

11. See, for example, Rupert Chetwynd, *Yesterday's Enemy: Freedom Fighters or Terrorists?* (Ronkonhoma, NY: Impala Press 2005).

12. On Romanticism and race, see Pratima Prasad, *Colonialism, Race, and the French Romantic Imagination* (New York: Routledge, 2009); Paul Youngquist, ed., *Race, Romanticism, and the Atlantic* (Burlington: Ashgate, 2013); Peter J. Kitson, *Romantic Literature, Race, and Colonial Encounter* (New York: Palgrave Macmillan, 2007).

13. William L. Van Deburg, *New Day in Babylon: The Black Power Movement and American Culture, 1965–1975* (Chicago: University of Chicago Press, 1993); James Smethurst, *The Black Arts Movement: Literary Nationalism in the 1960s and 1970s* (Chapel Hill: University of North Carolina Press, 2005).

14. On transnational history, see Akira Iriye, "The Internationalization of History," *The American Historical Review* 94, no. 1 (February 1989); Ian Tyrell, *Transnational Nation: United States History in Global Perspective since 1789* (New York: Palgrave Macmillan, 2007); Thomas Bender, *A Nation among Nations: America's Place in World History* (New York: Hill and Wang, 2006); Tyler Stovall, *Transnational France: the Modern History of a Universal Nation* (New York: Routledge, 2015).

15. For example, see Thomas J. Schaeper, *France and America in the Revolutionary Era: The Life of Jacques-Donatien Leray de Chaumont, 1725–1803* (New York: Berghahn, 1995); Steve Sainlaude, *France and the American Civil War: A Diplomatic History* (Chapel Hill: University of North Carolina Press, 2019); André Kaspi, *Le temps des Américains: Le concours américain à la France en 1917–1918* (Paris: Publications de la Sorbonne, 1976); Richard F. Kuisel, *Seducing the French: the Dilemma of Americanization* (Berkeley: University of California Press, 1997); Mary-Louise Roberts, *What Soldiers Do: Sex and the American GI in World War II France* (Chicago: University of Chicago Press, 2013); Tyler Stovall, *Paris Noir: African Americans in the City of Light* (Boston: Houghton-Mifflin, 1996); Jean-Philippe Mathy, *French Resistance: The French-American Culture Wars* (Minneapolis: University of Minnesota Press, 2000).

16. Paul Hoffmann, *Théories et modèles de la liberté au XVIIIème siècle* (Paris: Presses Universitaires de France, 1996); Pierre Rosanvallon, *The Demands of Liberty: Civil Society in France since the Revolution* (Cambridge, MA: Harvard University Press, 2007); Sue Peabody and Tyler Stovall, eds., *The Color of Liberty: Histories of Race in France* (Durham: Duke University Press, 2003); Gary Wilder, *Freedom Time: Negritude, Decolonization, and the Future of the World* (Durham: Duke University Press, 2015).

17. Foner, *Give Me Liberty!: An American History* (New York: W. W. Norton, 2005), p. xxiii.

18. On universalism in France, see Roger Celestin and Eliane DalMolin, *France from 1851 to the Present: Universalism in Crisis* (New York: Palgrave Macmillan, 2007); Maurice Samuels, *The Right to Difference: French Universalism and the Jews* (Chicago: University of Chicago Press, 2017); Stovall, *Transnational France*; Mary Dewhurst Lewis, *The Boundaries of the Republic: Migrant Rights and the Limits of Universalism in France, 1918–1940* (Stanford: Stanford University Press, 2007). In the United States universalism is somewhat more complex, since it interacts with another intellectual tradition that at first blush would seem to contradict it: American exceptionalism. See, for example, Godfrey Hodgson, *The Myth of American Exceptionalism* (New Haven: Yale University Press, 2009).

19. Jane Samson, *Race and Empire* (New York: Routledge, 2004); Tony Ballantyne, *Orientalism and Race: Aryanism in the British Empire* (New York: Palgrave, 2002); Philippa Levine, *Prostitution, Race, and Politics: Policing Venereal Disease in the British Empire* (New York: Routledge, 2003).

20. Horst Junginger, *The Scientification of the "Jewish Question" in Nazi Germany* (Boston: Brill, 2017); Devin O. Pendas et al., *Beyond the Racial State: Rethinking Nazi Germany* (Washington, DC: The German Historical Institute, 2017); Aaron Gillette, *Racial Theories in Fascist Italy* (New York: Routledge, 2001).

21. On whiteness studies see, among others, David Roediger, *The Wages of Whiteness: Race and the Making of the American Working Class* (London: Verso, 2007); Theodore W. Allen, *The Invention of the White Race*, 2 vols. (London: Verso, 2012); Noel Ignatiev, *How the Irish Became White* (London: Routledge, 2008); Karen Brodkin, *How Jews Became White Folks, and What That Says About Race in America* (New Brunswick: Rutgers University Press, 1998).

22. Morgan, *American Slavery, American Freedom*, 4.

23. Ibid., 376.

24. Ibid., 386.

25. Eric Foner, *The Story of American Freedom* (New York and London: W. W. Norton, 1998). He might have added the ways in which a tremendous range of consumer products in twentieth-century American society, ranging from washing machines to automobiles, have promised not just clean clothes or efficient transport but above all freedom to those who buy them. See, for example, Stuart Ewen, *Captains of Consciousness: Advertising and the Social Roots of the Consumer Culture* (New York: Basic Books, 2001).

26. Ultimately, to raise such questions is to shift from the terrain of the historian to that of the philosopher. The classic study is Rudolf Steiner, *The Philosophy of Freedom: A Basis of a Modern World Conception* (London: Rudolf Steiner Press, 1979). Themes of freedom are also central to the existentialist philosophy of Jean-Paul Sartre, notably in *Being and Nothingness* and *A Critique of Dialectical Reason*.

27. See, for example, Herbert J. Muller, *Freedom in the Ancient World* (New York: Harper, 1961); Max Pohlenz, *Freedom in Greek Life and Thought* (Dordrecht: D. Reidel, 1966); Moses I. Finley, *Ancient Slavery and Modern Ideology* (New York: Penguin, 1980).

28. John Stuart Mill, *On Liberty* (London: John Parker & Sons, 1859); John Emerich Edward Dalberg, Lord Acton, *The History of Freedom and Other Essays* (London: Macmillan & Co, 1907); Isaiah Berlin, *Four Essays on Liberty* (New York: Oxford University Press, 1970).

29. See Gertrude Himmelfarb, "Liberty: 'One Very Simple Principle'?," *The American Scholar* 62, no. 4 (Autumn 1993): 531–50.

30. Orlando Patterson, *Freedom*, vol. 1, *Freedom in the Making of Western Culture* (New York: Basic Books, 1991), ix.

31. See The Making of Modern Freedom, a book series published by Stanford University Press. Edited by R. W. Davis, it began in 1991 with hopes of completing the work of Lord Acton on freedom and eventually reached thirteen volumes.

32. Donald W. Treadgold, *Freedom: A History* (New York and London: New York University Press, 1990), 5.

33. Joseph Klaits and Michael H. Haltzel, eds., *Liberty/Liberté: The American and French Experiences* (Baltimore and London: The Johns Hopkins University Press, 1991).

34. On the history of liberal democracy, see C. B. Macpherson, *The Life and Times of Liberal Democracy* (Oxford: Oxford University Press, 1977); William E. Scheuerman, *Liberal Democracy and the Social Acceleration of Time* (Baltimore: Johns Hopkins University Press, 2004).

35. John Hope Franklin, *From Slavery to Freedom: A History of Negro Americans* (New York: A. A. Knopf, 1947).

36. Henry Hampton and Steve Fayer: *Voices of Freedom: An Oral History of the Civil Rights Movement from the 1950s through the 1980s* (Bantam: 1990); Robin D. G. Kelly, *Freedom Dreams: The Black Radical Imagination* (Boston: Beacon Press, 2003); Gary Wilder, *Freedom Time: Negritude, Decolonization, and the Future of the World* (Durham and London: Duke University Press, 2015).

37. Sara Evans, *Born for Liberty: A History of Women in America* (1989); Mark Thompson and Randy Shilts, *Long Road to Freedom: The Advocate History of the Gay and Lesbian Movement* (New York: St Martin's Press, 1995).

38. Patterson, *Freedom in the Making of Western Culture*; and, by the same author, *Slavery and Social Death: A Comparative Study* (Cambridge, MA: Harvard University Press, 1982).

39. See Peter A. Dorsey, *Common Bondage: Slavery as Metaphor in Revolutionary America* (Knoxville: University of Tennessee Press, 2009).

40. See Frank M. Snowden Jr., *Before Color Prejudice: The Ancient View of Blacks* (Cambridge, MA: Harvard University Press, 1983); Benjamin Isaac, *The Invention of Racism in Classical Antiquity* (Princeton: Princeton University Press, 2006).

41. Ivan Hannaford, *Race: The History of an Idea in the West* (Baltimore: Johns Hopkins University Press, 1996).

42. See, for example, George M. Frederickson, *Racism: A Short History* (Princeton: Princeton University Press, 2002); Thomas Gossett, *Race: The History of an Idea in America* (New York: Oxford University Press, 1963); Neil MacMaster, *Racism in Europe, 1870–2000* (New York: Palgrave, 2001); Ann Laura Stoler, *Carnal Knowledge and Imperial Power: Race and the Intimate in Colonial Rule* (Berkeley: University of California Press, 2002).

43. Emmanuel Eze, *Race and the Enlightenment: A Reader*; see also Justin E. H. Smith, *Nature, Human Nature, and Human Difference: Race in Early Modern Philosophy* (Princeton: Princeton University Press, 2015); Deborah K. Heikes, *Rationality, Representation, and Race* (London: Palgrave Macmillan, 2016); Pierre Pluchon, *Nègres et juifs au XVIIIe siècle: Le racisme au Siècle des Lumières* (Paris: Tallandier, 1984).

44. Léon Poliakov, *The Aryan Myth: A History of Racist and Nationalist Ideas in Europe* (New York: Basic Books, 1974); George Mosse, *Toward the Final Solution: A History of European Racism* (New York: H. Fertig, 1978). Other major histories of anti-Semitism include Léon Poliakov, *The History of Anti-Semitism* (New York: Vanguard Press, 1985); Albert S. Lindemann and Richard S. Levy, *Antisemitism: A History* (Oxford and New York: Oxford University Press, 2010).

45. On the history of African American studies, see Fabio Rojas, *From Black Power to Black Studies: How a Radical Social Movement became an Academic Discipline* (Baltimore: Johns Hopkins University Press, 2007).

46. See, for example, Ronald Takaki, *A Different Mirror: A History of Multicultural America* (Boston: Little, Brown, 1993); Roxanne Dunbar-Ortiz, *An Indigenous People's History of the United States* (Boston: Beacon, 2014); Juan Poblete, *Critical Latino and Latin American Studies* (Minneapolis: University of Minnesota Press, 2003).

47. Janice A. Radway et al., *American Studies: An Anthology* (Wiley-Blackwell, 2009); George Lipsitz, *American Studies in a Moment of Danger* (Minneapolis: University of Minnesota Press, 2001).

48. Eduardo Bonilla-Silva, *Racism without Racists: Color-Blind Racism and the Persistence of Racial Inequality in America* (Lanham, MD: Rowman and Littlefield, 2009); Bryan K. Fair, *Notes of a Racial Caste Baby: Color Blindness and the End of Affirmative Action* (New York: New York University Press, 1999).

49. Alain Finkelkraut, *La defaite de la pensée* (Paris: Gallimard, 1987); Tzvetan Todorov, *Nous et les autres: La reflexion française sur la diversité humaine* (Paris: Seuil, 1989); Maxim Silverman, *Deconstructing the Nation: Immigration, Racism, and Citizenship in Modern France* (New York: Routledge, 2014); John R. Bowen, *Why the French Don't Like Headscarves: Islam, the State, and Public Space* (Princeton: Princeton University Press, 2010); Mayanthi L. Fernando, *The Republic Unsettled: Muslim French and the Contradictions of Secularism* (Durham: Duke University Press, 2014); Joan W. Scott, *Parité: Sexual Equality and the Crisis of French Universalism* (Chicago: University of Chicago Press, 2005).

50. See, for example, Tessa Blackstone, Bhikhu Parekh, and Peter Saunders, eds., *Race Relations in Britain* (London: Routledge, 1997); Annie Phizacklea, "A Sociology of Migration or 'Race Relations'? A View from Britain," *Current Sociology* 32, no. 3 (Winter 1984); University of Birmingham Centre for Contemporary Cultural Studies, *The Empire Strikes Back: Race and Racism in 70s Britain* (London: Hutchinson, 1982); Zig Layton-Henry, *The Politics of Immigration: Immigration, "Race," and "Race" Relations in Postwar Britain* (Oxford: Blackwell Publishers, 1992).

51. Not all; recently some geneticists and other scientists have argued that race does have a certain objective biological reality. See, for example, Nicholas Wade, *A Troublesome Inheritance: Genes, Race and Human History* (New York: Penguin Books, 2015); David Reich, *Who We Are and How We Got Here: Ancient DNA and the New Science of the Human Past* (New York: Pantheon, 2018).

Chapter 1

1. As Barrie himself made clear, there were no lost girls because female infants were too smart to fall out of their baby carriages. Here masculinity and savagery coincide.

2. The racial portrayal of the Native Americans, frequently called pickaninnies and often referring to Peter Pan as the great white father, is complex. See Sarah Laskow, "The Racist History of Peter Pan's Indian Tribe," *Smithsonian Magazine* (December 2, 2014).

3. J. M. Barrie, *Peter Pan*, https://www.gutenberg.org/files/16/16-h/16-h.htm#link2 HCH0005 (last accessed June 26, 2020).

4. And yet, one must note that Peter Pan remains a lost boy, outside the conventional structures of Edwardian society. White freedom must triumph over savage freedom, but at the same time alternate fantasies of liberty retain an important place in its world.

5. For a good overview of the scholarship on freedom, see Treadgold, *Freedom: A History*; for the scholarship on race, see John Stone, "New Paradigms for Old? Ethnic and Racial Studies on the Eve of the Millennium," *Ethnic and Racial Studies* #21 (1998).

6. Isaiah Berlin, *Four Essays on Liberty* (New York: Oxford University Press, 1970), xlv.

7. See, for example, Paul Gilroy, *Against Race: Imagining Political Culture Beyond the Color Line* (Cambridge, MA: Harvard University Press, 2000).

8. On the history of nationalism, see Benedict Anderson, *Imagined Communities: Reflections on the Origin and Spread of Nationalism* (London and New York: Verso, 2006); Eric Hobsbawm, *Nations and Nationalism since 1780: Programme, Myth, Reality* (Cambridge: Cambridge University Press, 2012); Ernest Gellner, *Nations and Nationalism* (Ithaca: Cornell University Press, 2009); Liah Greenfeld, *Nationalism: Five Roads to Modernity* (Cambridge, MA: Harvard University Press, 1993).

9. See Gary Gerstle, *American Crucible: Race and Nation in the Twentieth Century* (rev. ed. Princeton: Princeton University Press, 2001); Mariana Ortega and Linda Alcoff, *Constructing the Nation: A Race and Nationalism Reader* (Albany: SUNY Press, 2009); Eric D. Weitz, *A Century of Genocide: Utopias of Race and Nation* (Princeton: Princeton University Press, 2003).

10. Marc Redfield, *The Politics of Aesthetics: Nationalism, Gender, Romanticism* (Stanford: Stanford University Press, 2003); W. M. Verhoeven, *Revolutionary Histories: Transatlantic Cultural Nationalism, 1775–1815* (Palgrave Macmillan, 2002).

11. On *völkisch* ideology, see Mosse, *Toward a Final Solution*; Roderick Stackelberg, *Idealism Debased: From "Völkisch" Ideology to National Socialism* (Kent, OH: Kent State University Press, 1981).

12. Ernest Renan, "What Is a Nation?," in Homi Bhabha, ed., *Nation and Narration* (London and New York: Routledge, 1990).

13. Carole Paligot-Reynaud, *De l'identité nationale: Science, race, et politique en Europe et aux États-Unis, XIXe-XXe siècles* (Paris: Presses Universitaires de France, 2011).

14. Theodor Herzl, *The Jewish State* (Mineola, NY: Dover, 1989); Walter Laqueur, *A History of Zionism: From the French Revolution to the Establishment of the State of Israel* (New York: Shocken: 2003); Arthur Hertzberg, *The Zionist Idea* (New York: Doubleday, 1959).

15. Klytus Smith et al., *The Harlem Cultural Political Movements 1960–1970: From Malcolm X to Black Is Beautiful* (New York: Gumbs and Thomas, 1994); William L. Van Deburg, *New Day in Babylon: The Black Power Movement and American Culture, 1965–1975* (Chicago: University of Chicago Press, 1993).

16. Andre Neher, *They Made Their Souls Anew* (Albany: State University of New York Press, 1990), 149–51.

17. Pap Ndiaye, *La condition noire: Essai sur une minorité française* (Paris: Calmann-Lévy, 2008).

18. Thomas B. Allen, *Tories: Fighting for the King in America's First Civil War* (New York: Harper Paperbacks, 2011).

19. Cited in Oxford online dictionary, www.oxforddictionnaries.com.

20. Ibid.

21. George Woodcock, *Anarchism: A History of Libertarian Ideas and Movements* (Cleveland: The World Publishing Company, 1962); Paul Avrich and Barry Pateman, *Anarchist Voices: An Oral History of Anarchism in America* (AK Press, 2005). John M. Merriman, *The Dynamite Club: How a Bombing in Fin-de-Siècle Paris Ignited the Age of Modern Terror* (New Haven: Yale University Press, 2016).

22. Charles Johnson, *Historie der Engelsche Zee-Rovers* (Amsterdam: Hermann Uytwerf, 1725). See Marcus Rediker's discussion of this contrast in *Villains of All Nations: Atlantic Pirates in the Golden Age* (Boston: Beacon Press, 2005).

23. On women and piracy, see Joan Druett, *She Captains: Heroines and Hellions of the Sea* (New York: Simon and Schuster, 2001); David Cordingly, *Seafaring Women: Adventures of Pirate Queens, Female Stowaways, and Sailors' Wives* (New York: Random House, 2002).

24. Henry A. Ormerod, *Piracy in the Ancient World: An Essay in Mediterranean History* (Totowa, NJ: Rowman and Littlefield, 1978).

25. Adrian Tinniswood, *Pirates of Barbary: Corsairs, Conquests and Captivity in the Seventeenth-Century Mediterranean* (London: Jonathan Cape, 2010); Jacques Heers, *The Barbary Corsairs: Warfare in the Mediterranean, 1480–1580* (London: Greenhill Books, 2003); C. S. Forester, *The Barbary Pirates* (New York: Random House, 1953).

26. Brian Kilmeade and Don Yaeger, *Thomas Jefferson and the Tripoli Pirates: The Forgotten War That Changed American History* (New York: Sentinel, 2015); Frank Lambert, *The Barbary Wars: American Independence in the Atlantic World* (New York: Hill and Wang, 2007).

27. Rediker, *Villains of All Nations*; David Cordingly, *Under the Black Flag: The Romance and the Reality of Life among the Pirates* (New York: Random House, 2006).

28. Harry Kelsey, *Sir Francis Drake, the Queen's Pirate* (New Haven: Yale University Press, 1998); John Sugden, *Sir Francis Drake* (New York: Henry Holt and Co., 1991).

29. Angus Konstam, *Blackbeard: America's Most Notorious Pirate* (Hoboken: Wiley, 2007).

30. David Cordingly, *Life among the Pirates: The Romance and the Reality* (Boothbay Harbor: Abacus, 1996).

31. Cited in Charles Johnson, *A General History of the Robberies and Murders of the Most Notorious Pyrates* (Conway Maritime Press, 1724), 213–14; Richard Sanders, *If a Pirate I Must Be . . . : The True Story of "Black Bart," King of the Caribbean Pirates* (New York: Skyhorse Publishing, 2009).

32. In fact, some have argued that one of the main reasons for suppressing piracy was to make the Caribbean safe for the slave trade. See Sanders, *If a Pirate I Must Be.*

33. On the history of maroons, see Richard Price, *Maroon Societies: Rebel Slave Communities in the Americas* (Baltimore: Johns Hopkins University Press, 1996); Karla Lewis Gottlieb, *The Mother of Us All: A History of Queen Nanny, Leader of the Jamaican Windward Maroons* (Lawrenceville, NJ: Africa World Press, 2000).

34. Peter Leeson, *The Invisible Hook: The Hidden Economics of Pirates* (Princeton: Princeton University Press, 2009).

35. Marcus Rediker, *Between the Devil and the Deep Blue Sea: Merchant Seamen, Pirates, and the Anglo-American Maritime World, 1700–1750* (Cambridge, UK: Cambridge University Press, 1989); Marcus Rediker, *Outlaws of the Atlantic: Sailors, Pirates, and Motley Crews, in the Age of Sail* (Boston: Beacon Press, 2015); Peter Linebaugh and Marcus Rediker, *The Many-Headed Hydra: Sailors, Slaves, Commoners, and the Hidden History of the Revolutionary Atlantic* (Boston: Beacon Press, 2013); Colin Woodard, *The Republic of Pirates: Being the True and Surprising Story of the Pirates and the Man Who Brought Them Down* (Mariner Press: 2008).

36. Johnson, *A General History of the Robberies and Murders.*

37. Melinda Long, *Pirates Don't Change Diapers* (Boston: Houghton Mifflin Harcourt, 2007). Part of the attraction of piracy, of course, represents a masculine revolt against domesticity, one frequently criticized as yet another form of men refusing to grow up. This emphasis on delayed maturity, and its representation in a children's book, underscores the link between piracy and

childhood later in this chapter. See Barbara Ehrenreich, *The Hearts of Men: American Dreams and the Flight from Commitment* (New York: Anchor Books, 1983).

38. The Confederate flag represents an interesting and complex example of white freedom. On the one hand, like the pirate flag it symbolizes a kind of alternate, even subversive liberty. On the other, it also clearly represents whiteness and white privilege. The debate between proponents and opponents of the flag often comes down to whether one sees it as a symbol of freedom or racism; in line with this book's broader argument, I suggest it is both. See John M. Coski, *The Confederate Battle Flag: America's Most Embattled Emblem* (Cambridge, MA: Belknap Press, 2006).

39. On the idea of the rebel, see Howard Mumford Jones, *Revolution and Romanticism* (Cambridge, MA: Harvard University Press, 1974).

40. Aram Sinnreich, *The Piracy Crusade: How the Music Industry's War on Sharing Destroys Markets and Erodes Civil Liberties* (Amherst and Boston: University of Massachusetts Press, 2013), 1, 4.

41. Michael Strangelove, *The Empire of Mind: Digital Piracy and the Anti-Capitalist Movement* (Toronto: University of Toronto Press, 2005), 56.

42. Analysts have hotly debated the extent to which the rise of Napster and free file sharing precipitated the downturn in music industry profits in the early years of the twenty-first century. For music industry representatives the relationship is clear; others, however, have argued that file sharing actually prompted consumers to buy more music. See on this point Sinnreich, *The Piracy Crusade*, part 2.

43. Mathew Burkart, *Pirate Politics* (Cambridge, MA: The MIT Press, 2014), 51.

44. Internet pirates also protested against corporate control, of course; one Pirate Bay poster showed a pirate ship firing on the famous Hollywood sign in Los Angeles.

45. Sinnreich, *The Piracy Crusade*, 179–80.

46. Cited in Ben Jones, "The Swedish Pirate Party Presents Their Election Manifesto," *TF*, August 29, 2006. https://torrentfreak.com/the-swedish-pirate-party-presents-their-election-manifesto/ (last accessed June 26, 2020).

47. Strangelove, *The Empire of Mind*.

48. See James L. Huston, *Calculating the Value of the Union: Slavery, Property Rights, and the Economic Origins of the Civil War* (Chapel Hill: University of North Carolina Press, 2003).

49. See David Brion Davis, *The Problem of Slavery in Western Culture* (Ithaca: Cornell University Press, 1966), 391–421.

50. On piracy and childhood, see Bradley Deane, "Imperial Boyhood: Piracy and the Play Ethic," *Victorian Studies* 53, no. 4 (Summer 2011); Anne Petersen, "'You Believe in Pirates, Of Course . . .': Disney's Commodification and 'Closure' vs. Johnny Depp's Aesthetic Piracy of 'Pirates of the Caribbean,'" *Studies in Popular Culture* 29, no. 2 (April 2007).

51. Robert Louis Stevenson, *Treasure Island* (Mineola, NY: Dover, 1993).

52. From children fantasizing about life on the unfenced prairie to New Age philosophers entranced by Native American spirituality, American Indians have had a key relationship to ideas of freedom as well as modern childhood. See, for example, Bruce E. Johansen, *Debating Democracy: Native American Legacy of Freedom* (Santa Fe: Clear Light Publishers, 1998); Joshua David Bellin, *The Demon of the Continent: Indians and the Shaping of American Literature* (Philadelphia: University of Pennsylvania Press, 2001); Caroline Levander, *Cradle of Liberty: Race, the Child,*

and National Belonging from Thomas Jefferson to W.E.B. DuBois (Durham: Duke University Press, 2006); Anna Mae Duane, *Suffering Childhood in Early America: Violence, Race, and the Making of the Child Victim* (Athens: University of Georgia Press, 2011).

53. J. M. Barrie, *Peter Pan* (London: Hodder and Stoughton, 1911). The novel was based upon the 1904 play, *Peter Pan, or the Boy Who Wouldn't Grow Up*, and on characters from an earlier novel, *The Little White Bird* (1902). See also Andrew Birkin, *J. M. Barrie and the Lost Boys: the Real Story of Peter Pan* (New Haven: Yale University Press, 2003).

54. Thus the Peter Pan Syndrome, or rejecting adulthood. See, for example, Dan Kiley, *The Peter Pan Syndrome: Men Who Have Never Grown Up* (New York: Dodd, Mead, 1983).

55. The classic study of the history of childhood is Philippe Ariès, *Centuries of Childhood: A Social History of Family Life*, translated by Robert Baldick (New York: Alfred A. Knopf, 1962). See also Colin Heywood, *A History of Childhood: Children and Childhood in the West from Medieval to Modern Times* (Cambridge: Polity Press, 2001); C. John Sommerville, *The Rise and Fall of Childhood* (Beverly Hills: Sage Publications, 1982); Peter Stearns, *Childhood in World History* (London and New York: Routledge, 2006).

56. Philippe Ariès, *Centuries of Childhood*, 413.

57. Colin Heywood, *A History of Childhood: Children and Childhood in the West from Medieval to Modern Times* (Cambridge, UK: Polity Press, 2001); Peter N. Stearns, *Childhood in World History* (New York and London: Routledge, 2006).

58. John Locke, *Some Thoughts Concerning Education* and *Of the Conduct of Understanding*, edited by Ruth Grant and Nathan Tarcov (Indianapolis: Hackett, 1996).

59. Jean-Jacques Rousseau, *The Émile of Jean-Jacques Rousseau*, translated by William Boyd (New York: Columbia University Press, 1965).

60. Nathan Tarcov, *Locke's Education for Liberty* (Lanham, MD: Lexington Books, 1999).

61. Jimmy Casas Klaussen, *Fugitive Rousseau: Slavery, Primitivism, and Freedom* (New York: Fordham University Press, 2014).

62. Anja Muller, ed., *Fashioning Childhood in the Eighteenth Century: Age and Industry* (Burlington, VT: Ashgate, 2006); Judith Plotz, *Romanticism and the Vocation of Childhood* (New York: Palgrave, 2001); Anne Higonnet, *Pictures of Innocence: The History and Crisis of Ideal Childhood* (New York: Thames and Hudson, 1998).

63. On child labor, see Jane Humphries, *Childhood and Child Labour in the British Industrial Revolution* (Cambridge: Cambridge University Press, 2011); Hugh D. Hindman, *Child Labor: An American History* (New York and London: Routledge, 2002); Beverly C. Grier, *Invisible Hands: Child Labor and the State in Colonial Zimbabwe* (New York: Heinemann, 2005).

64. On the history of education, see Antoine Prost, *Histoire de l'enseignement en France, 1800–1967* (Paris: Colin, 1968); Nicholas Touloudis, *Teaching Marianne and Uncle Sam: Public Education, State Centralization, and Teacher Unionism in France and the United States* (Philadelphia: Temple University Press, 2011); William J. Reese, *America's Public Schools: From the Common School to No Child Left Behind* (Baltimore: Johns Hopkins University Press, 2005); Mary Stuart, *The Education of the People: A History of Primary Education in England and Wales during the Nineteenth Century* (London and New York: Routledge, 2013); Fritz K. Ringer, *Education and Society in Modern Europe* (Bloomington: Indiana University Press, 1978).

65. Higonnet, *Pictures of Innocence*.

66. See, for example, Helene Guldberg, *Reclaiming Childhood: Freedom and Play in an Age of Fear* (London and New York: Routledge, 2009).

67. Jerrold Siegel, *Bohemian Paris: Culture, Politics, and the Boundaries of Bourgeois Life, 1830–1930* (Baltimore: Johns Hopkins University Press, 1999).

68. Cited in Jon Savage, *Teenage: The Prehistory of Youth Culture: 1875–1945* (New York: Penguin, 2008), xv.

69. Michael H. Kater, *Hitler Youth* (Cambridge MA: Harvard University Press, 2004); H. W. Koch, *The Hitler Youth: Origins and Development, 1922–1945* (New York: Cooper Square Press, 2000).

70. Kelly Jakes, *Strains of Dissent: Popular Music and Everyday Resistance in World War II France, 1940–1945* (East Lansing: Michigan State University Press, 2019); Luis Alvarez, *The Power of the Zoot: Youth Culture and Resistance during World War II* (Berkeley: University of California Press, 2008); Kathy Peiss, *Zoot Suit: The Enigmatic Career of an Extreme Style* (Philadelphia: University of Pennsylvania Press, 2011).

71. Daniel Singer, *Prelude to Revolution: France in May 1968* (Boston: South End Press, 2002); Kristin Ross, *May '68 and its Afterlives* (Chicago: University of Chicago Press, 2002).

72. David Maraniss: *They Marched into Sunlight: War and Peace Vietnam and American October 1967* (New York: Simon and Schuster, 2004); Robert Cohen, *Freedom's Orator: Mario Savio and the Radical Legacy of the 1960s* (Oxford: Oxford University Press, 2009).

73. John R. Gillis, *Youth and History: Tradition and Change in European Age Relations, 1770-Present* (Cambridge, MA: Academic Press, 1974); Stuart Hall, *Resistance Through Rituals: Youth Subcultures in Postwar Britain* (New York and London: Routledge, 2006); Uta Poiger, *Jazz, Rock, and Rebels: Cold War Politics and American Culture in a Divided Germany* (Berkeley: University of California Press, 2000).

74. See, for example, Mathew Thomson, *Lost Freedom: The Landscape of the Child and the British Post-War Settlement* (Oxford: Oxford University Press, 2013).

75. Hyman Rickover, *Education for Freedom* (Dutton, 1959); bell hooks, *Teaching to Transgress: Education as the Practice of Freedom* (New York and London: Routledge, 1994).

76. Robert S. Gildea, *Education in Provincial France, 1800–1914: A Study of Three Departments* (Oxford: Oxford University Press, 1983): Jo Burr Margadant, *Madame le Professeur: Women Educators in the Third Republic* (Princeton: Princeton University Press, 1990); Mona Siegel, *The Moral Disarmament of France: Education, Pacifism, and Patriotism, 1914–1940* (Cambridge, UK: Cambridge University Press, 2011).

77. Cited in David S. Landes, *The Unbound Prometheus: Technological Change and Industrial Development in Western Europe from 1750 to the Present* (Cambridge, UK: Cambridge University Press, 1972), 342.

78. For a recent statement of this opposition, see Gary Cross, *Men to Boys: The Making of Modern Immaturity* (New York: Columbia University Press, 2010).

79. Adrian Tinniswood, *Pirates of Barbary: Corsairs, Conquests and Captivity in the Seventeenth-Century Mediterranean* (London: Jonathan Cape, 2010), xvi.

80. Gillian Weiss, *Captives and Corsairs: France and Slavery in the Early Modern Mediterranean* (Stanford: Stanford University Press, 2011).

81. Darcy Grimaldo Grigsby, *Extremities: Painting Empire in Post-Revolutionary France* (New Haven and London: Yale University Press, 2002).

82. Laurent Dubois and Richard Lee Turits, eds., *Freedom Roots: Histories from the Caribbean* (Chapel Hill: University of North Carolina Press, 2019); Hilary McD. Beckles, *The First Black Slave Society: Britain's "Barbarity Time" in Barbados, 1636–1876* (Kingston: University Press of the West Indies, 2016); Jennifer L. Palmer, *Intimate Bonds: Family and Slavery in the French Atlantic* (Philadelphia: University of Pennsylvania Press, 2016).

83. S. Derek Turner, *Digital Denied: The Impact of Systemic Racial Discrimination on Home-Internet Adoption* (New York: Free Press, 2016), 2.

84. Bahjat El-Darwiche, "Why Are 4 Billion People without the Internet?," *Strategy+Business* (May 31, 2016).

85. Mona Ozouf, *Jules Ferry: La liberté et la tradition* (Paris: Gallimard, 2014).

86. Karen Sands-O'Connor, "Primitive Minds: Anthropology, Children, and Savages in Andrew Lang and Rudyard Kipling," in Adrienne E. Gavin and Andrew F. Humphries, eds., *Children in Edwardian Fiction* (London: Palgrave Macmillan, 2009), 177.

87. Zohreh T. Sullivan, *Narratives of Empire: The Fictions of Rudyard Kipling* (New York: Cambridge University Press, 1993); David Gilmour, *The Long Recessional: The Imperial Life of Rudyard Kipling* (New York: Farrar, Straus and Giroux, 2002).

88. John Stuart Mill, *On Liberty*, cited in Foner, *The Story of American Freedom*, 71.

89. Elisabeth Wesseling, ed., *The Child Savage, 1890–2010: From Comics to Games* (Oxon and New York: Routledge, 2016), 9.

90. Mike Sell, "Bohemianism, the Cultural Turn of the Avantgarde, and Forgetting the Roma," *TDR* 51, no. 2 (Summer, 2007): 41–59.

91. Paula S. Fass, *The Damned and the Beautiful: American Youth in the 1920s* (New York: Oxford University Press, 1977).

92. Jon Savage, *Teenage*.

93. Norman Mailer, "The White Negro: Superficial Reflections on the Hipster," *Dissent* (Fall 1957). On beatniks and Black culture, see Stephen R. Duncan, *The Rebel Café: Sex, Race, and Politics in Cold War America's Nightclub Underground* (Baltimore: Johns Hopkins University Press, 2018).

94. On primitivism, see Marianna Torgovnick, *Gone Primitive: Savage Intellects, Modern Lives* (Chicago: University of Chicago Press, 1990); Daniel Sherman, *French Primitivism and the Ends of Empire, 1945–1975* (Chicago: University of Chicago Press, 2011).

Chapter 2

1. Rebecca M. Joseph, "The Black Statue of Liberty Rumor: An Inquiry into the History and Meaning of Bartholdi's *Liberté éclairant le Monde*," National Park Service, 2000; David Glassberg, "Rethinking the Statue of Liberty: Old Meanings, New Contexts," National Park Service, 2003; "Making the Case for the African-American Origins of the Statue of Liberty," *Journal of Blacks in Higher Education* (Spring 2000).

2. On the history of the Statue of Liberty, see in particular Marvin Trachtenberg, *The Statue of Liberty* (New York: Penguin, 1986); Edward Berenson, *The Statue of Liberty: A Transatlantic Story* (New Haven and London: Yale University Press, 2012); Yasmin Sabina Khan, *Enlightening the World: The Creation of the Statue of Liberty* (Ithaca and London: Cornell University Press, 2010); Wilton S. Dillon and Neil G. Kotler, eds., *The Statue of Liberty Revisited* (Washington and

London: Smithsonian Institution Press, 2010); John Bodnar, Laura Burt, Jennifer Stinson, and Barbara Truesdell, "The Changing Face of the Statue of Liberty," unpublished paper, National Park Service, Indiana University Center for the Study of History and Memory, 2005.

3. See Kirk Savage, *Standing Soldiers, Kneeling Slaves: Race, War and Monument in Nineteenth-Century America* (Princeton: Princeton University Press, 1997): Marilène Patrick Henry, *Monumental Accusations: The "monuments aux morts" as Expressions of Popular Resentment* (New York: Peter Lang, 1996).

4. Lee Bebout, *Mythohistorical Interventions: The Chicano Movement and Its Legacies* (Minneapolis and London: University of Minnesota Press, 2011). See also Joanne M. Braxton and Maria I. Diedrich, eds., *Monuments of the Black Atlantic: Slavery and Memory* (Rutgers and London: Transaction Publishers, 2004).

5. Albert Boime, *The Unveiling of the National Icons: A Plea for Patriotic Iconclasm in a Nationalist Era* (Cambridge and New York: Cambridge University Press, 1998). See in particular chapter 2 for Boime's discussion of the Statue of Liberty.

6. For an example of the latter, see Sieglinde Lemke, "Liberty: A Transnational Icon," in Winfried Flock et al., *Reframing the Transnational Turn in American Studies* (Hanover: Dartmouth College Press, 2011).

7. Berenson, *The Statue of Liberty*; Klaits and Haltzel, eds., *Liberty/Liberté*.

8. One important aspect of this, dating back to the medieval era, was the freedom principle, according to which all slaves brought onto French soil should become free. See Sue Peabody, *'There Are No Slaves in France': The Political Culture of Race and Slavery in the Ancien Régime* (Oxford: Oxford University Press, 1996).

9. Patrice Higonnet, *Sister Republics: The Origins of French and American Republicanism* (Cambridge, MA: Harvard University Press, 1988); Sudhir Hazareesingh, *Intellectual Founders of the Republic: Five Studies in Nineteenth-Century French Thought* (Oxford: Oxford University Press, 2001); Edward Berenson et al., *The French Republic: History, Values, Debates* (Ithaca and London: Cornell University Press, 2011); Emile Chabal, *A Divided Republic: Nation, State, and Citizenship in Contemporary France* (Cambridge, UK: Cambridge University Press, 2015).

10. William R. Everdell, *The End of Kings: A History of Republics and Republicans* (Chicago: University of Chicago Press, 2000); John W. Maynor, *Republicanism in the Modern World* (Cambridge: Polity, 2003).

11. Dena Goodman, *The Republic of Letters: A Cultural History of the French Enlightenment* (Ithaca and London: Cornell University Press, 1994); David Wootton, ed., *Republicanism, Liberty, and Commercial Society, 1649–1776* (Stanford: Stanford University Press, 1994).

12. Dan Edelstein, *The Terror of Natural Right: Republicanism, the Cult of Nature, and the French Revolution* (Chicago: University of Chicago Press, 2010); Andrew Jainchill, *Reimagining Politics after the Terror: The Republican Origins of French Liberalism* (Ithaca and London: Cornell University Press, 2008).

13. Jardin and Andre-Jean Tudesq, *Restoration and Reaction, 1815–1848* (Cambridge: Cambridge University Press, 1988); Maurice Agulhon, *The Republican Experiment, 1848–1852* (Cambridge: Cambridge University Press, 1983).

14. William H. Sewell, *Work and Revolution in France: The Language of Labor from the Old Regime to 1848* (Cambridge, UK: Cambridge University Press, 1980).

15. Philip Nord, *The Republican Moment: Struggles for Democracy in Nineteenth-Century France* (Cambridge, MA: Harvard University Press, 1995); Serge Berstein and Odile Rudelle, *Le Modèle républicain* (Paris: Presses Universitaires de France, 1992); Michel Borgetto and Robert Lafore, *La république sociale: Contribution à l'étude de la question démocratique en France* (Paris: Presses Universitaires de France, 2000); Alain Pessin, *Le mythe du people et la société française du XIXe siècle* (Paris: Presses Universitaires de France, 1992); Tyler Stovall, "The Myth of the Liberatory Republic and the Political Culture of Freedom in Imperial France," *Yale French Studies*, no. 111 (2007).

16. Alain Plessis, *The Rise and Fall of the Second Empire* (Cambridge, UK: Cambridge University Press, 1985); Sudhir Hazareesingh, *From Subject to Citizen: The Second Empire and the Emergence of Modern French Democracy* (Princeton: Princeton University Press, 1998); Roger Price, *The French Second Empire: An Anatomy of Political Power* (Cambridge, UK: Cambridge University Press, 2007).

17. Georges Valance, *Thiers: Bourgeois et révolutionnaire* (Paris: Flammarion, 2007).

18. Steward Edwards, *The Paris Commune, 1871* (New York: Quadrangle Books, 1973); John Merriman, *Massacre: The Life and Death of the Paris Commune* (New York: Basic Books, 2014); Kristin Ross, *Communal Luxury: The Political Imaginary of the Paris Commune* (London: Verso, 2015).

19. Nord, *The Republican Moment*.

20. On the life of Laboulaye, see Walter D. Gray, *Interpreting American Democracy in France: The Career of Édouard Laboulaye, 1811–1883* (Newark: University of Delaware Press, 1994).

21. See, for example, his *Histoire des États-Unis* (Paris: Charpentier, 1867); *Paris en Amérique* (Paris: Charpentier, 1866); *De l'esclavage* (Paris: Au Bureau du dictionnaire des arts et manufactures, 1855).

22. Michele Cunningham, *Mexico and the Foreign Policy of Napoleon III* (New York: Palgrave, 2001).

23. Cited in Trachtenberg, *The Statue of Liberty*, 26.

24. Cited in Édouard Laboulaye, *Paris in America*, translated by Mary L. Booth (New York: Charles Scribner, 1863), Translator's Preface, v.

25. Lawrence C. Jennings, *French Anti-Slavery: The Movement for the Abolition of Slavery in France* (Cambridge: Cambridge University Press, 2006); Françoise Vergès, "The Slave Trade, Slavery, and Abolitionism: The Unfinished Debate in France," in W. Mulligan and M. Bric, eds., *A Global History of Anti-Slavery Politics in the Nineteenth Century* (New York: Palgrave Macmillan, 2013); John Oldfield, *Transatlantic Abolitionism in the Age of Revolution* (Cambridge, UK, and New York: Cambridge University Press, 2013).

26. Historians have long contended that Laboulaye and Bartholdi first conceived of the Statue of Liberty at a dinner party in Laboulaye's home in 1865. This idea has since been refuted. See Joseph, "The Black Statue of Liberty Rumor."

27. Khan, *Enlightening the World*, 53; Berenson, *The Statue of Liberty*, 16–23.

28. Marina Warner, *Monuments and Maidens: The Allegory of Female Form* (New York: Atheneum, 1985); Barbara A. Babcock and John J. Macaloon, "Everybody's Gal: Women, Boundaries, and Monuments," in Dillon and Kotler, *The Statue of Liberty Revisited*.

29. See Maurice Agulhon, *Marianne into Battle: Republican Imagery and Symbolism in France, 1789–1880* (Cambridge, UK: Cambridge University Press, 1981).

30. Gilles Néret, *Eugène Delacroix, 1798–1863: The Prince of Romanticism* (Cologne: Taschen, 1999).

31. For example, the little-known second verse of "La Marseillaise" runs thus:

What do they want this horde of slaves

Of traitors and conspiratorial kings?

For whom these vile chains

These long-prepared irons?

Frenchmen, for us, ah! What outrage

What methods must be taken?

It is us they dare plan

To return to the old slavery!

32. Maurice Agulhon, *Marianne into Battle: Republican Imagery and Symbolism in France, 1789–1880* (Cambridge: Cambridge University Press, 1981), 139–56.

33. The *pétroleuse* was in fact a myth; no convincing evidence of their existence has ever came to light.

34. Carolyn Eichner, *Surmounting the Barricades: Women in the Paris Commune* (Bloomington: Indiana University Press, 2004); Gay L. Gullickson, *Unruly Women of Paris: Images of the Commune* (Ithaca: Cornell University Press, 1996); Edith Thomas, *The Women Incendiaries: The Inspiring Story of the Women of the Paris Commune* (Chicago: Haymarket Publishers, 2007).

35. Agulhon, *Marianne into Battle*, 158–59.

36. "She is not liberty with a red cap on her head and a pike in her hand, stepping over corpses." Laboulaye, cited in Don H. Doyle, *The Cause of All Nations: An International History of the Civil War* (New York: Basic Books, 2014), 311.

37. See Maurice Agulhon, "Bartholdi's *Liberty* in the French Political Context," in Klaits and Haltzel, *Liberty/Liberté*.

38. Stovall, "Faith, Freedom, and Frenchness?: Race, Class, and the Myth of the Liberatory French Republic," *Yale French Studies* no. 111 (2007).

39. Maurice Agulhon, *Marianne*.

40. See the discussion of this issue in chapter 4.

41. Cited in Katz, *From Appomattox to Montmartre: Americans and the Paris Commune* (Cambridge, MA: Harvard University Press, 1998), 98.

42. Michael D. Biddis, *Father of Racist Ideology: The Social and Political Thought of Count Gobineau* (New York: Weybright and Talley, 1970); Mosse, *Toward the Final Solution*.

43. On race and colonialism in France, see among many studies Alice Conklin, *A Mission to Civilize: The Republican Idea of Empire in France and West Africa, 1895–1930* (Stanford: Stanford University Press, 1997); Gary Wilder, *The French Imperial Nation-State: Negritude and Colonial Humanism between the Two World Wars* (Chicago: University of Chicago Press, 2005); Richard Fogarty, *Race and War in France: Colonial Subjects in the French Army, 1914–1918* (Baltimore: Johns Hopkins University Press, 2012).

44. Gordon S. Wood, *Empire of Liberty: A History of the Early Republic* (Oxford: Oxford University Press, 2009); Scott J. Kester, *The Haunted Philosophe: James Madison, Republicanism, and Slavery* (Lanham, MD: Lexington Books, 2008).

45. John R. Vile, ed., *American Immigration and Citizenship: A Documentary History* (Lanham: Rowman and Littlefield, 2016).

46. Earl M. Maltz, *Dred Scott and the Politics of Slavery* (Lawrence: University Press of Kansas, 2007); Mark A. Graber, *Dred Scott and the Problem of Constitutional Evil* (Cambridge, UK: Cambridge University Press, 2006).

47. For a general history of the Civil War, see Allen C. Guelzo, *Fateful Lightning: A New History of the Civil War and Reconstruction* (Oxford: Oxford University Press, 2012).

48. On nineteenth-century Black struggles for equality and citizenship, see Stephen Kantrowitz, *More than Freedom: Fighting for Black Citizenship in a White Republic, 1829–1889* (New York: Penguin, 2012).

49. Eric Foner, *The Fiery Trial: Abraham Lincoln and American Slavery* (New York: W. W. Norton, 2010).

50. Annette Gordon-Reed, *Andrew Johnson* (New York: Henry Holt, 2011); David Warren Bowen, *Andrew Johnson and the Negro* (Knoxville: University of Tennessee Press, 1989).

51. Hans L. Trefousse, *The Radical Republicans: Lincoln's Vanguard for Racial Justice* (New York: Knopf, 1968); Philip B. Lyons, *Statesmanship and Reconstruction: Moderate vs. Radical Republicans on Restoring the Union after the Civil War* (Lanham, MD: Lexington Books, 2014); Deborah Beckel, *Radical Reform: Interracial Politics in Post-Emancipation North Carolina* (Charlottesville: University of Virginia Press, 2011).

52. Charles Lane, *The Day Freedom Died: the Colfax Massacre, the Supreme Court, and the Betrayal of Reconstruction* (New York: Henry Holt and Co., 2008).

53. On the history of Reconstruction, see Eric Foner, *A Short History of Reconstruction* (New York: Harper, 2015); A. J. Langguth, *After Lincoln: How the North Won the Civil War and Lost the Peace* (New York: Simon and Schuster, 2015); Douglas R. Egerton, *The Wars of Reconstruction: The Brief, Violent History of America's Most Progressive Era* (London: Bloomsbury, 2015); David Roediger, *Seizing Freedom: Slave Emancipation and Liberty for All* (London: Verso, 2015).

54. On the achievements of the Reconstruction, see Egerton, *The Wars of Reconstruction*; Eric Foner, *Reconstruction: America's Unfinished Revolution* (New York: Harper and Row, 1988).

55. *Charlottesville Weekly Chronicle*, April 7, 1871, cited in Katz, *From Appomattox to Montmartre*, 112.

56. C. Vann Woodward, *Reunion and Reaction: The Compromise of 1877 and the End of Reconstruction* (New York: Oxford University Press, 1991).

57. Carol A. Horton, *Race and the Making of American Liberalism* (Oxford: Oxford University Press, 2005).

58. Roediger, *The Wages of Whiteness: Race and the Making of the American Working Class* (London: Verso, 1999), 167–68; Alexander Saxton, *The Indispensable Enemy: Labor and the Anti-Chinese Movement in California* (Berkeley: University of California Press, 1975).

59. Andrew Gyory, *Closing the Gate: Race, Politics, and the Chinese Exclusion Act* (Chapel Hill: University of North Carolina Press, 1998); Erika Lee, *At America's Gates: Chinese Immigration during the Exclusion Era, 1882–1943* (Chapel Hill: University of North Carolina Press, 2003).

60. Dee Brown, *Bury My Heart at Wounded Knee: An Indian History of the American West* (New York: Bantam, 1972); Roxanne Dunbar-Ortiz, *An Indigenous People's History of the United States* (Boston: Beacon, 2015).

61. Matthew Frye Jacobson, *Barbarian Virtues: The United States Encounters Foreign Peoples at Home and Abroad, 1876–1917* (New York: Hill and Wang, 2001); Richard H. Immerman,

Empire for Liberty: A History of American Imperialism from Benjamin Franklin to Paul Wolfowitz (Princeton: Princeton University Press, 2012).

62. Roediger, *The Wages of Whiteness*; Alexander Saxton, *The Rise and Fall of the White Republic: Class Politics and Mass Culture in Nineteenth-Century America* (London: Verso, 1991).

63. David Blight, *Race and Reunion: The Civil War in American Memory* (Cambridge, MA: Harvard University Belknap Press, 2002).

64. Khan, *Enlightening the World*, 104–109.

65. Ibid., 147–176; Berenson, *op. cit.*, 69–89.

66. Mary Ryan, *Cradle of the Middle Class: The Family in Oneida City, New York, 1790–1865* (Cambridge: Cambridge University Press, 1983); Nancy Cott, *The Bonds of Womanhood: "Women's Sphere" in New England, 1780–1831* (New Haven: Yale University Press, 1997).

67. As Gloria Steinem famously quipped, "A pedestal is as much a prison as any small, confined space."

68. Cited in Elizabeth Cady Stanton et al., *History of Women's Suffrage . . . 1883–1900* (New York: Fowler & Wells, 1902), 107.

69. Marvin Trachtenberg, *The Statue of Liberty*, 196.

70. Michael Mason, *The Making of Victorian Sexual Attitudes* (Oxford: Oxford University Press, 1986); Judith R. Walkowitz, *City of Dreadful Delight: Narratives of Sexual Danger in Late-Victorian London* (Chicago: University of Chicago Press, 1992); Anne McClintock, *Imperial Leather: Race, Gender, and Sexuality in the Colonial Contest* (London: Routledge, 1995).

71. The classic image is that of Miss Sadie Thompson in W. Somerset Maugham's short story *Rain*.

72. Margaret Strobel, *European Women and the Second British Empire* (Bloomington: Indiana University Press, 1995); Margaret MacMillan, *Women of the Raj: The Mothers, Wives, and Daughters of the British Empire in India* (New York: Random House, 2007); Julia Clancy-Smith and Frances Gouda, eds., *Domesticating the Empire: Race, Gender, and Family Life in French and Dutch Colonialism* (Charlottesville: University of Virginia Press, 1998); Ann Laura Stoler, *Carnal Knowledge and Imperial Power: Race and the Intimate in Colonial Rule* (Berkeley: University of California Press, 2010).

73. Linda Peavey, *Pioneer Women: The Lives of Women on the Frontier* (Norman: University of Oklahoma Press, 1998); Julie Jeffrey, *Frontier Women: "Civilizing" the West? 1840–1880* (New York: Hill and Wang, 1998).

74. Stephanie E. Jones-Rogers, *They Were Her Property: White Women as Slave Owners in the American South* (New Haven: Yale University Press, 2019); Elizabeth Fox-Genovese, *Within the Plantation Household: Black and White Women of the Old South* (Chapel Hill: University of North Carolina Press, 1988); Catherine Clinton, *The Plantation Mistress: Woman's World in the Old South* (New York: Pantheon, 1984); Drew Gilpin Faust, *Mothers of Invention: Women of the Slaveholding South in the American Civil War* (Chapel Hill: University of North Carolina Press, 2004).

75. Elise Lemire, *"Miscegenation": Making Race in America* (Philadelphia: University of Pennsylvania Press, 2009); Peggy Pascoe, *What Comes Naturally: Miscegenation Law and the Making of Race in America* (Oxford: Oxford University Press, 2010).

76. Cited in Bob Herbert, "The Blight That Is Still With Us," *The New York Times,* January 22, 2008. See Stephen Kantrowitz, *Ben Tillman and the Reconstruction of White Supremacy* (Chapel Hill: University of North Carolina Press, 2000).

77. Ida B. Wells, *Southern Horrors and Other Writings: The Anti-Lynching Campaign of Ida B. Wells, 1892–1900*, edited by Jacqueline Jones Royster (New York: Bedford/St. Martin's, 1996); Crystal N. Feimster, *Southern Horrors: Women and the Politics of Rape and Lynching* (Cambridge, MA: Harvard University Press, 2011).

78. Cited in Berenson, *The Statue of Liberty*, 100.

79. *St. Louis Post-Dispatch*, April 17, 1906, 12.

80. See the discussion of this incident in John Bodnar, Laura Burt, Jennifer Stinson, and Barbara Truesdell, "The Changing Face of the Statue of Liberty," 186–88.

81. Jenny Fillmer, "1906 Lynchings Grew from Tensions, Racism—Thriving Black Community Died," *The Springfield News-Leader*, April 14, 2006; Harriet C. Frazier, *Lynchings in Missouri, 1803–1981* (Jefferson, North Carolina: McFarland Press, 2009); Kimberly Harper, *White Man's Heaven: The Lynching and Expulsion of Blacks in the Southern Ozarks, 1894–1909* (Fayetteville: University of Arkansas Press, 2010).

82. "The Immigrant's Statue," National Park Service, https://www.nps.gov/stli/learn /historyculture/the-immigrants-statue.htm.

83. Berenson, *The Statue of Liberty*,104.

84. David Roediger, *Working toward Whiteness: How America's Immigrants Became White: The Strange Journey from Ellis Island to the Suburbs* (New York: Basic Books, 2006); Ignatiev, *How the Irish Became White*; Brodkin, *How Jews Became White Folks*.

85. John Higham, *Coming to America*, 124; Berenson, *The Statue of Liberty*, 105.

86. On the history of European immigration to the United States in the late nineteenth and early twentieth centuries, see Roger Daniels, *Coming to America: A History of Immigration and Ethnicity in American Life* (New York: Harper, 2002); Leonard Dinnerstein and David M. Reimers, *Ethnic Americans: A History of Immigration* (New York: Columbia University Press, 2009); Vincent J. Cannato, *American Passage: The History of Ellis Island* (New York: Harper, 2010); Marianne Debouzy, ed., *In the Shadow of the Statue of Liberty: Immigrants, Workers, and Citizens in the American Republic* (Urbana: University of Illinois Press, 1992).

87. Eileen Putnam, "Immigrants Wept for Joy As They Saw The Statue," *The Dispatch*, Lexington, North Carolina, June 18, 1986.

88. Peter Schrag, *Not Fit for Our Society: Nativism and Immigration* (Berkeley: University of California, 2010), 1.

89. Ibid. See also John Higham, *Strangers in the Land: Patterns of American Nativism 1860–1925* (Westport, CT: Greenwood Publishers, 1981).

90. Thomas Bailey Aldrich, "Unguarded Gates," *The Atlantic Monthly*, no. 60 (July 1892).

91. See the further discussion of this issue in chapter 4.

92. Cited in Khan, *Enlightening the World*, 172.

93. Rudolph J. Vecoli, "The Lady and the Huddled Masses: The Statue of Liberty as a Symbol of Immigration," in Dillon and Kotler, *The Statue of Liberty Revisited*, 41.

94. Berenson, *The Statue of Liberty*, 115–16.

95. On Emma Lazarus, see Esther Schor, *Emma Lazarus* (New York: Schocken, 2006); Daniel Marom, "Who Is the 'Mother of Exiles'? An Inquiry into Jewish Aspects of Emma Lazarus's 'The New Colossus,'" *Prooftexts* 20, no. 3 (Fall 2000). My thanks to Bruce Thompson for this reference.

96. Reproduced in Tony Allan, *Paris, The Glamour Years, 1919–1940* (New York: Gallery Books, 1977), 24.

97. John Higham, *Strangers in the Land: Patterns of American Nativism, 1860–1925* (New York: Atheneum, 1973).

98. David Roediger, *Working toward Whiteness*.

99. Matthew Frye Jacobsen, *Whiteness of a Different Color: European Immigrants and the Alchemy of Race* (Cambridge, MA: Harvard University Press, 1999).

100. *Detroit Free Press*, June 19, 1941. Ironically, the cartoon appeared on Juneteenth, the African American holiday celebrating the end of slavery.

101. That museum opened on Liberty Island in 1972, then closed in 1991 following the opening of the Ellis Island immigration museum in 1990.

102. Richard Stengl, "The Party of the Century," *Time*, July 7, 1986. See the discussion of Liberty Weekend in Berenson, *The Statue of Liberty*, 181–93.

103. In this context it is worth noting that New York City itself was one of America's great slave ports, at times second only to Charleston South Carolina, a history that the Statue of Liberty helps to obscure. Lisa Sturm-Lind, *Actors of Globalization: New York Merchants in the Global Trade, 1784–1812* (Leiden and Boston: Brill, 2018); Leslie M. Harris, *In the Shadow of Slavery: African Americans in New York City, 1626–1863* (Chicago: University of Chicago Press, 2003).

104. https://en.wikipedia.org/wiki/Replicas_of_the_Statue_of_Liberty; Berenson, *The Statue of Liberty*, 189–90.

105. Jeffrey N. Wasserstrom and Elizabeth J. Perry, eds., *Popular Protest and Political Culture in Modern China* (Boulder: Westview Press, 1994); Robert V. Des Forges et al., *Chinese Democracy and the Crisis of 1989: Chinese and American Reflections* (Albany: State University of New York Press, 1993); Han Minzhu, ed., *Cries for Democracy: Writings and Speeches from the 1989 Chinese Democratic Movement* (Princeton: Princeton University Press, 1990).

106. The statue was modeled on a famous socialist realist sculpture, "A Worker and Collective Farm Woman," created by Soviet sculptor Vera Mukhina in 1937. See Tsao Hsingyan, "A Beijing Chronicle," in Dillon and Kotler, *The Statue of Liberty Revisited*, 104–5.

107. Ibid., 108.

108. Timothy Brook, *Quelling the People: The Military Suppression of the Beijing Democracy Movement* (New York: Oxford University Press, 1992).

109. Ibid.; Tsao Tsing-yuan, "Popular Culture and the Politics of Art: The Birth of the Goddess of Democracy," in Wasserstrom and Perry, *Popular Protest and Political Culture*.

110. George T. Crane, "Collective Identity, Symbolic Mobilization, and Student Protest in Nanjing, China, 1988–1989," *Comparative Politics* 26, no. 4 (July 1994).

111. Barry Sautman, "Anti-Black Racism in Post-Mao China," *The China Quarterly*, no. 138 (June 1994): 426.

Chapter 3

1. Wolfgang Amadeus Mozart, *The Magic Flute*, libretto (G. Schirmer, 1986); see also Malcolm S. Cole, "Monostatos and His 'Sister': Racial Stereotype in *Die Zauberflöte* and Its Sequel" in *Opera Quarterly* 21, no. 1 (2005): 2–26.

2. "It is certain that the *nègres* armed themselves in the name of the king: that they had a flag soiled by the fleur-de-lis, and by the motto 'Long live Louis XVI." Cited in Laurent Dubois, *Avengers of the New World: The Story of the Haitian Revolution* (Cambridge, MA, and London: The Belknap Press of Harvard University Press, 2004), 106.

3. Ibid., 96–97, 154–59.

4. The classic studies remain Eric Hobsbawm, *The Age of Revolution, 1789–1848* (New York: Vintage, 1996), and R. R. Palmer, *The Age of the Democratic Revolution: A Political History of Europe and America, 1760–1800* (Princeton: Princeton University Press, 2014). See also David Armitage and Sanjay Subrahmanyam, *The Age of Revolutions in Global Context, c 1760–1840* (London: Palgrave, 2009); and Ben Marsh and Mike Rapport, *Understanding and Teaching the Age of Revolutions* (Madison: University of Wisconsin Press, 2017).

5. The classic work on this is the great trilogy of David Brion Davis, especially its third volume, *The Problem of Slavery in the Age of Emancipation* (New York: Vintage, 2014).

6. For a recent example of a general history of the American Revolution that places such questions at the center of its narrative, see Alan Taylor, *American Revolutions: A Continental History, 1750–1804* (New York and London: W. W. Norton, 2016).

7. Black slavery was by no means the only issue that underscored the relationship between universal ideas of freedom and the continued subjugation of different social groups, of course. Historians have written extensively about the relationship of the Enlightenment universalist project to gender discrimination, anti-Semitism and changing perspectives on the Jews, the expropriation of Native Americans, and other issues. These are very important, but given that this is just one chapter in one book, I could only cover so much, and African slavery and the slave trade occupied a central place in discussions of freedom at the time and since.

8. Among the numerous histories of the Enlightenment, classics include Ernst Cassirer, *The Philosophy of the Enlightenment* (Princeton: Princeton University Press, 2009); and Peter Gay, *The Enlightenment: An Interpretation*, 2 vols. (New York: Knopf, 2013). One of the most prominent contemporary scholars of the movement is Jonathan I. Israel. See his *Radical Enlightenment: Philosophy and the Making of Modernity 1650–1750* (Oxford: Oxford University Press, 2002). Anthony Pagden's *The Enlightenment: And Why It Still Matters* (New York: Random House, 2013) is a wonderful overview.

9. On Enlightenment views of freedom, see Peter Gay, *The Enlightenment: An Interpretation*, vol. 2, *The Science of Freedom* (New York: Knopf, 2013); Mary Efrosini Gregory, *Freedom in French Enlightenment Thought* (New York: Peter Lang, 2010); Jonathan I. Israel, *A Revolution of the Mind: Radical Enlightenment and the Intellectual Origins of Modern Democracy* (Princeton: Princeton University Press, 2009).

10. On the Romantic critique of the Enlightenment, see Tim Blanning, *The Romantic Revolution: A History* (New York: Modern Library, 2011).

11. Max Horkheimer and Theodor Adorno, *The Dialectic of Enlightenment* (Stanford: Stanford University Press, 2007).

12. Emmanuel Chukwudi Eze, *Race and the Enlightenment: A Reader* (Malden, MA: Blackwell, 1997).

13. A classic example of this is Dipesh Chakrabarty, *Provincializing Europe: Postcolonial Thought and Historical Difference* (Princeton: Princeton University Press, 2007). See also Daniel

Gordon, ed., *Postmodernism and the Enlightenment: New Perspectives in Eighteenth-Century French Intellectual History* (New York and London: Routledge, 2000).

14. On the Enlightenment and political liberalism, see Dennis C. Rasmussen, *The Pragmatic Enlightenment: Recovering the Liberalism of Hume, Smith, Montesquieu, and Voltaire* (Cambridge, UK: Cambridge University Press, 2013).

15. Denis Diderot, *The Encyclopedia,* cited in Mary Efrosini Gregory, *Freedom in French Enlightenment Thought*, 82.

16. See, for example, Christie M. Donald and Stanley Hoffman, eds., *Rousseau and Freedom* (Cambridge, UK: Cambridge University Press, 2010); Peter A. Shouls, *Reasoned Freedom: John Locke and Enlightenment* (Ithaca: Cornell University Press, 1992).

17. Jonathan I. Israel, *Democratic Enlightenment: Philosophy, Revolution, and Human Rights, 1750–1790* (Oxford: Oxford University Press, 2013).

18. Jean-Jacques Rousseau, *The Social Contract* and *The First and Second Discourses*, edited by Susan Dunn (New Haven and London: Yale University Press, 2002).

19. Ibid., 157. Such a condemnation of slavery also left open the door to excusing African slavery on the grounds that Africans were not human; as Rousseau puts it, "To conclude that the son of a slave is born a slave is to conclude that he is not born a man" (229).

20. Davis, *The Problem of Slavery in the Age of Revolution, 1770–1823* (Oxford: Oxford University Press, 1999), 263.

21. On slavery and the Enlightenment, see Dorinda Outram, *The Enlightenment* (Cambridge: Cambridge University Press, 2005), chapter 5; Louis Sala-Molins, *Dark Side of the Light: Slavery and the French Enlightenment* (Minneapolis and London: University of Minnesota Press, 2006); Andrew S. Curran, *The Anatomy of Blackness: Science and Slavery in an Age of Enlightenment* (Baltimore: The Johns Hopkins University Press, 2011); Justin Roberts, *Slavery and the Enlightenment in the British Atlantic, 1750–1807* (Cambridge, UK: Cambridge University Press, 2013); Nick Nesbitt, *Universal Emancipation: The Haitian Revolution and the Radical Enlightenment* (Charlottesville and London: University of Virginia Press, 2008).

22. Eric Williams, *Capitalism and Slavery* (Chapel Hill: University of North Carolina Press, 1994); Barbara Lewis Solow and Stanley L. Engerman, *British Capitalism and Caribbean Slavery: The Legacy of Eric Williams* (Cambridge: Cambridge University Press, 1994); S.H.H. Carrington and Heather Cateau, eds., *Capitalism and Slavery Fifty Years Later: Eric Eustace Williams—A Reassessment of the Man and His Work* (New York: Peter Lang, 2000).

23. Edward Baptist, *The Half Has Never Been Told: Slavery and the Making of American Capitalism* (New York: Basic Books, 2016); Sven Beckert, *Empire of Cotton: A Global History* (New York: Vintage, 2014).

24. David Richardson, Susan Schwarz, and Anthony Tibbles, eds., *Liverpool and Transatlantic Slavery* (Liverpool: Liverpool University Press, 2008); Madge Dresser, *Slavery Obscured: The Social History of the Slave Trade in an English Provincial Port* (London: Bloomsbury Academic, 2016); Robert Stein, "The Profitability of the Nantes Slave Trade, 1783–1792," *The Journal of Economic History* 35, no. 2 (1975). See also Catherine A. Reinhardt, *Claims to Memory: Beyond Slavery and Emancipation in the French Caribbean* (New York and Oxford: Berghahn Books, 2006).

25. Louis Sala-Molins, *Le Code Noir, ou le Calvaire de Canaan* (Paris, 1987), 244. Historical estimates vary widely on this point, but most modern historians agree that slavery and the slave trade played a major role in the economy of eighteenth-century France.

26. Voltaire, *Candide, or Optimism* (New York: Penguin, 1947), chapter 19.

27. Louis Sala-Molins, *Le Code Noir*, 239–41.

28. Christopher L. Miller, *The French Atlantic Triangle: Literature and Culture of the Slave Trade* (Durham: Duke University Press, 2007), 124.

29. Susan Buck-Morss, *Hegel, Haiti, and Universal History* (Pittsburgh: University of Pittsburgh Press, 2009).

30. Simon Schama, *The Embarrassment of Riches: An Interpretation of Dutch Culture in the Golden Age* (New York: Vintage, 1997).

31. Wayne Glausser, "Three Approaches to Locke and the Slave Trade," *Journal of the History of Ideas* 51, no. 2 (April–June 1990).

32. Eze, *Race and the Enlightenment*; on the history of scientific racism in this period, see Mosse, *Toward the Final Solution*; Stephen Jay Gould, *The Mismeasurement of Man* (New York: Norton, 1981); Nicolas Bancel, Thomas David, and Dominic Thomas, eds., *The Invention of Race: Scientific and Popular Representations* (New York and London: Routledge, 2014).

33. See Pierre H. Boulle, "François Bernier and the Origins of the Modern Concept of Race," in Sue Peabody and Tyler Stovall, eds., *The Color of Liberty: Histories of Race in France* (Durham: Duke University Press, 2003).

34. Cited in Eze, *Race and the Enlightenment*, 55.

35. Ibid., 4.

36. Cited in Sala-Molins, *Le Code Noir*, 17–18.

37. Sala-Molins, *Dark Side of the Light*, 29.

38. Thomas Jefferson, *Notes on the State of Virginia*, edited by Willam Peden (Chapel Hill: University of North Carolina Press, 1955), 138–43; see also John Chester Miller, *The Wolf by the Ears: Thomas Jefferson and Slavery* (New York: Free Press, 1977); Henry Wiencek, *Master of the Mountain: Thomas Jefferson and His Slaves* (New York: Farrar, Straus and Giroux, 2012).

39. Cited in Susan Buck-Morss, "Hegel and Haiti," *Critical Inquiry* 26, no. 4 (Summer 2000): 832–33.

40. Edmund S. Morgan, *American Slavery, American Freedom: The Ordeal of Colonial Virginia* (New York: W. W. Norton, 2005).

41. See, for example, Robert G. Parkinson, *The Common Cause: Creating Race and Nation in the American Revolution* (Chapel Hill: The University of North Carolina Press, 2016); David Waldstreicher, *Runaway America: Benjamin Franklin, Slavery, and the American Revolution* (New York: Hill and Wang, 2004); Patricia Bradley, *Slavery, Propaganda, and the American Revolution* (Jackson: University Press of Mississippi, 1998); Duncan J. MacLeod, *Slavery, Race and the American Revolution* (London and New York: Cambridge University Press, 1974).

42. Sylvia R. Frey, *Water from the Rock: Black Resistance in a Revolutionary Age* (Princeton: Princeton University Press, 1991); Gerald Horne, *The Counter-Revolution of 1776: Slave Resistance and the Origins of the American Revolution* (New York: NYU Press, 2014); Simon Schama, *Rough Crossings: Britain, the Slaves, and the American Revolution* (New York: HarperCollins Publishers, 2006).

43. Alfred Blumrosen and Ruth Blumrosen, *Slave Nation: How Slavery United the Colonies and Sparked the American Revolution* (Naperville: Sourcebooks, Inc., 2005), chapter 13.

44. Horne, *The Counter-Revolution of 1776*, 239–40.

45. Parkinson, *The Common Cause*; Colin Galloway, *The American Revolution in Indian Country: Crisis and Diversity in Native American Communities* (Cambridge, UK: Cambridge University Press, 1995); Richard D. Blackmon, *Dark and Bloody Ground: The American Revolution along the Southern Frontier* (Yardley, PA: Westholme, 2012); Kathleen DuVal, *Independence Lost: Lives on the Edge of the American Revolution* (New York: Random House, 2015).

46. Bernard Bailyn, *The Ideological Origins of the American Revolution* (Cambridge, MA: Belknap Press of Harvard University Press, 1992); Garry Wills, *Inventing America: Jefferson's Declaration of Independence* (New York: Doubleday, 2017).

47. Cited in Patricia Bradley, *Slavery, Propaganda, and the American Revolution* (Jackson: University Press of Mississippi, 1999), 29.

48. Cited in Morgan, *American Slavery, American Freedom*, 3.

49. See Eric Foner, *Give Me Liberty! An American History* (London and New York: W. W. Norton & Co.), 222. See also Peter Dorsey, *Common Bondage: Slavery as Metaphor in Revolutionary America* (Knoxville: University of Tennessee Press, 2009).

50. Samuel Johnson, "Taxation No Tyranny: An Answer to the Resolutions and Address of the American Congress," 1775.

51. Cited in MacLeod, *Slavery, Race, and the American Revolution*, 16.

52. Cited in Foner, *Give Me Liberty!*, 224.

53. On the general history of slave revolts in America, see Herbert Aptheker, *American Negro Slave Revolts* (New York: International Publishers, 1983); Eugene Genovese, *From Rebellion to Revolution: Afro-American Slave Revolts in the Making of the Modern World* (Baton Rouge: Louisiana State University Press, 1981).

54. Foner, *Give Me Liberty!*, 133; Mark M. Smith, ed., *Stono: Documenting and Interpreting a Southern Slave Revolt* (Columbia: University of South Carolina Press, 2005).

55. Frey, *Water from the Rock*, 54.

56. Blumrosen and Blumrosen, *Slave Nation*; Schama, *Rough Crossings*, 44–57.

57. Schama, *Rough Crossings*, 68.

58. Frey, *Water from the Rock*, 59.

59. Ibid., 63; Schama, *Rough Crossings*, 70–88.

60. Foner, *Give Me Liberty!*, 227.

61. Thomas Jefferson, *Notes on the State of Virginia* (New York: Penguin Classics, 1998).

62. Foner, *Give Me Liberty!*, 226.

63. Ibid; Schama, *Rough Crossings*, 74–76.

64. Cited in Frey, *Water from the Rock*, 59.

65. On the history of slavery in New York, see Leslie M. Harris, *In the Shadow of Slavery: African Americans in New York City, 1626–1863* (Chicago: University of Chicago Press, 2004). Jill Lepore, *New York Burning: Liberty, Slavery, and Conspiracy in Eighteenth Century Manhattan* (New York: Vintage, 2006).

66. See Alan Gilbert, *Black Patriots and Loyalists: Fighting for Emancipation in the War for Independence* (Chicago: University of Chicago Press, 2012).

67. Benjamin Quarles, *The Negro in the American Revolution* (Chapel Hill: University of North Carolina Press, 2012).

68. Foner, *Give Me Liberty!*, 227.

69. It is interesting to observe that most of the biographies of Crispus Attucks are popular studies written for children.

70. Note that Schama refers to Peters as the first African American political leader. Schama, *Rough Crossings*, 10.

71. The historiography of the French Revolution is of course immense, far too vast even to consider summarizing here. Let me instead just note a few classic studies I have found useful over the years: William Doyle, *The Oxford History of the French Revolution* (Oxford: Oxford University Press, 2003); Alexis de Tocqueville, *The Old Regime and the French Revolution* (Chicago: The University of Chicago Press, 2015); Albert Soboul, *The Sans-Culottes* (New York: Anchor Books, 1972); François Furet, *Interpreting the French Revolution* (Cambridge, UK: Cambridge University Press, 1981); Lynn Hunt, *The Family Romance of the French Revolution* (Berkeley and Los Angeles: University of California Press, 1993); and Eric Hobsbawm, *Echoes of the Marseillaise: Two Centuries Look Back on the French Revolution* (New Brunswick: Rutgers University Press, 1990).

72. On universalism as a theme and legacy of the French Revolution, see Alyssa Goldstein Sepinwall, *The Abbé Grégoire and the French Revolution: The Making of Modern Universalism* (Berkeley and Los Angeles: The University of California Press, 2005); Naomi Schor, "The Crisis of French Universalism," *Yale French Studies*, no. 100 (2001); Suzanne Desan, Lynn Hunt, and William Max Nelson, eds., *The French Revolution in Global Perspective* (Ithaca: Cornell University Press, 2013); Maurice Samuels, *The Right to Difference: French Universalism and the Jews* (Chicago: The University of Chicago Press, 2016); Tyler Stovall, *Transnational France: The Modern History of a Universal Nation* (Boulder: Westview Press, 2015).

73. On the history of the Haitian Revolution, see James, *Black Jacobins: Toussaint L'Ouverture and the San Domingo Revolution* (New York: Vintage, 1989); Dubois, *Avengers of the New World.*; Carolyn Fick, *The Making of Haiti: The Saint-Domingue Revolution from Below* (Knoxville: University of Tennessee Press, 1990); Jeremy D. Popkin, *A Concise History of the Haitian Revolution* (Malden, MA: Wiley-Blackwell, 2012); Malick W. Ghachem, *The Old Regime and the Haitian Revolution* (Cambridge, UK: Cambridge University Press, 2012); David Patrick Geggus, ed., *Haitian Revolutionary Studies* (Bloomington: Indiana University Press, 2002).

74. See Desan, Hunt, and Nelson, eds., *The French Revolution*; Alan Forrest and Matthias Middell, eds., *The Routledge Companion to the French Revolution in World History* (London and New York: Routledge, 2015).

75. On this point, see, for example, Frederick Cooper and Ann Laura Stoler, *Tensions of Empire: Colonial Cultures in a Bourgeois World* (Berkeley and Los Angeles: University of California Press, 1997); Gary Wilder, *The French Imperial Nation-State: Negritude and Colonial Humanism Between the Two World Wars* (Chicago: University of Chicago Press, 2005); Elizabeth Heath, *Wine, Sugar, and the Making of Modern France: Global Economic Crisis and the Racialization of French Citizenship, 1870–1910* (Cambridge, UK: Cambridge University Press, 2014).

76. I will take up this topic more fully in the next chapter, but it is worth noting here the substantial literature on working-class politics and antislavery movements. See Betty Lorraine Fladeland, *Abolitionists and Working-Class Problems in the Age of Industrialization* (London: Macmillan, 1984); Bernard Mandel, *Labor Free and Slave: Workingmen and the Anti-Slavery*

Movement in the United States (Urbana: University of Illinois Press, 2007); Eric Foner, "Abolitionism and the Labor Movement in Ante-Bellum America," in Foner, *Politics and Ideology in the Age of the Civil War* (Oxford: Oxford University Press, 1980).

77. See Laurent Dubois, "Atlantic Freedoms," *The Aeon Newsletter*, November 7, 2016; also Ada Ferrer, *Freedom's Mirror: Cuba and Haiti in the Age of Revolution* (Cambridge: Cambridge University Press, 2014).

78. On the history of the freedom principle in France, see Peabody, *"There Are No Slaves in France."*

79. Ibid., 12.

80. John Garrigus, *Before Haiti: Race and Citizenship in French Saint-Domingue* (New York: Palgrave Macmillan, 2006).

81. Peabody, *"There Are No Slaves in France."*

82. Cited in Hugh Thomas, *The Slave Trade* (New York: Simon and Schuster, 1997), 522.

83. *Address to the National Assembly in Favor of the Abolition of the Slave Trade*, cited in Lynn Hunt, ed., *The French Revolution and Human Rights: A Brief History with Documents* (Boston and New York: Bedford/St. Martin's, 2016).

84. David R. Geggus, "Racial Equality, Slavery, and Colonial Secession during the Constituent Assembly," *The American Historical Review*, 94, no. 5 (December, 1989).

85. Dubois, *Avengers of the New World*; Yves Bénot, *La révolution française et la fin des colonies* (Paris: Éditions la Découverte, 1988).

86. See Stewart R. King, *Blue Coat or Powdered Wig: Free People of Color in Pre-Revolutionary Saint-Domingue* (Athens: University of Georgia Press, 2007).

87. John Garrigus, "'Thy Coming Fame, Ogé! Is Sure': New Evidence on Ogé's 1790 Revolt and the Beginnings of the Haitian Revolution," in John Garrigus and Chris Morris, eds., *Assumed Identities: The Meanings of Race in the Atlantic World* (Texas A&M University Press, 2010).

88. David Geggus, "The Slaves and Free Coloreds of Martinique during the Age of the French and Haitian Revolutions: Three Moments of Resistance," in Robert Paquette and Stanley Engerman, eds., *The Lesser Antilles in the Age of European Expansion* (Gainesville: University of Florida Press, 1996).

89. Cited in Laurent Dubois and John D. Garrigus, eds., *Slave Revolution in the Caribbean 1789–1804: A Brief History with Documents* (Boston and New York: Bedford/St. Martin's, 2006), 126.

90. Shanti Singham, "Betwixt Cattle and Men: Jews, Blacks and Women and the Declaration of the Rights of Man," in Dale Van Kley, ed., *The French Idea of Freedom. The Old Regime and the Declaration of Rights of 1789* (Stanford: Stanford University Press, 1994).

91. Dubois, *Avengers of the New World*, 130.

92. Jeremy Popkin, *You Are All Free: The Haitian Revolution and the Abolition of Slavery* (Cambridge, UK: Cambridge University Press, 2010).

93. On Napoleon Bonaparte's restoration of slavery and its impact in the Caribbean, see Laurent Dubois, *A Colony of Citizens: Revolution and Slave Emancipation in the French Caribbean, 1787–1804* (Chapel Hill: University of North Carolina Press, 2004).

94. On the White Terror, see Stephen Clay, "The White Terror: Factions, Reactions, and the Politics of Vengeance," in Peter McPhee, ed., *A Companion to the French Revolution* (Malden, MA: Wiley-Blackwell, 2012).

95. Victor Hugo, *Les misérables* (Project Gutenberg EBook, 2016), vol. 4, *Saint-Denis*, chapter 5.

96. See Soboul, *The Sans-Culottes*.

97. The Haitian government continued to pay this compensation to France until 1947. Only in 2010 did the French government finally cancel Haiti's outstanding debt and issue a belated apology for the ravages of Caribbean slavery. One can hardly imagine a more outrageous example of further victimizing the victim. See Ishaan Tharoor, "Is It Time for France to Pay Its Real Debt to Haiti?," *The Washington Post*, May 13, 2015; "M. Sarkozy, rendez à Haiti son argent extorqué," *Libération*, August 16, 2010.

98. Laurent Dubois, *Haiti: The Aftershocks of History* (New York: Metropolitan, 2012); Julia Gaffield, *Haitian Connections in the Atlantic World: Recognition after Revolution* (Chapel Hill: The University of North Carolina Press, 2015).

99. Ashli White, *Encountering Revolution: Haiti and the Making of the Early Republic* (Baltimore: Johns Hopkins University Press, 2012); Elizabeth Maddock Dillon and Michael Drexler, eds., *The Haitian Revolution and the Early United States: Histories, Textualities, Geographies* (Philadelphia: University of Pennsylvania Press, 2016); James Alexander Dun, *Dangerous Neighbors: Making the Haitian Revolution in Early America* (Philadelphia: University of Pennsylvania Press, 2016); Maurice Jackson and Jacqueline Bacon, *African Americans and the Haitian Revolution: Selected Essays and Historical Documents* (New York and London: Routledge, 2009).

100. Michel-Rolph Trouillot, *Silencing the Past: Power and the Production of History* (Boston: Beacon Press, 1995), 106–7.

101. Alex Dupuy, *Haiti: From Revolutionary Slaves to Powerless Citizens: Essays on the Politics and Economics of Underdevelopment, 1804–2013* (London and New York: Routledge, 2014).

102. Historians have noted that Thomas Jefferson tried to include a more substantial clause condemning slavery into the Declaration, but was blocked from doing so by pro-slavery delegates. David Brion Davis, *Was Thomas Jefferson an Authentic Opponent of Slavery?* (Oxford: Oxford University Press, 1970).

103. There is now a substantial literature on women in the Age of Revolution. See Harriet B. Applewhite and Darlene G. Levy, eds., *Women and Politics in the Age of the Democratic Revolution* (Ann Arbor: University of Michigan Press, 1991); Carla Hesse, *The Other Enlightenment: How French Women Became Modern* (Princeton: Princeton University Press, 2003); Mary Beth Norton, *Liberty's Daughters: The Revolutionary Experience of American Women, 1750–1800* (Ithaca: Cornell University Press, 1996); Joan B. Landes, *Women and the Public Sphere in the Age of the French Revolution* (Ithaca: Cornell University Press, 1988).

104. On the history of abolitionism, see Manisha Sinha, *The Slave's Cause: A History of Abolition* (New Haven: Yale University Press, 2016); John Oldfield, *Transatlantic Abolitionism in the Age of Revolution* (Cambridge, UK: Cambridge University Press, 2013); Seymour Drescher, *Abolition: A History of Slavery and Antislavery* (Cambridge: Cambridge University Press, 2009); Kathryn Kish Sklar and James Brewer Stewart, *Women's Rights and Transatlantic Slavery in the Era of Emancipation* (New Haven: Yale University Press, 2007); Gelien Matthews, *Caribbean Slave Revolts and the British Abolitionist Movement* (Baton Rouge: Louisiana State University Press, 2006).

Chapter 4

1. Katie Donlington et al., eds., *Britain's History and Memory of Transatlantic Slavery: Local Nuances of a 'National Sin'* (Liverpool: Liverpool University Press, 2017); Anthony Tibbles, *Liverpool and the Slave Trade* (Liverpool: Liverpool University Press, 2018); Suzanne Schwarz, ed., *Slave Captain: The Career of James Irving in the Liverpool Slave Trade* (Liverpool: Liverpool University Press, 2008).

2. Emily Brontë, *Wuthering Heights* (London: Puffin Books, Penguin, 2009), 80.

3. Corinne Fowler, "Was Emily Brontë's Heathcliff Black? ," *The Conversation*, October 25, 2017; "Heathcliff and the Ghosts of Slavery," *The Yorkshire Post*, November 7, 2011. See also the novel by Caryl Phillips, *The Lost Child* (New York: Farrar, Straus and Giroux, 2015).

4. Xiaoyan Tong, "Heathcliff's Freedom in Emily Brontë's *Wuthering Heights*," *Brontë Studies: The Journal of the Brontë Society* 41, no. 3 (2016).

5. James A. Rawley, *London: Metropolis of the Slave Trade* (Columbia: University of Missouri Press, 2003).

6. Ibid., 297. Shortly thereafter Heathcliff addresses his son by saying, "Now, don't wince, and colour up! Though it *is* something to see you have not white blood" (299).

7. In its theme of a poor outcast returning as a wealthy man bent on revenge, *Wuthering Heights* strongly resembles another nineteenth-century romantic potboiler, *The Count of Monte Cristo*, a novel written by a Black man who modeled the book's eponymous hero on his own father. Alexandre Dumas, *The Count of Monte Cristo* (New York: Penguin Classics, 2003); see also Tom Reiss, *The Black Count: Glory, Revolution, Betrayal, and the Real Count of Monte Cristo* (New York: Crown Books, 2012).

8. Brontë, *Wuthering Heights*, 64.

9. Classic studies include Joseph A. Schumpeter, *Capitalism, Socialism, and Democracy* (New York: Harper, 2008); Barrington Moore Jr., *Social Origins of Dictatorship and Democracy: Lord and Peasant in the Making of the Modern World* (Boston: Beacon, 1993); Karl Polanyi, *The Great Transformation: The Political and Economic Origins of Our Time* (Boston: Beacon, 2008); and Benedict Anderson, *Imagined Communities: Reflections on the Origin and Spread of Nationalism* (London: Verso, 2016).

10. On the history of liberal democracy, see Charles Tilly, *Democracy* (Cambridge: Cambridge University Press, 2007); John Dunn, *Democracy: A History* (New York: Atlantic Monthly Press, 2006); Temma Kaplan, *Democracy: A World History* (Oxford: Oxford University Press, 2014); Anthony Giddens, "Modernity, History, Democracy," *Theory and Society* 22, no. 2 (April 1993). For critiques of liberal democracy, see Domenico Losurdo, *Liberalism: A Counter-History* (London: Verso, 2011), translated by Gregor Elliott; and Marina Sitin, *They Can't Represent Us!: Reinventing Democracy from Greece to Occupy* (London: Verso, 2014).

11. Alan Sked, *The Decline and Fall of the Habsburg Empire, 1815–1918* (London: Taylor and Francis, 2001); Dominic Lieven, ed., *The Cambridge History of Russia*, vol. 2 (Cambridge: Cambridge University Press, 2006); Iván Zoltán Dénes, ed., *Liberty and the Search for Identity: Liberal Nationalisms and the Legacy of Empires* (Budapest: Central European University Press, 2006).

12. Jeremy Adelman, *Sovereignty and Revolution in the Iberian Atlantic* (Princeton: Princeton University Press, 2009); Jaime E. Rodriguez, *The Independence of Spanish America* (Cambridge, UK: Cambridge University Press, 1998); John Lynch, *The Spanish American Revolutions 1808–1826* (New York: W. W. Norton, 1986).

13. Tyler Stovall, "Empires of Democracy," in Graham Huggins, ed., *The Oxford Handbook of Postcolonial Studies* (Oxford: Oxford University Press, 2014). For overviews of the history of the British and French empires, see Philippa Levine, *The British Empire: Sunrise to Sunset* (Harlow: Pearson, 2007); Robert Aldrich, *Greater France: A History of French Overseas Expansion* (Houndmills: Macmillan Press, 1996).

14. Alexis de Tocqueville, *Democracy in America*, 102.

15. John Rawls, *Political Liberalism* (New York: Columbia University Press, 2005); Edmund Fawcett, *Liberalism: The Life of an Idea* (Princeton: Princeton University Press, 2018); Alan Thomas, *Republic of Equals: Predistribution and Property-Owning Democracy* (Oxford: Oxford University Press, 2016); Martin O'Neill, *Property-Owning Democracy: Rawls and Beyond* (Hoboken: Wiley-Blackwell, 2014).

16. Michael Levin, *The Spectre of Democracy: The Rise of Modern Democracy as Seen by Its Critics* (New York: Palgrave Macmillan, 1992).

17. John Stuart Mill, *On Liberty* (Mineola, NY: Dover Publications, 2002), 3. Edmund Burke, *Reflections on the Revolution in France* (Oxford: Oxford University Press, 2009); Yuval Levin, *The Great Debate: Edmund Burke, Thomas Paine, and the Birth of Right and Left* (New York: Basic Books, 2013).

18. See, for example, Lani Guinier, *The Tyranny of the Majority: Fundamental Fairness in Representative Democracy* (New York: Free Press, 1995). For a contemporary account that replicates the classic liberal fear of democracy, see Fareed Zakaria, "The Rise of Illiberal Democracy," *Foreign Affairs*, November/December 1997.

19. Cited in W. H. Greenleaf, *The British Political Tradition*, vol. 1, *The Rise of Collectivism* (London and New York: Routledge, 1983), 218. See on this point Richard Pipes, *Property and Freedom* (New York: Vintage, 2000).

20. This is the essence of much of the modern conservative attack on taxation, that it represents the expropriation of private property by the state. For a classic statement, see Milton Friedman and Rose Friedman, *Free to Choose: A Personal Statement* (Boston: Mariner Books, 1990).

21. James Madison, debates in the Constitutional Convention, Philadelphia, June 26, 1787.

22. E. A. Smith, *The House of Lords in British Politics and Society, 1815–1911* (London and New York: Longman, 1992); Antony Taylor, *Lords of Misrule: Hostility to Aristocracy in Late Nineteenth and Early Twentieth Century Britain* (New York: Palgrave Macmillan, 2004).

23. Zachary D. Clopton and Seven E. Art, "The Meaning of the Seventeenth Amendment and a Century of State Defiance," *Northwestern University Law Review* 107, no. 3 (Spring 2013); Jay S. Bybee, "Ulysses at the Mast: Democracy, Federalism, and the Sirens' Song of the Seventeenth Amendment," *Scholarly Works*, Paper 350 (1997). It is worth noting that, because each state has the same number of senators regardless of its population size, the American Senate still retains some of this undemocratic character: California with nearly 40 million people has the same number of senators as Wyoming with less than 600,000. Jay Willis, "The Case for Abolishing the US Senate," *GQ*, October 16, 2018.

24. Alexander Keyssar, *The Right to Vote: The Contested History of Democracy in the United States* (New York: Basic Books, 2000); Roger D. Congleton, *Perfecting Parliament; Constitutional Reform, Liberalism, and the Rise of Western Democracy* (Cambridge, UK: Cambridge University Press, 2011); John Hostettler and Brian P. Block, *Voting in Britain: A History of the Parliamentary Franchise* (Chichester: Barry Rose, 2001); Pierre Rosanvallon, *Democracy Past and Future* (New York: Columbia University Press, 2006).

25. On the history of literacy, see the work of Harvey J. Graff, especially *The Literacy Myth: Literacy and Social Structure in the Nineteenth Century City* (New York: Academic Press, 1979).

26. Eugen Weber, *Peasants into Frenchmen: The Modernization of Rural France, 1870–1914* (Stanford: Stanford University Press, 1976). On French education during the Third Republic, see Linda L. Clark, *Schooling the Daughters of Marianne: Textbooks and the Socialization of Girls in Modern French Primary Schools* (Albany: State University of New York Press, 1984); Jo Burr Margadant, *Madame le Professeur: Women Educators in the Third Republic* (Princeton: Princeton University Press, 1990).

27. John C. Courtney, "Right to Vote in Canada," *Historica Canada*, March 2007.

28. Paul Lewinson, *Race, Class and Party: A History of Negro Suffrage and White Politics in the South* (New York: Grosset and Dunlap, 1965); Phyllis F. Field, *The Politics of Race in New York: The Struggle for Black Suffrage in the Civil War Era* (Ithaca: Cornell University Press, 1982).

29. Douglas Lorimer, *Colour, Class and the Victorians: English Attitudes to the Negro in the Mid-Nineteenth Century* (New York: Holmes and Meier, 1978); Alastair Bonnett, "How the British Working Class Became White: The Symbolic (Re)formation of Racialized Capitalism," *Journal of Historical Sociology* 11, no. 3 (September 1998).

30. Quoted in Susan Thorne, "'The Conversion of Englishman and the Conversion of the World Inseparable': Missionary Imperialism and the Language of Class in Early Industrial Britain," in Frederick Cooper and Ann L. Stoler, eds., *Tensions of Empire: Colonial Cultures in a Bourgeois World* (Berkeley: University of California Press, 1997), 238.

31. John M. Merriman, *The Margins of City Life: Explorations on the French Urban Frontier, 1815–1851* (Oxford: Oxford University Press, 1991); Tyler Stovall, "From Red Belt to Black Belt: Race, Class, and Urban Marginality in Twentieth-Century Paris," in Sue Peabody and Tyler Stovall, eds., *The Color of Liberty: Histories of Race in France* (Durham: Duke University Press, 2003).

32. Emmanuel Chukwudi Eze, ed., *Race and the Enlightenment* (Cambridge, MA: Blackwell, 1997); Mosse, *Toward the Final Solution*.

33. Catherine Hall et al., *Defining the Victorian Nation: Class, Race, Gender and the Reform Act of 1867* (Cambridge, UK: Cambridge University Press, 2000); Anne McClintock, *Imperial Leather: Race, Gender, and Sexuality in the Colonial Conquest* (New York: Routledge, 1995); Gareth Stedman Jones, *Outcast London: A Study in the Relationship between Classes in Victorian Society* (London: Verso, 2014); Elinor Accampo, *Industrialization, Family Life, and Class Relations: Saint-Chamond, 1815–1914* (1989).

34. Michel Foucault, *"Society Must Be Defended": Lectures at the Collège de France, 1975–1976* (New York: Picador, 2003); Ann Laura Stoler, *Race and the Education of Desire: Foucault's History of Sexuality and the Colonial Order of Things* (Durham: Duke University Press, 1995).

35. Ernest Gellner, *Nations and Nationalism* (Ithaca: Cornell University Press, 2009); Rogers Brubaker, *Citizenship and Nationhood in France and Germany* (Cambridge, MA: Harvard Uni-

versity Press, 1998); Richard McMahon, *The Races of Europe: Construction of National Identities in the Social Sciences, 1839–1939* (London: Palgrave, 2016).

36. H. G. Wells, *The Time Machine* (Mineola, NY: Dover Publications, 1995).

37. Linda P. Clark, *Social Darwinism in France* (Tuscaloosa: University of Alabama Press, 1984); Mike Hawkins, *Social Darwinism in European and American Thought 1860–1945: Nature as Model and Nature as Threat* (Cambridge, UK: Cambridge University Press, 1997).

38. Michael D. Biddiss, *Father of Racist Ideology: The Social and Political Thought of Count Gobineau* (New York: Weybright and Talley, 1970).

39. Hugh Cunningham, *The Challenge of Democracy: Britain, 1832–1918* (London: Routledge, 2001); Philip Nord, *The Republican Moment: Struggles for Democracy in Nineteenth-Century France* (Cambridge, MA: Harvard University Press, 1998); John Breuilly, *The Formation of the First German Nation-State* (New York: St. Martin's Press, 1996).

40. Seymour Drescher, *Abolition: A History of Slavery and Antislavery* (Cambridge, UK: Cambridge University Press, 2009); Manisha Sinha, *The Slave's Cause: A History of Abolition* (New Haven: Yale University Press, 2016); Eric Metaxas, *Amazing Grace: William Wilberforce and the Heroic Campaign to End Slavery* (New York: HarperOne, 2007); William Mulligan and Maurice Bric, eds., *A Global History of Antislavery Politics in the Nineteenth Century* (New York: Palgrave Macmillan, 2013).

41. Lord Acton, *The History of Freedom* (London: Macmillan & Co., 1907); Orlando Patterson, *Freedom*, vol. 1, *Freedom and the Making of Western Culture* (New York: Basic Books, 1991); Treadgold, *Freedom: A History.*

42. Anthony Bogues, *Empire of Liberty: Power, Desire, and Freedom* (Hanover, NH: Dartmouth, 2010); Richard Hussey, *Freedom Burning: Anti-Slavery and Empire in Victorian Britain* (Ithaca: Cornell University Press, 2012).

43. J. R. Oldfield, *Popular Politics and British Anti-Slavery: The Mobilization of Public Opinion against the Slave Trade* (New York: St. Martin's Press, 1998).

44. Hussey, *Freedom Burning.*

45. Emilia Viotti Da Costa, *Crowns of Glory, Tears of Blood: The Demerara Slave Rebellion of 1823* (New York: Oxford University Press, 1994).

46. Simon Morgan, "The Anti-Corn Law League and British Anti-Slavery in Transatlantic Perspective, 1838–1846," *The Historical Journal*, 52, no. 1 (2009).

47. Lawrence C. Jennings, *French Anti-Slavery: The Movement for the Abolition of Slavery in France, 1802–1848* (Cambridge, UK: Cambridge University Press, 2000).

48. Alice Conklin, *A Mission to Civilize: The Republican Idea of Empire in France and West Africa, 1895–1930* (Stanford: Stanford University Press, 1997); Matthew Stanard, *European Overseas Empire, 1879–1999: A Short History* (Hoboken: Wiley, 2018); Harald Fischer Tiné and Michael Mann, eds., *Colonialism and the Civilizing Mission: Cultural Ideology in British India* (London: Anthem Press, 2004); Osama Abi-Mershed, *Apostles of Modernity: Saint-Simonians and the Civilizing Mission in Algeria* (Stanford: Stanford University Press, 2010).

49. Martin A. Klein, *Slavery and Colonial Rule in French West Africa* (New York: Cambridge University Press, 1998); Deirdre Coleman, *Romantic Colonization and British Anti-Slavery* (New York: Cambridge University Press, 2004).

50. Conklin, *A Mission to Civilize.*

51. David H. Pinkney, *The French Revolution of 1830* (Princeton: Princeton University Press, 1972); Pamela M. Pilbeam, *The French Revolution of 1830* (London: Macmillan, 1991); Jennifer E. Sessions, *By Sword and Plow: France and the Conquest of Algeria* (Ithaca: Cornell University Press, 2011).

52. Abi-Mershed, *Apostles of Modernity*; Patricia M. E. Lorcin, *Imperial Identities: Stereotyping, Prejudice, and Race in Colonial Algeria* (New York: St Martin's Press, 1995); Benjamin Stora, *Algeria, 1830–2004: A Short History* (Ithaca: Cornell University Press, 2004).

53. Quoted in Jennifer Pitts, *A Turn to Empire: The Rise of Imperial Liberalism in Britain and France* (Princeton: Princeton University Press, 2005).

54. Alain Plessis, *The Rise and Fall of the Second Empire, 1852–1871* (Cambridge, UK: Cambridge University Press, 1988); Roger D. Price, *Napoleon III and the Second Empire* (London: Routledge, 1997); Hazareesingh, *From Subject to Citizen*.

55. Cited in Mary Margaret McAllen, *Maximilian and Carlota: Europe's Last Empire in Mexico* (San Antonio, Texas: Trinity University Press, 2014), 7–8. See also Jasper Ridley, *Maximilian and Juárez* (New York: Ticknor and Fields, 1992); Edward Shawcross, *France, Mexico, and Informal Empire in Latin America, 1820–1867* (Cham, Switzerland: Palgrave Macmillan, 2018).

56. Thomas Francis Power, *Jules Ferry and the Renaissance of French Imperialism* (New York: Octagon Books, 1966); Jean-Michel Gaillard, *Jules Ferry* (Paris: Fayard, 1989).

57. Conklin, *A Mission to Civilize*; Gary Wilder, *The French Imperial Nation-State: Negritude and Colonial Humanism between the Wars* (Chicago: University of Chicago Press, 2005); Jacques Thobie et al., *Histoire de la France colonial, 1914–1990* (Paris: Armand Colin, 1990); Alice L. Conklin, "Histories of Colonialism: Recent Studies of the Modern French Empire," *French Historical Studies* 30, no. 2 (2011).

58. Weber, *Peasants into Frenchmen*.

59. Raymond Betts, *Assimilation and Association in French Colonial Theory* (New York: Columbia University Press, 1961).

60. Lorimer, *Colour, Class and the Victorians*; Catherine Hall et al., *Defining the Victorian Nation: Class, Race, Gender, and the British Reform Act of 1867* (Cambridge, UK: Cambridge University Press, 2000).

61. Guenther Roth, *The Social Democrats in Imperial Germany* (New York: Arno Press, 1979).

62. Albert S. Lindemann, *A History of European Socialism* (New Haven: Yale University Press, 1984); William Smaldone, *European Socialism: A Concise History with Documents* (Lanham, MD: Rowman and Littlefield, 2014).

63. Stephen Howe, *Ireland and Empire: Colonial Legacies in Irish History and Culture* (New York: Oxford University Press, 2000); Kevin Kenny, ed., *Ireland and the British Empire* (New York: Oxford University Press, 2006).

64. Michael De Nie, *The Eternal Paddy: Irish Identity and the British Press, 1798–1882* (Madison: University of Wisconsin Press, 2004); Richard Lebo, *White Britain and Black Ireland: The Impact of Stereotypes on Colonial Policy* (Philadelphia: Institute for the Study of Human Issues, 1976).

65. James Epstein, *Lion of Freedom: Feargus O'Connor and the Chartist Movement* (London: Croom Helm, 1982); Rachel O'Higgins, "The Irish Influence in the Chartist Movement," *Past and Present* 1, no. 20 (1961).

66. Terry McCarthy, ed., *The Great Dock Strike 1889* (London: Weidenfeld and Nicolson, 1988).

67. McClintock, *Imperial Leather*.

68. John Merriman, *Massacre: The Life and Death of the Paris Commune* (New York: Basic Books, 2014); Danny Gluckstein, *The Paris Commune: A Revolution in Democracy* (Chicago: Haymarket Books, 2011); Kristin Ross, *Communal Luxury: The Political Imaginary of the Paris Commune* (London: Verso, 2016).

69. Gay Gullickson, *Unruly Women of Paris: Images of the Commune* (Ithaca: Cornell University Press, 1996).

70. Alice Bullard, *Exile to Paradise: Savagery and Civilization in Paris and the South Pacific, 1790–1900* (Stanford: Stanford University Press, 2000).

71. Claire Midgley, *Women against Slavery: The British Campaigns, 1780–1870* (London and New York: Routledge, 1995).

72. Claire Midgley, "British Abolition and Feminism in Transatlantic Perspective," in Kathryn Kish Sklar and James Brewer Stewart, eds., *Women's Rights and Transatlantic Antislavery in the Era of Emancipation* (New Haven: Yale University Press, 2007).

73. See, for example, Antoinette Burton, "The White Woman's Burden: British Feminists and the Indian Woman, 1865–1915," in *Women's Studies International. Forum* (1990); Susan Pedersen, "The Maternalist Moment in British Colonial Policy: The Controversy over 'Child Slavery' in Hong Kong, 1917–1941," *Past and Present*, no. 171 (May 2002); Ian Christopher Fletcher et al., *Women's Suffrage in the British Empire: Citizenship, Nation, and Race* (London and New York: Routledge, 2000).

74. Harold L. Smith, *The British Women's Suffrage Campaign 1866–1928* (London and New York: Routledge, 2009); Laura E. Nym Mayhall, *The Militant Suffrage Movement: Citizenship and Resistance in Britain, 1860–1930* (Oxford: Oxford University Press, 2003).

75. Cited in Antoinette Burton, *Burdens of History: British Feminists, Indian Women, and Imperial Culture, 1865–1915* (Chapel Hill and London: The University of North Carolina Press, 1994), 148.

76. See, for example, Julie Evans, *Equal Subjects, Unequal Rights: Indigenous People in British Settler Colonies, 1830–1910* (Manchester: Manchester University Press, 2003).

77. James Chiriyankandath, "'Democracy' under the Raj: Elections and Separate Representation in British India," *Journal of Commonwealth & Comparative Politics* 30, no. 1 (March 1992): 39–64.

78. Thomas Holt, *The Problem of Freedom: Race, Labor, and Politics in Jamaica and Britain, 1832–1938* (Baltimore: Johns Hopkins University Press, 1992), 216.

79. John C. Courtney, *Elections* (Vancouver: University of British Columbia Press, 2004); Martin Plaut, *Promise and Despair: The First Struggle for a Non-Racial South Africa* (Johannesburg: Jacana Media, 2016).

80. Silyane Larcher, *L'autre citoyen: L'idéal républicain et les Antilles après l'esclavage* (Paris: Armand Colin, 2014); Heath, *Wine, Sugar, and the Making of Modern France*; Dale W. Tomich, *Slavery in the Circuit of Sugar: Martinique and the World Economy, 1830–1848* (Albany: State University of New York Press, 2017); Armand Nicolas, *Histoire de la Martinique*, vol. 2, *De 1848 à 1939* (Paris: L'Harmattan, 1996).

81. Ed Naylor, *France's Modernising Mission: Citizenship, Welfare and the Ends of Empire* (London: Palgrave Macmillan UK, 2018).

82. Conklin, "Histories of Colonialism"; William B. Cohen, *The French Encounter with Africans: White Response to Blacks, 1530–1880* (Bloomington: Indiana University Press, 2003); Owen White, *Children of the French Empire: Miscegenation and Colonial Society in French West Africa, 1895–1960* (Oxford: Clarendon Press, 1999).

83. Aldrich, *Greater France*; Patricia Lorcin, *Imperial Identities: Stereotyping, Prejudice, and Race in Colonial Algeria* (London: I. B. Tauris, 1999).

84. One important exception was the case of the Jews of Algeria, who received French citizenship in 1870. See Sophie B. Roberts, *Citizenship and Antisemitism in French Colonial Algeria, 1870–1962* (Cambridge, UK: Cambridge University Press, 2018); Joshua Schreier, *Arabs of the Jewish Faith: The Civilizing Mission in Colonial Algeria* (New Brunswick: Rutgers University Press, 2010).

85. Harry Gamble, *Contesting French West Africa: Battles over Schools and the Colonial Order* (Lincoln: University of Nebraska Press, 2017); Clive Whitehead, *Colonial Educators: The British Indian and Colonial Education Service 1858–1983* (London: I. B. Tauris, 2003); Spencer D. Segalla, *The Moroccan Soul: French Education, Colonial Ethnology, and Muslim Resistance* (Lincoln: University of Nebraska Press, 2009); Peter Kallaway and Rebecca Swartz, eds., *Empire and Education in Africa: The Shaping of a Comparative Perspective* (New York: Peter Lang, 2016).

86. The classic study remains Alexis de Tocqueville, *Democracy in America*. On the history of liberal democracy in America, see also Foner, *Give Me Liberty!*; Gottfried Dietze, *American Democracy: Aspects of Practical Liberalism* (Baltimore: Johns Hopkins University Press, 1993).

87. August H. Mintz Jr., *Marx, Tocqueville, and Race in America: The 'Absolute Democracy' or 'Defiled Republic'* (Lanham, MD: Lexington Books, 2003); Mary Dudziak, *Cold War Civil Rights: Race and the Image of American Democracy* (Princeton: Princeton University Press, 2001); John Milton Cooper and Thomas J. Knock, eds., *Jefferson, Lincoln, and Wilson: The American Dilemma of Race and Democracy* (Charlottesville: University of Virginia Press, 2010).

88. On the idea of the American South as a colony, see Natalie Ring, *The Problem South: Region, Empire, and the New Liberal State, 1880–1930* (Athens, GA: University of Georgia Press, 2012).

89. Cited in Garrett Epps, "Voting, Right or Privilege?," *The Atlantic*, September 18, 2012.

90. On the history of voting in America, see Keyssar, *The Right to Vote*; Michael Waldman, *The Fight to Vote* (New York: Simon and Schuster, 2016); Donald W. Rogers, ed., *Voting and the Spirit of American Democracy: Essays on the History of Voting and Voting Rights in America* (Urbana: University of Illinois Press, 1992).

91. Keyssar, *The Right to Vote*.

92. Albert Edward Mckinley, *The Suffrage Franchise in the Thirteen English Colonies in America* (Boston: Ginn and Co., 1905); Robert J. Dinkin, *Voting in Provincial America: A Study of Elections in the Thirteen Colonies, 1689–1776* (New York: Praeger, 1977); Gary B. Nash, *The Urban Crucible: Social Change, Political Consciousness, and the Origins of the American Revolution* (Cambridge, MA: Harvard University Press, 1979).

93. Thomas Paine, *Dissertation of First Principles of Government* (London: Daniel Isaac Eaton, 1795), 21.

94. Gordon S. Wood, *The Radicalism of the American Revolution* (New York: Vintage, 1993); Robert J. Dinkin, *Voting in Revolutionary America: A Study of Elections in the Original Thirteen States, 1776–1789* (New York: Praeger, 1982); Elisha P. Douglass, *Rebels and Democrats: The Struggle for Equal Political Rights and Majority Rule During the American Revolution* (Chapel Hill: University of North Carolina Press, 1955).

95. Keyssar, *The Right to Vote*, chapter 2; Daniel Walker Howe, *What Hath God Wrought: The Transformation of America, 1815–1848* (Oxford: Oxford University Press, 2009); Harry L. Watson, *Liberty and Power: The Politics of Jacksonian America* (New York: Hill and Wang, 2006).

96. On the struggle for women's suffrage in nineteenth century America, see Ellen Carol DuBois, *Feminism and Suffrage: The Emergence of an Independent Women's Movement in America, 1848–1869* (Ithaca: Cornell University Press, 1998); Nancy Isenberg, *Sex and Citizenship in Antebellum America* (Chapel Hill: University of North Carolina Press, 1998).

97. Leon F. Litwack, *North of Slavery: The Negro in the Free States, 1790–1860* (Chicago: University of Chicago Press, 1965); Ira Berlin, *Slaves without Masters: The Free Negro in the Antebellum South* (New York: Random House, 1974); Leslie M. Harris, *In the Shadow of Slavery: African Americans in New York City, 1626–1863* (Chicago: University of Chicago Press, 2004); Patrick Rael, *Black Identity and Black Protest in the Antebellum North* (Chapel Hill: University of North Carolina Press, 2002).

98. Keyssar, *The Right to Vote*, 54–55; Rogers M. Smith, *Civic Ideals: Conflicting Visions of Citizenship in U.S. History* (New Haven: Yale University Press, 1999).

99. Keyssar, *The Right to Vote*, 57.

100. On the *Dred Scott* decision, see Don E. Fehrenbacher, *The Dred Scott Case: Its Significance in American Law and Politics* (Oxford: Oxford University Press, 2001); David Thomas King, et al., *The Dred Scott Case: Historical and Contemporary Perspectives on Race and Law* (Athens: Ohio University Press, 2010); Andrew P. Napolitano, *Dred Scott's Revenge: A Legal History of Race and Freedom in America* (Nashville: HarperCollins, 2009).

101. Cited in Kenneth Roff, "Brooklyn's Reaction to Black Suffrage in 1860," *Afro-Americans in New York Life and History (1977–1989)* 2, no. 11 (1978): 29.

102. Laura Gomez, *Manifest Destinies: The Making of the Mexican American Race* (New York: New York University Press, 2008).

103. Keyssar, *The Right to Vote*, 59–60; Jeannette Wolfley, "Jim Crow, Indian Style: The Disenfranchisement of Native Americans," *American Indian Law Review* 16 (1991).

104. Peter Guardino, *The Dead March: A History of the Mexican-American War* (Cambridge, MA: Harvard University Press, 2017); Amy S. Greenberg, *A Wicked War: Polk, Clay, Lincoln, and the 1846 U.S. Invasion of Mexico* (New York: Vintage, 2013); Timothy J. Henderson, *A Glorious Defeat: Mexico and Its War with the United States* (New York: Hill and Wang, 2008).

105. On the history of Mexican Americans in Texas, see David Montejano, *Anglos and Mexicans in the Making of Texas, 1836–1986* (Austin: University of Texas Press, 1987); Paul A. Ramos, *Beyond the Alamo: Forging Mexican Ethnicity in San Antonio, 1821–1861* (Chapel Hill: University of North Carolina Press, 2010); Arnoldo De Leon, *The Tejano Community, 1836–1900* (Dallas: Southern Methodist University, 1997).

106. Cited in "The Anti-Slavery Society," *The New York Times,* May 11, 1865, 2.

107. The historiography of the Civil War and slavery is of course immense. Books I've used include James M. McPherson, *Battle Cry of Freedom: The Civil War Era* (Oxford: Oxford

University Press, 1988); David Williams, *A People's History of the Civil War: Struggles for the Meaning of Freedom* (New York: The New Press, 2005); Bruce Levine, *The Fall of the House of Dixie: The Civil War and the Social Revolution That Transformed the South* (New York: Random House, 2013); David Roediger, *Seizing Freedom: Slave Emancipation and Liberty for All* (London: Verso, 2014); David S. Cecelski, *The Fire of Freedom: Abraham Galloway and the Slaves' Civil War* (Chapel Hill: University of North Carolina Press, 2012).

108. Cited in McPherson, *Battle Cry of Freedom*, 312.

109. Cited in Foner, *Give Me Liberty!*, 533.

110. Cited in McPherson, *Battle Cry of Freedom*, 241.

111. Cecelski, *The Fire of Freedom*; James M. McPherson, *The Negro's Civil War: How American Blacks Felt and Acted During the War for the Union* (New York: Vintage, 2003); John David Smith, ed., *Black Soldiers in Blue: African American Troops in the Civil War Era* (Chapel Hill: University of North Carolina Press, 2002); Gabor Boritt and Scott Hancock, eds., *Slavery, Resistance, Freedom* (Oxford: Oxford University Press, 2007).

112. James M. McPherson, *The Struggle for Equality: Abolitionists and the Negro during the Civil War and Reconstruction* (Princeton: Princeton University Press, 2014); Stanley Harrold, *Lincoln and the Abolitionists* (Carbondale: Southern Illinois University Press, 2018).

113. Hugh Dubrulle, *Ambivalent Nation: How Britain Imagined the American Civil War* (Baton Rouge: Louisiana State University Press, 2018); Richard J. M. Blackett, *Divided Hearts: Britain and the American Civil War* (Baton Rouge: Louisiana State University Press, 2000); Mary Ellison, *Support for Secession: Lancashire and the American Civil War* (Chicago: University of Chicago Press, 1973).

114. W.E.B. DuBois, *Black Reconstruction in America* (New York: Russell and Russell, 1963), 121.

115. Cited in Bruce Levine, *The Fall of the House of Dixie*, 171. On the history of the Emancipation Proclamation, see John Hope Franklin, *The Emancipation Proclamation* (New York: Wiley-Blackwell, 1994); Allen C. Guelzo, *Lincoln's Emancipation Proclamation: The End of Slavery in America* (New York: Simon and Schuster, 2004); Louis P. Masur, *Lincoln's Hundred Days: The Emancipation Proclamation and the War for the Union* (Cambridge, MA: The Belknap Press of Harvard University Press, 2012).

116. J. D. Dickey, *Rising in Flames: Sherman's March and the Fight for a New Nation* (New York: Pegasus, 2018); Burke Davis, *Sherman's March: The First Full-Length Narrative of General William Tecumseh Sherman's Devastating March Through Georgia and the Carolinas* (New York: Vintage, 1988).

117. That day is still celebrated and commemorated as the African American holiday of Juneteenth. See Randolph B. Campbell, *An Empire for Slavery: the Peculiar Institution in Texas, 1821–1865* (Baton Rouge: Louisiana State University Press, 1989).

118. On the history of Reconstruction, see W.E.B. DuBois, *Black Reconstruction*; Foner, *Reconstruction*; Leon F. Litwack, *Been in the Storm So Long: The Aftermath of Slavery* (New York: Knopf, 1979); Thomas J. Brown, ed., *Reconstructions: New Perspectives on the Postbellum United States* (Oxford: Oxford University Press, 2006).

119. Eric Foner, *Nothing but Freedom: Emancipation and Its Legacy* (Baton Rouge: Louisiana State University Press, 1983); Vincent Harding, *There Is a River: The Black Struggle for Freedom in America* (New York: Harcourt Brace Jovanovich, 1981); John David Smith, *We Ask Only for*

Even-Handed Justice: Black Voices From Reconstruction, 1863–1877 (Amherst: University of Massachusetts, 2014).

120. Hilary Green, *Education Reconstruction: African American Schools in the Urban South, 1865–1900* (New York: Fordham University Press, 2016); Ronald E. Butchart, *Northern Schools, Southern Blacks, and Reconstruction: Freedmen's Education, 1862–1875* (New York: Praeger, 1980).

121. Cited in Litwack, *Been in the Storm So Long,* 209.

122. Claude F. Oubre, *Forty Acres and a Mule: The Freedman's Bureau and Black Land Ownership* (Baton Rouge: Louisiana State University Press, 2012).

123. Hans L. Trefousse, *The Radical Republicans: Lincoln's Vanguard for Racial Justice* (New York: Knopf, 1969); Earl M. Maltz, *Civil Rights, the Constitution, and Congress, 1863–1869* (Lawrence: University Press of Kansas, 1990); Howard N. Meyer, *The Amendment That Refused to Die: Equality and Justice Deferred: A History of the Fourteenth Amendment* (Lanham, MD: Rowman and Littlefield, 2000).

124. Cited in Foner, *Reconstruction,* 199.

125. Elaine Frantz Parsons, *Ku-Klux: The Birth of the Klan during Reconstruction* (Chapel Hill: University of North Carolina Press, 2016); David M. Chalmers, *Hooded Americanism: The History of the Ku Klux Klan* (New York: F. Watts, 1981).

126. C. Vann Woodward, *Reunion and Reaction: The Compromise of 1877 and the End of Reconstruction* (Oxford: Oxford University Press, 1991).

127. Douglas A. Blackmon, *Slavery by Another Name: The Re-Enslavement of Black Americans from the Civil War to World War II* (New York: Doubleday, 2008); C. Vann Woodward, *The Strange Career of Jim Crow* (Oxford: Oxford University Press, 2001); Richard Wormser, *The Rise and Fall of Jim Crow* (New York: St. Martin's Press, 2003); David M. Oshinsky, *Worse than Slavery: Parchman Farm and the Ordeal of Jim Crow Justice* (New York: Free Press, 1997).

128. R. Volney Riser, *Defying Disfranchisement: Black Voting Right Activism in the Jim Crow South, 1890–1908* (Baton Rouge: Louisiana State University Press, 2013); Edmund Drago, *Black Politicians and Reconstruction in Georgia: A Splendid Failure* (Athens: University of Georgia Press, 1992).

129. "Defense of the Negro Race—Charges Answered," Speech of the Honorable George H. White of North Carolina, House of Representatives, January 29, 1901.

130. Joseph Roth, *The Wandering Jews* (New York: W. W. Norton, 2001), 102.

131. Cited in Foner, *Reconstruction,* 33.

132. Harris, *In the Shadow of Slavery;* Iver Bernstein, *The New York City Draft Riots: Their Significance for American Society and Politics in the Age of Civil War* (Oxford: Oxford University Press, 1990); Adrian Cook, *The Armies of the Streets: The New York City Draft Riots of 1863* (Lexington: University Press of Kentucky, 1982).

133. Foundational texts of whiteness studies include David Roediger, *The Wages of Whiteness: Race and the Making of the American Working Class* (London: Verso, 2007); Theodore W. Allen, *The Invention of the White Race,* 2 vols. (London: Verso, 2012); George Lipsitz, *The Possessive Investment in Whiteness: How White People Profit from Identity Politics* (Philadelphia: Temple University Press, 2006); Ruth Frankenberg, *White Women, Race Matters: The Social Construction of Whiteness* (Minneapolis: University of Minnesota Press, 1993); Matthew Frye Jacobson, *Whiteness of a Different Color: European Immigrants and the Alchemy of Race* (Cambridge, MA:

Harvard University Press, 1998). For a critical overview of whiteness studies, see Eric Arnesen, "Whiteness and the Historians' Imagination," *International Labor and Working Class History*, no. 60 (Fall 2001).

134. Ignatiev, *How the Irish Became White*; Brodkin, *How Jews Became White Folks*; Thomas A. Gugliemo, *White on Arrival: Italians, Race, Color, and Power in Chicago, 1890–1945* (Oxford: Oxford University Press, 2003).

135. Russell A. Kazal, *Becoming Old Stock: The Paradox of German-American Identity* (Princeton: Princeton University Press, 2004); Stanley Nadel, *Little Germany: Ethnicity, Religion, and Class in New York City* (Urbana: University of Illinois Press, 1994); Kathleen Neils Conzen, *Immigrant Milwaukee, 1836–1860: Accommodation and Community in a Frontier City* (Cambridge, MA: Harvard University Press, 1976).

136. Ignatiev, *How the Irish Became White*, 41. On the Irish in America, see Kerby A. Miller, *Emigrants and Exiles: Ireland and the Irish Exodus to North America* (Oxford: Oxford University Press, 1983); David T. Gleason, ed., *The Irish in the Atlantic World* (Columbia, SC: University of South Carolina Press, 2010).

137. Ignatiev, *How the Irish Became White*, 6–31; Angela F. Murphy, *American Slavery, Irish Freedom: Abolition, Immigrant Citizenship, and the Transatlantic Movement for Irish Repeal* (Baton Rouge: Louisiana State University Press, 2010); Daniel O'Connell, *Liberty or Slavery? Daniel O'Connell on American Slavery. Reply to O'Connell by Hon. S.P. Chase* (Ithaca: Cornell University Library, 1863); Christine Kinealy, *Daniel O'Connell and the Anti-Slavery Movement. The Saddest People the Sun Sees* (London: Pickering and Chatto, 2010).

138. Cited in Ignatiev, *How the Irish Became White*, Frontispiece

139. Richard White, *Railroaded: The Transcontinentals and the Making of Modern America* (New York: W. W. Norton, 2012); Walter R. Borneman, *Rival Rails: The Race to Build America's Greatest Transcontinental Railroad* (New York: Random House, 2010); David Haward Bain, *Empire Express: Building the First Transcontinental Railroad* (New York: Viking, 1999).

140. Elliott Young, *Alien Nation: Chinese Migration in the Americas from the Coolie Era through World War II* (Chapel Hill: University of North Carolina Press, 2014); Peter Kwong and Dusanka Miscevic, *Chinese America: A History in the Making* (New York: The New Press, 2005); Erika Lee, *At America's Gates: Chinese Immigration During the Exclusion Era, 1882–1943* (Chapel Hill: University of North Carolina Press, 2003); Yong Chen, *Chinese San Francisco, 1850–1943* (Stanford: Stanford University Press, 2000).

141. Beth Lew-Williams, *The Chinese Must Go: Violence, Exclusion, and the Making of the Alien in America* (Cambridge, MA: Harvard University Press, 2018); Alexander Saxton, *The Indispensable Enemy: Labor and the Anti-Chinese Movement in California* (Berkeley: University of California Press, 1971).

142. Lee, *At America's Gates*; John Soennichsen, *The Chinese Exclusion Act of 1882* (Rochester: Greenwood Books, 2011); Andrew Gyory, *Closing the Gate: Race, Politics, and the Chinese Exclusion Act* (Chapel Hill: University of North Carolina Press, 1998).

143. Gyory, *Closing the Gate*; Najia Aarim-Heriot, *Chinese Immigrants, African Americans, and Racial Anxiety in the United States, 1848–1882* (Urbana: University of Illinois Press, 2003). See also Edlie L. Wong, *Racial Reconstruction: Black Inclusion, Chinese Exclusion, and the Fictions of Citizenship* (New York: New York University Press, 2015).

144. Gyory, *Closing the Gate*, 228–29.

145. Aarim-Heriot, *Chinese Immigrants*, 219–21.

146. Gugliemo, *White on Arrival*, 6.

147. Eli N. Evans, *Judah P. Benjamin, the Jewish Confederate* (New York: Free Press, 1988).

148. Jacobsen, *Whiteness of a Different Color*, chapter 7.

149. Gugliemo, *White on Arrival*, 3.

150. On urban machine politics in America, see Seymour J. Mandelbaum, *Boss Tweed's New York* (New York: Praeger, 1982); Steven P. Erie, *Rainbow's End: Irish-Americans and the Dilemmas of Urban Machine Politics, 1840–1985* (Berkeley: University of California Press, 1990); Rick Su, "Urban Politics and the Assimilation of Immigrant Voters," *William and Mary Bill of Rights Journal* 21, no. 2 (2012).

151. Keyssar, *The Right to Vote*, 170.

Chapter 5

1. *The Washington Post*, June 13, 2020; Allan M. Winkler, "The Philadelphia Transit Strike of 1944," *The Journal of American History*, 59, no. 1 (June 1972).

2. *The New York Age*, September 2, 1944; NAACP, 1940–1955, General Office File. Lynching, Liberty Mississippi, 1944, reel 25, frame 0431–0464.

3. For overviews of the era of the two world wars, see Mark Mazower, *Dark Continent: Europe's Twentieth Century* (New York: Vintage Books, 2000); Eric Hobsbawm, *The Age of Extremes: A History of the World, 1914–1991* (New York: Vintage Books, 1996); Volker Berghahn, *Europe in the Era of Two World Wars: From Militarism and Genocide to Civil Society, 1900–1950* (Princeton: Princeton University Press, 2006).

4. See, for example, Arthur Herman, *Freedom's Forge: How American Business Produced Victory in World War II* (New York: Random House, 1994); Joseph H. Alexander et al., *One of Freedom's Finest Hours: Statesmanship and Soldiership in World War II* (Hillsdale Michigan: Hillsdale College Press, 2002); Margaret T. Bixler, *Winds of Freedom: The Story of the Navajo Code Talkers of World War II* (Darien, CT: Two Bytes Publishing, 1992).

5. Gary Wilder, *Freedom Time: Negritude, Decolonization and the Future of the World* (Durham: Duke University Press, 2014); David Ryan and Victor Pungong, eds., *The United States and Decolonization: Power and Freedom* (New York: Palgrave Macmillan, 2000); Dominique Lapierre and Larry Collins, *Freedom at Midnight* (New York: Simon and Schuster, 1975).

6. African Americans in particular have deployed the language of freedom struggles. See Clayborne Carson and Emma J. Lapsansky-Werner, *The Struggle for Freedom: A History of African Americans*, two vols. (London: Pearson Press, 2014); Charles Payne, *I've Got the Light of Freedom: The Organizing Tradition and the Mississippi Freedom Struggle* (Berkeley and Los Angeles: University of California Press, 2007); Vincent Harding, *There Is a River: The Black Struggle for Freedom in America* (New York: Mariner Books, 1993).

7. On war and race in the modern era, see, for example, Nikhil Pal Singh, *Race and America's Long War* (Berkeley and Los Angeles: University of California Press, 2017); John W. Dower, *Race and Power in the Pacific War* (New York: Pantheon, 1987); Richard S. Fogarty, *Race and War in France: Colonial Subjects in the French Army, 1914–1918* (Baltimore: Johns Hopkins University Press, 2008); Takashi Fujitani, *Race for Empire: Koreans as Japanese and Japanese as*

Americans during World War II (Berkeley and Los Angeles: University of California Press, 2013).

8. Fogarty, *Race and War in France*; Fujitani, *Race for Empire*; Chad L. Williams, *Torchbearers of Democracy: African American Soldiers in the World War I Era* (Chapel Hill: University of North Carolina Press, 2010); Tarak Barkawi, *Soldiers of Empire: Indian and British Armies in World War II* (Cambridge, UK: Cambridge University Press, 2017); Ruth Ginio, *The French Army and its African Soldiers: The Years of Decolonization* (Lincoln: University of Nebraska Press, 2017).

9. Stefan Zweig, *The World of Yesterday* (Lincoln: University of Nebraska Press, 2013), 192–93.

10. On the Belle Époque, see Barbara Tuchman *The Proud Tower: A Portrait of the World Before the War, 1890–1918* (New York: Random House, 2011); Arno Mayer, *The Persistence of the Old Regime: Europe to the Great* War (New York: Pantheon Books, 1981); Eric Hobsbawm, *The Age of Empire, 1875–1914* (New York: Vintage 1989); Stephen Kern, *The Culture of Time and Space, 1880–1918* (Cambridge, MA: Harvard University Press, 2003). The classic literary source on the era is Marcel Proust, *A Remembrance of Things Past*, translated by Andreas Mayor, 3 vols. (New York: Vintage, 1982).

11. On America in the Progressive era, see Steven Diner, *A Very Different Age: Americans of the Progressive Era* (New York: Hill and Wang, 1997); Jackson Lears, *Rebirth of a Nation: the Making of Modern America, 1877–1920* (New York: Harper Vintage, 2010); Henry James, *The American Scene* (New York: Scribner's and Sons, 1946).

12. On the history of democracy, see Temma Kaplan, *Democracy: A World History* (Oxford: Oxford University Press, 2014); Brian S. Roper, *The History of Democracy: A Marxist Interpretation* (London: Pluto Press, 2012).

13. See, for example, (Senator) Mike Lee, *Written Out of History: The Forgotten Founders Who Fought Big Government* (New York: Penguin Random House, 2017).

14. On the idea of the freeborn Englishman, see Edward Thompson, "The Free-born Englishman," *New Left Review* 1, no. 15 (May–June 1962); Michael Braddick, *The Common Freedom of the People: John Lilburne and the English Revolution* (Oxford: Oxford University Pres, 2018); John Rees, *The Leveller Revolution: Radical Political Organization in England, 1640–1650* (London: Verson, 2017).

15. E. P. Thompson, *The Making of the English Working Class* (New York: Vintage, 1966).

16. On freedom in French political culture, see Dale Van Kley, *The French Idea of Freedom: The Old Regime and the Declaration of Rights of 1789* (Stanford: Stanford University Press, 1997); David Andress, *The Terror: The Merciless War for Freedom in the French Revolution* (New York: Farrar, Straus and Giroux, 2006).

17. See "Americanism," in Michael Kazin, ed., *The Concise Princeton Encyclopedia of American Political History* (Princeton: Princeton University Press, 2011).

18. See, for example, Stephen Wilkes, *Ellis Island: Ghosts of Freedom* (New York: W. W. Norton, 2006). A particular focus has been the idea of religious freedom, above all with the history of the founding of Puritan Massachusetts. See, for example, Rebecca Fraser, *The Mayflower: The Families, the Voyage, and the Founding of America* (New York: St. Martin's Press, 2007).

19. On the history of modern nationalism, see Benedict Anderson, *Imagined Communities: Reflections on the Origin and Spread of* Nationalism (London: Verso, 2016); Eric Hobsbawm, *Nations and Nationalism since 1870: Programme, Myth, Reality* (Cambridge: Cambridge Univer-

sity Press, 1992); Rogers Brubaker, *Citizenship and Nationhood in France and Germany* (Cambridge, MA: Harvard University Press, 1992); Liah Greenfeld, *Nationalism: Five Roads to Modernity* (Cambridge, MA: Harvard University Press, 1993).

20. On the origins of World War I, see Barbara Tuchman, *The Guns of August* (New York: Random House, 1986); Margaret Macmillan, *The War That Ended Peace: The Road to 1914* (New York: Random House, 2013); Christopher Clark, *The Sleepwalkers: How Europe Went to War in 1914* (New York: Harper, 2013). For a somewhat different perspective on popular attitudes, see Michael S. Neiberg, *Dance of the Furies: Europe and the Outbreak of World War I* (Cambridge, MA: Belknap Press, 2011); Modris Eksteins, *Rites of Spring: The Great War and the Birth of the Modern Age* (New York: Mariner Press, 2000).

21. Geoffrey R. Stone, *War and Liberty: An American Dilemma, 1790 to the Present* (New York: W. W. Norton, 2007); Paul L. Murphy, *World War I and the Origin of Civil Liberties in the United States* (New York: W. W. Norton, 1979).

22. George Q. Flynn, *Conscription and Democracy: The Draft in France, Great Britain, and the United States* (New York: Praeger, 2001); Dorit Geva, *Conscription, Family, and the Modern State: A Comparative Study of France and the United States* (Cambridge: Cambridge University Press, 2013); Ute Frevert, *A Nation in Barracks: Conscription, Military Service, and Civil Society in Modern Germany* (Oxford: Berg, 2004); Joshua A. Sanborn, *Drafting the Russian Nation: Military Conscription, Total War, and Mass Politics, 1905–1925* (DeKalb, IL: Northern Illinois University Press, 2011).

23. Cited in Bruce Baum, *The Rise and Fall of the Caucasian Race: A Political History of Racial Identity* (New York: New York University Press, 2006), 118.

24. On the history of World War I, see, for example, Marc Ferro, *The Great War 1914–1918* (London and New York: Routledge, 2001); Paul Fussell, *The Great War and Modern Memory* (Oxford: Oxford University Press, 2013); Jay Winter, *Sites of Memory, Sites of Mourning: The Great War in European Cultural History* (Cambridge: Cambridge University Press, 2014): John Keegan, *The First World War* (New York: Knopf, 1999).

25. See, for example, Jacques Barzun, *The French Race: Theories of Its Origins and their Social and Political Implications Prior to the Revolution* (New York: Columbia University Press, 1932). On the interplay of nation and race, see Gary Gerstle, *American Crucible: Race and Nation in the Twentieth Century* (Princeton: Princeton University Press, 2017); Elisa Camiscioli, *Reproducing the French Race: Immigration, Intimacy, and Embodiment in the Early Twentieth Century* (Durham: Duke University Press, 2009).

26. See Fogarty, *Race and War in France*; Williams, *Torchbearers of Democracy*; Adriane Danette Lentz-Smith, *Freedom Struggles: African Americans and World War I* (Cambridge, MA: Harvard University Press, 2010); Santanu Das, ed., *Race, Empire and First World War Writing* (Cambridge, UK: Cambridge University Press, 2011); Andrew D. Evans, *Anthropology at War: World War I and the Science of Race in Germany* (Chicago: University of Chicago Press, 2010).

27. Richard F. Hamilton, Holger H. Herwig, *The Origins of World War I* (Cambridge: Cambridge University Press, 2003); Richard Overy, *The Origins of the Second World War* (New York: Routledge, 2017); Jeffrey W. Taliaferro, *Balancing Risks: Great Power Intervention in the Periphery* (Ithaca: Cornell University Press, 2004).

28. On the Sykes-Picot Agreement, see David Fromkin, *A Peace to End All Peace: The Fall of the Ottoman Empire and the Creation of the Modern Middle East* (New York: Owl, 1989); J. C.

Hurewitz, *The Middle East and North Africa in World Politics: A Documentary Record. British-French Supremacy, 1914–1945* (New Haven: Yale University Press, 1979), 60–65.

29. On Germany's overseas empire, see Sebastian Conrad, *German Colonialism: A Short History* (Cambridge, UK: Cambridge University Press, 2011); Woodruff D. Smith, *The German Colonial Empire* (Chapel Hill: University of North Carolina Press, 1978); Lora Wildenthal, *German Women for Empire, 1884–1945* (Durham: Duke University Press, 2001); Jeff Bowersox, *Raising Germans in the Age of Empire: Youth and Colonial Culture, 1871–1914* (Oxford: Oxford University Press, 2013).

30. On race and German colonialism, see Arne Perras, *Carl Peters and German Imperialism, 1856–1918* (Oxford: Clarendon Press, 2004); Volker Langbehn and Mohammad Salama, eds., *German Colonialism: Race, the Holocaust, and Postwar Germany* (New York: Columbia University Press, 2011).

31. Marie-Eve Chagnon, "Le Manifeste des 93: La mobilization des academies françaises et allemandes au déclenchement de la Prèmiere Guerre Mondiale (1914–1915)," *French Historical Studies* 35, no. 1 (2012).

32. Larry Zuckerman, *The Rape of Belgium: the Untold Story of World War I* (New York: New York University Press, 2004).

33. Library of Congress Control Number 2010652057.

34. Celia M. Kingsbury, *For Home and Country: World War I Propaganda on the Home Front* (Lincoln: University of Nebraska Press, 2010); Troy Paddock, ed., *World War I and Propaganda* (Leiden: Brill, 2014); David Welch, *Germany and Propaganda in World War I: Pacifism, Mobilization and Total War* (London: I. B. Tauris, 2014).

35. Das, *Race, Empire and First World War Writing*; Robert Gewarth and Erez Manela, eds., *Empires at War, 1911–1923* (Oxford: Oxford University Press, 2014); George Morton Jack, *Army of Empire: The Untold Story of the Indian Army in World War I* (New York: Basic Books, 2018).

36. Charles Mangin, *La force noire* (Ann Arbor: University of Michigan Library, 1910).

37. On France's use of African soldiers in World War I, see Marc Michel, *Les Africains et la Grande Geurre: L'appel à l'Afrique (1914–1918)* (Paris: Karthala, 2014); Joe H. Lunn, *Memoirs of the Maelstrom: A Senegalese Oral History of the First World War* (New York: Heinemann, 1999); Gregory Mann, *Native Sons: West African Veterans and France in the Twentieth Century* (Durham: Duke University Press, 2006).

38. John Horne, "Immigrant Workers in France during World War I," *French Historical Studies* 14, no. 1 (Spring 1985); Jean Vidalenc, "La main d'oeuvre étrangère en france et la première guerre mondiale (1901–1926)," *Francia* 2 (1974); Bertrand Nogaro and Lucien Weil, *La main-d'oeuvre étrangère et colonial pendant la guerre* (Paris, PUF, 1926); Tyler Stovall, "Colour-blind France? Colonial Workers during the First World War," *Race and Class* 35, no. 2 (October–December, 1993).

39. John Howard Morrow, *The Great War: An Imperial History* (London and New York: Routledge, 2004), 82–84. On British colonial soldiers in World War I, see also "'All in the Same Uniform'? The Participation of Black Colonial Residents in the British Armed Forces in the First World War," *Journal of Imperial and Commonwealth History* 40, no. 2 (June 2012); Philippa Levine, "Battle Colors: Race, Sex, and Colonial Soldiery in World War I," *Journal of Women's History* 9, no. 4 (1998); George Morton-Jack, *Army of Empire: The Untold Story of the Indian Army in World War I* (New York: Basic Books, 2018).

40. Fogarty, *Race and War in France*; Lunn, *Memoirs of the Maelstrom*.

41. Tyler Stovall, "The Color Line Behind the Lines: Racial Violence in France during the Great War," *The American Historical Review* 103, no. 3 (June 1998).

42. On African American soldiers in World War I, see Lentz-Smith, *Freedom Struggles*; Williams, *Torchbearers of Democracy*; Arthur E. Barbeau and Florette Henri, *The Unknown Soldiers: African-American Troops in World War I* (Philadelphia: Temple University Press, 1974); Jeffrey T. Sammons and John H. Morrow Jr., *Harlem's Rattlers and the Great War: The Undaunted 369th Regiment and the African American Quest for Equality* (Lawrence: University Press of Kansas, 2014).

43. Cited in Tyler Stovall, *Paris Noir: African Americans in the City of Light* (Boston: Houghton-Mifflin, 2006), 13.

44. Lunn, *Memoirs of the Maelstrom*.

45. Neil Richardson, *A Coward if I Return, a Hero if I Fall: Stories of Irishmen in World War I* (Dublin: O'Brien Press, 2010); Fearghal McGarry, *The Rising: Ireland: Easter 1916* (Oxford: Oxford University Press, 2010); Michael Hopkinson, *The Irish War of Independence* (Montreal: McGill-Queen's University Press, 2002).

46. *The Crisis*, July 1918.

47. Among the many studies of the Russian Revolution, see Sheila Fitzpatrick, *The Russian Revolution* (Oxford: Oxford University Press, 2017); Richard Pipes, *The Russian Revolution* (New York: Vintage, 1991); Orlando Figes, *A People's Tragedy: A History of the Russian Revolution* (New York: Viking, 1997); Mark D. Steinberg, *The Russian Revolution, 1905–1921* (Oxford: Oxford University Press, 2017).

48. On Woodrow Wilson, see Patricia O'Toole, *The Moralist: Woodrow Wilson and the World He Made* (New York: Simon and Schuster, 2018); Richard Striner, *Woodrow Wilson and World War I: A Burden Too Great to Bear* (Lanham, MD: Rowman and Littlefield, 2016); August Heckscher, *Woodrow Wilson: A Biography* (New York: Scribner's, 1991).

49. John David Smith and J. Vincent Lowery, eds., *The Dunning School: Historians, Race, and the Meaning of Reconstruction* (Lexington: University Press of Kentucky, 2013).

50. Eric S. Yellin, *Racism in the Nation's Service: Government Workers and the Color Line in Woodrow Wilson's America* (Chapel Hill: University of North Carolina Press, 2013).

51. On the intersections of progressivism and race, see David W. Southern, *The Progressive Era and Race: Reaction and Reform, 1900–1917* (New York: Wiley-Blackwell, 2005).

52. On the Paris peace talks, see Margaret MacMillan, *Paris 1919: Six Months That Changed the World* (New York: Random House, 2003); Arno J. Mayer, *Politics and Diplomacy of Peacemaking: Containment and Counterrevolution at Versailles 1918–1919* (New York: Vintage, 1969); Michael S. Neiberg, *The Treaty of Versailles: A Concise History* (Oxford: Oxford University Press, 2017).

53. Mazower, *Dark Continent*.

54. Erez Manela, *The Wilsonian Moment: Self-Determination and the Origins of Anticolonial Nationalism* (Oxford: Oxford University Press, 2009); David Fromkin, *A Peace to End All Peace: The Fall of the Ottoman Empire and the Creation of the Modern Middle East* (New York: Henry Holt, 2009).

55. Susan Pedersen, *The Guardians: The League of Nations and the Crisis of Empire* (Oxford: Oxford University Press, 2015).

56. On the 1919 Pan-African Congress, see Clarence G. Contee, "Du Bois, the NAACP, and the Pan-African Congress of 1919," *The Journal of Negro History* 57, no. 1 (January 1972); John D. Hargreaves, "Maurice Delafosse on the Pan-African Congress of 1919," *African Historical Studies* 1, no. 2 (1968); H. F. Worley and C. G. Contee, "The Worley Report on the Pan-African Congress of 1919," *The Journal of Negro History* 55, no. 2 (April 1970). On the Japanese proposal for racial equality, see Naoko Shimazu, *Japan, Race and Equality: The Racial Equality Proposal of 1919* (London and New York: Routledge, 1998).

57. Tyler Stovall, *Paris and the Spirit of 1919: Consumer Struggles, Transnationalism, and Revolution* (Cambridge, UK: Cambridge University Press, 2012); William Klingaman, *1919: The Year Our World Began* (New York: HarperCollins, 1989); David J. Mitchell, *1919: Red Mirage: Year of Desperate Rebellion* (London: Cape, 1970); Anthony Read, *A World on Fire: 1919 and the Battle with Bolshevism* (New York and London: W. W. Norton, 2008).

58. Jad Adams, *Women and the Vote: A World History* (Oxford: Oxford University Press, 2014); Doris Stevens, *Jailed for Freedom: American Women Win the Vote* (Troutdale, OR: Newsage Press, 1995).

59. Cynthia Neverdon-Morton et al., *African American Women and the Vote-1837–1965* (Amherst: University of Massachusetts, 1997); Rosalyn Terborg-Penn, *African-American Women in the Struggle for the Vote, 1850–1920* (Bloomington: Indiana University Press, 1998).

60. On the March First movement in Korea, see Michael D. Shin, *Korean National Identity under Japanese Colonial Rule: Yi Gwangsu and the March First Movement of 1919* (London and New York: Routledge, 2018).

61. On the Amritsar massacre, see Nick Lloyd, *The Amritsar Massacre: The Untold Story of One Fateful Day* (London: I.B. Tauris, 2011); Robert McLain, *Gender and Violence in British India: The Road to Amritsar 1914–1919* (New York: Palgrave Macmillan, 2014).

62. Ellis Goldberg, "Peasants in Revolt—Egypt 1919," *International Journal of Middle East Studies* 24, no. 2 (1992); Joel Beinin and Zachary Lockman, *Workers on the Nile: Nationalism, Communism, Islam, and the Egyptian Working Class, 1882–1954* (Princeton: Princeton University Press, 1987).

63. Charles Townshend, *The Republic: The Fight for Irish Independence* (London: Penguin UK, 2014); Michael Hopkinson, *The Irish War of Independence* (Montreal: McGill-Queen's University Press, 2002); R. F. Foster, *Vivid Faces: The Revolutionary Generation in Ireland, 1890–1923* (New York: W. W. Norton, 2015).

64. Isabel Wilkerson, *The Warmth of Other Suns: The Epic Story of America's Great Migration* (New York: Vintage, 2011); Nicholas Lemann, *The Promised Land: The Great Black Migration and How it Changed America* (New York: Vintage, 1992); Eric Arnesen, *Black Protest and the Great Migration: A Brief History with Documents* (New York: Bedford/St. Martin's, 2002).

65. Jeremy Krikler, *The Rand Revolt: The 1922 Insurrection and Racial Killing in South Africa* (Johannesburg: Jonathan Ball Publishers, 2007); Keith Breckenridge, "Fighting for a White South Africa: White Working-Class Racism and the 1922 Rand Revolt," *South African Historical Journal* 57, no. 1 (January 1, 2007).

66. Laura Tabili, *"We Ask for British Justice": Workers and Racial Difference in Late Imperial Britain* (Ithaca: Cornell University Press, 1994). On Red Clydeside, see Henry Bell, *John Maclean: Hero of Red Clydeside* (London: Pluto Press, 2018); William Gallacher, *Revolt on the Clyde: The Classic Autobiography of Red Clydeside* (London: Lawrence and Wishart, 2017).

67. Annie Kriegel, *Aux origines du communisme français, 1914–1920: Contribution à l'histoire du mouvement ouvrier français*, 2 vols. (Paris: Mouton & Co., 1964); Robert Wohl, *French Communism in the Making, 1914–1924* (Stanford: Stanford University Press, 1966).

68. Stovall, *Paris and the Spirit of 1919*; Benjamin F. Martin, *France and the Après Guerre, 1918–1924* (Baton Rouge: Louisiana State University Press, 1999); Sian Reynolds, *France Between the Wars: Gender and Politics* (London and New York: Routledge, 1996); Mary Louise Roberts, *Civilization without Sexes: Reconstructing Gender in Postwar France, 1917–1927* (Chicago: University of Chicago Press, 1994).

69. *Bulletin du Ministère du Travail* (Jan.–Feb. 1920), cited in Jean-Louis Robert, "Ouvriers et mouvement ouvrier parisiens pendant la Grande Guerre et l'immédiat après-guerre: Histore et anthropologie," doctoral thesis, Université de Paris—I, 1989, 474.

70. Tyler Stovall, "Remaking the French Working Class: The Postwar Exclusion of Colonial Labor," *Representations* (November 2003): 52–72.

71. *The Crisis*, founded by W.E.B. Dubois in 1910, was the official publication of the National Association for the Advancement of Colored People and remains so to this day.

72. Cited in Lentz-Smith, *Freedom Struggles*, 83.

73. Cited in Cameron McWhirter, *Red Summer: The Summer of 1919 and the Awakening of Black America* (New York: Henry Holt & Co., 2011), 56.

74. On the history of lynching in America, see Karlos K. Hill, *Beyond the Rope: The Impact of Lynching on Black Culture and Memory* (New York: Cambridge University Press, 2016); Manfred Berg, *Popular Justice: A History of Lynching in America* (Chicago: Ivan R. Dee publishers, 2011); Amy Kate Bailey and Stewart E. Tolnay, *Lynched: The Victims of Southern Mob Violence* (Chapel Hill: University of North Carolina Press, 2015).

75. Robert V. Haynes, *A Night of Violence: The Houston Riot of 1917* (Baton Rouge: Louisiana State University Press, 1976); Garna L. Christian, *Black Soldiers in Jim Crow Texas 1899–1917* (College Station: Texas A&M University Press, 1995); Elliot M. Rudwick, *Race Riot at East St. Louis, July 2, 1917* (Carbondale: Southern Illinois University Press, 1964); Charles Lumpkins, *American Pogrom: The East St. Louis Race Riot and Black Politics* (Athens, OH: Ohio University Press, 2008).

76. McWhirter, *Red Summer*; Robert Whitaker, *On the Laps of Gods: The Red Summer of 1919 and the Struggle for Justice That Remade a Nation* (Portland, OR: Broadway Books, 2009); Jan Voogd, *Race Riots and Resistance: The Red Summer of 1919* (New York: Peter Lang, 2008); William M. Tuttle Jr., *Race Riot: Chicago in the Red Summer of 1919* (Urbana: University of Illinois Press, 1996); David F. Krugler, *1919, The Year of Racial Violence: How African Americans Fought Back* (Cambridge: Cambridge University Press, 2014).

77. Grif Stockley, *Blood in Their Eyes: The Elaine Race Massacre of 1919* (Fayetteville: University of Arkansas Press, 2004).

78. Linda Gordon, *The Second Coming of the KKK: The Ku Klux Klan of the 1920s and the American Political Tradition* (New York: Liveright, 2017); Felix Harcourt, *Ku Klux Kulture: America and the Klan in the 1920s* (Chicago: University of Chicago Press, 2017).

79. Madison Grant, *The Passing of the Great Race* (Eastford, CT: Martino Fine Books, 2017).

80. Cited in Foner, *Give Me Liberty!*, 770. On the Sacco and Vanzetti case, see Susan Tejada, *In Search of Sacco and Vanzetti: Double Lives, Troubled Times, and the Massachusetts Murder Case That Shook the World* (Boston: Northeastern University Press, 2012); Moshik Temkin,

The Sacco-Vanzetti Affair: America on Trial (New Haven: Yale University Press, 2009); Felix Frankfurter, *The Case of Sacco and Vanzetti* (Boston: Little, Brown, 1961).

81. On the Johnson-Reed Act, see Mae M. Ngai, *Impossible Subjects: Illegal Aliens and the Making of Modern America* (Princeton: Princeton University Press, 2014).

82. In America, one result of this was the Red Scare that began in 1919. See Roberta Strauss Feuerlicht, *America's Reign of Terror: World War I, the Red Scare, and the Palmer Raids* (New York: Random House, 1971); Kenneth D. Ackerman, *Young J. Edgar: Hoover, the Red Scare, and the Assault on Civil Liberties* (Boston: Da Capo Press, 2007).

83. Theodore Kornweibel Jr., *"Seeing Red:" Federal Campaigns Against Black Militancy, 1919–1925* (Bloomington: Indiana University Press, 1998).

84. John Riddell, ed., *To See The Dawn: Baku, 1920, First Congress of the Peoples of the East* (New York: Palgrave, 1993).

85. Adolf Hitler, *Mein Kampf*, translated by Ralph Manheim (Boston: Houghton Mifflin, 1943). See also Albrecht Koschorke, *On Hitler's Mein Kampf: The Poetics of National Socialism*, translated by Erik Butler (Cambridge, MA: MIT Press, 2017); Hans Staudinger, *The Inner Nazi: A Critical Analysis of "Mein Kampf"* (Baton Rouge: Louisiana State University Press, 1982).

86. On the Freikorps, see Robert G. L. Waite, *Vanguard of Nazism: The Free Corps Movement in Postwar Germany 1918–1923* (New York: W. W. Norton, 1969); Robert Gewarth and John Horne, eds., *War in Peace: Paramilitary Violence in Europe after the Great War* (Oxford: Oxford University Press, 2013). On the Palmer Raids, see Roberta Strauss Feuerlicht, *America's Reign of Terror: World War I, the Red Scare, and the Palmer Raids* (New York: Random House, 1971).

87. Gaetano Salvemini, *The Origins of Fascism in Italy* (New York: Harper and Row, 1973); A. James Gregor, *Young Mussolini and the Intellectual Origins of Fascism* (Berkeley and Los Angeles: University of California Press, 1979); Simon Levis Sullam, *Giuseppe Mazzini and the Origins of Fascism* (New York: Palgrave Macmillan, 2015).

88. Richard J. Evans, *The Coming of the Third Reich* (New York: Penguin Books, 2005); Benjamin Carter Hett, *The Death of Democracy: Hitler's Rise to Power and the Downfall of the Weimar Republic* (New York: Henry Holt, 2018); William Brustein, *The Logic of Evil: The Social Origins of the Nazi Party, 1925–1933* (New Haven: Yale University Press, 1998); Peter Fritzsche, *Germans into Nazis* (Cambridge, MA: Harvard University Press, 1999).

89. Timothy Mitchell, *Bloodlands: Europe Between Hitler and Stalin* (New York: Basic Books, 2012).

90. Benito Mussolini, *The Doctrine of Fascism* (1932): http://www.worldfuturefund.org /wffmaster/Reading/Germany/mussolini.htm.

91. As Mussolini argued in a footnote to *The Doctrine of Fascism*: "Freedom is not a right, it is a duty. It is not a gift, it is a conquest; it is not equality, it is a privilege." http://www.worldfuturefund .org/wffmaster/Reading/Germany/mussolini.htm#bookmark13.

92. See, for example, Ruth Ben-Ghiat, *Fascist Modernities: Italy, 1922–1945* (Berkeley and Los Angeles: University of California Press, 2001).

93. Aaron Gillette, *Racial Theories in Fascist Italy* (London and New York: Routledge, 2001).

94. Cited in ibid., 41.

95. Michael Burleigh and Wolfgang Wippermann, *The Racial State: Germany 1933–1945* (Cambridge, UK: Cambridge University Press, 1991); Mosse, *Towards the Final Solution*; Leon Poliakov, *The Aryan Myth: A History of Racist and Nationalist Ideas in Europe* (New York: Basic

Books, 1974). See also David Theo Goldberg, *The Racial State* (Hoboken: Wiley-Blackwell, 2001).

96. Hitler, *Mein Kampf*, 290.

97. Ibid., 232

98. On Nazi anti-Semitism, see Götz Aly, *Why the Germans? Why the Jews? Envy, Race Hatred, and the Prehistory of the Holocaust* (New York: Metropolitan, 2014); Philippe Burrin, *Nazi Anti-Semitism: From Prejudice to the Holocaust* (New York: The New Press, 2005).

99. In German, *25-Punkte-Programm*. The full text can be found at https://alphahistory.com/nazigermany/nazi-party-25-points-1920/.

100. Aly, *Why the Germans?*; Burleigh and Wippermann, *The Racial State*.

101. Andree Gerrits, *The Myth of Jewish Communism: A Historical Interpretation* (Bern: Peter Lang, 2009); Michael Kellogg, *The Russian Roots of Nazism: White Emigrés and the Making of National Socialism, 1917–1945* (Cambridge: Cambridge University Press, 2008).

102. Hermann Rauschning, *Hitler Speaks: A Series of Political Conversations with Adolf Hitler on His Real Aims* (London: Thornton Butterworth, 1939), 234.

103. Mosse, *Towards the Final Solution*; Poliakov, *The Aryan Myth*.

104. Hannah Arendt, *The Origins of Totalitarianism* (New York: Harcourt, Brace & World, 1951); see also Richard H. King and Dan Stone, eds., *Hannah Arendt and the Uses of History: Imperialism, Nation, Race, and Genocide* (New York and Oxford: Berghahn Books, 2007).

105. Arendt, *The Origins of Totalitarianism*, 206. On the boomerang effect, see Patricia Owens, *Between War and Politics: International Relations and the Thought of Hannah Arendt* (Oxford: Oxford University Press, 2007).

106. Cited in King and Stone, *Hannah Arendt and the Uses of History*, 55.

107. Hitler, *Mein Kampf*, 439–440.

108. James Q. Whitman, *Hitler's American Model: The United States and the Making of Nazi Race Law* (Princeton: Princeton University Press, 2017); Stefan Kühl, *The Nazi Connection: Eugenics, American Racism, and German National Socialism* (Oxford: Oxford University Press, 2002).

109. Cited in Alex Ross, "How American Racism Influenced Hitler," *The New Yorker* (April 30, 2018): 16.

110. Shelley Baranowski, *Nazi Empire: German Colonialism and Imperialism from Bismarck to Hitler* (Cambridge: Cambridge University Press, 2011), 64. Edward B. Westermann, *Hitler's Ostkrieg and the Indian Wars: Comparing Genocide and Conquest* (Norman: University of Oklahoma Press, 2016); Carroll P. Kakel III, *The American West and the Nazi East: A Comparative and Interpretive Perspective* (New York: Palgrave Macmillan, 2011).

111. Cited in Alex Ross, "How American Racism Influenced Hitler." See also David E. Stannard, *American Holocaust: The Conquest of the New World* (Oxford: Oxford University Press, 1993).

112. King and Stone, *Hannah Arendt and the Uses of History*; Birthe Kundrus, "Colonialism, Imperialism, National Socialism: How Imperial Was the Third Reich?," in Bradley Naranch and Geoff Eley, *German Colonialism in a Global Age* (Durham: Duke University Press, 2014); Samuel Kalman, *French Colonial Fascism: The Extreme Right in Algeria, 1919–1939* (New York: Palgrave Macmillan, 2013).

113. Robert Young, *White Mythologies: Writing History and the West* (New York and London: Routledge, 1991), 8.

114. Lora Wildenthal, *German Women for Empire, 1884–1945* (Durham: Duke University Press, 2001); George Steinmetz, *The Devil's Handwriting: Precoloniality and the German Colonial State in Qingdao, Samoa, and Southwest Africa* (Chicago: University of Chicago Press, 2007); Bradley Naranch and Geoff Eley, eds., *German Colonialism in a Global Age* (Durham: Duke University Press, 2015).

115. Langbehn and Salama, *German Colonialism.*

116. Arne Perras, *Carl Peters and German Imperialism 1856–1918: A Political Biography* (Oxford: Clarendon Press, 2004).

117. Jurgen Zimmerer and Joachim Zeller, eds., *Genocide in German South-West Africa: The Colonial War of 1904–1908 and Its Aftermath* (London: Merlin Press, 2011); David Olusoga and Casper W. Erichsen, *The Kaiser's Holocaust: Germany's Forgotten Genocide* (London: Faber and Faber, 2011).

118. *Journal of the International Institute* (University of Michigan), 12, no. 2 (Winter 2005).

119. Aaron Gillette, *Racial Theories in Fascist Italy.*

120. Robert M. Mallett, *Mussolini in Ethiopia, 1919–1935: The Origins of Fascist Italy's African War* (Cambridge, UK: Cambridge University Press, 2015); Alberto Sbacchi, *Legacy of Bitterness: Ethiopia and Fascist Italy 1935–1941* (Trenton, NJ: Red Sea Press, 1997); James Dugan *Days of Emperor and Clown: The Italo-Ethiopian War 1935–1936* (New York: Doubleday, 1973).

121. Cited in Gillette, *Racial Theories in Fascist Italy*, 58.

122. Cited in Luigi Reale, *Mussolini's Concentration Camps for Civilians: An Insight into the Nature of Fascist Racism* (Middlesex, UK, and Portland, OR: Vallentine Mitchell Press, 2011), 31.

123. On the Holocaust in Italy, see Simon Levis Sullam, *The Italian Executioners: The Genocide of the Jews of Italy,* (Princeton: Princeton University Press, 2018); Michele Sarfatti, *The Jews in Mussolini's Italy: From Equality to Persecution* (Madison: University of Wisconsin Press, 2006); Susan Zuccotti, *Under His Very Windows: The Vatican and the Holocaust in Italy* (New Haven: Yale University Press, 2002).

124. Hitler, *Mein Kampf*, 139.

125. Baranowski, *Nazi Empire*; Mark Mazower, *Hitler's Empire: How the Nazis Ruled Europe* (New York: Penguin Books, 2009); Eberhard Jäckel, *Hitler's World View* (Cambridge MA: Harvard University Press, 1981).

126. Hugh Ragsdale, *The Soviets, the Munich Crisis, and the Coming of World War II* (Cambridge: Cambridge University Press, 2009); Mirna Zakic, *Ethnic Germans and National Socialism in Yugoslavia in World War II* (Cambridge, UK: Cambridge University Press, 2017).

127. Martyn Housden, *Hans Frank: Lebensraum and the Holocaust* (New York: Palgrave Macmillan, 2003).

128. Baranowski, *Nazi Empire*; Mazower, *Hitler's Empire*; Timothy Snyder, *Bloodlands: Europe Between Hitler and Stalin* (New York: Basic Books, 2012).

129. Snyder, *Bloodlands*; Stephen G. Fritz, *Ostkrieg: Hitler's War of Extermination in the East* (Lexington: University Press of Kentucky, 2011); Alex J. Kay et al.; *Nazi Policy on the Eastern Front, 1941: Total War, Genocide, and Radicalization* (Rochester: University of Rochester Press, 2012).

130. Christian Gerlach, *The Extermination of the European Jews* (Cambridge, UK: Cambridge University Press, 2016), chapter 4; Yitzhak Arad, *The Holocaust in the Soviet Union* (Lincoln: University of Nebraska Press, 2013); A. Anatoli Kuznetsov, *Babi Yar: A Document in the Form of a Novel* (New York: Farrar, Straus and Giroux, 1970).

131. On Manifest Destiny, see Anders Stephanson, *Manifest Destiny: American Expansion and the Empire of Right* (New York: Hill and Wang, 1996); Reginald Horsman, *Race and Manifest Destiny: The Origins of American Racial Anglo-Saxonism* (Cambridge, MA: Harvard University Press, 1981); John Mack Faragher, ed., *Rereading Frederick Jackson Turner: "The Significance of the Frontier in American History" and Other Essays* (New Haven: Yale University Press, 1999).

132. Westermann, *Hitler's Ostkrieg and the Indian Wars*; Kakel, *The American West and the Nazi East*.

133. Cited in Timothy Snyder, "Hitler's American Dream," *Slate*, March 8, 2017.

134. Ibid.

135. To a certain extent the death camps were the exception to this, but they too developed in the context of total war. On the death camps, see Saul Friedlander, *The Years of Extermination: Nazi Germany and the Jews, 1939–1945* (New York: Harper, 2007); Eugen Kogon, *The Theory and Practice of Hell: The German Concentration Camps and the System Behind Them* (New York: Farrar, Straus and Giroux, 2006); Primo Levi, *Survival in Auschwitz* (New York: Random House, 2007).

136. Cited in M. K. Dziewanowski, *War at Any Price: World War II in Europe, 1939–1945* (Englewood Cliffs, NJ: Prentice-Hall, 1987), 260.

137. Cited in Michael Neiberg, *The Blood of Free Men: The Liberation of Paris, 1944* (New York: Basic Books, 2012), 237.

138. Cited in "Gandhi's 1942 Letter to FDR, Asking for Support for Indian Independence," *The Vault, Slate*, July 23, 2014.

139. On the general history of World War II, see Snyder, *Bloodlands*; Dziewanowski, *War at Any Price*; Gerhard L. Weinberg, *A World at Arms: A Global History of World War II* (Cambridge, UK: Cambridge University Press, 1994); John Keegan, *The Second World War* (New York: Penguin, 2016); Gordon Craig, *The Ordeal of Total War* (New York: Harper and Row, 1968).

140. On the Stalinist dictatorship, see Stephen Kotkin, *Stalin: Waiting for Hitler, 1929–1941* (New York: Penguin, 2017); Jorg Baberowski, *Scorched Earth: Stalin's Reign of Terror* (New Haven: Yale University Press, 2016); Oleg V. Khlevniuk, *The History of the Gulag: From Collectivization to the Great Terror* (New Haven: Yale University Press, 2004).

141. On the Soviet Union in World War II, see Chris Bellamy, *Absolute War: Soviet Russia in the Second World War* (New York: Vintage, 2008); Richard Overy, *Russia's War: A History of the Soviet War Effort, 1941–1945* (New York: Penguin Books, 1998); David Stahel, *Operation Barbarossa and Germany's Defeat in the East* (Cambridge: Cambridge University Press, 2011).

142. On the United States in World War II, see Michael C. C. Adams, *The Best War Ever: America and World War II* (Baltimore: Johns Hopkins University Press, 2015); David M. Kennedy, *Freedom from Fear: The American People in Depression and War, 1929–1945* (Oxford: Oxford University Press, 1999); Studs Terkel, *"The Good War": An Oral History of World War II* (New York: Pantheon, 1984); John Dower, *War without Mercy: Race and Power in the Pacific War* (New York: Pantheon, 1987).

143. See Donny Gluckstein, *A People's History of the Second World War: Resistance versus Empire* (London: Pluto Press, 2012).

144. *The Militant*, November 11, 1944.

145. *Lettres de fusillés*, edited by Jacques Duclos (Paris: Éditions Sociales, 1970).

146. Winston S. Churchill, *Memoirs of the Second World War* (Boston: Houghton Mifflin, 1991), 285.

147. Barkawi, *Soldiers of Empire*; Andrew Stewart, *Empire Lost: Britain, The Dominions and the Second World War* (London: Bloomsbury Academic, 2008); Ashley Jackson et al., eds., *An Imperial World at War: Aspects of the British Empire's War Experience, 1939–1945* (London and New York: Routledge, 2008).

148. Iain E. Johnston-White, *The British Commonwealth and Victory in the Second World War* (New York: Palgrave Macmillan, 2016); T. J. Copp, *No Price Too High: Canadians and the Second World War* (Whitby, Ontario: McGraw-Hill Ryerson, 1996).

149. Barkawi, *Soldiers of Empire*; Srinath Raghavan, *India's War: World War II and the Making of Modern South Asia* (New York: Basic Books, 2016); Yasmin Khan, *India at War: The Subcontinent and the Second World War* (Oxford: Oxford University Press, 2015).

150. Charles De Gaulle, *The Complete War Memoirs of Charles De Gaulle* (New York: Carroll and Graf, 1998), 84.

151. Eric T. Jennings, *Free French Africa in World War II: The African Resistance* (Cambridge, UK: Cambridge University Press, 2015); Brian Weinstein, *Eboué* (Oxford: Oxford University Press, 1972).

152. Martin Thomas, *The French Empire at War, 1940–1945* (Manchester, UK: Manchester University Press, 2007); Eric T. Jennings, *Vichy in the Tropics: Petain's National Revolution in Madagascar, Guadeloupe, and Indochina, 1940–1944* (Stanford: Stanford University Press, 2001).

153. Meredith L. Scott-Weaver, "Networks and Refugees: Salomon Grumbach's Activism in Late Third-Republic France," *French History* 28, no. 4 (2014); William Wiser, *The Twilight Years: Paris in the 1930s* (New York: Carroll and Graf, 2000); Erich Maria Remarque, *Arch of Triumph* (New York: D. Appleton-Century Co., 1945).

154. Denis Peschanski, *Des étrangers dans la Résistance* (Paris: Eds. de l'Atelier-Musée de la Résistance, 2002).

155. On the Vél d'Hiv raid, see Maurice Rajsfus, *Operation Yellow Star: Black Thursday, The Round-up of July 16, 1942* (Los Angeles: Doppelhaus Press, 2017); Claude Lévy and Paul Tillard, *Betrayal at the Vél d'Hiv* (New York: Hill and Wang, 1969).

156. Philippe Robrieux, *L'Affaire Manouchian: Vie et Mort d'un Héros Communiste* (Paris: Fayard, 1986); Greg Lamazeres, *Marcel Langer, une vie de combats, 1903–1943: Juif, communiste, résistant . . . et guillotiné* (Toulouse: Privat, 2003).

157. Cited in Julian Jackson, *France: The Dark Years, 1940–1944* (Oxford: Oxford University Press, 2001).

158. Anny Latour, *The Jewish Resistance in France, 1940–1944* (Washington, DC: US Holocaust Museum, 1981); Lazare Lucien, *La résistance juive en France* (Paris: Stock, 1987); Jacques Adler, *The Jews of Paris and the Final Solution* (New York and Oxford: Oxford University Press, 1987).

159. Renée Poznanski, *Jews in France during World War II* (Waltham, MA: Brandeis University Press, 2001); Michael R. Marrus and Robert O. Paxton, *Vichy France and the Jews* (Stanford: Stanford University Press, 1995); Susan Zucotti, *The Holocaust, The French, and The Jews* (New York: Basic Books, 1993).

160. Stefanie Wichhart, *Britain, Egypt and Iraq During World War II: The Decline of Imperial Power in the Middle East* (London: I. B. Tauris, 2018).

161. Christopher Somerville, *Our War: The Story of the Unsung Heroes of Her Majesty's Foreign Legions* (London: Orion, 1998); Ben Bousquet and Colin Douglas, *West Indian Women at War: British Racism in World War II* (London: Lawrence and Wishart, 1991).

162. "Paris Liberation Made 'Whites Only,'" BBC, April 6, 2009; Tyler Stovall, "Bogey Goes Colonial: Hollywood, World War II, and *la France Outre-Mer*," unpublished paper.

163. A. J. Baime, *The Arsenal of Democracy: FDR, Detroit, and an Epic Quest to Arm an America at War* (New York: Mariner Books, 2015); Herman, *Freedom's Forge*; Nelson Lichtenstein, *Labor's War at Home: The CIO in World War II* (Philadelphia: Temple University Press, 2008).

164. Kevin J. McMahon, *Reconsidering Roosevelt on Race: How the Presidency Paved the Road to Brown* (Chicago: University of Chicago Press, 2003); Patrick D. Lukens, *A Quiet Victory for Latino Rights: FDR and the Controversy over "Whiteness"* (Tucson: University of Arizona Press, 2012).

165. On African American soldiers in World War II, see Neil A. Wynn, *The African American Experience during World War II* (Lanham, MD: Rowman and Littlefield, 2010); Mary P. Motley, *The Invisible Soldier: The Experience of the Black Soldier, World War II* (Detroit: Wayne State University Press, 1987); J. Todd Moye, *Freedom Flyers: The Tuskegee Airmen of World War II* (Oxford: Oxford University Press, 2012); Phillip McGuire, Ed., *Taps for a Jim Crow Army: Letters from Black Soldiers in World War II* (Lexington: University Press of Kentucky, 1993).

166. On the bracero program, see Mireya Loza, *Defiant Braceros: How Migrant Workers Fought for Racial, Sexual, and Political Freedom* (Chapel Hill: University of North Carolina Press, 2016); Deborah Cohen, *Braceros: Migrant Citizens and Transnational Subjects in the Postwar United States and Mexico* (Chapel Hill: University of North Carolina Press, 2011); Kitty Calavita, *Inside the State: The Bracero Program, Immigration, and the I.N.S.* (London and New York: Routledge, 1992).

167. Steven Rosales, *Soldados Razos at War: Chicano Politics, Identity, and Masculinity in the U.S. Military from World War II to Vietnam* (Tucson: University of Arizona Press, 2017); Bixler, *Winds of Freedom*; Chester Nez, *Code Talker: The First and Only Memoir by One of the Original Navajo Code Talkers of WWII* (New York: Dutton Caliber, 2011); Kevin Scott Wong, *Americans First: Chinese Americans and the Second World War* (Cambridge, MA: Harvard University Press, 2005).

168. Erika Lee, *At America's Gates: Chinese Immigration during the Exclusion Era* (Chapel Hill: University of North Carolina Press, 2003), 240–51.

169. Mason B. Williams, *City of Ambition: FDR, LaGuardia, and the Making of Modern New York* (New York: W. W. Norton, 2014); Lawrence Elliott, *Little Flower: The Life and Times of Fiorello LaGuardia* (New York: William Morrow, 1983).

170. Esther Schor, *Emma Lazarus* (New York: Schocken, 2006).

171. "My Children!," *Detroit Free Press*, June 19, 1941.

172. On Hollywood in World War II, see Robert L. McLaughlin and Sally E. Parry, *We'll Always Have the Movies: American Cinema during World War II* (Lexington: University Press of Kentucky, 2006); Thomas Doherty, *Projections of War: Hollywood, American Culture, and World War II* (New York: Columbia University Press, 1999); Clayton R. Koppes and Gregory D. Black,

Hollywood Goes to War: How Politics, Profits, and Propaganda Shaped World War II Movies (Berkeley and Los Angeles: University of California Press, 1990).

173. Mary Elizabeth Basile Chopas, *Searching for Subversives: The Story of Italian Internment in Wartime America* (Chapel Hill: University of North Carolina Press, 2017); Stephen Fox, *America's Invisible Gulag: A Biography of German American Internment and Exclusion in World War II* (New York: Peter Lang, 2000).

174. Andrew E. Kersten and Clarence Lang, eds., *Reframing Randolph: Labor, Black Freedom, and the Legacies of A. Philip Randolph* (New York: NYU Press, 2015), David Lucander, *Winning the War for Democracy: The March on Washington Movement, 1941–1946* (Urbana: University of Illinois Press, 2014).

175. Adolph Reed Jr., "Race and the New Deal Coalition," *The Nation*, March 20, 2008; Andor Skotnes, *A New Deal for All? Race and Class Struggles in Depression-Era Baltimore* (Durham: Duke University Press, 2012); Harvard Sitkoff, *A New Deal for Blacks: The Emergence of Civil Rights as a National Issue: The Depression Decade* (Oxford: Oxford University Press, 1978).

176. Wynn, *The African American Experience*; Morris J. MacGregor Jr., *Integration of the Armed Forces, 1940–1965* (Washington, DC: Government Printing Office, 1981); Stephen E. Ambrose, *The U.S. Army from the Normandy Beaches to the Bulge to the Surrender of Germany, June 7, 1944 to May 7, 1945* (New York: Simon and Schuster, 1998).

177. Eduardo Obregón Pagán, *Murder at the Sleepy Lagoon: Zoot Suits, Race, and Riot in Wartime L.A.* (Chapel Hill: University of North Carolina Press, 2003); Mark A. Weitz, *The Sleepy Lagoon Murder Case: Race Discrimination and Mexican-American Rights* (Lawrence: University Press of Kansas, 2010).

178. Dominic J. Capeci Jr. and Martha Wilkerson, *Layered Violence: The Detroit Rioters of 1943* (Jackson: University Press of Mississippi, 2009); Nat Brandt, *Harlem at War: The Black Experience in World War II* (Syracuse: Syracuse University Press, 1996).

179. On Japanese American history, see Frank Chin, *Born in the USA: A Story of Japanese America, 1889–1947* (Lanham, MD: Rowman and Littlefield, 2002); Roger Daniels, *Asian America: Chinese and Japanese in the United States since 1850* (Seattle: University of Washington Press, 1988); Ronald Takaki, *Strangers from a Different Shore: A History of Asian America* (New York: Little, Brown, 1998).

180. Richard Reeves, *Infamy: The Shocking Story of the Japanese-American Internment in World War II* (New York: Henry Holt, 2015); Roger Daniels, *Prisoners without Trial: Japanese Americans in World War II* (New York: Hill and Wang, 2004); Alice Yang Murray, *Historical Memories of the Japanese American Internment and the Struggle for Redress* (Stanford: Stanford University Press, 2007).

181. Robert Asahina, *Just Americans: How Japanese Americans Won a War at Home and Abroad; The Story of the 100th Battalion/442nd Regimental Combat Team in World War II* (New York: Gotham, 2006); Masayo Duus, *Unlikely Liberators: The Men of the 100th and 442nd* (Honolulu: University of Hawaii Press, 1987); Brenda L. Moore, *Serving Our Country: Japanese American Women in the Military during World War II* (New Brunswick, NJ: Rutgers University Press, 2003).

182. Donald Warren, *Radio Priest: Charles Coughlin, the Father of Hate Radio* (New York: The Free Press, 1996).

183. Stephen Dorril, *Blackshirt: Sir Oswald Mosley and British Fascism* (New York: Viking Publishing, 2006); Martin Pugh, *Hurrah for the Blackshirts!: Fascists and Fascism in Britain between the Wars* (New York: Random House, 2005).

184. Deborah Dash Moore, *GI Jews: How World War II Changed a Generation* (Cambridge, MA: Belknap Press, 2006); Martin Sugarman, *Fighting Back: British Jewry's Military Contribution in the Second World War* (London: Vallentine Mitchell, 2010); Richard Goldstein, "Max Fuchs, G.I. Cantor in Historic Battlefield Service, is Dead at 96," *The New York Times*, July 4, 2018.

185. *The Pittsburgh Courier*, January 31, 1942.

186. *The Pittsburgh Courier*, February 14, 1942.

187. Patrick S. Washburn, "The Pittsburgh Courier's Double V Campaign in 1942," Annual Meeting of the Association for Education in Journalism (East Lansing: Michigan State University, 1981); Rawn James Jr., *The Double V: How Wars, Protest, and Harry Truman Desegregated America's Military* (New York: Bloomsbury, 2013); Ronald Takaki, *Double Victory: A Multicultural History of America in World War II* (New York: Little, Brown, 2000).

188. Laurence Rees, *Horror in the East: Japan and the Atrocities of World War II* (New York: Da Capo Press, 2002).

189. Dower, *War without Mercy*; Nakano Satoshi, *Japan's Colonial Moment in Southeast Asia 1942–1945: The Occupier's Experience* (London and New York: Routledge, 2018); Ramon Hawley Myers and Mark R. Peattie, *The Japanese Colonial Empire, 1895–1945* (Princeton: Princeton University Press, 1984).

190. Cited in Pankaj Mishra, *From the Ruins of Empire: The Revolt Against the West and the Remaking of Asia* (New York: Penguin, 2013), 249–50.

191. Jan A. Krancher, *The Defining Years of the Dutch East Indies, 1942–1949: Survivors Accounts of Japanese Invasion and Enslavement of Europeans and the Revolution That Created Free Indonesia* (Jefferson, NC: McFarland, 2003); Boudewign van Oort, *Tjideng Reunion: A Memoir of World War II on Java* (Brooklyn, NY: Seaside Press, 2017).

192. Ikehata Setsuho and Ricardo Trota Jose, eds., *The Philippines under Japan: Occupation Policy and Reaction* (Manila: Ateneo De Manila University Press, 2000).

193. Jen Green, *Days of Decision: Gandhi and the Quit India Movement* (Chicago: Heinemann, 2013); Francis G. Hutchins, *India's Revolution: Gandhi and the Quit India Movement* (Cambridge, MA: Harvard University Press, 1973).

194. Joyce Chapman Lebra, *The Indian National Army and Japan* (Singapore: Institute of Southeast Asian Studies, 2008); Peter Ward Fay, *The Forgotten Army: India's Armed Struggle for Independence 1942–1945* (Ann Arbor: University of Michigan Press, 1994).

195. Jennings, *Vichy in the Tropics*; Sébastien Verney, *L'Indochine sous Vichy: Entre révolution nationale, collaboration, et identités nationales* (Paris: Riveneuve, 2012).

196. William J. Duiker, *Ho Chi Minh: A Life* (Westport, CT: Hyperion, 2001); Geoffrey C. Gunn, *Rice Wars in Colonial Vietnam: The Great Famine and the Viet Minh Road to Power* (Lanham, MD: Rowman and Littlefield, 2014).

Chapter 6

1. On the Sétif massacres, see Kamel Benaiche, *Sétif, la fosse commune: Massacres du 8 mai 1945* (Algiers: El Ibriz Editions, 2016); Roger Vétillard, *Sétif, mai 1945: Massacres en Algérie* (Versailles: Éditions de Paris, 2008); Jean-Louis Planche, *Sétif 1945: Histoire d'un massacre annoncé* (Paris: Perrin, 2006).

2. United Nations *Charter*, Article 1 Section 3 (San Francisco, 1945).

3. Frank Capra, *Prelude to War*, 1942; on Hollywood during World War II, see David Welky, *The Moguls and the Dictators: Hollywood and the Coming of World War II* (Baltimore: Johns Hopkins University Press, 2008); Thomas Doherty, *Projections of War: Hollywood, American Culture, and World War II* (New York: Columbia University Press, 1993); Clayton R. Koppes, *Hollywood Goes to War: How Politics, Profits, and Propaganda Shaped World War II Movies* (Berkeley: University of California Press, 1990); Michael Birdwell, *Celluloid Soldiers: The Warner Bros. Campaign against Nazism* (New York: New York University Press, 1998).

4. On the history of the cold war, see Melvyn P. Leffler, *The Cambridge History of the Cold War*, 3 vols. (Cambridge: Cambridge University Press, 2012); John Lewis Gaddis, *The Cold War: A New History* (New York: Penguin, 2006); Elizabeth Edwards Spalding, *The First Cold Warrior: Harry Truman, Containment, and the Remaking of Liberal Internationalism* (Lexington: University Press of Kentucky, 2006); Frances Stonor Saunders, *The Cultural Cold War: The CIA and the World of Arts and Letters* (New York: The New Press, 1999).

5. Cited in Denise M. Bostdorff, *Proclaiming the Truman Doctrine: The Cold War Call to Arms* (College Station: Texas A&M Press, 2008), 4–5.

6. Winston Churchill, "Sinews of Peace," speech given at Fulton Missouri, March 5, 1946, https://www.thoughtco.com/winston-churchills-iron-curtain-speech-1779492.

7. Konni Zilliacus, *Tito of Yugoslavia* (London: M. Joseph, 1952); Richard West, *Tito and the Rise and Fall of Yugoslavia* (London: Carroll and Graf, 1995).

8. Churchill, "Sinews of Peace."

9. On the revisionist school of cold war historiography, see William Appleman Williams, *The Tragedy of American Diplomacy* (New York: W. W. Norton, 2009); Gar Alperovitz, *Atomic Diplomacy: Hiroshima and Potsdam* (London: Pluto Press, 1994); Gabriel Kolko, *The Politics of War: The World and United States Foreign Policy, 1943–1945* (New York: Pantheon, 1990).

10. Williams, *The Tragedy of American Diplomacy*, 9–10. On the revisionist historiography of the Cold War, see also Walter LaFeber, *America, Russia, and the Cold War* (New York: McGraw Hill, 2002); Gabriel Kolko, *The Politics of War: The World and United States Foreign Policy, 1943–1945* (New York: Pantheon, 1990).

11. On the idea of captive nations, see John Coert Campbell, *American Policy Toward Communist Eastern Europe: The Choices Ahead* (Minneapolis: University of Minnesota Press, 1965).

12. Ibid.; Andrei Tsygankov, *Russophobia: Anti-Russian Lobby and American Foreign Policy* (New York: Palgrave-Macmillan, 2009).

13. Joint Resolution of the US Congress, Public Law 86–90, July 17, 1959.

14. Tsygankov, *Russophobia*.

15. NSC-68, "United States Objectives and Programs for National Security," April 14, 1950, 5.

16. On the history of NSC-68, see John Lewis Gaddis, "NSC 68 and the Problem of Ends and Means," *International Security* 4, no. 4 (Spring 1980); Curt Cardwell, *NSC 68 and the Political Economy of the Early Cold War* (Cambridge, UK: Cambridge University Press, 2011).

17. Stephen Brooke, *Labour's War: The Labour Party during the Second World War* (New York: Oxford University Press, 1992); Basil Davidson, *Special Operations Executive: Scenes from the Anti-Nazi War* (London: V. Gollancz, 1980).

18. William H. Beveridge, *Full Employment in a Free Society: A Report* (London: Routledge, 2015); Rodney Lowe, *The Welfare State in Britain since 1945* (New York: St. Martin's Press, 1993).

19. *Conseil National de la Résistance, Programme, 15 mars, 1944* https://fr.wikisource.org/wiki/Programme_du_Conseil_national_de_la_R%C3%A9sistance. On the history of the French Resistance, see Olivier Wieviorka, *The French Resistance*, translated by Jane Marie Todd (Cambridge, MA: Harvard University Press, 2016); Robert Gildea, *Fighters in the Shadows: A New History of the French Resistance* (Cambridge, MA: Harvard University Press, 2015).

20. Stephanie Haboush Plunkett and James J. Kimble, co-curators, *Enduring Ideals: Rockwell, Roosevelt, and the Four Freedoms* (New York and London: Abbeville Press, 2018).

21. Michael J. Hogan, *The Marshall Plan: America, Britain, and the Reconstruction of Western Europe, 1947–1952* (New York: Cambridge University Press, 1987); Martin Schain, *The Marshall Plan, Fifty Years After* (New York: Palgrave, 2001); Benn Steil, *The Marshall Plan: Dawn of the Cold War* (New York: Simon and Schuster, 2018).

22. On cold war in Asia, see Christopher E. Goscha and Christian F. Ostermann, *Connecting Histories: Decolonization and the Cold War in Southeast Asia, 1945–1962* (Stanford: Stanford University Press, 2009); Jian Chen, *Mao's China and the Cold War* (Chapel Hill: University of North Carolina Press, 2001); Carole K. Fink, *Cold War: An International History* (London: Routledge, 2013).

23. Jean-Paul Sartre, Preface, in Frantz Fanon, *The Wretched of the Earth* (New York: Grove Press, 2005), xliii.

24. Lawrence James, *Churchill and Empire: A Portrait of an Imperialist* (New York: Pegasus Books, 2014); Richard Toye, *Churchill's Empire: The World That Made Him and the World He Made* (New York: Henry Holt, 2010).

25. On the history of decolonization see, among many studies, Jan C. Jansen, *Decolonization: A Short History* (Princeton: Princeton University Press, 2017); Dane Kennedy, *Decolonization: A Short Introduction* (New York: Oxford University Press, 2016); Raymond F. Betts, *Decolonization* (New York: Routledge, 2004); Todd Shepard, *The Invention of Decolonization: the Algerian War and the Remaking of France* (Ithaca: Cornell University Press, 2006).

26. "Resolution adopted by the Indian National Congress at Ramgarh, March 18, 1940," *Labour Monthly*, April 1940.

27. Kwame Nkrumah, *I Speak of Freedom: A Statement of African Ideology* (New York: Praeger, 1961).

28. For example, *Freedom and Liberation: A Selection from Speeches, 1974–1999* (New York: Oxford University Press, 2011), and *Freedom and Socialism: Uhuru na ujamaa; A Selection from Writings and Speeches, 1965–1967* (New York: Oxford University Press, 1968).

29. Julius K. Nyerere, "Freedom and Development," in *Freedom and Development: A Selection from Writings and Speeches, 1968–1973* (London, Oxford, and New York: Oxford University Press, 1973), 58.

30. See the discussions of these issues in the preceding two chapters.

31. The classic statement on colonialism and racism is Frantz Fanon, *Black Skin, White Masks* (London: Pluto, 2008); see also Ann L. Stoler, *Carnal Knowledge and Imperial Power: Race and the Intimate in Colonial Rule* (Berkeley: University of California Press, 2002); Jane Samson, *Race and Empire* (New York: Routledge, 2005); John Rex, *Race, Colonialism, and the City* (London: Routledge and Kegan Paul, 1973).

32. Nancy L. Clark and William H. Worger, *South Africa: The Rise and Fall of Apartheid* (New York: Routledge, 2016); Martin Loney, *Rhodesia: White Racism and Imperial Response* (New York: Penguin, 1975).

33. Tom Mboya, *Freedom and After* (Boston: Little, Brown, 1963), 22.

34. See, for example, Adria Lawrence, *Imperial Rule and the Politics of Nationalism: Anti-Colonial Protests in the French Empire* (New York: Cambridge University Press, 2013); Joseph Sramek, *Gender, Morality, and Race in Company India, 1765–1858* (New York: Palgrave Macmillan, 2011); Hilary Jones, *The Métis of Senegal: Urban Life and Politics in French West Africa* (Bloomington: Indiana University Press, 2013).

35. Ramachandra Guha, *Gandhi Before India* (New York: Alfred A. Knopf, 2014); Judith M. Brown and Martin Prozesky, eds., *Gandhi and South Africa: Principles and Politics* (New York: St. Martin's Press, 1996).

36. Sean Chabot, *Transnational Roots of the Civil Rights Movement: African American Explorations of the Gandhian Repertoire* (Lanham: Lexington Books, 2012); Sudarshan Kapur, *Raising Up a Prophet: The African-American Encounter with Gandhi* (Boston: Beacon Press, 1992).

37. On the history of the Indian National Congress, see Ranjan Ray, *A Concise History of the Indian National Congress, 1885–1947* (New Delhi: Vikas Publishing House, 1985); Mike Shepperdson, *The Indian National Congress and the Political Economy of India* (Brookfield: Avebury Press, 1988).

38. See, for example, Lawrence, *Imperial Rule and the Politics of Nationalism*; Jones, *The Métis of Senegal*.

39. On anticolonialism, see Edward H. Judge and John W. Langdon, *The Struggle against Imperialism: Anticolonialism and the Cold War* (London: Verso, 2018).

40. Nkrumah, *Speak Now*, 127.

41. See Thomas E. Smith, *Emancipation without Equality: Pan-African Activism and the Global Color Line* (Amherst: University of Massachusetts, 2018); Lara Putnam, *Radical Moves: Caribbean Migrants and the Politics of Race in the Jazz Age* (Chapel Hill: University of North Carolina Press, 2013); UNESCO, *Sociological Theories: Race and Colonialism* (Paris: UNESCO, 1980).

42. See, for example, Madhu Dubey, "The 'True Lie' of the Nation: Fanon and Feminism," *differences: A Journal of Feminist Cultural Studies*, 10, no. 2 (1998); John Mowitt, "Algerian Nation: Fanon's Fetish," *Cultural Critique*, no. 22 (Fall 1992).

43. Rozina Visram, *Women in India and Pakistan: The Struggle for Independence from British Rule* (Cambridge: Cambridge University Press, 1993); Stephen Legg, "Gendered Politics and Nationalised Homes: Women and the Anti-colonial Struggle in Delhi, 1930–1947," *Gender, Place and Culture*, 10, no. 1 (2003).

44. Tanya Lyons, *Guns and Guerrilla Girls: Women in the Zimbabwean National Liberation Struggle* (London: Africa World Press, 2004).

45. Tyler Stovall, "Empires of Democracy"; Andrew W. M. Smith and Chris Jeppensen, eds., *Britain, France, and the Decolonization of Africa: Future Imperfect?* (London: UCL Press, 2017); Miles Kahler, *Decolonization in Britain and France: The Domestic Consequences of International relations* (Princeton: Princeton University Press, 1984); Frederick Cooper, *Decolonization and African Society: The Labor Question in French and British Africa* (Cambridge: Cambridge University Press, 1996).

46. On the end of British rule in India, see Yasmin Khan, *The Great Partition: The Making of India and Pakistan* (New Haven: Yale University Press, 2007); Ian Talbot, *The Partition of India* (Cambridge: Cambridge University Press, 2009); Larry Collins and Dominique Lapierre, *Free-*

dom at Midnight: The Epic Drama of India's Struggle for Independence (New York: HarperCollins, 1997).

47. James L. Gelvin, *The Israel-Palestine Conflict: One Hundred Years of War* (Cambridge, UK: Cambridge University Press, 2014); Ian Black, *Enemies and Neighbors: Arabs and Jews in Palestine and Israel, 1917–2017* (New York: Grove Press, 2018).

48. Anthony C. Alessandrini, *Frantz Fanon and the Future of Cultural Politics: Finding Something Different* (Lanham: Lexington Books, 2016); David Macey, *Frantz Fanon: A Biography* (New York: Picador, 2001); Lewis R. Gordon et al., *Fanon: A Critical Reader* (Hoboken: Wiley-Blackwell, 1996).

49. Benjamin John Grob-Fitzgibbon, *Imperial Endgame: Britain's Dirty Wars and the End of Empire* (London and New York: Palgrave Macmillan, 2011); Ruth Ginio, *The French Army and Its African Soldiers: The Years of Decolonization* (Lincoln: University of Nebraska Press, 2017); Caroline Elkins, *Imperial Reckoning: The Untold Story of Britain's Gulag in Kenya* (New York: Henry Holt, 2005); Anthony Clayton, *The Wars of French Decolonization* (London and New York: Longman, 1994).

50. Fanon, *The Wretched of the Earth* (New York: Grove Press, 2005), 5.

51. Elkins, *Imperial Reckoning*; David Anderson, *Histories of the Hanged: The Dirty War in Kenya and the End of Empire* (New York: W. W. Norton, 2005).

52. Martin S. Alexander et al., *The Algerian War and the French Army, 1954–1962: Experiences, Images, Testimonies* (New York: Palgrave Macmillan, 2002).

53. Jim House, *Paris 1961: Algerians, State Terror, and Memory* (Oxford: Oxford University Press, 2006); Jean-Luc Einaudi, *La bataille de Paris: 17 octobre 1961* (Paris: Éditions du Seuil, 2001).

54. See, for example, Robert Mason, *Legacies of Violence: Rendering the Unspeakable Past in Modern Australia* (New York: Berghahn Books, 2017).

55. Classic examples of this literature include Alice Conklin, *A Mission to Civilize: The Republican Idea of Empire in France and West Africa, 1895–1930* (Stanford: Stanford University Press, 1997); Catherine Hall, *Civilising Subjects: Metropole and Colony in the English Imagination 1830–1867* (Chicago: University of Chicago Press, 2002); Lora Wildenthal, *German Women for Empire, 1884–1945* (Durham: Duke University Press, 2001). For an excellent overview of this literature, see Frederick Cooper and Ann Laura Stoler, eds., *Tensions of Empire: Colonial Cultures in a Bourgeois World* (Berkeley: University of California Press, 1997).

56. Kristin Ross, *Fast Cars, Clean Bodies: Decolonization and the Reordering of French Culture* (Cambridge, MA: The MIT Press, 1996).

57. Stephen Howe, *Anticolonialism in British Politics: The Left and the End of Empire, 1918–1964* (Oxford: Clarendon Press, 1993); Partha Sarathi Gupta, *Imperialism and the British Labour Movement, 1914–1964* (New Delhi: Sage, 2002).

58. Jean-Pierre Rioux, *The Fourth Republic, 1944–1958* (Cambridge: Cambridge University Press, 1987); Philip Williams, *Crisis and Compromise: Politics in the Fourth Republic* (Hamden, CT: Anchor Books, 1964); Bruce D. Graham, *The French Socialists and Tripartism* (Toronto: University of Toronto Press, 1965).

59. John Darwin, *The End of the British Empire: The Historical Debate* (London: Wiley Blackwell, 2006).

60. Clayton, *The Wars of French Decolonization*; Ross, *Fast Cars, Clean Bodies*, Raymond F. Betts, *France and Decolonization* (London: Macmillan, 1991); Tony Chafer, *The End of Empire*

in French West Africa: France's Successful Decolonization? (New York: Berg, 1992); Todd Shepard, *The Invention of Decolonization: The Algerian War and the Remaking of France* (Ithaca: Cornell University Press, 2006).

61. This was the path chosen by the French West Indies in 1946, for example. See Max-Auguste Dufrénot, *Nous, les naufragés de l'indépendance* (Goubeyre: Les Éditions Nestor, 2015).

62. Gary Wilder, *Freedom Time: Negritude, Decolonization, and the Future of the World* (Durham: Duke University Press, 2015).

63. Stovall, "Empires of Democracy," 39.

64. Bonny Ibhawoh, "Testing the Atlantic Charter: Linking Anticolonialism, Self-Determination and Universal Human Rights," *The International Journal of Human Rights*, September 30, 2014; Elizabeth Borgwardt, *A New Deal for the World: America's Vision for Human Rights* (Cambridge, MA: Belknap Press of Harvard University Press, 2005); W. Louis, "American Anti-Colonialism and the Dissolution of the British Empire," *International Affairs* 61, no. 3 (1985).

65. Stanley Karnow, *In Our Image: America's Empire in the Philippines* (New York: Ballantine Books, 1990); Theodore Friend, *Between Two Empires: The Ordeal of the Philippines, 1929–1946* (New Haven: Yale University Press, 1966).

66. Dean Itsuji Saranillio, *Unsustainable Empire: Alternative Histories of Hawai'i Statehood* (Durham: Duke University Press, 2018); John S. Whitehead, *Completing the Union: Alaska, Hawai'i, and the Battle for Statehood* (Albuquerque: The University of New Mexico Press, 2004).

67. James Le Sueur, ed., *The Decolonization Reader* (New York: Routledge, 2003), 51.

68. William Roger Louis and Ronald Robinson, "The Imperialism of Decolonization," in Le Sueur, *The Decolonization Reader*.

69. Ibid., 53.

70. Daniel Kurtz-Phelan, *The China Mission: George Marshall's Unfinished War, 1945–1947* (New York: W. W. Norton, 2019).

71. On France's war in Indochina, see Ivan Cadeau, *La guerre d'Indochine: De l'Indochine française aux adieux à Saigon, 1940–1956* (Paris: Tallandier, 2015); Fredrik Logevall, *Embers of War: The Fall of an Empire and the Making of American's Vietnam* (New York: Random House, 2012); Bernard B. Fall, *Street Without Joy: The French Debacle in Indochina* (Mechanicsburg, PA: Stackpole Books, 2018).

72. On Tripartism, see Isser Woloch, *The Postwar Moment: Progressive Forces in Britain, France, and the United States after World War II* (New Haven: Yale University Press, 2019).

73. Timothy J. Lomperis, *The War Everyone Lost—and Won: America's Intervention in Viet Nam's Twin Struggles* (Washington, DC: CQ Press, 1984); George C. Herring, *America's Longest War: The United States and Vietnam, 1950–1975* (New York: Knopf, 1986).

74. Nick Turse, *Kill Anything That Moves: The Real American War in Vietnam* (New York: Metropolitan Books, 2013); Daniel S. Lucks, *Selma to Saigon: The Civil Rights Movement and the Vietnam War* (Lexington: University Press of Kentucky, 2014).

75. Cited in David J. Garrow, *Bearing the Cross: Martin Luther King Jr, and the Southern Christian Leadership Conference* (New York: William Morrow, 1986), 91.

76. William O. Walker, *The Rise and Decline of the American Century* (Ithaca: Cornell University Press, 2018); Alan Brinkley, *The Publisher: Henry Luce and his American Century* (New York: Alfred A. Knopf, 2010); Robert Edwin Herzstein, *Henry R. Luce: A Political Portrait of the Man Who Created the American Century* (New York: C. Scribner's Sons, 1994).

77. For example, during the late 1940s the US government sponsored the "Freedom Train," a traveling exhibit of documents symbolizing American freedom, that toured around the country. See Foner, *Give Me Liberty!*, 893–95; Erik Christiansen, *Channeling the Past: Politicizing History in Postwar America* (Madison: The University of Wisconsin Press, 2013).

78. Brenda Gayle Plummer, *Rising Wind: Black Americans and U.S. Foreign Affairs, 1935–1960* (Chapel Hill: The University of North Carolina Press, 1996); Penny M. Von Eschen, *Satchmo Blows up the World: Jazz Ambassadors Play the Cold War* (Cambridge, MA: Harvard University Press, 2004); Mary Dudziak, *Cold War Civil Rights: Race and the Image of American Democracy* (Princeton: Princeton University Press, 2011).

79. The historiography of the civil rights movement is of course vast. Some useful explorations include Steven F. Lawson, "Freedom Then, Freedom Now: The Historiography of the Civil rights Movement," *The American Historical Review* 96, no. 2 (April 1991); Jacquelyn Dowd Hall, "The Long Civil Rights Movement and the Political Uses of the Past," *The Journal of American History* 91, no. 4 (March 2005); Kevin Gaines, "The Historiography of the Struggle for Black Equality since 1945," in Jean-Christophe Agnew and Roy Rosenzweig, eds., *A Companion to Post-1945 America* (Hoboken: Wiley-Blackwell, 2002).

80. John Munro, *The Anticolonial Front: The African American Freedom Struggle and Global Decolonization, 1945–1960* (Cambridge: Cambridge University Press, 2017); Brenda Gayle Plummer, *In Search of Power: African Americans in the Era of Decolonization, 1956–1974* (Cambridge, UK: Cambridge University Press, 2013); Gerald Horne, *Black Revolutionary: William Patterson and the Globalization of the African American Freedom Struggle* (Urbana: University of Illinois Press, 2013); Penny M. Von Eschen, *Race against Empire: Black Americans and Anticolonialism, 1937–1957* (Ithaca: Cornell University Press, 1997).

81. Adriane Lentz-Smith, *Freedom Struggles: African Americans and World War I* (Cambridge, MA: Harvard University Press, 2009); Chad Louis Williams, *Torchbearers of Democracy: African American Soldiers and the Era of the First World War* (Chapel Hill: The University of North Carolina Press, 2010); Rawn James Jr., *The Double V: How Wars, Protest, and Harry Truman Desegregated America's Military* (New York: Bloomsbury, 2013); Takaki, *Double Victory*.

82. Plummer, *In Search of Power*; Stephen G. N. Tuck and Robin D. G. Kelley, eds., *The Other Special Relationship: Race, Rights, and Riots in Britain and the United States* (New York: Palgrave Macmillan, 2015).

83. See, for example, Janet Dewart Bell, *Lighting the Fires of Freedom: African American Women in the Civil Rights Movement* (New York: The New Press, 2018); Faith S. Holsaert et al., *Hands on the Freedom Plow: Personal Accounts by Women in SNCC* (Urbana: University of Illinois Press, 2012); Henry Hampton et al., *Voices of Freedom: An Oral History of the Civil Rights Movement from the 1950s through the 1980s* (New York: Bantam, 1991); Danielle L. Mcguire and John Dittmer, eds., *Freedom Rights: New Perspectives on the Civil Rights Movement* (Lexington: University Press of Kentucky, 2011).

84. Cited in Conrad Cherry, ed., *God's New Israel: Religious Interpretations of American Destiny* (Chapel Hill: The University of North Carolina Press, 1998), 350; Martin Luther King Jr, *Letter from Birmingham Jail* (New York: Penguin Random House, 2018); Jonathan Rieder, *Gospel of Freedom: Martin Luther King, Jr.'s Letter from Birmingham Jail and the Struggle That Changed a Nation* (New York: Bloomsbury, 2013).

85. Cited in Foner, *Give Me Liberty!*, 966.

86. On the history of the Black church, see Albert J. Raboteau, *African-American Religion* (Oxford: Oxford University Press, 2001). On its role in the civil rights movement, see Garrow, *Bearing the Cross*; Gary J. Dorrien, *Breaking White Supremacy: Martin Luther King Jr. and the Black Social Gospel* (New Haven: Yale University Press, 2018).

87. Foner, *Give Me Liberty!*, 970–71.

88. Kathleen J. Frydl, *The G.I. Bill* (Cambridge: Cambridge University Press, 2009); Glenn Altschuler and Stuart Blumin, *The GI Bill: The New Deal for Veterans* (Oxford: Oxford University Press, 2009); Edward Humes, *Over Here: How the G.I. Bill Transformed the American Dream* (New York: Harcourt, 2006).

89. Clark Kerr, *The Gold and the Blue: A Personal Memoir of the University of California, 1949–1967*, 2 vols. (Berkeley: University of California Press, 2001); Hannah Holborn Gray, *Searching for Utopia: Universities and their Histories* (Berkeley: University of California Press, 2011); David F. Labaree, *A Perfect Mess: the Unlikely Ascendancy of American Higher Education* (Chicago: University of Chicago Press, 2017).

90. Cited in Andrew Hartman, *Education and the Cold War: The Battle for the American School* (New York: Palgrave Macmillan, 2008), 2.

91. Diane J. Macunovich, *Birth Quake: the Baby Boom and its Aftershocks* (Chicago: University of Chicago Press, 2002); Janet Lynne Golden, *Babies Made Us Modern: How Infants Brought America into the Twentieth Century* (New York: Cambridge University Press 2018); Elaine Tyler May, *Homeward Bound: American Families in the Cold War Era* (New York: Basic Books, 1988).

92. Wayne J. Urban, *More than Science and Sputnik: The National Defense Education Act of 1958* (Tuscaloosa: University of Alabama Press, 2008); Peter Dow, *Schoolhouse Politics: Lessons from the Sputnik Era* (Cambridge, MA: Harvard University Press, 1991).

93. Dow, *Schoolhouse Politics*; John L. Rudolph, *Scientists in the Classroom: The Cold War Reconstruction of American Science Education* (New York: Palgrave Macmillan, 2002).

94. James T. Patterson, *Brown v. Board of Education: A Civil Rights Milestone and Its Troubled Legacy* (Oxford: Oxford University Press, 2001), xiv, xvi.

95. Richard Rothstein, *The Color of Law: A Forgotten History of How Our Government Segregated America* (New York: Liveright, 2017). See also Ira Katznelson, *When Affirmative Action Was White: An Untold History of Racial Inequality in Twentieth-Century America* (New York: W. W. Norton, 2006).

96. Steven Luxenberg, *Separate: The Story of Plessy v Ferguson, and America's Journey from Slavery to Segregation* (New York: W. W. Norton, 2019); Williamjames Hull Hoffer, *Plessy v. Ferguson: Race and Inequality in Jim Crow America* (Lawrence: University Press of Kansas, 2012); Saidiya V. Hartman, *Scenes of Subjection: Terror, Slavery, and Self-Making in Nineteenth-Century America* (Oxford: Oxford University Press, 1997).

97. Patterson, *Brown v. Board of Education*; Richard Kluger, *Simple Justice: The History of Brown v. Board of Education and Black America's Struggle for Equality* (New York: Vintage, 2004); Waldo E. Martin Jr., *Brown v. Board of Education: A Brief History with Documents* (New York: Bedford/St. Martin's, 1998); Clare Cushman and Melvin I. Urofsky, eds., *Black, White, and Brown: The Landmark School Desegregation Case in Retrospect* (Washington, DC: CQ Press, 2014).

98. Melba Patillo Beals, *Warriors Don't Cry: A Searing Memoir of the Battle to Integrate Little Rock's Central High* (New York: Washington Square Press, 1995); Joseph Bagley, *The Politics of White Rights: Race, Justice, and Integrating Alabama's Schools* (Athens: University of Georgia Press, 2018); Rachel Devlin, *A Girl Stands at the Door: The Generation of Young Women Who Desegregate America's Schools* (New York: Basic Books, 2018).

99. Steward Burns, *Daybreak of Freedom: The Montgomery Bus Boycott* (Chapel Hill: The University of North Carolina Press, 1997); Donnie Williams and Wayne Greenhaw, *The Thunder of Angels: The Montgomery Bus Boycott and the People Who Broke the Back of Jim Crow* (Chicago: Lawrence Hill, 2006); Mary Stanton, *Journey toward Justice: Juliette Hampton Morgan and the Montgomery Bus Boycott* (Athens: University of Georgia Press, 2006).

100. M. J. O'Brien, *We Shall Not Be Moved: The Jackson Woolworth's Sit-in and the Movement It Inspired* (Jackson: University Press of Mississippi, 2014); Christopher W. Schmidt, *The Sit-ins: Protest and Legal Change in the Civil Rights Era* (Chicago: University of Chicago Press, 2018).

101. Raymond Arsenault, *Freedom Riders: 1961 and the Struggle for Racial Justice* (Oxford: Oxford University Press, 2007); Eric Etheridge, *Breach of Peace: Portraits of the 1961 Mississippi Freedom Riders* (Nashville: Vanderbilt University Press, 2018); Carol Ruth Silver, *Freedom Rider Diary: Smuggled Notes from Parchman Prison* (Jackson: University Press of Mississippi, 2014); B. J. Hollars, *The Road South: Personal Stories of the Freedom Riders* (Tuscaloosa: University of Alabama Press, 2018).

102. Holsaert, *Hands on the Freedom Plow*; Clayborne Carson, *In Struggle: SNCC and the Black Awakening of the 1960s* (Cambridge, MA: Harvard University Press, 1981); Hasan Kwame Jeffries, *Bloody Lowndes: Civil Rights and Black Power in Alabama's Black Belt* (New York: NYU Press, 2010); Laura Visser-Maessen, *Robert Parris Moses: A Life in Civil Rights and Leadership at the Grassroots* (Chapel Hill: The University of North Carolina Press, 2016).

103. Carson, *In Struggle*; James P. Marshall, *Student Activism and Civil Rights in Mississippi: Protest Politics and the Struggle for Racial Equality, 1960–1965* (Baton Rouge: LSU Press, 2013).

104. Cited in Carson, *In Struggle*, 89.

105. Doug McAdam, *Freedom Summer* (Oxford: Oxford University Press, 1988); Bruce Watson, *Freedom Summer: The Savage Season of 1964 That Made Mississippi Burn and Made America a Democracy* (New York: Penguin Books, 2011).

106. Kenneth T. Andrews, *Freedom Is a Constant Struggle: The Mississippi Civil Rights Movement and Its Legacy* (Chicago: University of Chicago Press, 2004); Jon N. Hale, *The Freedom Schools: Student Activists in the Mississippi Civil Rights Movement* (New York: Columbia University Press, 2016).

107. Howard Ball, *Murder in Mississippi: United States v. Price and the Struggle for Civil Rights* (Lawrence: University Press of Kansas, 2004); Seth Cagin and Philip Dray, *We Are Not Afraid: The Story of Goodman, Schwerner, and Chaney and the Civil Rights Campaign for Mississippi* (New York: Macmillan, 1988); William Bradford Huie, *Three Lives for Mississippi* (Jackson: University Press of Mississippi, 2000).

108. Clay Risen, *The Bill of the Century: The Epic Battle for the Civil Rights Act* (New York: Bloomsbury Press, 2014); Robert D. Loevy, *To End All Segregation: The Politics of the Passage of the Civil Rights Act of 1964* (Lanham: University Press of America, 1990); Todd S. Purdum, *An Idea Whose Time Has Come: Two Presidents, Two Parties, and the Battle for the Civil Rights Act of 1964* (New York: Henry Holt, 2014).

109. Charles E. Fager, *Selma, 1965: The March That Changed the South* (Boston: Beacon, 1985); David J. Garrow, *Protest at Selma: Martin Luther King, Jr., and the Voting Rights Act of 1965* (New Haven: Yale University Press, 1978); Joe Street and Henry Knight, eds., *The Shadow of Selma* (Gainesville: University of Florida Press, 2018).

110. Charles S. Bullock et. al., *The Rise and Fall of the Voting Rights Act* (Norman: University of Oklahoma Press, 2016); Richard M. Valelly, ed., *The Voting Rights Act: Securing the Ballot* (Washington, DC: CQ Press, 2006); Chandler Davidson and Bernard Grofman, eds., *Quiet Revolution in the South: The Impact of the Voting Rights Act 1965–1990* (Princeton: Princeton University Press, 1994); Michael Waldman, *The Fight to Vote* (New York: Simon and Schuster, 2016).

111. Cited in Leo Zeilig, *Lumumba: Africa's Lost Leader* (London: Haus, 2008), 103.

112. Emmanuel Gerard and Bruce Kuklick, *Death in the Congo: Murdering Patrice Lumumba* (Cambridge, MA: Harvard University Press, 2015); Georges Nzongola-Ntalaja, *Patrice Lumumba* (Athens: Ohio University Press, 2014).

113. Kwame Nkrumah, *Neo-Colonialism, the Highest Stage of Imperialism* (London: Thomas Nelson and Sons, 1965), 1.

114. Guy Vanthemsche, *Belgium and the Congo, 1885–1980* (Cambridge, UK: Cambridge University Press, 2012).

115. Krishnan Srinivasan, *The Rise, Decline and Future of the British Commonwealth* (New York: Palgrave Macmillan, 2005); William D. McIntyre, *British Decolonization, 1946–1997: When, Why, and How Did the British Empire Fall?* (New York: St. Martin's Press, 1998).

116. Alice L. Conklin et al., *France and Its Empire Since 1870* (New York and Oxford: Oxford University Press, 2011), 285.

117. Ginio, *The French Army*; Tony Chafer, *The End of Empire in French West Africa: France's Successful Decolonization?* (New York: Berg, 2002); Frederick Cooper, *Citizenship between Empire and Nation: Remaking France and French Africa, 1945–1960* (Princeton: Princeton University Press, 2014).

118. Jean-Claude Djereke, *Abattre la Françafrique ou périr: Le dilemma de l'Afrique francophone* (Paris: Harmattan, 2014); Fanny Pigeaud and Ndongo Samba Sylla, *L'arme invisible de la Françafrique* (Paris: La Découverte, 2018).

119. Frédéric Turpin, *Jacques Foccart: Dans l'ombre du pouvoir* (Paris: Éditions du CNRS, 2015); Pierre Péan, *L'homme de l'ombre: Éléments d'enquête autour de Jacques Foccart, l'homme le plus mystérieus et le plus puissant de la Ve république* (Paris: Fayard, 1990).

120. Thomas Deltombe et al., *Kamerun!: Une guerre cachée aux origines de la Françafrique (1948–1971)* (Paris: La Découverte, 2011).

121. Nathaniel K. Powell, "Battling Instability? The Recurring Logic of French Military Interventions in Africa," *African Security* 10, no. 1 (January 2017); Victor-Manuel Vallin, "France as the Gendarme of Africa, 1960–2014," *Political Science Quarterly* 30, no. 1 (2015).

122. Kwame Nkrumah, "On the Coup in Ghana," *The Black Scholar* 3, no. 9 (May 1972); Basil Davidson, *Black Star: A View of The Life and Times of Kwame Nkrumah* (London: Allen Lane, 1973).

123. Benjamin Stora, *Algeria 1830–2000, A Short History* (Ithaca: Cornell University Press, 2001).

124. Thomas C. Wright, *Latin America in the Era of the Cuban Revolution and Beyond* (New York: Praeger, 2018); Alfred C. Stepan, *The Military in Politics: Changing Patterns in Brazil*

(Princeton: Princeton University Press 1971); Deborah L. Norden, *Military Rebellion in Argentina: Between Coups and Consolidation* (Lincoln: University of Nebraska Press, 1996); J. Samuel Valenzuela, *Military Rule in Chile: Dictatorship and Oppositions* (Baltimore: Johns Hopkins University Press, 1986).

125. Tuong Vu, *Vietnam's Communist Revolution: The Power and Limits of Ideology* (Cambridge, UK: Cambridge University Press, 2016); Rebecca E. Karl, *Mao Zedong and China in the Twentieth-Century World: A Concise History* (Durham: Duke University Press, 2010); Aviva Chomsky, *A History of the Cuban Revolution* (Hoboken: Wiley-Blackwell, 2015).

126. Bidyut Chakrabarty, *Constitutional Democracy in India* (London: Routledge, 2018); Emily Rook-Koepel, *Democracy and Unity in India: Understanding the All India Phenomenon, 1940–1960* (London: Routledge, 2019).

127. *Boston Globe*, March 3, 1976.

128. See Louis P. Masur, *The Soiling of Old Glory: The Story of a Photograph That Shocked America* (London: Bloomsbury Press, 2008).

129. "Strom Thurmond, Foe of Integration, Dies at 100," *The New York Times*, June 27, 2003; Joseph Crespino, *Strom Thurmond's America* (New York: Hill and Wang, 2012).

130. Cited in Ronald Takaki, *A Different Mirror: A History of Multicultural America* (New York: Back Bay Books, 2008), 408; Margaret Sands Orchowski, *The Law That Changed the Face of America: The Immigration and Nationality Act of 1965* (Boston: Rowman and Littlefield, 2015); Gabriel Chin and Rose Cuison Villazor, eds., *The Immigration and Nationality Act of 1965: Legislating a New America* (Cambridge, UK: Cambridge University Press, 2015).

131. Tom Gjelten, *A Nation of Nations: A Story of America after the 1965 Immigration Law* (New York: Simon and Schuster, 2015). For a controversial statement about the dangers of the new shape of immigration, one that underscores the relationship between whiteness and freedom, see Samuel P. Huntington, *Who Are We? The Challenges to America's National Identity* (New York: Simon and Schuster, 2005).

132. Robert Cohen, *Freedom's Orator: Mario Savio and the Radical Legacy of the 1960s* (Oxford: Oxford University Press, 2009); Robert Cohen and Reginald E. Zelnik, eds., *The Free Speech Movement: Reflections on Berkeley in the 1960s* (Berkeley: University of California Press, 2002); W. J. Rorabaugh, *Berkeley at War: The 1960s* (Oxford: Oxford University Press, 1989).

133. Key texts include Simone de Beauvoir, *The Second Sex* (orig. 1949; New York: Knopf, 2010); Betty Friedan, *The Feminine Mystique* (orig. 1963; New York: W. W. Norton, 2013); Sheila Rowbotham, *Women, Resistance, and Revolution: A History of Women and Revolution in the Modern World* (orig. 1972; London: Verso, 2014); Zillah Eisenstein, ed., *Capitalist Patriarchy and the Case for Socialist Feminism* (New York: Monthly Review Press, 1978).

134. A classic example of the latter was Stokely Carmichael's infamous remark about the only position for women in the movement being "prone." Stokely Carmichael, *Ready for Revolution: The Life and Struggles of Stokely Carmichael* (New York: Scribner, 2003), 432.

135. David J. Garrow, editor, *The Montgomery Bus Boycott and the Women Who Started It: The Memoir of Jo Ann Gibson Robinson* (Knoxville: The University of Tennessee Press, 1987).

136. Benita Roth, *Separate Roads to Feminism: Black, Chicana, and White Feminist Movements in America's Second Wave* (Cambridge: Cambridge University Press, 2003); Zillah R. Eisenstein, *The Color of Gender: Reimaging Democracy* (Berkeley: University of California Press, 1994); bell hooks, *Ain't I a Woman?: Black Women and Feminism* (Boston: South End Press, 1981); Cherríe

Moraga and Gloria E. Anzaldúa, eds., *This Bridge Called My Back: Writings by Radical Women of Color* (Watertown, MA: Persephone Press, 1981).

137. Sam Kushner, *Long Road to Delano: A Century of Farmworker's Struggle* (New York: International Publishers, 1975); Jacques E. Levy, *Cesar Chavez: Autobiography of La Causa* (Minneapolis: University of Minnesota Press, 2007); David Montejano, *Quixote's Soldiers: A Local History of the Chicano Movement* (Austin: University of Texas Press, 2010); Marc S. Rodriguez, *Rethinking the Chicano Movement* (New York: Routledge, 2015).

138. Dee Brown, *Bury My Heart at Wounded Knee: An Indian History of the American West* (New York: Picador, 2007); David E. Stannard, *American Holocaust: The Conquest of the New World* (New York: Oxford University Press, 1992); R. David Edmunds, "Native Americans, New Voices: American Indian History, 1895–1995," *The American Historical Review* 100, no. 3 (1995).

139. Martin Duberman, *Stonewall* (New York: Dutton, 1993); George Chauncey, *Gay New York: Gender, Urban Culture, and the Making of the Gay Male World* (New York: Basic Books, 1995); Michael Bronski, *A Queer History of the United States* (Boston: Beacon Press, 2012); Lilian Faderman, *The Gay Revolution: The Story of the Struggle* (New York: Simon and Schuster, 2015).

140. David R. Farber, *The Sixties: From Memory to History* (Chapel Hill: The University of North Carolina Press, 1994); Marianne DeKoven, *The Sixties and the Emergence of the Postmodern* (Durham: Duke University Press, 2004); Christopher B. Strain, *The Long Sixties: America, 1955–1973* (Hoboken: Wiley, 2017).

141. Mary Lou Finley et al., *The Chicago Freedom Movement: Martin Luther King Jr. and Civil Rights Activism in the North* (Lexington: University Press of Kentucky, 2016); James R. Ralph, Jr. *Northern Protest: Martin Luther King, Jr., Chicago, and the Civil Rights Movement* (Cambridge, MA: Harvard University Press, 1993).

142. Joshua Bloom and Waldo E. Martin Jr., *Black against Empire: The History and Politics of the Black Panther Party* (Berkeley: University of California Press, 2016); Robyn C. Spencer, *The Revolution Has Come: Black Power Gender, and the Black Panther Party in Oakland* (Durham: Duke University Press, 2016); Bobby Seale and Stephen Shames, *Power to the People: The World of the Black Panthers* (New York: Harry N. Abrams, 2016).

143. Cited in Patterson, *Brown v. Board of Education*, 229.

144. Matthew F. Delmont, *Why Busing Failed: Race, Media, and the National Resistance to School Desegregation* (Berkeley: University of California Press, 2016).

145. Ibid., 6.

146. Ibid., 49–52.

147. Ibid.; Ronnie A. Dunn, et al., *Boycotts, Busing, AND Beyond: The History AND Implications of School Desegregation in the Urban North* (Dubuque: Kendall Hunt Publishing, 2016).

148. Edward Keynes, *The Court vs. Congress: Prayer, Busing, and Abortion* (Durham: Duke University Press, 1989); Bernard Schwartz, *Swann's Way: The School Busing Case and the Supreme Court* (Oxford: Oxford University Press, 1986); Joyce A. Baugh, *The Detroit School Busing Case: Miliken v. Bradley and the Controversy over Desegregation* (Lawrence: University Press of Kansas, 2011).

149. Cited in Delmont, *Why Busing Failed*, 2.

150. Jesse L. Jackson, "It's Not the Bus, It's Us," *The New York Times*, March 8, 1992.

151. Jeff Zeleny, "Letters from Joe Biden Reveal How He Sought Support of Segregationists in Fight against Busing," CNN, April 11, 2019.

152. Cited in *The Washington Post,* March 7, 2019. See also Brett Gadsden, *Between North and South: Delaware, Desegregation, and the Myth of American Sectionalism* (Philadelphia: University of Pennsylvania Press, 2012).

153. Malcolm X, "The Ballot or the Bullet," April, 1964.

154. The full text of the Southern Manifesto (formally titled "Declaration of Constitutional Principles") appears at Wikisource: https://en.wikisource.org/wiki/Southern_Manifesto.

155. Charles T. Clotfelter, *After Brown: The Rise and Retreat of School Desegregation* (Princeton: Princeton University Press, 2006), 103.

156. See Christopher Bonastia, "The Racist History of the Charter School Movement," *Alternet,* March 9, 2012. See also Pete Tucker, "Diane Ravitch on School Choice: From Segregation Academies to Charters," https://www.pete-tucker.com/blog/2018/12/3/from-segregation -academies-to-charter-schools-a-conversation-with-diane-ravitch, December 3, 2018.

157. Elizabeth Gillespie McRae, *Mothers of Massive Resistance: White Women and the Politics of White Supremacy* (Oxford: Oxford University Press, 2018), Conclusion.

158. Delmont, *Why Busing Failed,* 146, 148.

159. Ronald P. Formisano, *Boston against Busing: Race, Class, and Ethnicity in the 1960s and 1970s* (Chapel Hill: The University of North Carolina Press, 2004); Lawrence S. DiCara, *Turmoil and Transition in Boston: A Political Memoir from the Busing Era* (Falls River: Hamilton Books, 2013); J. Anthony Lukas, *Common Ground: A Turbulent Decade in the Lives of Three American Families* (New York: Vintage, 1986).

160. See, for example, Howard Bryant, *Shut Out: A Story of Race and Baseball in Boston* (Boston: Beacon Press, 2003).

161. Cited in Kathleen Banks Nutter, "'Militant Mothers': Boston, Busing, and the Bicentennial of 1976," *Historical Journal of Massachusetts* 38, no. 2 (Fall 2010): 62.

162. Ibid., 67–68.

163. Baugh, *The Detroit Busing Case.*

164. Rucker Johnson, *Children of the Dream: Why School Integration Works* (New York: Basic Books, 2019); Erica Frankenberg et al., *School Integration Matters: Research-Based Strategies to Advance Equity* (New York: Teachers College Press, 2016); Hope C. Rias, *St. Louis School Desegregation: Patterns of Progress and Peril* (Cham, Switzerland: Palgrave Macmillan, 2019); Toni Morrison, *Remember: The Journey to School Integration* (Boston: Houghton-Mifflin, 2004).

165. "Brown v. Board of Education," *The New York Times,* May 16, 2004.

166. Cited in Rick Perlstein, "Exclusive: Lee Atwater's Infamous 1981 Interview on the Southern Strategy," *The Nation,* November 13, 2012.

167. Lisa McGirr, *Suburban Warriors: The Origins of the New American Right* (Princeton: Princeton University Press, 2015); Robert O. Self, *All in the Family: The Realignment of American Democracy Since the 1960s* (New York: Hill and Wang, 2013); Matthew D. Lassiter, *The Silent Majority: Suburban Politics in the Sunbelt South* (Princeton: Princeton University Press, 2007).

168. Alvin S. Felzenberg, *A Man and His Presidents: The Political Odyssey of William F. Buckley Jr.* (New Haven: Yale University Press, 2017).

169. Milton Friedman, *Capitalism and Freedom* (Chicago: University of Chicago Press, 2002).

170. John A. Andrew III, *The Other Side of the Sixties: Young Americans for Freedom and the Rise of Conservative Politics* (New Brunswick: Rutgers University Press, 1996); Wayne Thorburn,

Young Americans for Freedom: Igniting A Movement (Herndon, VA: Young America Foundation, 2017).

171. See the full text at: http://www.yaf.org/news/the-sharon-statement/.

172. Cite Jerome L. Himmelstein, *To the Right: The Transformation of American Conservatism* (Berkeley: University of California Press, 1990); George W. Carey, "Conservatives and Libertarians View Fusionism: Its Origins, Possibilities, and Problems," *Modern Age* 26 (1982).

173. Cited in Himmelstein, *To the Right*, 56.

174. Frances FitzGerald, *The Evangelicals: The Struggle to Shape America* (New York: Simon and Schuster, 2017); Matthew Avery Sutton, *Jerry Falwell and the Rise of the Religious Right: A Brief History with Documents* (New York: Bedford/St. Martin's, 2012); Andrew R. Lewis, *The Rights Turn in Conservative Christian Politics: How Abortion Transformed the Culture Wars* (Cambridge: Cambridge University Press, 2017); Emily Suzanne Johnson, *This Is Our Message: Women's Leadership in the New Christian Right* (Oxford: Oxford University Press, 2019).

175. "IRS vs. 'Segregation Academies,'" *The Christian Science Monitor*, May 27, 1980; Jennifer Eaton Dyer, *The Core Beliefs of Southern Evangelicals: A Psycho-Social Investigation of the Evangelical Megachurch Phenomenon*, PhD dissertation, Vanderbilt University, 2007.

176. Cited in Joseph E. Lowndes, *From the New Deal to the New Right: Race and the Southern Origins of Modern Conservatism* (New Haven: Yale University Press, 2008), 52.

177. Ibid.; Amy Elizabeth Ansell, *New Right, New Racism: Race and Reaction in the United States and Britain* (New York: New York University Press, 1997).

178. Cited in Lowndes, *From the New Deal to the New Right*, 71.

179. John C. Skipper, *The 1964 Republican Convention: Barry Goldwater and the Beginning of the Conservative Movement* (Jefferson, NC: McFarland, 2016); J. William Middendorf II, *A Glorious Disaster: Barry Goldwater's Presidential Campaign and the Origins of the Conservative Movement* (New York: Basic Books, 2006).

180. See Glenn Feldman, *The Irony of the Solid South: Democrats, Republicans, and Race, 1865–1944* (Tuscaloosa: University of Alabama Press, 2013).

181. Kari A. Frederickson, *The Dixiecrat Revolt and the End of the Solid South* (Chapel Hill: University of North Carolina Press, 2001); William D. Barnard, *Dixiecrats and Democrats: Alabama Politics, 1942–1950* (Tuscaloosa: University of Alabama Press, 1950).

182. Earl and Merle Black, *The Rise of Southern Republicans* (Cambridge, MA: Harvard University Press, 2003); Edward H. Miller, *Nut Country: Right-Wing Dallas and the Birth of the Southern Strategy* (Chicago: University of Chicago Press, 2015); Edward O. Frantz, *The Door of Hope: Republican Presidents and the First Southern Strategy, 1877–1933* (Gainesville: University Press of Florida, 2011).

183. Cited in Bill Moyers, *Moyers on America: A Journalist and His Times* (New York: New Press 2004), 167.

184. Theodore H. White, *The Making of the President, 1968* (New York: Atheneum, 1969); Lawrence O'Donnell, *Playing with Fire: The 1968 Election and the Transformation of American Politics* (New York: Penguin, 2017); Aram Goudsouzian, *The Men and the Moment: The Election of 1968 and the Rise of Partisan Politics in America* (Chapel Hill: The University of North Carolina Press, 2019).

185. The National Advisory Commission on Civil Disorders, *The Kerner Report* (Princeton: Princeton University Press, 2016); Peter B. Levy, *The Great Uprising: Race Riots in Urban*

America during the 1960s (Cambridge: Cambridge University Press, 2018); Gerald Horne, *The Fire This Time: The Watts Uprising and the 1960s* (Charlottesville: University of Virginia Press, 1995).

186. Kevin Phillips, *The Emerging Republican Majority* (New York: Arlington House, 1969), 31–32.

187. David Hamilton Golland, *Constructing Affirmative Action: The Struggle for Equal Employment Opportunity* (Lexington: University Press of Kentucky, 2011).

188. In fact, all the Democratic presidents between JFK and Obama—Lyndon Johnson, Jimmy Carter, and Bill Clinton—came from the South.

189. Himmelstein, *To the Right*, 147–50.

190. Jacob Heilbrunn, *They Knew They Were Right: The Rise of the Neocons* (New York: Doubleday, 2008); Jean-François Drolet, *America Neoconservatism: The Politics and Culture of a Reactionary Idealism* (New York: Columbia University Press, 2011); Justin Vaisse, *Neoconservatism: The Biography of a Movement* (Cambridge, MA: Harvard University Press, 2010); Irving Kristol, *Neo-Conservatism: The Autobiography of an Idea* (New York: Free Press, 1995).

191. Stuart E. Eizenstat, *President Carter: The White House Years* (New York: Thomas Dunne, 2018); Burton I. Kaufman and Scott Kaufman, *The Presidency of James Earl Carter, Jr.* (Lawrence: University Press of Kansas, 2006); Jimmy Carter, *Keeping Faith: Memoirs of a President* (New York: Bantam, 1982).

192. Cited in Himmelstein, *To the Right*, 84.

193. Garry Wills, *Reagan's America: Innocents at Home* (Garden City, NY: Doubleday, 1987); Troy Gil, *The Reagan Revolution: A Very Short Introduction* (Oxford: Oxford University Press, 2009); Henry Olsen, *The Working Class Republican: Ronald Reagan and the Return of Blue-Collar Conservatism* (Northampton, MA: Broadside Books, 2017); Ronald Reagan, *An American Life: The Autobiography* (New York: Simon and Schuster, 2011).

194. Jeremy D. Mayer, *Running on Race: Racial Politics in Presidential Campaigns, 1960–2000* (New York: Random House, 2002), 152–53.

195. Ibid.,152.

196. William Raspberry, "Reagan's Race Legacy," *The Washington Post*, June 14, 2004.

197. Cited in Ian Haney-Lopez, *Dog Whistle Politics: How Coded Racial Appeals Have Reinvented Racism and Wrecked the Middle Class* (Oxford: Oxford University Press, 2014), 58.

198. Cited in *American Rhetoric*, https://www.americanrhetoric.com/speeches/ronaldreaganbrandenburggate.htm; Paul Kengor, *The Crusader: Ronald Reagan and the Fall of Communism* (New York: Harper, 2006).

199. William F. Buckley Jr., *The Fall of the Berlin Wall* (Hoboken: Wiley, 2004); Michael Meyer, *The Year That Changed the World: The Untold Story Behind the Fall of the Berlin Wall* (New York: Scribner, 2009); Tim Mohr: *Burning Down the Haus: Punk Rock, Revolution, and the Fall of the Berlin Wall* (Chapel Hill: Algonquin Books, 2018).

200. Timothy Garton Ash, *The Magic Lantern: The Revolution of '89 Witnessed in Warsaw, Budapest, Berlin, and Prague* (New York: Random House, 1990); Victor Sebestyen, *Revolution 1989: The Fall of the Soviet Empire* (New York: Pantheon, 2009); Padraic Kenneyk, *A Carnival of Revolution: Central Europe 1989* (Princeton: Princeton University Press, 2002); Constantine Pleshakov, *There Is No Freedom Without Bread! 1989 and the Civil War That Brought Down Communism* (New York: Farrar, Straus and Giroux, 2009).

201. Patti Waldmeir, *Anatomy of a Miracle: The End of Apartheid and the Birth of the New South Africa* (New York: W. W. Norton, 1997); Nelson Mandela, *Long Walk to Freedom: The Autobiography of Nelson Mandela* (Boston: Back Bay Books 2013); Minzhu Han, *Cries for Democracy: Writings and Speeches from the 1989 Chinese Democracy Movement* (Princeton: Princeton University Press, 1990); Suzanne Ogden, Kathleen Hartford, Lawrence Sullivan, and David Zweig, eds., *China's Search for Democracy: The Students and Mass Movement of 1989* (New York: Routledge, 1992).

202. https://www.sup.org/books/series/?series=The%20Making%20of%20Modern%20Freedom.

203. Stephen Kotkin, *Armageddon Averted: The Soviet Collapse 1970–2000* (Oxford: Oxford University Press, 2008); Chris Miller, *The Struggle to Save the Soviet Economy: Mikhail Gorbachev and the Collapse of the USSR* (Chapel Hill: The University of Carolina Press, 2016); Serhii Plokhy, *The Last Empire: The Final Days of the Soviet Union* (New York: Basic Books, 2014).

204. Buckley, *The Fall of the Berlin Wall*; William J. Bennett, *America: The Last Best Hope*, vol. 8, *From the Collapse of Communism to the Rise of Radical Islam* (Nashville: Thomas Nelson, 2011); Francis Fukuyama et al., "The Strange Death of Soviet Communism," *National Interest* 31 (April 1993).

205. Ramón E. Arango, *Spain: Democracy Regained* (Boulder: Westview Press, 1995); Kostis Kornetis, *Children of the Dictatorship: Student Resistance, Cultural Politics and the "Long 1960s" in Greece* (New York: Berghahn, 2013); Pedro Ramos Pinto, *Lisbon Rising: Urban Social Movements in the Portuguese Revolution, 1974–1975* (Manchester, UK: Manchester University Press, 2013).

206. Luis Schenoni and Scott Mainwaring, "Hegemonic Effects and Regime Change in Latin America," *Democratization* 26, no. 2 (2019).

207. Samuel P. Huntington, *The Third Wave: Democratization in the Late Twentieth Century* (Norman: University of Oklahoma Press 1991), 5.

208. John P. McKay et al., *A History of Western Society*, eighth ed. (Boston: Houghton-Mifflin, 2006), 1043.

209. Ronald Grigor Suny, *The Soviet Experiment: Russia, the USSR, and the Successor States* (Oxford: Oxford Unversity Press, 1997); Abel Polese, Jeremy Morris, Emilia Pawlusz, Oleksandra Seliverstova, eds., *Identity and Nation Building in Everyday Post-Socialist Life* (New York: Routledge, 2017); Robert R. Kaufman, *Reforming the State: Fiscal and Welfare Reform in Post-Socialist Countries* (Cambridge: Cambridge University Press, 2001).

210. Norman Naimark, *Fires of Hatred: Ethnic Cleansing in Twentieth-Century Europe* (Cambridge, MA: Harvard University Press, 2002).

211. Misha Glenny, *The Fall of Yugoslavia: The Third Balkan War* (New York: Penguin, 1996); Slavenka Drakulic, *The Balkan Express: Fragments from the Other Side of the War* (New York: W. W. Norton, 1993); Laura Silber and Allan Little, *Yugoslavia: Death of a Nation* (New York: Penguin, 1997); V. P. Gagnon Jr., *The Myth of Ethnic War: Serbia and Croatia in the 1990s* (Ithaca: Cornell University Press, 2004).

212. David Rohde, *Endgame: The Betrayal and Fall of Srebrenica, Europe's Worst Massacre Since World War II* (New York: Penguin, 2012); Selma Leydesdorff, *Surviving the Bosnian Genocide: The Women of Srebrenica Speak* (Bloomington: Indiana University Press, 2011).

213. Claude Cahn, "End Europe's Ugly Racism toward the Roma," *The New York Times*, March 1, 2005.

214. Stephen Kinzer, "A Wave of Attacks on Foreigners Stirs Shock in Germany," *The New York Times*, October 1, 1991; Steven Schäller, *PEGIDA and New Right-Wing Populism in Germany* (Cham, Switzerland: Springer International, 2018).

215. Berna Turam, *Gaining Freedoms: Claiming Space in Istanbul and Berlin* (Stanford: Stanford University Press, 2015); Kira Kosnick, *Migrant Media: Turkish Broadcasting and Multicultural Politics in Berlin* (Bloomington: Indiana University Press, 2007).

216. Nancy Foner, *Jamaica Farewell: Jamaican Migrants in London* (Berkeley: University of California Press, 1978); Stephen Castles and Godula Kosack, *Immigrant Workers and Class Structure in Western Europe* (Oxford: Oxford University Press, 1985); Alec Hargreaves, *Immigration, "Race," and Ethnicity in Contemporary France* (New York: Routledge, 1995); Rogers Brubaker, *Citizenship and Nationhood in France and Germany* (Cambridge, MA: Harvard University Press, 1992).

217. Christopher T. Husbands, *Racial Exclusionism and the City: The Urban Support of the National Front* (London: Routledge, 2007); Peter Davies, *The National Front in France: Ideology, Discourse, and Power* (New York: Routledge, 1999); Françoise Gaspard, *A Small City in France* (Cambridge, MA: Harvard University Press, 1995).

218. Robert Leiken *Europe's Angry Muslims: The Revolt of The Second Generation* (Oxford: Oxford University Press, 2011); Hanif Kureishi, *The Buddha of Suburbia* (London: Faber and Faber, 1990); Trica Danielle Keaton, *Muslim Girls and the Other France: Race, Identity Politics, and Social Exclusion* (Bloomington: Indiana University Press, 2006); Gilles Kepel, *Les banlieues de l'Islam: Naissance d'une religion en France* (Paris: Points, 2015).

219. Brendan Evans, *Thatcherism and British Politics, 1975–1997* (London: Sutton, 2000); Stuart Hall and Martin Jaques, eds., *The Politics of Thatcherism* (London: Lawrence and Wishart, 1983); Margaret Thatcher, *Margaret Thatcher: The Autobiography* (New York: Harper, 2013).

220. Alexander F. Day, *The Peasant in Postsocialist China: History, Politics, and Capitalism* (Cambridge, UK: Cambridge University Press, 2013); Ezra F. Vogel, *Deng Xiaoping and the Transformation of China* (Cambridge, MA: Belknap Press, 2011).

Conclusion

1. *The Washington Post*, September 20, 2001.

2. Martin Gitlin, ed., *The Border Wall with Mexico* (New York: Greenhaven, 2018); Alan I Abramovitz, *The Great Alignment: Race, Party Transformation, and the Rise of Donald Trump* (New Haven: Yale University Press, 2018).

3. In 2012, for example, future caucus chairman Mark Meadows vowed to send Barack Obama home to Kenya. William Cummings, "After Denying Racism, Videos of Meadows Vowing to Send Obama 'Home to Kenya' Resurface," *USA Today*, February 28, 2019.

4. Matthew Green, *Legislative Hardball: The House Freedom Caucus and the Power of Threat-Making in Congress* (Cambridge: Cambridge University Press, 2019).

5. Connor D. Wolf, "House Freedom Caucus Demands Border Wall Funding as Shutdown Deadline Looms," *LifeZette*, December 19, 2018.

6. Matt Mayer, "Not the Berlin Wall," *US News and World Report*, April 17, 2017.

7. William Faulkner, *Requiem for a Nun* (New York: Random House, 1951).

8. Among many others, two works that have inspired me are Gary Wilder, *The French Imperial Nation-State: Negritude and Colonial Humanism between the Wars* (Chicago: University of

Chicago Press, 2005), and Edward E. Baptist, *The Half Has Never Been Told: Slavery and the Making of American Capitalism* (New York: Basic Books, 2014).

9. National Commission on Terrorist Attacks, *The 9/11 Commission Report: Final Report of the National Commission on Terrorist Attacks on the United States* (New York: W. W. Norton, 2004); Lawrence Wright, *The Looming Tower: Al-Qaeda and the Road to 9/11* (New York: Vintage, 2007).

10. Kurt Anderson, "The Best Decade Ever? The 1990s, Obviously," *The New York Times*, February 6, 2015.

11. Jeffrey W. Paller, *Democracy in Ghana: Everyday Politics in Urban Africa* (Cambridge: Cambridge University Press, 2019).

12. Larry Diamond and Marc F. Plattner, eds., *Democratization in Africa* (Baltimore: Johns Hopkins University Press, 1999).

13. Huntington, *The Third Wave*; Francis Fukuyama, *The End of History and the Last Man* (New York: Free Press, 1992).

14. On Islamophobia in America, see Khaled A. Beydoun, *American Islamophobia: Understanding the Roots and Rise of Fear* (Berkeley and Los Angeles: University of California Press, 2018); Erik Love, *Islamophobia and Racism in America* (New York: NYU Press, 2017); Carl W. Ernst, ed., *Islamophobia in America: The Anatomy of Intolerance* (New York: Palgrave Macmillan, 2013).

15. Edward Morrissey, "Falluja-sur-Seine," *The Weekly Standard*, November 8, 2005. Tyler Stovall, "Outer Cities: Visions américaines de la banlieue française," in Bernard Wallon, ed., *Banlieues Vues d'Ailleurs* (Paris: CNRS Editions, 2016); Andrew Hussey, *The French Intifada: The Long War between France and Its Arabs* (London: Granta Books, 2014).

16. Quoted in *The Daily Telegraph*, December 26, 2010.

17. On the French National Front, see J. G. Shields, *The Extreme Right in France: From Pétain to LePen* (New York: Routledge, 2007); Jonathan Marcus, *The National Front and French Politics: The Resistible Rise of Jean-Marie LePen* (New York: NYU Press, 1996); Françoise Gaspard, *A Small City in France* (Cambridge, MA: Harvard University Press, 1995).

18. On contemporary authoritarian populism, see Pippa Norris, *Cultural Backlash: Trump, Brexit and Authoritarian Populism* (Cambridge, UK: Cambridge University Press, 2019); Roger Eatwell and Matthew Goodwin, *National Populism: The Revolt against Liberal Democracy* (New York: Penguin, 2018); John B. Judis, *The Populist Explosion: How the Great Recession Transformed American and European Politics* (New York: Columbia Global Reports, 2016).

19. Dalibor Rohac et al., "Drivers of Authoritarian Populism in the United States: A Primer," Report co-sponsored by the Center for American Progress and the American Enterprise Institute, May 10, 2018.

20. Cited in *The Guardian*, March 29, 2019. The hoplites were generally free citizens and the foot soldiers of the armies of ancient Greece.

21. "France's LePen Announces Far-Right Bloc of Anti-EU MEPs," *BBC News*, June 16, 2015.

SELECT BIBLIOGRAPHY

This bibliography does not list all the works used in preparing this study. For more information, the reader is kindly requested to consult the notes in the text.

Aarim-Heriot, Najia. *Chinese Immigrants, African Americans, and Racial Anxiety in the United States, 1848–1882.* Urbana: University of Illinois Press, 2003.

Abi-Mershed, Osama. *Apostles of Modernity: Saint-Simonians and the Civilizing Mission in Algeria.* Stanford: Stanford University Press, 2010.

Abramovitz, Alan I. *The Great Alignment: Race, Party Transformation, and the Rise of Donald Trump.* New Haven: Yale University Press, 2018.

Adams, Jad. *Women and the Vote: A World History.* Oxford: Oxford University Press, 2014.

Adams, Michael C. C. *The Best War Ever: America and World War II.* Baltimore: Johns Hopkins University Press, 2015.

Agulhon, Maurice. *Marianne into Battle: Republican Imagery and Symbolism in France, 1789–1880.* Cambridge: Cambridge University Press, 1981.

Allen, Theodore W. *The Invention of the White Race,* 2 vols. London: Verso, 2012.

Anderson, Benedict. *Imagined Communities: Reflections on the Origin and Spread of Nationalism.* London and New York: Verso, 2006.

Ansell, Amy Elizabeth. *New Right, New Racism: Race and Reaction in the United States and Britain.* New York: New York University Press, 1997.

Applewhite, Harriet B., and Darlene G. Levy, eds. *Women and Politics in the Age of the Democratic Revolution.* Ann Arbor: University of Michigan Press, 1991.

Ariès, Philippe. *Centuries of Childhood: A Social History of Family Life.* New York: Vintage, 1965.

Arsenault, Raymond. *Freedom Riders: 1961 and the Struggle for Racial Justice.* Oxford: Oxford University Press, 2007.

Ash, Timothy Garton. *The Magic Lantern: The Revolution of '89 Witnessed in Warsaw, Budapest, Berlin, and Prague.* New York: Random House, 1990.

Baberowki, Jörg, et al. *Scorched Earth: Stalin's Reign of Terror.* New Haven: Yale University Press, 2016.

Baptist, Edward E. *The Half Has Never Been Told: Slavery and the Making of American Capitalism.* New York: Basic Books, 2014.

Baranowski, Shelley. *Nazi Empire: German Colonialism and Imperialism from Bismarck to Hitler.* Cambridge, UK: Cambridge University Press, 2011.

Barkawi, Tarak. *Soldiers of Empire: Indian and British Armies in World War II*. Cambridge, UK: Cambridge University Press, 2017.

Barzun, Jacques. *The French Race: Theories of Its Origins and Their Social and Political Implications Prior to the Revolution*. New York: Columbia University Press, 1932.

Beauvoir, Simone de. *The Second Sex*. New York: Knopf, 2010.

Beckert, Sven. *Empire of Cotton: A Global History*. New York: Vintage, 2014.

Bell, Janet Dewart. *Lighting the Fires of Freedom: African American Women in the Civil Rights Movement*. New York: The New Press, 2018.

Ben-Ghiat, Ruth. *Fascist Modernities: Italy, 1922–1945*. Berkeley and Los Angeles: University of California Press, 2001.

Benaiche, Kamel. *Sétif, la fosse commune: Massacres du 8 mai 1945*. Algiers: El Ibriz Editions, 2016.

Bender, Thomas. *A Nation among Nations: America's Place in World History*. New York: Hill and Wang, 2006.

Berenson, Edward. *The Statue of Liberty: A Transatlantic Story*. New Haven and London: Yale University Press, 2012.

Berghahn, Volker. *Europe in the Era of Two World Wars: From Militarism and Genocide to Civil Society, 1900–1950*. Princeton: Princeton University Press, 2006.

Berlin, Isaiah. *Four Essays on Liberty*. New York: Oxford University Press, 1970.

Bernstein, Iver. *The New York City Draft Riots: Their Significance for American Society and Politics in the Age of the Civil War*. Oxford: Oxford University Press, 1990.

Betts, Raymond. *Assimilation and Association in French Colonial Theory*. New York: Columbia University Press, 1961.

Birdwell, Michael. *Celluloid Soldiers: The Warner Bros. Campaign against Nazism*. New York: New York University Press, 1998.

Birkin, Andrew. *J. M. Barrie and the Lost Boys: The Real Story of Peter Pan*. New Haven: Yale University Press, 2003.

Blackmon, Douglas A. *Slavery by Another Name: The Re-Enslavement of Black Americans from the Civil War to World War II*. New York: Doubleday, 2008.

Blanning, Tim. *The Romantic Revolution: A History*. New York: Modern Library, 2011.

Bloom, Joshua, and Waldo E. Martin Jr. *Black against Empire: The History and Politics of the Black Panther Party*. Berkeley: University of California Press, 2016.

Blumrosen, Alfred, and Ruth Blumrosen. *Slave Nation: How Slavery United the Colonies and Sparked the American Revolution*. Naperville: Sourcebooks, Inc., 2005.

Bradley, Patricia. *Slavery, Propaganda, and the American Revolution*. Jackson: University Press of Mississippi, 1999.

Brodkin, Karen. *How Jews Became White Folks, and What That Says about Race in America*. New Brunswick: Rutgers University Press, 1998.

Brook, Timothy. *Quelling the People: The Military Suppression of the Beijing Democracy Movement*. New York: Oxford University Press, 1992.

Brown, Dee. *Bury My Heart at Wounded Knee: An Indian History of the American West*. New York: Picador, 2007.

Brubaker, Rogers. *Citizenship and Nationhood in France and Germany*. Cambridge, MA: Harvard University Press, 1998.

Buck-Morss, Susan. *Hegel, Haiti, and Universal History*. Pittsburgh: University of Pittsburgh Press, 2009.

Bullard, Alice. *Exile to Paradise: Savagery and Civilization in Paris and the South Pacific, 1790-1900.* Stanford: Stanford University Press, 2000.

Burkart, Patrick. *Pirate Politics.* Cambridge, MA: The MIT Press, 2014.

Burleigh, Michael, and Wolfgang Wippermann. *The Racial State: Germany 1933–1945.* Cambridge, UK: Cambridge University Press, 1991.

Burns, Steward. *Daybreak of Freedom: The Montgomery Bus Boycott.* Chapel Hill: University of North Carolina Press, 1997.

Burrin, Philippe. *Nazi Anti-Semitism: From Prejudice to the Holocaust.* New York: The New Press, 2005.

Camiscioli, Elisa. *Reproducing the French Race: Immigration, Intimacy, and Embodiment in the Early Twentieth Century.* Durham: Duke University Press, 2009.

Capeci, Dominic J., Jr., and Martha Wilkerson. *Layered Violence: The Detroit Rioters of 1943.* Jackson: University Press of Mississippi, 2009.

Cardwell, Curt. *NSC 68 and the Political Economy of the Early Cold War.* Cambridge, UK: Cambridge University Press, 2011.

Carson, Clayborne. *In Struggle: SNCC and the Black Awakening of the 1960s.* Cambridge, MA: Harvard University Press, 2016.

Cecelski, David S. *The Fire of Freedom: Abraham Galloway and the Slaves' Civil War.* Chapel Hill, University of North Carolina Press, 2012.

Chabal, Emile. *A Divided Republic: Nation, State, and Citizenship in Contemporary France.* Cambridge, UK: Cambridge University Press, 2015.

Chabot, Sean. *Transnational Roots of the Civil Rights Movement: African American Explorations of the Gandhian Repertoire.* Lanham: Lexington Books, 2012.

Chafer, Tony. *The End of Empire in French West Africa: France's Successful Decolonization?* New York: Berg, 1992.

Clark, Christopher. *The Sleepwalkers: How Europe Went to War in 1914.* New York: Harper, 2013.

Clotfelter, Charles T. *After Brown: The Rise and Retreat of School Desegregation.* Princeton: Princeton University Press, 2006.

Cohen, William. *The French Encounter with Africans: White Response to Blacks, 1530–1880.* Bloomington: Indiana University Press, 2003.

Conklin, Alice. *A Mission to Civilize: the Republican Idea of Empire in France and West Africa, 1895–1930.* Stanford: Stanford University Press, 1997.

Cooper, Frederick, and Ann Laura Stoler, eds. *Tensions of Empire: Colonial Cultures in a Bourgeois World.* Berkeley and Los Angeles: University of California Press, 1997.

Cooper, Frederick. *Citizenship between Empire and Nation: Remaking France and French Africa, 1945–1960.* Princeton: Princeton University Press, 2014.

Cordingly, David. *Seafaring Women: Adventures of Pirate Queens, Female Stowaways, and Sailors' Wives.* New York: Random House, 2002.

———. *Under the Black Flag: The Romance and Reality of Life among the Pirates.* New York: Random House, 2006.

Crenshaw, Kimberlé. "Mapping the Margins: Intersectionality, Identity Politics, and Violence against Women of Color." *Stanford Law Review* 43, no. 6 (1993).

Cunningham, Hugh. *The Challenge of Democracy: Britain, 1832–1918.* London: Routledge, 2001.

Dalberg, John Emerich Edward, Lord Acton. *The History of Freedom and Other Essays*. London: Macmillan and Co., 1907.

Daniels, Roger. *Coming to America: A History of Immigration and Ethnicity in American Life*. New York: Harper, 2002.

Das, Santu, ed. *Race, Empire, and First World War Writing*. Cambridge: Cambridge University Press, 2011.

Davis, David Brion. *The Problem of Slavery in the Age of Revolution, 1770–1823*. New York: Oxford University Press, 1999.

———. *The Problem of Slavery in Western Culture*. Ithaca, NY: Cornell University Press; repr. Oxford University Press, 1988.

Delmont, Matthew F. *Why Busing Failed: Race, Media, and the National Resistance to School Desegregation*. Berkeley: University of California Press, 2016.

Desan, Suzanne, et al., eds. *The French Revolution in Global Perspective*. Ithaca: Cornell University Press, 2013.

Dickey, J. D. *Rising in Flames: Sherman's March and the Fight for a New Nation*. New York: Pegasus, 2018.

Doherty, Thomas. *Projections of War: Hollywood, American Culture, and World War II*. New York: Columbia University Press, 1993.

Dorsey, Peter A. *Common Bondage: Slavery as Metaphor in Revolutionary America*. Knoxville: University of Tennessee Press, 2009.

Dower, John. *Race and Power in the Pacific War*. New York: Pantheon, 1987.

Doyle, William. *The Oxford History of the French Revolution*. Oxford: Oxford University Press, 2003.

Drescher, Seymour. *Abolition: A History of Slavery and Antislavery*. Cambridge, UK: Cambridge University Press, 2009.

DuBois, Ellen Carol. *Feminism and Suffrage: The Emergence of an Independent Women's Movement in America, 1848–1869*. Ithaca: Cornell University Press, 1998.

DuBois, Laurent. *Avengers of the New World: The Story of the Haitian Revolution*. Cambridge, MA, and London: The Belknap Press of Harvard University Press, 2004.

DuBois, W.E.B. *Black Reconstruction in America, 1860–1880*. New York: Free Press, 1988.

Dubrulle, Hugh. *Ambivalent Nation: How Britain Imagined the American Civil War*. Baton Rouge: Louisiana State University Press, 2018.

Dudziak, Mary. *Cold War Civil Rights: Race and the Image of American Democracy*. Princeton: Princeton University Press, 2001.

Dun, James Alexander. *Dangerous Neighbors: Making the Haitian Revolution in Early America*. Philadelphia: University of Pennsylvania Press, 2016.

Dunbar-Ortiz, Roxanne. *An Indigenous People's History of the United States*. Boston: Beacon, 2014.

Ehrenreich, Barbara. *The Hearts of Men: American Dreams and the Flight from Commitment*. New York: Anchor Books, 1983.

Eisenstein, Zillah R. *The Color of Gender: Reimagining Democracy*. Berkeley: University of California Press, 1994.

Eksteins, Modris. *Rites of Spring: The Great War and the Birth of the Modern Age*. New York: Mariner Press, 2000.

Erie, Steven P. *Rainbow's End: Irish-Americans and the Dilemmas of Urban Machine Politics, 1840–1985*. Berkeley: University of California Press, 1990.

Evans, Richard J. *The Coming of the Third Reich*. New York: Penguin Books, 2005.

Evans, Sara. *Born for Liberty: A History of Women in America*. New York: Free Press, 1997.

Eze, Emmanuel. *Race and the Enlightenment: A Reader*. London: Wiley-Blackwell, 1997.

Faderman, Lilian. *The Gay Revolution: The Story of the Struggle*. New York: Simon and Schuster, 2015.

Fanon, Frantz. *Black Skin, White Masks*. London: Pluto, 2008.

———. *The Wretched of the Earth*. New York: Grove Press, 2005.

Fernando, Mayanthi L. *The Republic Unsettled: Muslim French and the Contradictions of Secularism*. Durham: Duke University Press, 2014.

Ferro, Marc. *The Great War 1914–1918*. London and New York: Routledge, 2001.

Fink, Carole K. *Cold War: An International History*. London: Routledge, 2013.

Finley, Moses I. *Ancient Slavery and Modern Ideology*. New York: Penguin, 1980.

Flynn, Gregory Q. *Conscription and Democracy: The Draft in France, Great Britain, and the United States*. New York: Praeger, 2001.

Foner, Eric. *Give Me Liberty!: An American History*. New York: W. W. Norton and Co., 2005.

———. *A Short History of Reconstruction*. New York: Harper, 2015.

Formisano, Ronald P. *Boston against Busing: Race, Class, and Ethnicity in the 1960s and 1970s*. Chapel Hill: University of North Carolina Press, 2004.

Fox-Genovese, Elizabeth. *Within the Plantation Household: Black and White Women of the Old South*. Chapel Hill: University of North Carolina Press, 1988.

Franklin, John Hope. *From Slavery to Freedom: A History of Negro Americans*. New York: A. A. Knopf, 1947.

Frederickson, George M. *Racism: A Short History*. Princeton: Princeton University Press, 2002.

Frey, Silvia R. *Water from the Rock: Black Resistance in a Revolutionary Age*. Princeton: Princeton University Press, 1991.

Friedan, Betty. *The Feminine Mystique*. New York: W. W. Norton, 2013.

Friedlander, Saul. *The Years of Extermination: Nazi Germany and the Jews, 1939–1945*. New York: Harper, 2007.

Friedman, Milton, and Rose Friedman. *Free to Choose: A Personal Statement*. Boston: Mariner Books, 1990.

Fritz, Stephen G. *Ostkrieg: Hitler's War of Extermination in the East*. Lexington: University Press of Kentucky, 2011.

Fritzsche, Peter. *Germans into Nazis*. Cambridge, MA: Harvard University Press, 1999.

Frydl, Kathleen J., *The G.I. Bill*. Cambridge, UK: Cambridge University Press, 2009.

Fussell, Paul. *The Great War and Modern Memory*. Oxford: Oxford University Press, 2013.

Gaddis, John Lewis. *The Cold War: A New History*. New York: Penguin 2006.

Galloway, Colin. *The American Revolution in Indian Country: Crisis and Diversity in Native American Communities*. Cambridge, UK: Cambridge University Press, 1995.

Garrigus, John. *Before Haiti: Race and Citizenship in French Saint-Domingue*. New York: Palgrave Macmillan, 2006.

Garrow, David J. *Bearing the Cross: Martin Luther King Jr. and the Southern Christian Leadership Conference*. New York: William Morrow, 1985.

————. *Protest at Selma: Martin Luther King, Jr., and the Voting Rights Act of 1965*. New Haven: Yale University Press, 1978.

Gaspar, David Barry, and David Patrick Geggus, eds. *A Turbulent Time: The French Revolution in the Greater Caribbean*. Bloomington: Indiana University Press, 1997.

Gaspard, Françoise. *A Small City in France*. Cambridge, MA: Harvard University Press, 1995.

Gay, Peter. *The Enlightenment: An Interpretation*. Vol. 2: *The Science of Freedom*. New York: Knopf, 2013.

Geggus, David Patrick. *The Impact of the Haitian Revolution in the Atlantic World*. Columbia: University of South Carolina Press, 2001.

Gellner, Ernest. *Nations and Nationalism*. Ithaca: Cornell University Press, 2009.

Gerard, Emmanuel, and Bruce Kuklick. *Death in the Congo: Murdering Patrice Lumumba*. Cambridge, MA: Harvard University Press, 2015.

Gerlach, Christian. *The Extermination of the European Jews*. Cambridge, UK: Cambridge University Press, 2016.

Ghachem, Malick W. *The Old Regime and the Haitian Revolution*. Cambridge: Cambridge University Press, 2012.

Gilbert, Alan. *Black Patriots and Loyalists: Fighting for Emancipation in the War for Independence*. Chicago: University of Chicago Press, 2012.

Gildea, Robert. *Fighters in the Shadows: A New History of the French Resistance*. Cambridge, MA: Harvard University Press, 2015.

Gillette, Aaron. *Racial Theories in Fascist Italy*. New York: Routledge, 2001.

Gillis, John R. *Youth and History: Tradition and Change in European Age Relations, 1770- Present*. Cambridge, MA: Academic Press, 1974.

Ginio, Ruth. *The French Army and its African Soldiers: The Years of Decolonization*. Lincoln: University of Nebraska Press, 2017.

Gluckstein, Donny. *A People's History of the Second World War: Resistance versus Empire*. London: Pluto Press, 2012.

Gomez, Laura. *Manifest Destinies: The Making of the Mexican American Race*. New York: New York University Press, 2008.

Gordon, Linda. *The Second Coming of the KKK: The Ku Klux Klan of the 1920s and the American Political Tradition*. New York: Liveright, 2017.

Gordon-Reed, Annette. *Thomas Jefferson and Sally Hemings: An American Controversy*. Charlottesville: University of Virginia Press, 1997.

Gray, Hannah Holborn. *Searching for Utopia: Universities and their Histories*. Berkeley: University of California Press, 2011.

Gray, Walter D. *Interpreting American Democracy in France: The Career of Édouard Laboulaye, 1811–1833*. Newark: University of Delaware Press, 1994.

Gregory, Mary Efrosini. *Freedom in French Enlightenment Thought*. New York: Peter Lang, 2010.

Grigsby, Darcy Grimaldo. *Extremities: Painting Empire in Post-Revolutionary France*. New Haven and London: Yale University Press, 2002.

Gugliemo, Thomas. *White on Arrival: Italians, Race, Color, and Power in Chicago, 1890–1945*. Oxford: Oxford University Press, 2003.

Gyorgy, Andres. *Closing the Gate: Race, Politics, and the Chinese Exclusion Act*. Chapel Hill: University of North Carolina Press, 1998.

Hall, Catherine, et al. *Defining the Victorian Nation: Class, Race, Gender, and the British Reform Act of 1867*. Cambridge, UK: Cambridge University Press, 2000.

Hannaford, Ivan. *Race: The History of an Idea in the West*. Baltimore: Johns Hopkins University Press, 1996.

Harding, Vincent. *There Is a River: the Black Struggle for Freedom in America*. New York: Harcourt Brace and Jovanovich, 1981.

Harper, Kimberly. *White Man's Heaven: The Lynching and Expulsion of Blacks in the Southern Ozarks, 1894–1909*. Fayetteville: University of Arkansas Press, 2010.

Harris, Leslie M. *In the Shadow of Slavery: African Americans in New York City, 1626–1863*. Chicago: University of Chicago Press, 2004.

Hazareesingh, Sudhir. *From Subject to Citizen: The Second Empire and the Emergence of Modern French Democracy*. Princeton: Princeton University Press, 1998.

Heywood, Colin. *A History of Childhood: Children and Childhood in the West from Medieval to Modern Times*. Cambridge: Polity Press, 2001.

Higham, John. *Strangers in the Land: Patterns of American Nativism 1860–1925*. Westport, CT: Greenwood Publishers, 1981.

Higonnet, Anne. *Pictures of Innocence: The History and Crisis of Ideal Childhood*. New York: Thames and Hudson, 1998.

Higonnet, Patrice. *Sister Republics: The Origins of French and American Republicanism*. Cambridge, MA: Harvard University Press, 1988.

Hobsbawm, Eric. *Nations and Nationalism since 1780: Programme, Myth, Reality*. Cambridge, UK: Cambridge University Press, 2012.

Hogan, Michael J. *The Marshall Plan: America, Britain, and the Reconstruction of Western Europe, 1947–1952*. New York: Cambridge University Press, 1987.

———. *The Age of Revolution, 1789–1848*. New York: Vintage, 1996.

Holt, Thomas. *The Problem of Freedom: Race, Labor, and Politics in Jamaica and Britain, 1832–1938*. Baltimore: Johns Hopkins University Press, 1992.

Horkheimer, Max, and Theodor Adorno. *The Dialectic of Enlightenment*. Stanford: Stanford University Press, 2007.

Horne, Gerald. *The Counter Revolution of 1776: Slave Resistance and the Origins of the American Revolution*. New York: NYU Press, 2014.

Horsman, Reginald. *Race and Manifest Destiny: The Origins of American Racial Anglo-Saxonism*. Cambridge, MA: Harvard University Press, 1981.

Howe, Stephen. *Anticolonialism in British Politics: The Left and the End of Empire, 1918–1964*. Oxford: Clarendon Press, 1993.

Hussey, Richard. *Freedom Burning: Anti-Slavery and Empire in Victorian Britain*. Ithaca: Cornell University Press, 2012.

Ignatiev, Noel. *How the Irish Became White*. London: Routledge, 2008.

Immerman, Richard H. *Empire for Liberty: A History of American Imperialism from Benjamin Franklin to Paul Wolfowitz*. Princeton: Princeton University Press, 2012.

Iriye, Akira. "The Internationalization of History." *The American Historical Review*, 94, no. 1 (February 1989).

Israel, Jonathan I. *A Revolution of the Mind: Radical Enlightenment and the Intellectual Origins of Modern Democracy*. Princeton: Princeton University Press, 2009.

Jackson, Julian. *France: The Dark Years, 1940–1944*. Oxford: Oxford University Press, 2001.

Jacobsen, Matthew Frye. *Whiteness of a Different Color: European Immigrants and the Alchemy of Race*. Cambridge, MA: Harvard University Press, 1998.

Jainchill, Andrew. *Reimagining Politics after the Terror: The Republican Origins of French Liberalism*. Ithaca and London: Cornell University Press, 2008.

James, C.L.R. *Black Jacobins: Toussaint L'Ouverture and the San Domingo Revolution*. New York: Vintage, 1989.

James, Lawrence. *Churchill and Empire: A Portrait of an Imperialist*. New York: Pegasus Books, 2014.

James, Rawn Jr. *The Double V: How Wars, Protest, and Harry Truman Desegregated America's Military*. New York: Bloomsbury, 2013.

Jennings, Eric T. *Free French Africa in World War II: The African Resistance*. Cambridge, UK: Cambridge University Press, 2015.

———. *Vichy in the Tropics: Pétain's National Revolution in Madagascar, Guadeloupe, and Indochina, 1940–1944*. Stanford: Stanford University Press, 2001.

Jennings, Lawrence C. *French Anti-Slavery: The Movement for the Abolition of Slavery in France*. Cambridge, UK: Cambridge University Press, 2006.

Johansen, Bruce E. *Debating Democracy: Native American Legacy of Freedom*. Santa Fe: Clear Light Publishers, 1998.

Johnson, Charles. *A General History of the Robberies and Murders of the Most Notorious Pyrates*. London: Conway Maritime Press, 1724.

Johnson, Rucker. *Children of the Dream: Why School Integration Works*. New York: Basic Books, 2019.

Judis, John B. *The Populist Explosion: How the Great Recession Transformed American and European Politics*. New York: Columbia Global Reports, 2016.

Kahler, Miles. *Decolonization in Britain and France: The Domestic Consequences of International Relations*. Princeton: Princeton University Press, 1984.

Kakel, Carroll P., III. *The American West and the Nazi East: A Comparative and Interpretive Perspective*. New York: Palgrave Macmillan, 2011.

Kaplan, Temma. *Democracy: A World History*. Oxford: Oxford University Press, 2014.

Katz, Philip M. *From Appomattox to Montmartre: Americans and the Paris Commune*. Cambridge, MA: Harvard University Press, 1998.

Kantrowitz, Stephen. *More than Freedom: Fighting for Black Citizenship in a White Republic, 1829–1889*. New York: Penguin, 2012.

Keaton, Trica Danielle. *Muslim Girls and the Other France: Race, Identity Politics, and Social Exclusion*. Bloomington: Indiana University Press, 2006.

Kendi, Ibram X. *Stamped from the Beginning: The Definitive History of Racist Ideas in America*. New York: Perseus, 2016.

Kengor, Paul. *The Crusader: Ronald Reagan and the Fall of Communism*. New York: Harper, 2006.

Kennedy, Dane. *Decolonization: A Short Introduction*. New York: Oxford University Press, 2016.

Keyssar, Alexander. *The Right to Vote: The Contested History of Democracy in the United States*. New York: Basic Books, 2000.

Khan, Yasmin Sabina. *Enlightening the World: the Creation of the Statue of Liberty*. Ithaca and London: Cornell University Press, 2010.

Kinealy, Christine. *Daniel O'Connell and the Anti-Slavery Movement: The Saddest People the Sun Sees*. London: Pickering and Chatto, 2010.

King, Richard H., and Dan Stone, eds. *Hannah Arendt and the Uses of History: Imperialism, Nation, Race, and Genocide*. New York and Oxford: Berghahn Books, 2007.

Klaits, Joseph, and Michael H. Haltzel, eds. *Liberty/Liberté: The American and French Experiences*. Baltimore and London: The Johns Hopkins University Press, 1991.

Klaussen, Jimmy Casas. *Fugitive Rousseau: Slavery, Primitivism, and Freedom*. New York: Fordham University Press, 2014.

Klein, Martin A. *Slavery and Colonial Rule in French West Africa*. New York: Cambridge University Press, 1998.

Kluger, Richard. *Simple Justice: The History of Brown v. Education and Black America's Struggle for Equality*. New York: Vintage, 2004.

Kolko, Gabriel. *The Politics of War: The World and United States Foreign Policy, 1943–1945*. New York: Pantheon, 1990.

Koschorke, Albrecht. *On Hitler's Mein Kampf: The Poetics of National Socialism*. Cambridge, MA: MIT Press, 2017.

Kotkin, Stephen. *Armageddon Averted: The Soviet Collapse, 1970–2000*. Oxford: Oxford University Press, 2008.

Kühl, Stefan. *The Nazi Connection: Eugenics, American Racism, and German National Socialism*. Oxford: Oxford University Press, 2002.

Kuisel, Richard. *Seducing the French: the Dilemma of Americanization*. Berkeley: University of California Press, 1997.

Kushner, Sam. *Long Road to Delano: A Century of Farmworkers' Struggle*. New York: International Publishers, 1975.

Lake, Marilyn, and Henry Reynolds. *Drawing the Global Colour Line: White Men's Countries and the International Challenge of Racial Equality*. Cambridge: Cambridge University Press, 2008.

Lambert, Frank. *The Barbary Wars: American Independence in the Atlantic World*. New York: Hill and Wang, 2007.

Laqueur, Walter. *A History of Zionism: From the French Revolution to the Establishment of the State of Israel*. New York: Holt, Rinehart, and Winston, 1972.

Latour, Anny. *The Jewish Resistance in France 1940–1944*. Washington, DC: US Holocaust Museum, 1981.

Lawrence, Adria. *Imperial Rule and the Politics of Nationalism: Anti-Colonial Protests in the French Empire*. New York: Cambridge University Press, 2013.

Lebo, Richard. *White Britain and Black Ireland: The Impact of Stereotypes on Colonial Policy*. Philadelphia: Institute for the Study of Human Issues, 1976.

Lee, Erika. *At America's Gates: Chinese Immigration during the Exclusion Era, 1882–1943*. Chapel Hill: University of North Carolina Press, 2003.

Leiken, Robert. *Europe's Angry Muslims: The Revolt of the Second Generation*. Oxford: Oxford University Press, 2011.

Lentz-Smith, Adriane Danette. *Freedom Struggles: African Americans and World War I*. Cambridge, MA: Harvard University Press, 2010.

Lepore, Jill. *New York Burning: Liberty, Slavery, and Conspiracy in Eighteenth-Century Manhattan*. New York: Vintage, 2006.

Levine, Bruce. *The Fall of the House of Dixie: The Civil War and the Social Revolution That Transformed the South*. New York: Random House, 2013.

Levine, Philippa. *The British Empire: Sunrise to Sunset*. Harlow: Pearson, 2007.

Levander, Caroline. *Cradle of Liberty: Race, the Child, and National Belonging from Thomas Jefferson to W.E.B. DuBois*. Durham: Duke University Press, 2006.

Lewis, Mary Dewhurst. *The Boundaries of the Republic: Migrant Rights and the Limits of Universalism in France, 1918–1940*. Stanford: Stanford University Press, 2007.

Lezra, Esther. *The Colonial Art of Demonizing Others: A Global Perspective*. London and New York: Routledge, 2014.

Linebaugh, Peter, and Marcus Rediker. *The Many-Headed Hydra: Sailors, Slaves, Commoners, and the Hidden History of the Revolutionary Atlantic*. Boston: Beacon Press, 2015.

Lipsitz, George. *The Possessive Investment in Whiteness: How White People Profit from Identity Politics*. Philadelphia: Temple University Press, 2006.

Litwack, Leon F. *Been in the Storm So Long: The Aftermath of Slavery*. New York: Knopf, 1979.

———. *North of Slavery: The Negro in the Free States, 1790–1860*. Chicago: University of Chicago Press, 1965.

Lloyd, Nick. *The Amritsar Massacre: The Untold Story of One Fateful Day*. London: I. B. Tauris, 2011.

López, Alfred J. *Postcolonial Whiteness: A Critical Reader on Race and Empire*. Albany: State University of New York Press, 2005.

Lorimer, Douglas. *Colour, Class, and the Victorians: English Attitudes to the Negro in the Mid-Nineteenth Century*. New York: Holmes and Meier, 1978.

Love, Erik. *Islamophobia and Racism in America*. New York: NYU Press, 2017.

Lowndes, Joseph E. *From the New Deal to the New Right: Race and the Southern Origins of Modern Conservatism*. New Haven: Yale University Press, 2008.

Lucander, David. *Winning the War for Democracy: The March on Washington Movement, 1941–1946*. Urbana: University of Illinois Press, 2014.

Lunn, Joe H. *Memoirs of the Maelstrom: A Senegalese Oral History of the First World War*. New York: Heinemann, 1999.

Luxenberg, Steven. *Separate: The Story of Plessy v. Ferguson, and America's Journey from Slavery to Segregation*. New York: W. W. Norton, 2019.

Lynch, John. *The Spanish American Revolutions 1808–1826*. New York: W. W. Norton, 1986.

Macey, David. *Frantz Fanon: A Biography*. New York: Picador, 2001.

Macmillan, Margaret. *Paris 1919: Six Months That Changed the World*. New York: Random House, 2003.

———. *Women of the Raj: The Mothers, Wives, and Daughters of the British Empire in India*. New York: Random House, 2007.

Macpherson, C. B. *The Life and Times of Liberal Democracy*. Oxford: Oxford University Press, 1977.

Mailer, Norman. "The White Negro: Superficial Reflections on the Hipster." *Dissent*, Fall 1957.

Mallett, Robert M. *Mussolini in Ethiopia, 1919–1935: The Origins of Fascist Italy's African War*. Cambridge: Cambridge University Press, 2015.

Mandela, Nelson. *Long Walk to Freedom: The Autobiography of Nelson Mandela*. Boston: Back Bay Books, 2013.

Manela, Erez. *The Wilsonian Moment: Self-Determination and the Origins of Anticolonial Nationalism*. Oxford: Oxford University Press, 2009.

Masur, Louis P. *Lincoln's Hundred Days: The Emancipation Proclamation and the War for the Union*. Cambridge, MA: The Belknap Press of Harvard University Press, 2012.

———. *The Soiling of Old Glory: The Story of a Photograph That Shocked America*. London: Bloomsbury Press, 2008.

Marcus, Jonathan. *The National Front and French Politics: The Resistible Rise of Jean-Marie LePen*. New York: NYU Press, 1996.

Mathy, Jean-Philippe. *French Resistance: The French-American Culture Wars*. Minneapolis: University of Minnesota Press, 2000.

Mayer, Jeremy D. *Running on Race: Racial Politics in Presidential Campaigns, 1960–2000*. New York: Random House, 2002.

Mazower, Mark. *Dark Continent: Europe's Twentieth Century*. New York: Vintage Books, 2000.

———. *Hitler's Empire: How the Nazis Ruled Europe*. New York: Penguin Books, 2009.

McAdam, Doug. *Freedom Summer*. Oxford: Oxford University Press, 1988.

McClintock, Anne. *Imperial Leather: Race, Gender, and Sexuality in the Colonial Context*. New York: Routledge, 1995.

McGirr, Lisa. *Suburban Warriors: The Origins of the New American Right*. Princeton: Princeton University Press, 2015.

McIntyre, William D. *British Decolonization, 1946–1997: When, Why, and How did the Empire Fall?* New York: St. Martin's Press, 1998.

McPherson, James M. *Battle Cry of Freedom: The Civil War Era*. Oxford: Oxford University Press, 1988.

———. *The Struggle for Equality: Abolitionists and the Negro during the Civil War and Reconstruction*. Princeton: Princeton University Press, 2014.

McRae, Elizabeth Gillespie. *Mothers of Massive Resistance: White Women and the Politics of White Supremacy*. Oxford: Oxford University Press, 2018.

McWhirter, Cameron. *Red Summer: The Summer of 1919 and the Awakening of Black America*. New York: Henry Holt and Co., 2011.

Merriman, John. *The Dynamite Club: How a Bombing in Fin-de-Siècle Paris Ignited the Age of Modern Terror*. New Haven: Yale University Press, 2016.

———. *Massacre: The Life and Death of the Paris Commune*. New York: Basic Books, 2014.

Meyer, Michael. *The Year That Changed the World: The Untold Story Behind the Fall of the Berlin Wall*. New York: Scribner, 2009.

Michel, Marc. *Les Africains et la Grande Guerre: L'appel à l'Afrique; 1914–1918*. Paris: Karthala, 2014.

Mill, John Stuart. *On Liberty*. London: Parker and Sons, 1859.

Mitchell, Timothy. *Bloodlands: Europe Between Hitler and Stalin*. New York: Basic Books, 2012.

Montejano, David. *Anglos and Mexicans in the Making of Texas, 1836–1986*. Austin: University of Texas Press, 1987.

Moore, Barrington Jr. *Social Origins of Dictatorship and Democracy: Lord and Peasant in the Making of the Modern World*. Boston: Beacon Press, 1993.

Moore, Deborah Dash. *GI Jews: How World War II Changed a Generation*. Cambridge, MA: Belknap Press, 2006.

Morgan, Edmund. *American Slavery, American Freedom: The Ordeal of Colonial Virginia.* New York: W. W. Norton, 2005.

Moreton-Robinson, Aileen. *White Possessive: Property, Power, and Indigenous Sovereignty.* Minneapolis: University of Minnesota Press, 2015.

Mosse, George. *Toward the Final Solution: A History of European Racism.* New York: H. Fertig, 1978.

Moye, J. Todd. *Freedom Flyers: The Tuskegee Airmen of World War II.* Oxford: Oxford University Press, 2012.

Munro, John. *The Anticolonial Front: The African American Freedom Struggle and Global Decolonization, 1945–1960.* Cambridge: Cambridge University Press, 2017.

Murray, Alice Yang. *Historical Memories of the Japanese American Internment and the Struggle for Redress.* Stanford: Stanford University Press, 2007.

Naimark, Norman. *Fires of Hatred: Ethnic Cleansing in Twentieth-Century Europe.* Cambridge, MA: Harvard University Press, 2002.

Nash, Gary B. *The Urban Crucible: Social Change, Political Consciousness, and the Origins of the American Revolution.* Cambridge, MA: Harvard University Press, 1979.

Ndiaye, Pap. *La condition noire: Essai sur une minorité française.* Paris: Calmann-Lévy, 2008.

Nkrumah, Kwame. *I Speak of Freedom: A Statement of African Ideology.* New York: Praeger, 1961.

———. *Neo-Colonialism, the Highest Stage of Imperialism.* London: Thomas Nelson and Sons, 1965.

Nez, Chester. *Code Talker: The First and Only Memoir by One of the Original Navajo Code Talkers of WWII.* New York: Dutton Caliber, 2011.

Ngai, Mai M. *Impossible Subjects: Illegal Aliens and the Making of Modern America.* Princeton: Princeton University Press, 2014.

Nord, Philip. *The Republican Moment: Struggles for Democracy in Nineteenth-Century France.* Cambridge, MA: Harvard University Press, 1998.

Norris, Pippa. *Cultural Backlash: Trump, Brexit and Authoritarian Populism.* Cambridge, UK: Cambridge University Press, 2019.

Nyerere, Julius K. *Freedom and Development: A Section from Writings and Speeches, 1968- 1973.* London, Oxford, New York: Oxford University Press, 1973.

O'Neill, Martin, and Thad Williamson, eds. *Property-Owning Democracy: Rawls and Beyond.* Hoboken, NJ: Wiley-Blackwell, 2014.

Oldfield, John. *Transatlantic Abolitionism in the Age of Revolution.* Cambridge, UK, and New York: Cambridge University Press, 2013.

Olusoga, David, and Casper W. Erichsen. *The Kaiser's Holocaust: Germany's Forgotten Genocide.* London: Faber and Faber, 2011.

Orchowski, Margaret Sands. *The Law That Changed the Face of America: The Immigration and Nationality Act of 1965.* Boston: Rowman and Littlefield, 2015.

Oshinsky, David M. *Worse than Slavery: Parchman Farm and the Ordeal of Jim Crow Justice.* New York: Free Press, 1997.

O'Toole, Patricia. *The Moralist: Woodrow Wilson and the World He Made.* New York: Simon and Schuster, 2018.

Pagden, Anthony. *The Enlightenment: And Why It Still Matters.* New York: Random House, 2013.

Painter, Nell Irvin. *The History of White People.* New York: W. W. Norton, 2010.

Paligot-Reynaud, Carole. *De l'identité nationale: Science, Race, et Politique en Europe et aux États-Unis, XIXe-XXe siècles.* Paris: Presses Universitaires de France, 2011.

Palmer, R. R. *The Age of Democratic Revolution: A Political History of Europe and America, 1760–1800*. Princeton: Princeton University Press, 2014.

Parsons, Elaine Frantz. *Ku Klux: The Birth of the Klan during Reconstruction*. Chapel Hill: University of North Carolina Press, 2016.

Patterson, James. *Brown v. Board of Education: A Civil Rights Milestone and its Troubled Legacy*. Oxford: Oxford University Press, 2001.

Patterson, Orlando. *Freedom*. Vol. 1: *Freedom in the Making of Western Culture*. New York: Basic Books, 1991.

———. *Slavery and Social Death: A Comparative Study*. Cambridge, MA: Harvard University Press, 1982.

Peabody, Sue. *"There Are No Slaves in France": The Political Culture of Race and Slavery in the Ancien Regime*. Oxford: Oxford University Press, 2002.

———, and Tyler Stovall, eds. *The Color of Liberty: Histories of Race in France*. Durham: Duke University Press, 2003.

Perras, Arne. *Carl Peters and German Imperialism, 1856–1918*. Oxford: Clarendon Press, 2004.

Peschanski, Denis. *Des étrangers dans la Résistance*. Paris: Musée de la Résistance, 2002.

Phillips, Kevin. *The Emerging Republican Majority*. New York: Arlington House, 1969.

Pitts, Jennifer. *A Turn to Empire: The Rise of Imperial Liberalism in Britain and France*. Princeton: Princeton University Press, 2005.

Plummer, Brenda Gayle. *Rising Wind: Black Americans and U.S. Foreign Affairs, 1935–1960*. Chapel Hill: University of North Carolina Press, 1996.

Poliakov, Leon. *The Aryan Myth: A History of Racist and Nationalist Ideas in Europe*. New York: Basic Books, 1974.

Popkin, Jeremy. *You Are All Free: The Haitian Revolution and the Abolition of Slavery*. Cambridge, UK: Cambridge University Press, 2010.

Power, Thomas Francis. *Jules Ferry and the Renaissance of French Imperialism*. New York: Octagon Books, 1966.

Prasad, Pratima. *Colonialism, Race, and the French Romantic Imagination*. New York: Routledge, 2009.

Price, Richard. *Maroon Societies: Rebel Slave Communities in the Americas*. Baltimore: Johns Hopkins University Press, 1996.

Rawls, John. *Political Liberalism*. New York: Columbia University Press, 2005.

Rediker, Marcus. *Villains of all Nations: Atlantic Pirates in the Golden Age*. Boston: Beacon Press, 2011.

———. *Between the Devil and the Deep Blue Sea: Merchant Seamen, Pirates, and the Anglo-American Maritime World, 1700–1750*. Cambridge, UK: Cambridge University Press, 1989.

Reeves, Richard. *Infamy: The Shocking Story of the Japanese-American Internment in World War II*. New York: Henry Holt and Co., 2015.

Renan, Ernest. "What Is a Nation?" In Homi Bhabha, ed., *Nation and Narration*. London and New York: Routledge, 1990.

Richardson, Neil. *A Coward if I Return, A Hero if I Fall: Stories of Irishmen in World War I*. Dublin: O'Brien Press, 2002.

Ringer, Fritz K. *Education and Society in Modern Europe*. Bloomington: Indiana University Press, 1978.

Risen, Clay. *The Bill of the Century: The Epic Battle for the Civil Rights Act*. New York: Bloomsbury Press, 2014.

Roberts, Justin. *Slavery and the Enlightenment in the British Atlantic, 1750–1807*. New York: Cambridge University Press, 2013.

Roberts, Mary Louise. *What Soldiers Do: Sex and the American GI in World War II France*. Chicago: University of Chicago Press, 2013.

Roediger, David. *Seizing Freedom: Slave Emancipation and Liberty for All*. London: Verso, 2015.

———. *The Wages of Whiteness: Race and the Making of the American Working Class*. London: Verso, 2007.

Rosales, Steven. *Soldados Razos at War: Chicano Poitics, Identity, and Masculinity in the U.S. Military from World War II to Vietnam*. Tucson: University of Arizona Press, 2017.

Rosanvallon, Pierre. *The Demands of Liberty: Civil Society in France since the Revolution*. Cambridge, MA: Harvard University Press, 2007.

———. *Democracy Past and Future*. New York: Columbia University Press, 2006.

Ross, Kristin. *Communal Luxury: The Political Imaginary of the Paris Commune*. London: Verso, 2015.

———. *Fast Cars, Clean Bodies: Decolonization and the Reordering of French Culture*. Cambridge, MA: The MIT Press, 1996.

Roth, Joseph. *The Wandering Jews*. New York: W. W. Norton, 2001.

Rothstein, Richard. *The Color of Law: A Forgotten History of How Our Government Segregated America*. New York: Liveright, 2017.

Rousseau, Jean-Jacques. *The Emile of Jean-Jacques Rousseau*. Translated by William Boyd. New York: Columbia University Press, 1965.

———. *The Social Contract* and *The First and Second Discourses*. Edited by Susan Dunn. New Haven and London: Yale University Press, 2002.

Sala-Molins, Louis. *Dark Side of the Light: Slavery and the French Enlightenment*. Minneapolis: University of Minnesota Press, 2006.

Said, Edward W. *Orientalism*. New York: Vintage Books, 1978.

Samson, Jane. *Race and Empire*. New York: Routledge, 2004.

Samuels, Maurice. *The Right to Difference: French Universalism and the Jews*. Chicago: University of Chicago Press, 2017.

Savage, Jon. *Teenage: The Prehistory of Youth Culture: 1875–1945*. New York: Penguin, 2008.

Saxton, Alexander. *The Indispensable Enemy: Labor and the Anti-Chinese Movement in California*. Berkeley: University of California Press, 1971.

———. *The Rise and Fall of the White Republic: Class Politics and Mass Culture in Nineteenth-Century America*. London: Verso, 1991.

Schama, Simon. *Rough Crossings: Britain, the Slaves, and the American Revolution*. New York: HarperCollins, 2006.

Schor, Naomi. "The Crisis of French Universalism." *Yale French Studies*, no. 100 (2001).

Schrag, Peter. *Not Fit for Our Society: Nativism and Immigration*. Berkeley: University of California Press, 2010.

Scott, Joan W. *Parité: Sexual Equality and the Crisis of French Universalism*. Chicago: University of Chicago Press, 2005.

Sepinwall, Alyssa Goldstein. *The Abbé Grégoire and the Making of the French Revolution*. Berkeley: University of California Press, 2005.

Sessions, Jennifer E. *By Sword and Plow: France and the Conquest of Algeria*. Ithaca: Cornell University Press, 2011.

Sewell, William H. *Work and Revolution in France: The Language of Labor from the Old Regime to 1848*. Cambridge: Cambridge University Press, 1980.

Shepard, Todd. *The Invention of Decolonization: The Algerian War and the Remaking of France*. Ithaca: Cornell University Press, 2006.

Sherman, Daniel. *French Primitivism and the Ends of Empire, 1945–1975*. Chicago: University of Chicago Press, 2011.

Shouls, Peter A. *Reasoned Freedom: John Locke and Enlightenment*. Ithaca: Cornell University Press, 1992.

Silverman, Maxim. *Deconstructing the Nation: Immigration, Racism, and Citizenship in Modern France*. New York: Routledge, 2014.

Singh, Nikhil Pal. *Race and America's Long War*. Berkeley and Los Angeles: University of California Press, 2017.

Sinha, Manisha. *The Slave's Cause: A History of Abolition*. New Haven: Yale University Press, 2016.

Sinnreich, Aram. *The Piracy Crusade: How the Music Industry's War on Sharing Destroys Markets and Erodes Civil Liberties*. Amherst and Boston: University of Massachusetts Press, 2013.

Smedley, Audrey. *Race in North America: Origin and Evolution of a World View*. Boulder: Westview Press, 2007.

Smith, John David, ed. *Black Soldiers in Blue: African American Troops in the Civil War Era*. Chapel Hill: University of North Carolina Press, 2002.

Smith, Thomas E. *Emancipation without Equality: Pan-Africanism and the Global Color Line*. Amherst: University of Massachusetts, 2018.

Spalding, Elizabeth Edwards. *The First Cold Warrior: Harry Truman, Containment, and the Remaking of Liberal Internationalism*. Lexington: University Press of Kentucky, 2006.

Stahel, David. *Operation Barbarossa and Germany's Defeat in the East*. Cambridge, UK: Cambridge University Press, 2011.

Stearns, Peter. *Childhood in World History*. London and New York: Routledge, 2006.

Steinberg, Mark D. *The Russian Revolution, 1905–1921*. Oxford: Oxford University Press, 2017.

Steil, Ben. *The Marshall Plan: Dawn of the Cold War*. New York: Simon and Schuster, 2018.

Steiner, Rudolf. *The Philosophy of Freedom: A Basis of a Modern World Conception*. London: Rudolf Steiner Press, 1979.

Stewart, Andrew. *Empire Lost: Britain, the Dominions and the Second World War*. London: Bloomsbury Academic, 2008.

Stoler, Ann Laura. *Carnal Knowledge and Imperial Power: Race and the Intimate in Colonial Rule*. Berkeley: University of California Press, 2002.

Stora, Benjamin. *Algeria 1830–2000, A Short History*. Ithaca: Cornell University Press, 2001.

Stovall, Tyler. "Empires of Democracy," in Graham Huggins, ed, *The Oxford Handbook of Postcolonial Studies*. Oxford: Oxford University Press, 2014.

————. "Faith, Freedom, and Frenchness?: Race, Class, and the Myth of the Liberatory French Republic," *Yale French Studies* no. 111 (2007).

————. *Transnational France: The Modern History of a Universal Nation*. New York: Routledge, 2015.

Strangelove, Michael. *The Empire of the Mind: Digital Piracy and the Anti-Capitalist Movement*. Toronto: University of Toronto Press, 2005.

Striner, Richard. *Woodrow Wilson and World War I: A Burden too Great to Bear*. Lanham, MD: Rowman and Littlefield, 2016.

Tabili, Laura. *"We Ask for British Justice": Workers and Racial Difference in Late Imperial Britain*. Ithaca: Cornell University Press, 1994.

Takaki, Ronald. *A Different Mirror: A History of Multicultural America*. New York: Little, Brown and Co., 1993.

——. *Double Victory: A Multicultural History of America in World War II*. New York: Little, Brown and Co., 2000.

Talbot, Ian. *The Partition of India*. Cambridge, UK: Cambridge University Press, 2009.

Taylor, Alan. *American Revolutions: A Continental History, 1750–1804*. New York and London: W. W. Norton, 2016.

Thomas, Edith. *The Women Incendiaries: The Inspiring Story of the Women of the Paris Commune*. Chicago: Haymarket Publishers, 2007.

Thomas, Martin. *The French Empire at War, 1940–1945*. Manchester, UK: Manchester University Press, 2007.

Thomson, Mathew. *Lost Freedom: The Landscape of the Child and the British Post-War Settlement*. Oxford: Oxford University Press, 2013.

Tilly, Charles. *Democracy*. Cambridge, UK: Cambridge University Press, 2007.

Tinniswood, Adrian. *Pirates of Barbary: Corsairs, Conquests and Captivity in the Seventeenth-Century Mediterranean*. London: Jonathan Cape, 2010.

Todorov, Tzvetan. *Nous et les autres: La reflexion française sur la diversité humaine*. Paris: Seuil, 1989.

Torgovnick, Marianna. *Gone Primitive: Savage Intellects, Modern Lives*. Chicago: University of Chicago Press, 1990.

Trachtenberg, Marvin. *The Statue of Liberty*. New York: Penguin, 1986.

Treadgold, Donald W. *Freedom: A History*. New York and London: New York University Press, 1990.

Trefousse, Hans L. *The Radical Republicans: Lincoln's Vanguard for Racial Justice*. New York: Knopf, 1969.

Trouillot, Michel-Rolph. *Silencing the Past: Power and the Production of History*. Boston: Beacon Press, 1995.

Vaisse, Justin. *Neoconservatism: The Biography of a Movement*. Cambridge, MA: Harvard University Press, 2010.

Van Deburg, William L. *New Day in Babylon: The Black Power Movement and American Culture, 1965–1975*. Chicago: University of Chicago Press, 1993.

Van Kley, Dale. *The French Idea of Freedom: The Old Regime and the Declaration of Rights of 1789*. Stanford: Stanford University Press, 1997.

Vanthemsche, Guy. *Belgium and the Congo, 1885–1980*. Cambridge, UK: Cambridge University Press, 2012.

Viotti Da Costa, Emilia. *Crowns of Glory, Tears of Blood: The Demerara Slave Rebellion of 1823*. New York: Oxford University Press, 1994.

Von Eschen, Penny M. *Race Against Empire: Black Americans and Anticolonialism, 1937–1957*. Ithaca: Cornell University Press, 1997.

Waldman, Michael. *The Fight to Vote*. New York: Simon and Schuster, 2016.

Waldstreicher, David. *Runaway America: Benjamin Franklin, Slavery, and the American Revolution*. New York: Hill and Wang, 2004.

Weber, Eugen. *Peasants into Frenchmen: the Modernization of Rural France, 1870–1914*. Stanford: Stanford University Press, 1976.

Weinberg, Gerhard L. *A World at Arms: A Global History of World War II*. Cambridge, UK: Cambridge University Press, 1994.

Weiss, Gillian. *Captives and Corsairs: France and Slavery in the Early Modern Mediterranean*. Stanford: Stanford University Press, 2011.

Weitz, Eric. *A Century of Genocide: Utopias of Race and Nation*. Princeton: Princeton University Press, 2003.

Weitz, Mark. *The Sleepy Lagoon Murder Case: Race Discrimination and Mexican-American Rights*. Lawrence: University Press of Kansas, 2010.

Wells, Ida B. *Southern Horrors and Other Writings: The Anti-Lynching Campaign of Ida B. Wells, 1892–1900*. Edited by Jacqueline Jones Royster. New York: Bedford/St. Martin's, 1996.

Westermann, Edward B. *Hitler's Ostkrieg and the Indian Wars: Comparing Genocide and Conquest*. Norman: University of Oklahoma Press, 2016.

Whitman, James Q. *Hitler's American Model: The United States and the Making of Nazi Race Law*. Princeton: Princeton University Press, 2017.

Wiencek, Henry. *Master of the Mountain: Thomas Jefferson and His Slaves*. New York: Farrar, Straus and Giroux, 2012.

Wildenthal, Lora. *German Women for Empire, 1894–1945*. Durham: Duke University Press, 2001.

Wilder, Gary. *Freedom Time: Negritude, Decolonization, and the Future of the World*. Durham: Duke University Press, 2015.

———. *The French Imperial Nation-State: Negritude and Colonial Humanism between the Wars*. Chicago: University of Chicago Press, 2005.

Williams, Chad L. *Torchbearers of Democracy: African American Soldiers in the World War I Era*. Chapel Hill: University of North Carolina Press, 2010.

Williams, Eric. *Capitalism and Slavery*. Chapel Hill: University of North Carolina Press, 1994.

Williams, William Appleman. *The Tragedy of American Diplomacy*. New York: W. W. Norton, 2009.

Wills, Garry. *Negro President: Thomas Jefferson and the Slave Power*. Boston: Houghton-Mifflin, 2003.

Wong, Edlie L. *Racial Reconstruction: Black Inclusion, Chinese Exclusion, and the Fictions of Citizenship*. New York: New York University Press, 2015.

Wood, Gordon S. *Empire of Liberty: A History of the Early Republic*. Oxford: Oxford University Press, 2009.

———. *The Radicalism of the American Revolution*. New York: Vintage, 1993.

Woodward, C. Vann. *The Strange Career of Jim Crow*. Oxford: Oxford University Press, 2001.

Woodcock, George. *Anarchism: A History of Libertarian Ideas and Movements*. Cleveland: The World Publishing Company, 1962.

Young, Robert J. C. *White Mythologies: Writing History and the West*. London and New York: Routledge, 2004.

Zucotti, Susan. *The Holocaust, the French, and the Jews*. New York: Basic Books, 1993.

Zweig, Stefan. *The World of Yesterday*. Lincoln: University of Nebraska Press, 2013.

INDEX